DarkBASIC Pro Game Programming, Second Edition

Jonathan S. Harbour
Joshua R. Smith

D1501310

THOMSON

COURSE TECHNOLOGY™

Professional ■ Technical ■ Reference

ISBN-10: 1-59863-287-6
ISBN-13: 978-1-59863-287-3
Library of Congress Catalog Card Number: 2006927125
Printed in the United States of America
07 08 09 10 11 PH 10 9 8 7 6 5 4 3 2

Publisher and General Manager, Thomson Course Technology PTR:
Stacy L. Hiquet

Associate Director of Marketing:
Sarah O'Donnell

Manager of Editorial Services:
Heather Talbot

Marketing Manager:
Heather Hurley

Senior Acquisitions Editor:
Emi Smith

Project Editor:
Jenny Davidson

PTR Editorial Services Coordinator:
Erin Johnson

Interior Layout Tech:
Interactive Composition Corporation

Cover Designer:
Mike Tanamachi

CD-ROM Producer:
Brandon Penticuff

Indexer:
Kelly D. Henthorne

Proofreader:
Sara Gullion

Thomson Course Technology PTR,
a division of Thomson Learning Inc.
25 Thomson Place
Boston, MA 02210
http://www.courseptr.com

To the next generation: Jeremiah, April, Jason, Kayleigh, Stephen, Roseanna, Kaitlyn, and Liam.

—Jonathan

For my loving wife, Hope Smith, and my beautiful daughter Brianna.

—Joshua

FOREWORD

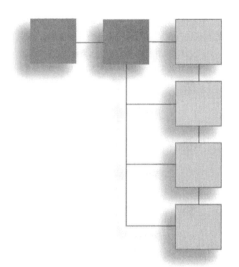

My first memory of a computer game was a set of paddles linked to a black and white TV; the object of the game was to bat the ball past your opponent to score points. I was a child at the time, but I played those paddles to pieces. My first memory of a computer was the VIC20, the property of my uncle who would let me play it from time to time. You can guess what my Christmas present was. Due to the price my parents had to pay, it was my only present, and it was the biggest present I would ever get. It was my future in a box.

My childhood was spent playing computer games. Every so often I would write one. They were all terrible, but because they were mine I was proud of every single one of them. Through childhood, school, university, and the workplace I learned lots of programming languages, though none ever had the same enjoyment factor as good old BASIC. At university, my games were good enough to sell and I made a little money. When it was time to enter the workplace, it was not the grades that got me the job, it was those terrible games I had made in my spare time. It was in the workplace that the idea for DarkBASIC was born.

I was working with Lego Media International when coding began for DarkBASIC. At the time, I was assisting in the creation of a programming language interface that would control the behavior and responses of robots built out of Lego. Prior to my time at Lego, I had been working on game creation tools that used drag and drop methodology to create 2D games and applications. I had also cobbled together in my spare time a 3D game called POBS, which taught me all the inner workings of a 3D game and how to code it on the PC. By the time my contract was complete for Lego, I resigned my position as software engineer and formed DarkBASIC Software Ltd. That Christmas, DarkBASIC was launched from a little known website in a corner of the Internet.

DarkBASIC was something I wanted as much for myself as anyone else. I had done no serious marketing, no advertising, and I was still learning the ropes. I was not at all sure anyone else would give it a second glance. I did not have much money, so I used every form of free advertising I could find. Website links, search engine submissions, magazine demos, and anything else that would spread the word. The website I designed and maintained myself, the orders were processed by a shareware company, the CDs were duplicated individually and labeled by hand. It was very much a cottage industry.

In the years that followed, DarkBASIC Software Ltd got bigger. I took on a commercial director, then an artist, then another project. That project took on seven more artists, two musicians, and several consultants. All the while DarkBASIC the language got bigger. Translations, new commands, and new media all formed part of a growing collection of software. As technology evolved, so did we. Starting from scratch we hired another programmer and artist to contribute to our next big project. To stay ahead of technology, we needed a new modern language that could be expanded for years to come. In the summer of 2002, DarkBASIC Professional was born and the company changed its name to The Game Creators. It did not stop there, with myriad related releases, including plug-ins for cloth, particles, advanced terrain, LUA, and scores of other add-ons, many written by third-party developers. In 2005 we launched FPS Creator, a drag and drop tool for making single and multiplayer FPS games, written entirely in DarkBASIC Professional, and the first product we self-published into shops.

I have come a long way since those early days with the bat and ball game I played so much. If those early computers had not come with BASIC, would I be writing this now? Perhaps. If I had not written those early (but terrible) games, would I have later been paid large sums of money to play on my computer? Probably not. Let's suppose a few years from now a programmer working for a game company will be asked to write the foreword to a book. Maybe this programmer will mention the early days, how a little-known language called DarkBASIC inspired that person to do great things. Might that programmer be you? If that happens, then I will be happy.

Best Regards,

Lee Bamber
The Game Creators

ACKNOWLEDGMENTS

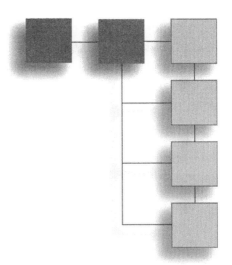

I would like to thank everyone who has made writing this book possible. I'd first and foremost like to thank God for giving me the skills and resolve to complete this book. Thanks to my family and friends for all their support. Thank you to my wife, Hope, for all the hours she's put up missing me for the sake of this book and for the valuable input she has provided.

I'd like to thank Jonathan for the opportunity to co-author with him. This has been a fun experience and I would gladly do it again. I'm thankful for our friendship.

—Joshua

I would like to thank everyone who helped make this book a reality. Thanks to my family and friends for their encouragement and patience. My wife, Jennifer; my kids, Jeremiah, Kayleigh, and Kaitlyn. Some day when you are old enough to read this, I want you to know that you are my inspiration.

Thank you to the editors and freelancers at Thomson Course Technology, who have been very supportive and encouraging. My deepest gratitude and appreciation go out to Jenny Davidson, Emi Smith, Kim Benbow, Kelly Henthorne, and Sara Gullion.

Many thanks to the team at The Game Creators for developing a great product; for eager support, suggestions, and free software, especially Lee Bamber and

Rick Vanner who have been very patient, understanding, and incredibly helpful. I am especially grateful to Reiner Prokein for allowing us the use of his tile and sprite animation sets from www.reinerstileset.de, and to Ari Feldman for the use of his SpriteLib at www.flyingyogi.com. And to all the DarkBASIC fans around the world, keep up the good work!

—Jonathan

About the Authors

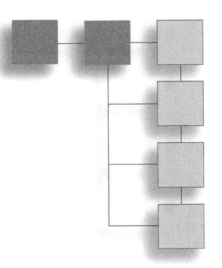

Joshua R. Smith is a Programmer Analyst for the County of Shasta. He worked as a professional game programmer at Semi-Logic Entertainments in Palo Cedro, California, for six years. During that time, he worked on several commercial games, including *Real War* and *Hot Wheels: Stunt Track Driver 2*. Joshua is an expert programmer, enjoys writing code in C#, and is a long-time fan of the BASIC language. He is currently living in Redding, California, with his wife, Hope, and daughter Brianna. In his spare time, Joshua enjoys playing and writing video games, reading science fiction, and spending time with his family and friends. He can be reached at www.delnar.com.

Jonathan S. Harbour is a senior instructor of game development at the University of Advancing Technology in Tempe, Arizona, where he teaches a variety of courses, from handhelds to consoles to game engines. When not teaching others about games, writing about games, or playing games, he enjoys video editing and working in the garage. His favorite game development tools are DarkBASIC, Allegro, and DirectX. Jonathan is the author of two recent books: *Beginning Java 5 Game Programming* and *The Gadget Geek's Guide to Your Xbox 360*. He is currently working on two more revisions: *Beginning Game Programming, Second Edition* and *Game Programming All In One, Third Edition*. He lives in the Arizona desert with his wife, Jennifer, and children, Jeremiah, Kayleigh, and Kaitlyn. He can be reached via www.jharbour.com.

Contents

INTRODUCTION

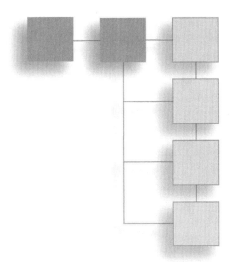

Congratulations, you have just found the one and only book you will need to learn the basics of game programming! Have you ever wanted to write your own *Half-Life* or *Quake III* mod? Why bother learning a complicated mod programming language when you can do the same thing with DarkBASIC Professional? DarkBASIC is a computer programming language and a complete integrated development environment that is totally focused and optimized for game development.

Does that sound complicated? Nothing could be further from the truth! DarkBASIC is the easiest compiled computer language in the world, hands down. You will be shocked by how much you can do right from the start, before you have learned any of the advanced tricks and techniques that the experts use. In case you were wondering, DarkBASIC is being used to create professional games that are sold today. You too will learn to use DarkBASIC to write your own games, and you will be able to get started right away. This book is not a manual on theory, but rather on practical tips for the aspiring game programmer. Will *you* write the next blockbuster game with DarkBASIC?

A Little Background...

My name is Jonathan Harbour, and I am a professional programmer, not just a writer. I have worked on real-world programs that impact others every day—in other words, I don't just write games. My work environment is one where phrases like "application development," "software specifications," "analysis and design," and "database schema" are used on a daily basis. My motto goes something like this: "Stop talking about it and just make it work." I have a very practical attitude toward computer programming because I like to do things that work well. Recently, I have made the move to teaching at the college level, as a senior instructor of game development at the University of Advancing Technology. I teach a course called *Introduction to Game Programming*, and much of the material I developed for that class made its way into this new revision. I also teach advanced courses in C++ game programming using Allegro and DirectX. Recently, I worked with a group of students to build a real-time strategy (RTS) game engine from scratch using Allegro. So, in a nutshell, I love this stuff! I hope my passion for it is evident as you read this book.

Joshua Smith, who co-authored this book, was a game programmer at Semi-Logic Entertainments in Northern California (http://www.slegames.com) for six years. He has worked on such games as *Real War, Real War: Rogue States, Guard Force*, and *Full-On Rally* for Planet Hot Wheels. Suffice it to say, Joshua knows his stuff, since he has had many years of experience working on retail games. Joshua understands what makes them tick, and how to write code that works. You will gain some of Joshua's insight into the video game industry in this book, and we believe much of the material you learn in this book is *real-world experience.*

Joshua and I have been buddies for about 20 years now. We are part of the "Nintendo generation" because we both grew up playing video games in the 1980s and 1990s. But playing was only part of the story. We both have a lifetime fascination with games and have spent much of our time over the years learning to write games, and then mastering the tricks of the trade. In the early days, we spent many a weekend playing games while trying to write our own. We used to take turns at *Super Mario World* or *Contra III* on the SNES, while the other would type away on the PC. At the time, the "PC" was a Tandy 1000, a Tandy Color Computer 3, a Timex Sinclair, a Commodore 64 or PET, or even an Apple II. At the time, video game consoles like the NES and Sega Master System were far more powerful than even a high-end PC. Back then, if you wanted to play a great game, you either went to an arcade or bought a console. How things have changed today!

Given our backgrounds, why do you suppose we are interested in DarkBASIC? Because DarkBASIC is awesome! You can do anything with it. You know, this might sound ridiculous, but you could write your own web browser with DarkBASIC! (In fact, DarkBASIC would be a great tool for developing a virtual reality style web browser, a gateway into cyberspace, due to the incredible 3D and TCP/IP commands built in.) Another reason why we enjoy programming with DarkBASIC is because it takes us back two decades to a time when the PC was new, and fun, and exciting, when the game industry was still a hobby for most people.

What I wouldn't have given back then for a product like DarkBASIC! It runs on the latest versions of Windows, supports DirectX 9.0, and features more than a thousand commands that are all geared for game development. The most compelling thing about DarkBASIC is that you can write solid, fast-running code, with a very short learning curve. Once you get started, and get a feel for what DarkBASIC can do, you will be hooked!

Consider yourself lucky, my friend. While it once was a black art just to get a sprite up on a PC screen, you can now load and draw a sprite in DarkBASIC with perhaps two lines of code. Two lines of code! I'm not talking about some hidden cache of game library code *in addition to* those two lines. I mean two lines of code, period! DirectX full-screen display with a sprite on the screen. Consider yourself privileged to have such an amazing tool as you start on the path of discovery in the art of writing games, because you will skip the frustration of a steep learning curve with a language like C++. Since the black art behind the technology is no longer a problem with DarkBASIC, aspiring game programmers can focus on the fun stuff—writing a game. Just think, in the early days of the video game industry, one had to write special code for every single video card and sound card, *individually!* Now, of course, DirectX has solved the problem of hardware standards, but DirectX itself is now incredibly complicated (sort of like coming full circle, don't you think?).

Instead of pulling your hair out just to get a pixel on the screen, with DarkBASIC you can load a complete 3D model of a car or an airplane and render it on the screen fully textured. You will be able to do this within a few minutes of installing DarkBASIC, instead of after days and weeks of determined coding.

Is This Book for You?

The goal of this book is to introduce beginners to the basics of writing games using a very simple language. We chose DarkBASIC because it meets these qualifications. You will be surprised by how easy it is to write a game in DarkBASIC. At the same time, you will be amazed by how many powerful features the language includes. DarkBASIC is suitable for more than just games, too. You will probably find, as I have, that DarkBASIC is great for all kinds of programs, such as graphics demos, business presentations, or even file viewers. It is a great resource for graphic art students who want to quickly and easily demonstrate their 3D models, scenes, and movies that they created with 3D Studio (which DarkBASIC supports natively). You can even use DarkBASIC to write your own MP3 player, because it can easily load and play MP3 music files!

This book was most certainly not written for experienced programmers. If you have a knack for new software and you are able to install DarkBASIC and within minutes write a simple program without breaking a sweat, then you are too advanced for this book. However, if you have experience writing code but would like to know more about DarkBASIC Professional, then I think you will find this book useful.

This book really starts at the beginning, and I mean *really*. I don't expect you to need another book or an online tutorial to get up to speed with DarkBASIC. On the contrary, I assume you know *nothing* about programming, period—let alone game programming. There are chapters in this book on basic statements, math, branching statements, basic language syntax, variables, data types, and looping—everything you need to get started, even if you have never written a program. In fact, I would prefer that you know nothing about programming because it is easier that way—you haven't learned any bad habits yet! Although many books make this claim, most fail miserably to cater to the complete beginner. Although we have renamed this book from the original title, *Beginner's Guide to Dark-BASIC Game Programming*, all of the key chapters from the original are still present in this new edition, and it still caters to the absolute beginner.

It is difficult to write a book without delving right into the advanced material and showing off what a product can do. It is easier to write an advanced book because you are able to get right to the point and you don't have to bother with any introductory material. That is probably the biggest hurdle for a computer book author—understanding the beginner. I hope that this book has succeeded in this regard, and that anyone who has not written any code will find it useful.

Educators

If you are a teacher of computer science, I think you will find this book useful for a wide variety of age groups, from junior high to high school to the college level. This book is especially helpful for adults who are just getting started in programming, as it presents all of the key concepts of computer programming in an easy-to-understand format, with lots of example programs in each chapter. I am using this book to launch students into the game programming curriculum at UAT, so it is definitely suitable for the college level as well.

If you would like to consider this book for your course, you may contact your local Thomson representative to request an evaluation copy. At the same time, be sure to ask about an Instructor Resource CD, containing a full course worth of assignments, exams, and PowerPoint presentations, which should be available soon after the book is released.

System Requirements

Most of the source code in this book will run on a low-end computer, with the exception of some of the high-end 3D commands. DarkBASIC supports advanced features found on the latest video cards, such as pixel shaders and vertex shaders. Obviously, you will need a video card that supports such features if you want to use them.

There is absolutely no way around the fact that you must have DirectX 9.0 runtime installed before running DarkBASIC. More than likely you already have DirectX installed if you are using Windows XP or Vista, but just in case you do not, it has been conveniently included on the CD-ROM under the \DirectX June 2006 folder. The programs in this book are pretty forgiving of computer hardware and will run on most systems without any trouble, but the latest DirectX runtime is *required*. Although the minimum system requirements are workable for DarkBASIC Professional, I would recommend a system with at least 512 MB of RAM and a high-end video card with at least 128 MB of video RAM.

- Windows 98, Me, 2000, XP

- Pentium II 300 MHz

- 128 MB of memory

- 1.0 GB of free hard drive space

- 32-MB 3D-accelerated video card with transform and lighting (T&L)

For the record, while developing the programs in this book, we used a GeForce 6400 128 MB DDR2 running on a *Pentium M* laptop and a GeForce 6600GT 128 MB DDR3 running on a *Pentium 4* desktop. I have tested the code on a variety of systems, from a *Pentium 3* to a dual-core *Pentium D*, and the only problem I ever encountered was on a system without the latest version of the DirectX runtime (June 2006 or later is recommended). So, if you write a cool game with DarkBASIC and want to put it up on a website, just be sure to include the disclaimer that the latest DirectX is recommended.

Book Summary

This book is divided into four parts, as described in the following paragraphs.

Part I—The Basics of Computer Programming

Part I will teach you how to get started programming DarkBASIC, with an introduction to the integrated development environment and the programming language. The first chapter is an overview of DarkBASIC, showing some of the capabilities of DarkBASIC. Chapters 2 through 7 provide a solid tutorial on basic computer programming concepts. If you have never written a program before, these early chapters will teach you how.

Part II—2D Game Programming

Part II includes the most important subjects for game programming with DarkBASIC. This Part begins with a chapter on basic graphics commands and moves on to chapters on bitmaps, sprites, input devices (keyboard, mouse, and joystick), sound effects, music, file access, and background scrolling. These chapters will take you step by step through the development of a complete 2D game called Darkanoid, and a game called Astro Gunner that demonstrates an advanced technique called angular velocity. This is truly the bulk of the material in the book; it is where you will likely learn the most about DarkBASIC.

Part III—3D Game Programming

Part III covers advanced game programming topics that extend your knowledge of DarkBASIC into the subjects of 3D graphics, lighting, camera control, bumpy terrain, and multiplayer programming. The final chapter of the book includes a

3D animated game called Battle Checkers that you learn how to create from scratch.

Part IV—Appendices

Part IV includes the appendices. This Part provides reference material that will be helpful as you are working through the book.

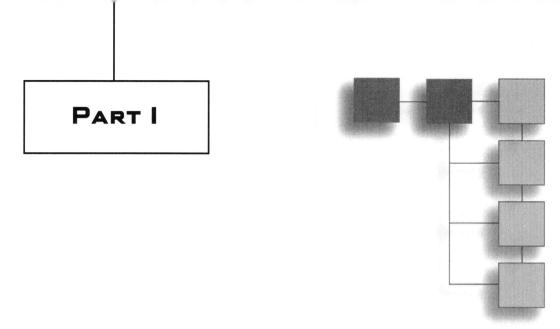

PART I

THE BASICS OF COMPUTER PROGRAMMING

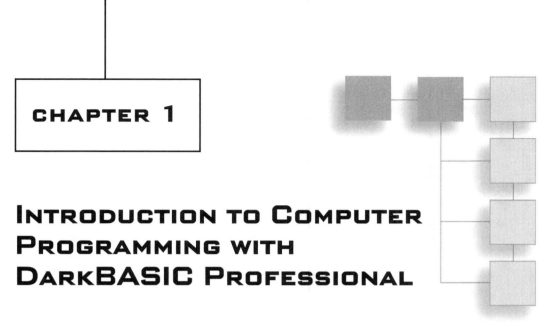

CHAPTER 1

INTRODUCTION TO COMPUTER PROGRAMMING WITH DARKBASIC PROFESSIONAL

DarkBASIC is a fantastic programming tool for creating games of any type and genre. Anyone who has at least minimal experience with a computer can use DarkBASIC to create many different types of games, from a 2D arcade game like the classic *Galaxian* to a modern first-person shooter like *Half-Life 2*. This chapter introduces you to DarkBASIC Professional with a tour of the integrated development environment and explains some of the basics of computer programming. Even if you have no programming experience, you should still be able to get the hang of programming with DarkBASIC over the next few chapters, because we're starting at the beginning. In this chapter I will help you to get started by explaining how to use DarkBASIC to write your first program. If you are an experienced programmer already, you might want to skip to the next chapter.

DarkBASIC Professional

DarkBASIC Professional is a tool that makes programming fun and intuitive and allows you to write intense graphics programs quickly and easily, without any formal knowledge or training in computer programming. DarkBASIC Professional is the perfect choice for prototyping software and creating presentations, product demonstrations, and especially games! DarkBASIC Professional completely hides the details of drawing 2D shapes and 3D objects and takes care of all the difficult work behind the scenes, allowing you to focus on solving problems rather than learning a new language or game library. DarkBASIC Professional

("DB") is a compiler with an integrated development environment (IDE) that lets you create, load, and save the source code files that make up programs and then compile them into standalone executable programs.

Note

For the sake of brevity, from this point forward, I will use the shorthand "DarkBASIC" or "DB" when referring to DarkBASIC Professional. There was a precursor product called DarkBASIC, from which the "Pro" edition was derived, but this older version has been completely replaced by DarkBASIC Professional. If you have the old DarkBASIC, you will not be able to use it to compile the programs in this book, in which case you should install DarkBASIC Professional off the book's CD-ROM.

This chapter—and those that follow—focuses on teaching you how to be a programmer, first and foremost. I make no assumptions about whether you know how a command works. The subjects in this book are organized so that basic topics are covered first, with each chapter covering a more challenging aspect of programming with the DB language. If you have never written a computer program before, you will have no trouble working your way through this chapter and those that follow. However, we do get into some very advanced topics in the second half of the book, so you may need to refer back to these early chapters as a reference while studying the 2D and 3D game projects.

Tip

If you have not done so yet, please open the CD-ROM enclosed with this book and install DB onto your computer. The installer is in the \software\DarkBASIC folder on the CD-ROM. This is a 30-day trial version of DB that is fully functional. The only drawback to the trial version is that it adds a small logo to the bottom-right corner of your programs. The full version of DB is available for purchase at http://www.thegamecreators.com, where you will be able to download it. At the time of this writing, DB costs $69.99—an incredible bargain for this fantastic game development tool.

What Is DarkBASIC Professional?

DB is essentially a scripting language sitting on top of a powerful 3D game engine. This engine provides many custom game-related commands that have been programmed in the DB engine, and this engine was created around DirectX. The DB engine is really a C++ function library. A function library is a source code file that has been compiled into a reusable object that other programs can use. As a C++ library, the DarkBASIC engine is powerful and fast, capable of handling millions of polygons per second and rendering realistic scenes such as the graphics found in commercial games.

The DB engine is updated regularly by The Game Creators (the company that created DarkBASIC) to take advantage of the latest features in DirectX. When the new "Professional" version of DB came out in late 2002, 3D shader technology was not yet common like it is today, so DB supported the "transform and lighting" (T&L) technology in 3D cards at the time, and it used DirectX 8. The latest version of DB now supports DirectX 9, and you can be sure that DB will support DirectX 10 in the near future (without requiring you to change any of your programs). For a single game development tool to have the ability to compile programs written four or five years ago is quite a spectacular feat in today's fast-paced world of software.

The DB compiler is actually not built into the integrated development environment (IDE); it is a separate program that the IDE runs whenever you compile your programs. The compiler takes your source code and translates it into machine language. The IDE is a graphical interface with an editor window that looks like a word processor, allowing you to type in the source code for a program. DB is more than just an editor, more than a compiler; it's a complete package with a built-in help system and project manager. The IDE keeps track of one or more source code files for each project, as well as settings for the project (such as the screen resolution to use for your game). See Figure 1.1.

You might think of the DB language as a "wrapper" for the game engine. The low-level functions in DarkBASIC (referring to the functions that do things like

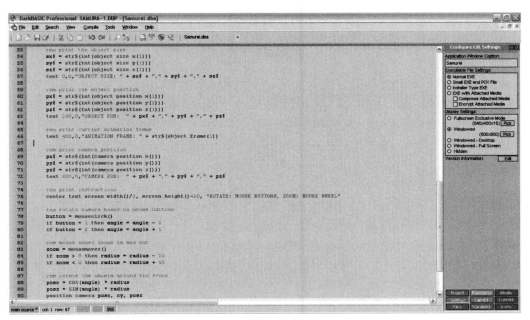

Figure 1.1
The DarkBASIC integrated development environment.

draw a bitmap onto the screen and read the mouse position) interface with DirectX below the scripting language. You use this language to tell the game engine what to do, and the result is a running game.

Since DarkBASIC was designed for writing games, it contains none of the complexity involved with languages such as Microsoft Visual C++ (the development tool used to develop most commercial games). DB is a scripted game engine, somewhat at the level of commercial game engines. Think of DB as one step above DirectX, which is the case with the *Doom III* and *Half-Life 2* engines. DB is not optimized like these other engines for a specific purpose (such as a first-person shooter); rather, it provides a general-purpose game engine for multiple genres.

Indeed, you can write any game that you can imagine using DB. But just as DB is not as fast or powerful as the *Unreal Tournament 2004* engine, you would be hard-pressed to write a 2D arcade game as a *UT2004* mod! You can use DarkBASIC for just about anything you can imagine, and it is a terrific tool for simulations, scientific visualizations, and even business presentations because it supports so many different media files.

Definition

A game "mod" is a game that uses an existing retail game engine (such as *Neverwinter Nights*) with your own supplied 3D models, levels, sound effects, and other game resources to develop a new game using the engine's modding features, the most prominent of which is usually a scripting language used to customize the new, unique game.

DB features a programming language with simple commands to invoke the awesome gaming power of Direct3D, which includes extensions for pixel and vertex shaders. A shader program is a small program loaded into the video card that is used to manipulate the polygons and even the individual pixels on the screen. Shader programs make it possible to add realistic effects like water to a game.

You don't need to know anything about DirectX to write a complete, professional game with DB! The programming language resembles Microsoft Quick-Basic, a descendant of the original BASIC (*Beginner's All-Purpose Symbolic Instruction Code*) language. QuickBasic itself actually evolved into what we know today as Visual Basic. The reason many programmers my age got started with BASIC and QuickBasic is because these lightweight programming tools came with many computers in the early days of personal computing—the '80s and early '90s. I got my start programming with a version of Microsoft BASIC that came with a Commodore PET (which used cassette tapes, before floppy disks or hard drives were available). My first PC was a Tandy 1000, sold by Radio Shack, which came with a newer version of Microsoft's seminal programming language called GW-BASIC. I spent hundreds of hours trying to make my first game using GW-BASIC, but I did not know how. Back then there were no game programming books and no Internet.

BASIC was the bread and butter of Microsoft when the company was young. Bill Gates and Paul Allen created a BASIC interpreter for the first PC, the Altair-8800, and then developed BASIC interpreters for many other makes and models of computers in the late '70s. Microsoft then developed a FORTRAN and a COBOL compiler for the CP/M operating system. FORTRAN is a business- and science-oriented language which stands for Formula Translator. COBOL is a database- and finance-oriented language commissioned by the Department of Defense in the '50s to be the de facto common programming language for business. Hence, the name stands for Common Business Oriented Language. These tools are used today only on a few old mainframe systems.

Compilers Versus Interpreters

A compiler is a program that converts source code into machine code that will run on a specific computer system. Programmers write the source code that makes up a program, but it must be compiled before it will run because computers don't execute English-like source code.

An interpreter, on the other hand, does not convert source code into machine code; instead, it executes the source code directly by reading each line of code and doing what it says. In this manner, an interpreter does read English. The benefit of an interpreted language is that a program will run on virtually any computer system without needing to be recompiled. Interpreted programs are much slower than compiled programs, but are more portable, and that is why languages like BASIC were so popular a few decades ago when every computer system was completely different.

DarkBASIC uses a compiler, not an interpreter, so your DarkBASIC programs will run as fast as possible in machine language on Windows systems.

DarkBASIC is a structured language with simple English-like commands. By combining the power of DirectX with the easy-to-use BASIC language, you can write a complete 3D game with only a few lines of source code. Compared to the several hundred lines of code you need to get even a rudimentary DirectX program up and running with C++, the power and convenience of DarkBASIC is its greatest strength. Who wants to spend six months working on a 3D engine when you could have created several complete games in that same timeframe?

Professional game developers are using DarkBASIC regularly to prototype their game designs. For instance, Peter Molyneux (the founder of Lionhead Studios and designer of *Black & White* and *The Movies*) has gone on record as being a fan of prototyping tools like DarkBASIC, having used them to prototype his games and get the artwork onto the screen as fast as possible. The irony of this is that many programmers are now using DarkBASIC for their finished games rather than using it just for the prototype.

Note

The DB engine is available as a C++ library. It is called Dark Game SDK, and it is the engine that powers DB (without the BASIC scripting language). You can use the Dark Game SDK in your own C++ projects to create games that have all the same advanced features as DB—such as the ability to load and animate 3D models. The difference is, you will be writing C++ code and calling functions in the Dark Game SDK instead of writing BASIC code in DB.

Most of the DB commands you will learn about in this book have equivalent functions in the Dark Game SDK, so it would be possible, for instance, to port your DB game to C++ without requiring a difficult rewrite. The URL for the Dark Game SDK is http://darkgamesdk.thegamecreators.com.

What makes DB so popular is that it provides users with the ability to quickly and easily write graphically intense programs that utilize the latest 3D graphics cards. It only takes a few simple commands to load a 3D model with full texturing and lighting enabled, and to move that model around on the screen. You will learn to write programs that do these things in due time.

Who Created DarkBASIC?

DarkBASIC was created by The Game Creators (formerly Dark Basic Software Ltd.). Most of The Game Creators' products are available for purchase on their website at http://www.thegamecreators.com. This site is helpful for keeping up to date on the latest news and upgrades to DB, as well as interacting with others in the web forum and accessing sample source code listings submitted by other programmers.

Windows and DirectX

Most games today are developed in C++ using development tools such as Microsoft Visual C++ or Borland C++ Builder. These are rich and complex tools, requiring extensive game libraries and "engines" that power the graphics system, usually implemented in 3D, to make a game. Before you can use DirectX, you must learn about Windows programming, which is no small task. I cover this subject in *Beginning Game Programming* (ISBN 1592005853) in as simple of terms as possible, but it is a daunting subject nonetheless.

Suppose you would like to write your own game in C++ using DirectX—the leading game development library for Windows today. The amount of work involved in writing a simple game using C++ is incredible. Not only must you interface with Windows, but you must also learn how to program the DirectX SDK, all before you are able to get started on your game. In contrast, DarkBASIC handles those details in the background and lets you start working on your game's design right away without learning a complex library of functions.

Note

> Microsoft's DirectX game development library is comprised of components that abstract the computer system, providing a common set of interfaces regardless of the underlying hardware (such as the video card and sound card). Hardware manufacturers, such as Nvidia (makers of the GeForce line of graphics chips) and Creative Labs (makers of the Sound Blaster line of sound cards) include DirectX drivers with their products so that all games developed in current or earlier versions of DirectX will run without incident. In the near future, physics cards will be a common component of a PC, featuring advanced physics chips.

Your First 3D Program

You can create a 3D object and animate it on the screen with five lines of code. Take a look at this code and the screenshot shown in Figure 1.2.

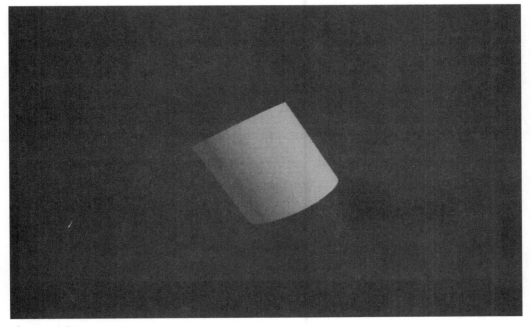

Figure 1.2
A spinning 3D object in only five lines of code (including timing).

```
make object cylinder 1, 100
do
  zrotate object 1, object angle z(1) + 5
  wait 20
loop
```

This is a good example of a command (make object cylinder) that you can use to construct a 3D world without having to load any 3D model files. However, this is a difficult way to make a game when DB can load up a 3D model so easily. As far as that goes, DB can load a *2D* object very easily too. But I find it helpful to learn how to construct things inside a program before loading objects from 2D and 3D files.

Your First 2D Program

Let's take a look at a simple program that uses 2D graphics. Here is the source code for the program shown in Figure 1.3. This program is a lot more complex than the 3D program, which demonstrates that the complexity of a game comes not from its graphics but from what the program does. In this case, a ball is bounding off the edges of the screen.

Figure 1.3
Bouncing a ball around on the screen in only 12 lines of code.

```
x as integer = 320
y as integer = 240
speedx as integer = 2
speedy as integer = 1
do
  cls
  inc x, speedx
  inc y, speedy
  if x < 50 or x > 599 then speedx = speedx * -1
  if y < 50 or y > 400 then speedy = speedy * -1
  circle x, y, 40
loop
```

I could have made this program much simpler by drawing a shape on the screen, which could be done with only two or three lines of code. But this interesting example of the bouncing ball actually does something that might be the precursor to an actual game. Can you think of all the different types of games you could make based on just this simple example program? I can! How about the classic game of *Pong*, for instance?

Your First Game

If we had a way to draw paddles on the screen along with the ball and then detect when the ball hits the paddles, we'd have a game. I'm kind of eager to try it. How about you? Let's give it a shot. Oh wait, this is only the first chapter. Well, it's never too early to start writing a game. Whatever you don't understand in this little game you will learn over the next few chapters—things like declaring variables, branching statements, drawing shapes, refreshing the screen, and collision testing. Go ahead and create a new DarkBASIC project and type the following code into the program, and then run it. You will be greeted with the game shown in Figure 1.4.

```
rem Simple Pong game

rem make some variables
ballx as integer = 320
bally as integer = 240
speedx as integer = -2
speedy as integer = 1
px1 as integer = 600
py1 as integer = 240
```

Figure 1.4
This complete game of Simple Pong requires 90 lines of code!

```
px2 as integer = 20
py2 as integer = 240
score1 as integer = 0
score2 as integer = 0

rem slow down the game
sync on
sync rate 40

rem the game runs in a loop
do
  cls

  rem check shift/ctrl keys to move the left paddle
  if shiftkey()
    dec py2, 2
    if py2 < 0 then py2 = 0
  endif
  if controlkey()
    inc py2, 2
```

```
      if py2 > 470 then py2 = 470
  endif

  rem check up/down keys to move the right paddle
  if upkey()
    dec py1, 2
    if py1 < 0 then py1 = 0
  endif
  if downkey()
    inc py1, 2
    if py1 > 470 then py1 = 470
  endif

  rem move the ball
  inc ballx, speedx
  inc bally, speedy

  rem bounce ball off top/bottom of the screen
  if bally < 0 or bally > 470 then speedy = speedy * -1

  rem see if left player missed the ball
  rem if so, player 2 scores, reset the ball
  if ballx < 0
    inc score2, 1
    ballx = 320
    bally = 240
    speedx = 2
    sleep 500
  endif

  rem see if right player missed the ball
  rem if so, player 1 scores, reset the ball
  if ballx > 630
    inc score1, 1
    ballx = 320
    bally = 240
    speedx = -2
    sleep 500
  endif

  rem draw the ball
  circle ballx, bally, 10
```

```
rem draw the paddles
box px1, py1, px1+16, py1+64
box px2, py2, px2+16, py2+64

rem let's see if the ball has hit a paddle
if point(ballx+5,bally+5) > 0
   speedx = speedx * -1
endif

rem print the scores
text 0, 0, "SCORE" + str$(score1)
text 550, 0, "SCORE" + str$(score2)

rem draw the screen
sync
loop
```

While typing in the source code for this Simple Pong project, did you get a good feel for some of the DB commands? There is a lot to writing a complete game, as you can see. But even this smallish game has a minimum size to it. There were a lot of comments in the program too (which start with the rem statement, which stands for "remark"). Out of the 90 lines of code in the Simple Pong game, the blank lines and comment lines took up 30 lines of code—a full third of the code listing!

The Importance of Commenting Code

Do you feel like this is a huge waste of space, taking up so much of the program just for comments? Imagine if I had just shown you the program without any comments . . . it would have been a long listing without any breaks, so it would have been *very* difficult to read the code. What's more, the *indentation* of the lines is also a form of comment, showing you that some lines of code belong under a certain logic statement. For instance, look at this example code:

```
if shiftkey()
  dec py2, 2
  if py2 < 0 then py2 = 0
endif
```

The lines between if . . . endif are indented so that it's easy to see that these lines of code are *only* executed if the if statement comes up with a true answer. I realize you have not been properly introduced to any of these concepts yet. Don't worry about these details; I will fully explain them in the chapters to come. Without any comments, blank spaces, or indenting, the program would look like this:

```
ballx as integer = 320
bally as integer = 240
speedx as integer = -2
speedy as integer = 1
px1 as integer = 600
py1 as integer = 240
px2 as integer = 20
py2 as integer = 240
score1 as integer = 0
score2 as integer = 0
sync on
sync rate 40
do
cls
if shiftkey()
dec py2, 2
if py2 < 0 then py2 = 0
endif
if controlkey()
inc py2, 2
if py2 > 470 then py2 = 470
endif
if upkey()
dec py1, 2
if py1 < 0 then py1 = 0
endif
if downkey()
inc py1, 2
if py1 > 470 then py1 = 470
endif
inc ballx, speedx
inc bally, speedy
if bally < 0 or bally > 470 then speedy = speedy * -1
if ballx < 0
```

```
inc score2, 1
ballx = 320
bally = 240
speedx = 2
sleep 500
endif
if ballx > 630
inc score1, 1
ballx = 320
bally = 240
speedx = -2
sleep 500
endif
circle ballx, bally, 10
box px1, py1, px1+16, py1+64
box px2, py2, px2+16, py2+64
if point(ballx+5,bally+5) > 0
speedx = speedx * -1
endif
text 0, 0, "SCORE " + str$(score1)
text 550, 0, "SCORE " + str$(score2)
sync
loop
```

Are you surprised by how bad the code listing looks? That is your first lesson in programming—remarks, blank lines, and indentations are all necessary and are not wasteful. If you do not properly comment your code, it will be absolutely unreadable and useless to anyone looking at it.

The ironic thing is, not even *you* will recognize your own code several months or years after you have written it if you have not commented your code properly. Use as much space as you feel is necessary to properly comment and document the progress within your source code. None of it is wasteful because the compiler ignores comments.

DarkBASIC Hides the Complexity

The way in which DarkBASIC hides the complexity of a 2D or 3D game might be thought of as engine encapsulation, to borrow a term from object-oriented programming (OOP). DarkBASIC doesn't support OOP, but it's the "big deal" for C++ programmers.

Suppose you have a great idea for a game that you want to develop. First you need to write your own DirectX library suited for the type of game you are planning. This library should include the 2D or 3D graphics engine that powers your game, as well as support for sound effects, background music, user input devices (including force-feedback joysticks, if applicable), and multi-player networking (if your game will support more than one player). It is a rare game today that is released with no built-in multiplayer capabilities.

Note

DarkBASIC supports DirectX 9.0, which is comprised of seven main components: DirectDraw, DirectSound (for sound effects), DirectSound3D (for positional 3D sound), DirectMusic (for music playback), DirectInput (for mouse, joystick, and keyboard input), DirectPlay (for multiplayer networking), and Direct3D (for 3D graphics).

By the time you have finished creating the core library and engine code needed to power your game, you probably will have given up on the game entirely and moved on to a new subject or game type—assuming you had the capabilities to develop a cutting-edge game engine in the first place. Writing a game engine, even for a 2D game, is very difficult and time consuming, and feels like re-inventing the wheel. An alternative is to use an existing game engine like Torque (developed by Garage Games—http://www.garagegames.com) to create a game. But even a game engine like Torque involves a difficult learning curve as you get up to speed on the engine's scripting language and functions, and then you must consider the game's resources as well—the 3D models, textures, sprites, and so on.

What you need is a way to *quickly*, *easily*, and *spontaneously* crank out the prototype version of your game idea before you lose interest and before the complexities of game programming overwhelm you and stifle the creative enthusiasm that you felt upon coming up with the new game idea. That's where DB comes in. Not only is DB a fantastic prototyping language that lets you get a minimal demonstration of your game up and running very quickly, it is also full-featured and loaded with awesome tools that will let you follow through and take the game to completion. Although you *can* (and will) write awesome games with DB, you could also use it to quickly prototype a game that you plan to eventually write in another (more difficult) language.

Figure 1.5 shows one example of a game you will develop as soon as you have learned about bitmaps and sprites. This game is called Darkanoid.

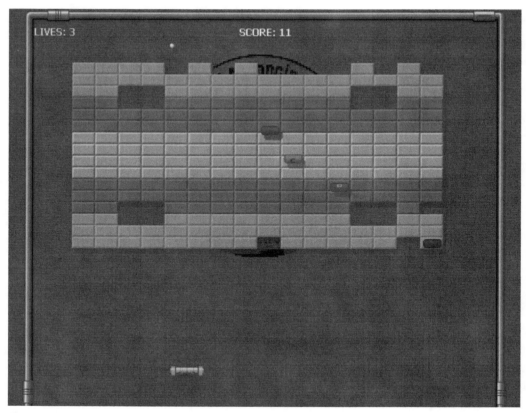

Figure 1.5
Darkanoid is a simple (but addictive) game!

Features of the DarkBASIC Language

DarkBASIC features automatic double buffering, which results in super-smooth animation at the highest possible frame rate using hardware 3D acceleration. There are many commands in the DB language that you will learn about in upcoming chapters. For instance, you will learn how to load and draw animated 3D models. But before you do that, you will first learn how to load and draw animated sprites. Probably one of the most interesting features of DarkBASIC is the compiler and how it creates standalone executable files that can be run on any PC without any special runtime file or DLL—DB programs are completely self-contained.

System Requirements

Okay now, what does it take to actually run DarkBASIC? I'll assume that you have a computer already because that's sort of a given, right? If you don't have a computer, I'll at least assume that you are using one at school, work, or a friend's house. You will need a Windows PC with DirectX 9.0 installed to run DarkBASIC or any program compiled with it. The latest version of DarkBASIC at the time of this writing is 1.062, which is referred to as "Update 6.2" or "U62" by DarkBASIC fans. All of the code in this book was written with 1.062, so I strongly recommend using that version (or a later version) to compile the code in this book. Here are the minimum recommended specifications for any PC running DarkBASIC.

- Windows 98, 2000, Me, or XP

- 300MHz Pentium II

- 64MB of RAM

- 400MB of hard disk space

- 4x CD-ROM drive

- 3D video card (32MB)

- DirectX 9.0 (April 2006 or later version)

- DirectX-compatible sound card

You will want a much more powerful system than the minimum specs; otherwise, your games will not run very fast. Most 3D code will not run at all on a 300 MHz computer, because a modern video card is required. The reason for these low minimum specifications is that you can compile and run a 2D game using DarkBASIC that has very low system requirements. However, I don't think DirectX 9.0 will function with a meager 32 MB video card, so this is related more to an original version of DarkBASIC Pro, circa 2002–2003. When it comes to writing games and graphics programs, you want a more powerful computer than the norm. Here are the specifications of the PC used to develop the example programs in this book, to give you an idea of the recommended specifications:

- Windows XP Professional SP2

- 2.8GHz Pentium 4 HT

- 1GB of DDR2 RAM

- GeForce 6600GT video card (128MB DDR3 RAM)

- Sound Blaster Audigy 2 ZS

Tip

If you are not familiar with terms such as T&L and shaders, you may want to pick up one of the excellent books by Course Technology dealing with Direct3D. You can find detailed information about these books at http://www.courseptr.com.

No Runtime Required

What happens after you have created a killer new game and you want to share it with your friends or send it to game companies to see whether they might publish it? Probably the most impressive feature of DB is that it can create standalone executable files that require no runtime library. A *runtime library* is a collection of functions that are built into a programming language and must be packaged with a program for it to run. Some languages (such as Visual Basic) store the runtime in one or more dynamic link library (DLL) files that must be installed before the program will run. DB programs, on the other hand, store the DB runtime library *inside* the executable, requiring no dependencies. You can zip your newly compiled DB program (such as MyGame.exe) into an archive file (such as MyGame.zip) and send it to a friend. That game will then run without needing an installer.

Note

Compiled DarkBASIC programs are standalone executables that do not require any runtime library because they are self-contained. The only requirement is that the DirectX 9.0+ runtime is installed.

There is another great feature of a DB program. DB programs can be compiled as standalone programs and distributed with all of the graphics and sounds needed by the game packaged together inside the executable file! Yes, you can compile an entire game—executable file, 3D model files, texture bitmap files, sound files, and music files—into the executable. DB handles the situation automatically. You don't need to modify anything to load files from disk or from inside the executable because it is done behind the scenes. All you have to do is check an option in the DB project settings to enable this feature and then add the files to a list that will be embedded inside the EXE file. This is a great feature, especially when you don't want others to steal your game artwork or music and use them in their own games without your permission.

BASIC Graphics

DarkBASIC includes all the commands you need to create 2D and 3D games, but it doesn't stop there. It also includes a bunch of example 3D models, textures, bitmaps, sound effects, and music that you can use in your own games. If you want to add even more resources to your game, there are support packages available for DB that provide you with hundreds of animated 3D models, buildings, houses, cars, military vehicles, spaceships, aliens, and many other objects for use in a game. These collections are called DarkMATTER, and are available for purchase for a very affordable price at The Game Creators' website. Figure 1.6 shows an example of the browser program that comes with DarkMATTER 2.

Tip

DarkMATTER is a series of 3D model collections available for sale by The Game Creators at http://darkmatter.thegamecreators.com. For about $40, you get a hundred or so models (most of which are animated) in each collection, which you may use in your own games royalty free.

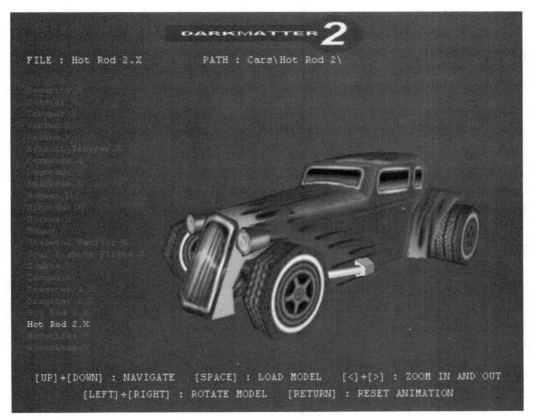

Figure 1.6
Browsing the 3D models in DarkMATTER 2.

OBJECT SIZE: 77,68,78   OBJECT POS: 0,0,0   ANIMATION FRAME: 2460   CAMERA POS: 94,34,-73

ROTATE: MOUSE BUTTONS, ZOOM: MOUSE WHEEL

Figure 1.7
An animated Samurai warrior that comes with DarkMATTER 2.

You can simply copy the 3D models from DarkMATTER to your game project folder and then load it into a game. Figure 1.7 shows an example program that loads the model of a Samurai warrior and animates it. This program helps to identify where the model is oriented in the X-Y-Z axes of 3D space by drawing a surface through each axis. The bottom surface on which the Samurai is standing is the X axis. The surface dividing the model front to back is the Z axis. The surface dividing the model side by side is the Y axis. You will learn all about 3D graphics starting in Chapter 18, "Fundamentals of 3D Graphics Programming"—one of the many chapters on 3D programming in the second half of the book.

Since we'll be working with 2D graphics before we get to 3D, I would be remiss if I didn't mention some of the 2D commands you'll be learning. DB has a large assortment of exciting commands for working with 2D graphics, bitmaps, and sprites, and you'll be creating arcade-style games in no time. DB has a built-in

Figure 1.8
This animated spider was loaded and drawn using only a few lines of code.

sprite engine that can load and draw animated sprites from image strips, such as the animated spider shown in Figure 1.8. Here is the source code for this short program.

```
color backdrop rgb(0,0,255)
backdrop on
set image colorkey 255, 0, 255
create animated sprite 1, "redspiderwalking.bmp", 8, 8, 5
size sprite 1, 256, 256
set current bitmap 0
do
   play sprite 1, 25, 25+7, 50
   x = screen width()/2 - sprite width(1)/2
   y = screen height()/2 - sprite height(1)/2
   paste sprite 1, x, y
loop
```

BASIC Commands

DB includes a rich assortment of commands used to write programs. What is a command? It is what other languages (such as C++) call an *intrinsic function*— something built into the language. DB makes the whole development process much easier than it is in C++, since there are no include files, library files, or other types of files that you must keep track of in a project. While you can break up large programs into multiple source code files (which is particularly useful when you want to share your custom code between programs), there is far less confusion when compiling and running programs developed with DB because the interface is so incredibly simple to use!

In a nutshell, DB uses a structured version of the classic BASIC language. By structured, I mean that it resembles QuickBasic more than old-school BASIC because it allows you to create your own subroutines and functions that return values. Old-school BASIC had the GoSub and Goto commands, which referred to line numbers. Not to worry, DB doesn't use line numbers. While DarkBASIC borrowed features of QuickBasic to make it easy to write programs, it utterly leaves QuickBasic in the dust beyond the core language. DB does use simple commands and supports concepts like functions and user-defined types (if you don't know what these things are, don't worry—you will in due time!).

Let me show you a simple program to demonstrate how DB can texture any object, including a sphere (shown in Figure 1.9). The following code creates a sphere and textures it with a bitmap of the Earth to simulate the planet rotating. This program is called SphereMap.

```
sync on
sync rate 0
color backdrop rgb(0,0,0)

make object sphere 1, 100, 40, 40
load image "earth_map.bmp", 1
texture object 1, 1

set ambient light 100
color ambient light rgb(255,255,255)
position camera 0, 20, -140

do
  yrotate object 1, object angle y(1) + 0.02
  sync
loop
```

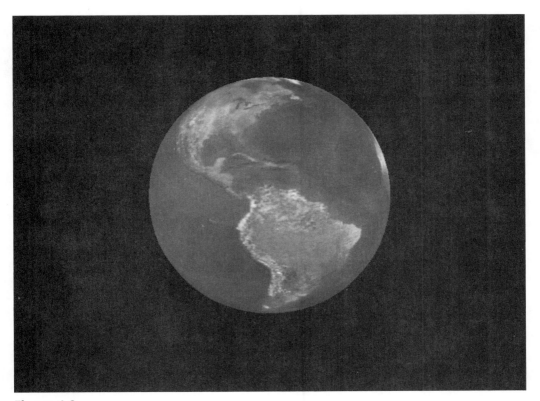

Figure 1.9
A 3D program that simulates a rotating planet Earth.

Summary

You have certainly been plunged into the depths of DarkBASIC programming already in this first chapter! The goal was to give you a feel for what is to come while getting you familiar with the DarkBASIC IDE and language. You will be learning the details behind all of the programs you've seen here in upcoming chapters, and you will soon be writing your own DarkBASIC programs without any help.

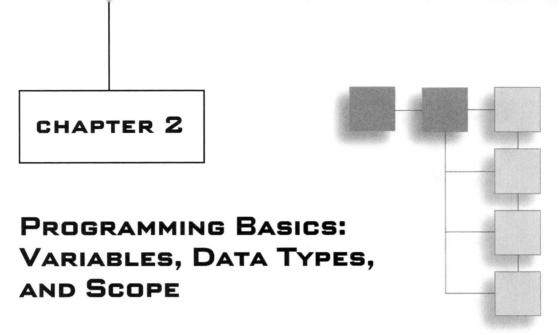

CHAPTER 2

PROGRAMMING BASICS: VARIABLES, DATA TYPES, AND SCOPE

There are many commands in DarkBASIC, and some are very easy to understand, while many are more complicated. But in order to understand those commands you will need to learn about variables. Programming is more than just knowing all the commands. You need to understand how to use variables and learn the basic data types. This chapter explains everything you need to know about variables—what they are, how they are defined, and how they are used. Data types are next. There are numerous data types to cover, including integer, decimal, and string.

The first thing aspiring programmers often discover is that programming looks really complicated. The truth is, computer programs are made up of hundreds of small parts—commands arranged in a specific order to accomplish a task. The program doesn't always have to be a game either. This chapter explains not only how to get started writing source code in DarkBASIC, but it also explains how programs work.

Here are the key topics you will learn:

- Overview of programming concepts

- The basics of a video game

- Using variables

- Learning about data types

- Understanding scope

Short Course on Programming

What's the best way to learn to write computer programs? You have probably been amazed and curious while playing the latest games. By the time you've finished reading this chapter, you'll have a much better understanding of programming and have a solid grasp on the answer! What I can tell you at this point is that it's a gradual process. First you learn the basics, and then you practice while learning more techniques, and with some diligence you will learn how the pros work their magic. Over time you will gain the experience needed to become an expert programmer, but you must invest a lot of time in studying and practicing your programming skills, learning new languages and tricks along the way. As with most things in life, it just boils down to a lot of work—not necessarily hard work, but it will take consistent effort. For that reason, it helps if you really enjoy programming in general—and you must *love* to play and write games to get really good at it. If you are not fascinated by something, how will you muster the will to keep at it?

What Is a Computer Program?

First of all, you might be asking this simple question: What exactly is a computer program? I have already hinted about the answer, but in a nutshell, a computer program is something that accepts input (like the keyboard), performs some computations (also called processing), and then outputs the result (usually to the screen). Figure 2.1 illustrates this point.

There are many different ways to write a computer program, and I'm not just talking about the programming language. You can use any language to write a computer program, although some languages are more suited for certain types of problems than others. When computer programs start to get really big, they tend to become unmanageable unless the programmer is well organized. For this reason, computer scientists came up with the fancy term *methodology*. This word refers to the steps one can take to describe how a program is written, and it is based on the way a programming language works. For instance, suppose you are

Figure 2.1
The basis for computer programming is input, process, and output.

writing a massively-multiplayer game like *World of Warcraft* that will be able to handle thousands of players online at the same time, interacting in a huge game world. The methodology for this game would describe how the computers will all be connected online in order for the game to work. One methodology might attempt to break up the game world into many smaller "worlds" that are linked together, while another methodology might describe a single huge game world.

Object-Oriented Programs

You might have heard of object-oriented programming (OOP) because it is used to write large and complex programs. Object-oriented programs are easy to handle when they get large because they are made up of many smaller related programs. Therefore, any time you need to solve a particular kind of problem in your program, you just plug in one of the smaller programs. As you might imagine, OOP excels at handling very large programs involving thousands or millions of lines of code, but it's more difficult to learn than other types of languages.

Structured Programs

Structured programming languages are easier to learn than OOP languages, which is one of the reasons why this book uses DarkBASIC. DB has a powerful structured programming language. Structured programs are also called *procedural programs* because they are made up of procedures, each of which is capable of solving a small problem. If this sounds similar to object-oriented programs, it's because OOP evolved from structured programming.

Structured programs tend to run faster than OOP programs. Although they are more difficult to manage when they get large, structured programs generally are easier to learn and use. Unlike OOP programs, structured programs don't require that you design an object before you can start writing the actual program. Figure 2.2 shows an illustration of structured programming.

DarkBASIC Is a Structured Language

DarkBASIC programs are completely self-contained executables that don't require any special runtime library because the library is built into the compiled program. (If you don't understand what I'm talking about, don't worry. I'll go over this information again in the next few chapters.) Figure 2.3 shows what the internal structure of a DarkBASIC program might look like in theory.

Procedural Programming

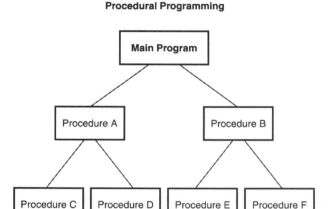

Figure 2.2
A visual representation of a structured program.

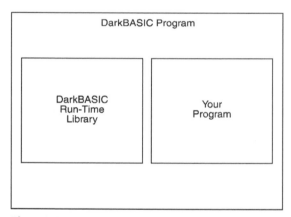

Figure 2.3
DarkBASIC executables include both your compiled code and the runtime library.

DarkBASIC allows you to compile your program to a standard Windows executable, which means that it runs like any other game you've played on your Windows PC, complete with support for DirectX. In fact, the greatest feature of DarkBASIC is that it lets you write DirectX games without even knowing any of the DirectX function calls. It's completely built in! Figure 2.4 shows the relationship among DarkBASIC, Windows, and DirectX.

Depending on your experience level, this might make sense or it might be something that you will pick up in time. A compiler is a program (like DB) that

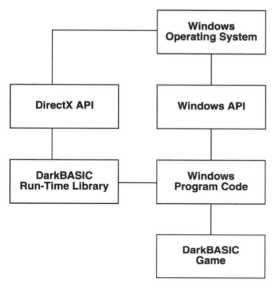

Figure 2.4
DarkBASIC programs are closely tied to Windows and DirectX.

converts your source code into an executable file. Like so many subjects involved in writing computer programs, this is one that I must defer until later in order to keep the subject matter more understandable and less rife with theory.

Definition of a Computer Program

In a more technical sense, a computer program is a series of instructions that tells the computer what to do, usually in the context of solving a problem. A web browser or word processing program is just a computer program made up of instructions—just like fast-action first-person shooter games such as *Doom III* and *Battlefield 2*. It's all about the *source code*.

What is code? You might have heard the word used before, but without a clear frame of reference, it can be somewhat confusing. *Code* refers to the source code instructions that make up a program. The instructions themselves are designed to perform simple operations such as math, logic, or memory movement. These very low-level instructions tell the computer what to do. Of course, it's very difficult for humans to read and write these instructions in the computer's native format, which is referred to as *machine language*. This format is completely binary—that is, it consists of streams of

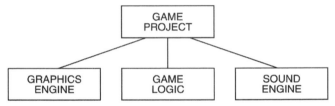

Figure 2.5
Computer programs are made up of separate parts, each of which accomplishes a task.

0s and 1s. These values are referred to as *bits*. A single bit can hold one piece of digital information.

Figure 2.5 shows a game project made up of several parts.

Video Game Bits

You might have heard the word *bit* used in the context of video games. Console makers, such as Nintendo, Sony, and Microsoft, love to talk about video games in terms of the bit strength of their consoles. For example, the Dreamcast was marketed as the very first 128-bit home video game machine. Where did the term "128-bit" come from? Generally, the number of bits that a video game system can handle is related to the computational power of the GPU (*Graphics Processing Unit*), which is different from the CPU (*Central Processing Unit*). This is really an interesting subject. Table 2.1 shows the specifications of the major video game machines on the market today.

Why do you suppose that a wide variety of console games seem to look and play so much better than PC games? Part of the reason is that console games are written very specifically for the hardware of the video game machine, while PC

Table 2.1 Video Game Console Comparison Chart

Console	CPU	GPU	Memory
Microsoft Xbox 360	3.2 GHz	256-bit, 500 MHz	512 MB
Microsoft Xbox	733 MHz	256-bit, 233 MHz	64 MB
Nintendo GameCube	485 MHz	128-bit, 162 MHz	40 MB
Sony PlayStation 2	295 MHz	128-bit, 150 MHz	40 MB

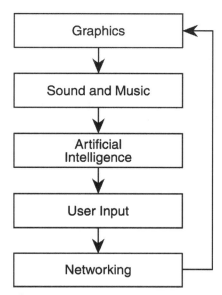

Figure 2.6
The game loop keeps the game running smoothly.

games have to support a wide variety of hardware configurations. Usually a high-end PC will totally blow away a console machine, but consoles generally attract a younger audience due to the lower price. This trend has changed in recent years, though, and the biggest consumer demographic of console systems today is males aged 18 to 34.

Since I'm on the subject of video games, what does it take to write a game? DarkBASIC excels at helping you write a game, thanks to all of the wonderful built-in commands that were tailored just for writing games. A game is basically a program that runs in a loop, which means that it keeps doing something over and over again until you tell the game to end. It's this looping feature that keeps the game running smoothly over time. When it comes to larger games that include animated graphics, artificial intelligence, sound effects, music, multiplayer support, and user input, the game loop can be quite complicated! On top of it all, the game needs to run as fast as possible—even with 3D graphics in most cases. Check out Figure 2.6 for an illustration of the game loop.

Solving Problems

Since computer programs are supposed to be written to solve a problem, what kinds of problems might need to be solved? There are innumerable problems that computer programs can help us solve. For example, there are computers and programs on airline jets that help the pilots take off, navigate, and land the aircraft. Computer programs operate streetlights. There are even programs running in modern cars that help to achieve better gas mileage. We are surrounded by problems, in fact! However, the process for solving a problem with a computer is similar to the processes humans use to solve real-life problems. Every decision you make involves one or more pieces of input that you must weigh in order to make a decision. The result of your decision is the output of your "program."

If you are a fan of *The Matrix* trilogy, then these concepts are probably very familiar to you. In fact, the philosophy of *The Matrix* borrows most of its concepts from simple software development methodology (and all the rest of the philosophy in the movies is just mumbo-jumbo to spruce up the script). In the matrix, everything from a bird to an A.I. agent is controlled by a program, and it is the complex interaction of all those millions of fictional programs that makes the matrix look and feel so real. Even the air in the matrix is a program, according to Morpheus (the character played by Lawrence Fishburne). The technology in *The Matrix* is not really that far beyond our technical capability today. The key technology we lack is a neural interface that allows a computer to communicate directly with a human brain. Even that technology is in its infancy today, as neural science is making great strides every year, performing miracles such as bringing sight to the blind and hearing to the deaf.

Progress in this field of science might startle you. For an example, look up the *BrainGate Neural Interface System* being developed by Cyberkinetics Neurotechnology Systems, Inc. at http://www.cyberkineticsinc.com. This company is working with the Rehabilitation Institute of Chicago to develop solutions for disabled and handicapped people, making it possible for them to control *robotic limbs* directly with their brains, just as we control our arms and legs. Ray Kurzweil predicted this technology in his 1999 book titled *The Age of Spiritual Machines*. Most futurists such as Kurzweil believe cybernetics will solve human disabilities in the next decade.

Beyond the hardware interfaces for anything from a keyboard to a neural connection, everything is controlled with software programs, and the basis for all programs is conditional logic. Figure 2.7 shows a simple illustration of a decision the way a computer sees it. You see, computers treat every decision as a single entity. Even when there are many details that must be considered before making a decision, the computer must think about every decision separately in this

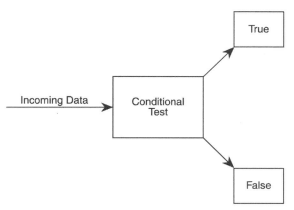

Figure 2.7
Computer problem solving involves making decisions using simple logic tests.

manner. Humans, on the other hand, have the ability to quickly draw conclusions, sometimes without looking at every factor involved.

Decisions, Decisions

Suppose you are purchasing a new video game console at the store. You want to buy a console with a large selection of games that appeal to you, but you also want it to last a long time before it becomes obsolete. Therefore, the game selection alone probably isn't a good single source of input for your decision. You intuitively weigh factors such as price, manufacturer, online multiplayer capabilities, and previous purchase decisions that went well or poorly before choosing a console.

Computer programs work in a similar way. A program is more limited than your mind, though, because programs have only a limited intelligence for adapting to new situations, whereas you are capable of adapting to any unforeseen condition. Computers excel at doing things precisely and quickly, but humans have intuition—we are able to see patterns and shapes that aren't apparent at the lowest detail, which is the narrow level that computers "see," so computers don't get the big picture like we do. To help with intuition, our minds like to categorize things as closely as possible, so we are able to recognize these patterns as quickly as possible.

As infants, one of the first patterns that our minds memorize is the face of our mother or father. Some of your mind's first problems involved seeing other faces and trying to decide whether it was Mom or Dad. That was a pattern-recognition problem that required a great deal of training and reinforcement—looking at familiar faces over and over again causes those memories to be remembered and used for comparison. So, when you think about it, our minds are already programmed when we are born and just need input. That is very similar to how a computer program works. First, you write the program and put as much or as little problem-solving ability into it as you choose, and then you send the program out into the world. Of course, another advantage we humans have over computers is the built-in ability to learn.

At present, computers are not very good at learning, but research into this field of science is also progressing at a staggering pace. There are already neural networks that are capable of learning a million times faster than a human brain. As scientists study the human brain and map more and more of it to learn how it works, they are able to build more powerful artificial neural networks.

Logic versus Intuition

Have you ever discovered something new and immediately found it difficult to compare that new thing with anything else you have seen in your life? Part of the enjoyment of discovering new things is the mystique of trying to categorize them. We leap upon solutions so quickly that it is fun to find something that is indescribable—at least at first. This is precisely why children have such a need to play, and why their lives are filled with such mystery, intrigue, and suspense. Children never know when something new will present itself to them. Adults are often not as fascinated by daily life, after having "seen it all." If you think about that observation for a minute, and note how it applies to your life, doesn't it start to make sense? The wonder of childhood is very closely tied to this built-in ability to categorize things in the world.

When a baby sees a new person's face, the baby might frown, look puzzled, or even cry, unhappy with the new situation. Often the baby is very quickly able to perform the "parent/not parent" test by comparing new faces with the most important faces in a baby's mind. The infant's mind is an extraordinarily complex neural network. To quickly summarize, a neural network is a pattern-recognition machine. Everything in the human mind is stored as a pattern, and it is our ability to organize and store patterns efficiently that determines our intelligence. Your ability to read the words on this page is an advanced exercise in pattern recognition. You recognize the letters that make up words so quickly that you don't even realize you are doing it. But at one time in your childhood you did not know how to read, and you had to painstakingly learn about phonemes and spelling and grammar. When you were learning to read, it might have been described as a painful process (in a limited sense), because you were rewiring your brain with the patterns of letters.

Today, we spend one-fourth to one-third of our lives just catching up to the current state of technology in our civilization. Past generations did not spend as much time in school and college as most of us do today because technology was not very advanced. Now, the technology of our civilization is increasing so rapidly that it takes at least 16 years—from age 5 until age 22 or so—to catch up, and even then we can only learn about a small segment of technology in that timeframe. The sum of human knowledge is incomprehensible to any individual person (and the rate at which that knowledge is increasing is itself increasing every year, a phenomenon called *entropy*).

Do you suppose your brain really stores every letter of the alphabet and then searches that list of 26 letters from start to finish while reading the words in this book? Take a moment to think about this, because it is more relevant to computer programming than you might imagine. No, you are reading these words and your mind is recognizing entire *words* as patterns, not just letters. Your mind will often misread words that have similar spelling (such as "grind" and "grand"), because a neural network seeks out solutions as fast as possible, and not always with perfect accuracy. That is intuition in a nutshell—grasping at the most likely pattern match. Our minds are able to wade through vast volumes of concepts, theories, and ideas to arrive at large-scale patterns, and these high-level insights lead to advances.

One reason why programmers are so fascinated with writing code is because it puts your mind through a constant workout as you try to reprogram your mind to stop making assumptions about things. You must put a conscious halt on some patterns and try to think like the computer thinks—how it processes data. That ability to quickly surmise the solution to a problem and write a program to do it is what makes a good programmer, and it does take practice. As you write more and more code and solve one problem after another, you will start to get the hang of it. At first, you will probably get frustrated when you realize how stupid computers are. They can't make any assumptions on their own—you must lead them every step of the way! But this will not always be the case in the future.

Methodology of the Mind

What I have learned over the years is that real programmers never get tired of writing code. No matter how boring the subject (like databases), a great programmer will find an inherent fascination with the "intuition bypass" that I described above. As you learn new techniques as a programmer, you find that many solutions simply involve challenging your assumptions about what the computer will do in a given situation. As you have lived your daily life, your mind has started to develop more advanced ways to store patterns. This is what you might call the "methodology of the mind," developed with experience. Not only is the human mind able to store and organize patterns efficiently, it is also able to completely reprogram the method by which it does these things—something that computer scientists may never be able to build into a computer.

I have mentioned categories already. A category is a sort of bin where your mind puts similar patterns, and there can be a hierarchy of these storage bins in your mind. For instance, you might lump shells, seaweed, and sand together in a category called "the beach." Since seaweed comes from the ocean, your mind doesn't need to add water to the category—it is just an assumption that water goes along with it.

Now, what if you have never seen a beach in your life, and you have likewise never seen a picture of the ocean? It is hard to imagine, somewhat like trying to imagine what it would be like to have been blind from birth. Without having ever used your eyes, how would you imagine the many colors in the world? You might imagine shades of color that resemble different scents or textures or temperatures, but you may never have any idea what different colors really look like.

As a programmer, you must learn to think outside of your assumptions in order to solve the most difficult problems in the best way. Not only will you become a better programmer, but you will be able to apply this skill to other areas of your life. After writing code for many years, I find that I am able to see things differently than other people. That is often what causes non-programmers to think of us as a little strange. While most people will look at a sports car and admire the paint and body style, a typical programmer will be interested in such things as the engine displacement, fuel economy, and gear ratios.

Three Steps to Solving Logical Problems

There are three basic steps to solving a problem—input, processing, and output. Consider a sample problem in which you are deciding which product to purchase at a store.

Input

Figure 2.8 shows three inputs for a decision that must be made. This represents the actual logic of a program (which could be the human brain or a computer, as

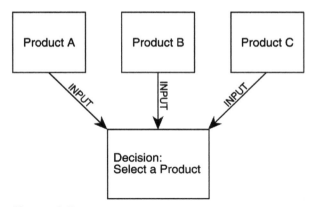

Figure 2.8
An illustration of a problem that needs to be solved

the case may be). This problem involves selecting a product. The square labeled "Decision: Select a Product" could be a program or a thought process that uses the incoming information.

Take a look at the sample problem to find the input. Input is nothing more than the data or facts that are available. In the sample problem, three products represent the input: Product A, Product B, and Product C. Each of these inputs might be stored in the program using a variable—a piece of data that the program can use.

Definition

A *variable* is a location in the computer's memory that stores some information that can be changed at any time.

Calculation

The next step to solving a problem is to do something with the input. This step is called the calculation step, or processing step, and usually involves some type of algorithm designed to solve a specific problem. Figure 2.9 shows how a product might be selected using specific criteria (also known as logic). This is really where all the action takes place, because the processing of the program occurs here. The program might run through many complex algorithms or just a simple equation.

Figure 2.9 shows a chain of test conditions involved in processing a decision. The decision is made only if all three conditions are true. Of course, in real life there might be any number of conditions, from just one to a hundred or even more.

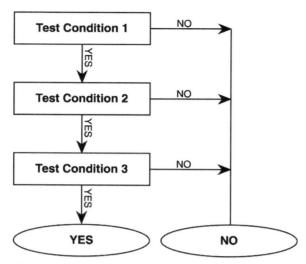

Figure 2.9
Several conditions must all be met before this decision returns true.

Naturally, computers are more efficient than humans when a decision involves a very large number of conditions.

Definition

> An *algorithm* is a step-by-step process for solving a problem.

Output

The output of a decision (or an entire program) is usually the most obvious part, where you clearly see something on the screen or printer or perhaps receive the answer to a decision. The output from one process is often also the input for another process. There are many different methods to map out a program. Thinking in the simple terms of input, process, and output will help you understand how programs work.

Video Game Basics

Well, I have covered many different aspects of computer programming without getting too technical. As you might have guessed from the title, this book is not just about writing computer programs; it is about writing games.

A computer game or video game is a program, written with a programming language such as C++ or DarkBASIC, which allows a player to interact within an imaginary world. The goal of a video game is to compete with other players in a cooperative or adversarial competition or to play solo, usually with an emphasis on setting a new high score (which other players will attempt to beat later).

Why Do We Play Video Games?

Video games are fun because they are very good at simulating another world and then drawing the player into that world. Video games are excellent for developing keen hand-eye coordination and problem-solving skills through the achievement of goals with specific rewards. Often the completion of the game is reward enough, but many games do not have a specific ending point. Rather, some games are suited for pitting two or more friends against each other, either at the same time or in turns.

Definition

Ludology is the formal name for the study of gameplay, and it attempts to answer the key question: "Why do we play games?" This subject is often discussed in game design books.

Competition helps to develop the skills you need to work with others and strive to better yourself, and video games are great at fostering competition. In addition, video games are wonderful works of art that reflect the often arcane imaginings of the game designer. As such, game designers are like painters with a virtual canvas, capable of transporting someone to another world. Once a game has achieved a minimum acceptable standard on the visual and audible level, players expect it to entertain through a gripping story or fantastic goal.

The Game Engine

Every game, from a simplistic card game like Solitaire to a complicated 3D strategy game like *Civilization IV,* has what is called a game engine. The *game engine* is the core set of commands that are executed repeatedly in a main game loop, which involves displaying images on the screen, playing sound effects, handling user input, and so on. Tall order, huh? Well, a game engine can be broken down into a few basic parts.

Game Graphics

In the old days, all games used two-dimensional images called sprites. It is a given that most games developed today will run entirely in 3D and feature three-dimensional objects throughout the game world rather than simply sprites. Not all games display 3D objects, but most games use a 3D world. DarkBASIC makes

3D programming easy by providing all the commands you need to load and draw 3D characters and worlds, as you'll see in later chapters!

Definition

A *sprite* is a small image that may or may not be animated, with properties that define how it will move around on the screen. The source image for a sprite usually has a background color that is defined as the *transparent* color that is not displayed when the sprite is drawn on the screen. The word sprite was originally coined by engineers at Atari.

Sound Effects and Music

Sound is quite often more important than the graphics in a game. It is clear that humans interact primarily through speech and sound. It should therefore be no surprise that sound is a vital part of any new game. In fact, it's no longer a great thing to have just sound and music in a game now that games use 3D sound. This provides the often eerie effect of being fully immersed in an environment filled with sounds from every direction.

Getting Input

User input is always needed, no matter what type of game you are writing. After all, a game without user input is nothing more than a technology demo! Dark-BASIC is capable of handling any number of input devices that you can plug into your PC, including the newer USB (universal serial bus) force-feedback joysticks. DarkBASIC handles the devices through a series of simple but robust commands, as you'll discover in Chapter 13.

Artificial Intelligence

Computer-controlled players are necessary for most types of games, and they are absolutely essential for single-player games. Some multiplayer games, such as first-person shooters, do not always have computer-controlled players, and thus do not need A.I. code. But the vast majority of games—especially strategy games—do, so it is important to learn the tricks and techniques for simulating intelligence and challenging the player with competitive computer players.

Writing Some DarkBASIC Code

I'd like to give you some experience playing around with DB. You should now have a basic grasp of what makes a computer program tick—even if you don't have a clue exactly how to put it to use yet. In other words, you have some theory but nothing useful yet! In this chapter and those that follow, you will be able to apply the Input-Process-Output model to game programming. First, I'll start with some basic concepts that will be useful in every DB programming project, regardless of the subject. You were introduced to several example programs in the previous chapter, but I'd like to start at the beginning nonetheless.

In most cases, DarkBASIC is located in the Windows Start menu under Program Files > The Game Creators or under Dark Basic Software. If you can't find DB in the Start menu, then you may want to make sure it was installed properly. The easiest way to tell is to run the install program again off the CD-ROM.

The "Hello World" Program

A program is made up of source code, which is the instruction manual that tells the computer what to do. When programming in DB, you will be typing in source code. Source code can be any text that instructs the computer what to do.

Typing in the "Hello World" Source Code

One of the hardest parts of writing a computer game is typing in the source code. You have to keep everything in mind, from what commands you want to use to what variables you want to create. Most programming languages are case sensitive, which means that you not only have to spell everything correctly, but the capitalization of each letter is important too. Fortunately, DB is not case sensitive, so you may use whatever capitalization you prefer. If it is easier for you to type in the source code using all lowercase, then DB won't mind.

The print command will work equally well as print, PRINT, or pRiNt.

Go ahead and type in the program yourself and see how it runs. Type the following two lines of source code into the DB editor exactly as shown.

```
print "Hello World"
wait key
```

Quick Keyboard Shortcuts

Sometimes the mouse just isn't convenient enough. Your fingers are just finishing up a long stream of code, and the little effort it takes to move the mouse up

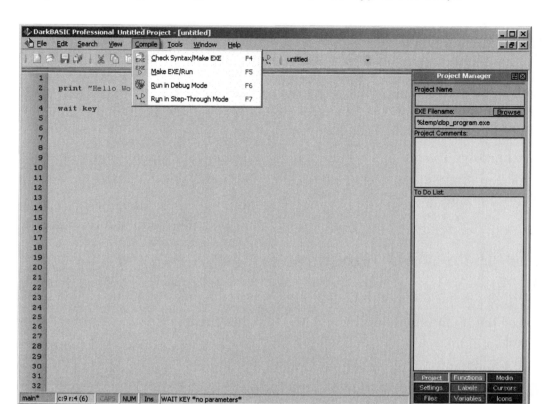

Figure 2.10
The Compile menu in the DarkBASIC IDE.

to the Run menu is just too much. Yes, I'm speaking from experience here. DB has that situation covered as well.

When you opened the Compile menu (shown in Figure 2.10), did you notice that each option has a function key listed next to it? The Compile option has F4, and the Run option has F5. This tells you that if you hit the F4 key while in DB, the program will compile. If you hit the F5 key, the program will run.

Saving the Program

Always be sure to save a program you've typed in before running it. Programming is always a scientific endeavor replete with mistakes, which will occasionally cause a compiler to crash—although DB is particularly user friendly and has never crashed in my experience. Another reason to save your work is that you never know when the power will go out after a long programming session. To

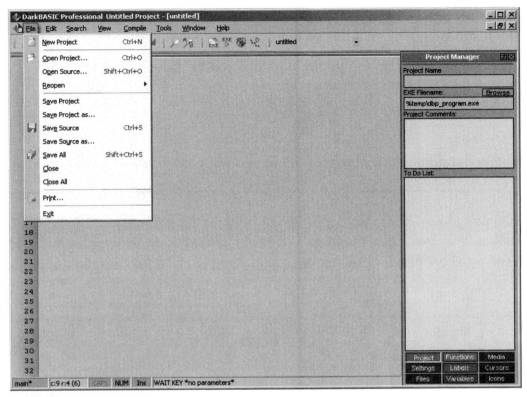

Figure 2.11
The File menu in DarkBASIC.

save the program, choose File > Save Project, as shown in Figure 2.11. You may also want to use the Save Source option to save your source code file with the project file.

Compiling the Program

You will need to check your source code for errors before running it. DB will not run the program if illegal commands have been entered. You can attempt to run the program, but it will not work if there is anything wrong. There is an easy way to compile and run your program—simply press the F5 key at any time and DarkBASIC will run your program (that is, if there are no errors).

DarkBASIC is a fun programming environment to use, as you have probably noticed. It just seems like everything was designed for writing games, and it's very immersive. DarkBASIC isn't overloaded with too many features that completely overwhelm anyone but an expert (which is the case with a complex tool like Microsoft Visual C++).

Now that you've saved the program, compile it to make sure there aren't any typos in it. To compile the program, open the Compile menu and select Run (or just press F5).

Definition

When you *compile* your source code, DB converts your source code into machine instructions that can be run on the computer.

Small programs such as this "Hello World" program compile in less than a second on most PCs, but larger programs can take a long time to compile. Figure 2.12 shows the compilation progress bar.

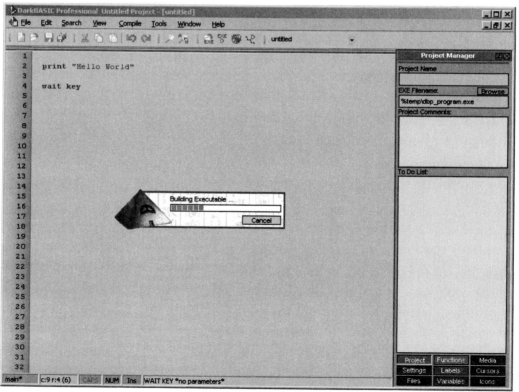

Figure 2.12
The compilation progress bar shows the progress while a program is being compiled.

Commenting Your Code

Some of the most important source code in a program consists of lines that are never executed, called *comments*—something that I emphasized strongly in the previous chapter. Adding comments to source code is helpful in two ways. First, it tells you what you were thinking when you wrote that particular section of code. Second, it helps you remove code that you do not want run but that you want to save for later. It's also useful to include blank lines in the source code to separate sections of code and make it easier to read. DB ignores blank lines and comment lines. There are three ways to add a comment to your source code.

The REM Statement

The REM command tells DarkBASIC that the line is a comment. The REM command must come first in the line, followed by the comment. The REM command is short for *remark*, and it allows you to include comments in a program that are ignored by DB.

```
REM This is a comment that doesn't do anything.
```

```
REM Comment lines are ignored by DarkBASIC.
```

The Reverse Apostrophe Comment Character

The reverse apostrophe character is the character normally associated with the ~ (tilde) key and is found to the left of the "1" key and above Tab on most keyboards. It is the most convenient way to add comments to your source code. After a few examples of using the other comment commands in upcoming chapters, I will use the reverse quote character more often.

```
' This is a comment that doesn't do anything.
```

```
' Comment lines are ignored by DarkBASIC.
```

The REMSTART. . .REMEND Statements

Often the REM command is just not enough to handle many lines in a lengthy comment. For example, you might want to add a header to your source code to give information about the program. You can include as many lines as you want in this header by defining those lines as comments. Adding REM to each line is easy to do, but there is a more elegant solution—the REMSTART and REMEND commands.

REMSTART indicates that a comment starts at that line. Anything following a REMSTART is considered a comment and is ignored by DarkBASIC—until it reaches a REMEND command. Here is an example of the REMSTART and REMEND commands.

```
remstart
   Program: Test.dba
   Author: Jonathan Harbour
   Date: April 20, 2006
   Description: Demonstrates the use of comments.
remend
```

Starting and Stopping the Program

Now let's talk about program flow. DarkBASIC executes the source code from the top to the bottom, executing each line of the program one at a time. That means the first command in the source code file is the first command that DarkBASIC executes. Since DarkBASIC executes code in this manner, there is an END command available that you can use to end the program from any point. Otherwise, the program will simply end after the last line of the program has executed.

The End Command

The END command ends the execution of your program wherever you put it. It can be placed in multiple locations. The following program shows how to use the END command.

```
REMSTART
   Program: Test.dba
   Author: Jonathan Harbour
   Date: April 20, 2006
   Description: Demonstrates the use of comments.
REMEND

REM print a message
print "Hello World"

REM wait for a key press
wait key

REM End the program!
END
```

This program might not do much, but it does demonstrate how you can comment your code effectively. It might seem like too many comments for such a short program, but small programs tend to grow large very quickly when you're on a coding marathon session. Why do you need an END command? Why not just place the last line of source code at the end of the file? So if you want to stop your program from running, you need to use the END command. Nothing after the END command will be run. You can also simply let the program end without this command, but there may be occasions when you need to end the program from any point in the source code.

Understanding Variables

I briefly mentioned variables in the last chapter (enough to tantalize you?), but this chapter is dedicated to the subject. One might go so far as to claim that variables are the foundation of computer programs. Variables provide a means to store data in a program. A variable is stored in memory and accessed through its name, like this:

```
HugeNumber = 3828549
DecimalNumber# = 3.14159265
Person$ = "Hayao Miyazaki"
```

As you can see, variables can store numbers or words (also called strings).

What Is a Variable?

In the old days when programmers used machine and assembly language, they would create variables by simply grabbing a chunk of memory and then storing a number in the newly acquired spot. This was called *memory allocation*, which is a valid term in software today. Reserving a space in the computer's memory was a manual process that required the programmer to keep track of exactly where that space was located by creating a pointer—which is where variables came from.

Definition

Assembly language is a very low-level programming language that uses mnemonics (symbols that are easy to remember) to represent the machine language instruction set of the computer. These mnemonic instructions allow the programmer to perform mathematical, logical, memory, and input-output related instruction. Assembly is normally used only to write high performance code that is time critical like device drivers, graphics algorithms, and operating system utility programs.

To make the task easier, programmers developed assembly language, made up of words and symbols that are very closely related to machine instructions but much easier to write. Assembly permitted the use of mnemonic words to replace the specific addresses in the memory where the information was stored. Rather than keep track of the address of a pointer, which in turn points to another address in memory where actual data is located, a mnemonic was used as the pointer. Mnemonics are easier to remember than physical addresses in memory, so this greatly eased the job of writing programs. Here is an example:

```
MOV AX, 03h

INT 33h
```

Those two commands together tell the computer to "get the mouse position." As you might imagine, assembly is difficult to master, and beginners always have an interrupt reference book handy. The first line "moves" the number 3 into the AX register. Registers are sort of like the piston chamber of a processor. Put something in the chamber and fire off an interrupt and something will happen (only in this case, it is a number instead of a spurt of gasoline and air). The second line is an interrupt call—the spark plug of assembly language. There are many interrupts in assembly that do all kinds of weird things, like polling the mouse.

Another popular old MS-DOS interrupt is INT 21h, which was very common in the "old days" when games were developed for MS-DOS (before Windows or DirectX came along). The "AX" in the first line above is the assembly equivalent of a variable, although that is a bit of a stretch, because AX is actually a physical part of the processor. If you were to take a processor and look at it through a microscope, you would theoretically be able to locate that "AX" register amidst a tight cluster of registers in the core of the chip.

Over time, assembly language and all the difficult-to-remember mnemonic words such as "MOV" and "INT" was replaced with more advanced languages that were closer to human language. DarkBASIC is what you might call an ultra high-level language, because it has so many features built in. In contrast, assembly language is extremely low-level because it is closer to machine language in form. Fortunately for us, DarkBASIC keeps track of all the variables in a program, including the type of data stored in variables.

Variable Notation

So how do you define a variable? You simply give it a name. There are rules for defining a variable name. You cannot start a variable with a number or punctuation mark, and you cannot have a space in a variable name. Other then that, the sky is the limit. For example, if you want to store the number of shots fired from a gun, you would define the variable like this.

```
ShotsFired = 5
```

You might also want to store how many shots are in the gun. To do so, just define another variable the keeps track of that value.

```
ShotsInGun = 6
```

Performing Basic Math Operations with Variables

You can also perform math functions on variables, including the four basic mathematical functions—addition, subtraction, multiplication, and division. Addition problems use the plus sign (+), subtraction problems use the minus sign (−), multiplication problems use the asterisk (*), and division problems use the forward slash (/).

Using More Than One Variable in a Formula

Now, here's a trick: Instead of using plain numbers (which are called *literals* in computer-speak) in a variable, you can use other variables. For example, to calculate the speed at which an object is traveling (such as your car), you need a variable for distance and a variable for time. The speed is just distance divided by time. The following program, called MathExample2, shows how to solve this simple problem with DarkBASIC.

```
Distance = 50
Time = 10
Speed = Distance / Time
PRINT "Distance is "; Distance
PRINT "Time is "; Time
PRINT "Speed is "; Speed
WAIT KEY
```

This short program outputs the following text:

```
Distance is 50
Time is 10
Speed is 5
```

Order of Operations

In DB, mathematical operations have an order to them. Division and multiplication are performed first, followed by addition and subtraction. You can bypass that order if you need to by enclosing your problem in parentheses. Parentheses tell DarkBASIC to evaluate a certain part of the problem first. For example, consider the following equation:

2 * 3 + 5

The answer is determined by first multiplying 2 by 3, and then adding 5 to arrive at an answer of 11. Imagine if you were to first add 5 to 3 and then multiply by 2. The answer would be 16, which is incorrect. By using parentheses, though, you can force DB to put priority on part of the calculation.

2 * (3 + 5) = 16

Here are some more examples of using parentheses:

```
REM this will evaluate to 3
Answer = 2 + 2 / 2
PRINT "2 + 2 / 2 ="; Answer

REM this will evaluate to 2
Answer = (2 + 2) / 2
PRINT "(2 + 2) / 2 ="; Answer
WAIT KEY
```

This is known as order of operations. The only way to bypass this order is by using parentheses. Let me throw a few more problems at you and see if you can figure them out. Use Table 2.2 if you need a guide to the order of operations.

A. 4 + 3 / 3

B. (4 + 4) / 2

C. 4 + 4 * 2

D. 4 * (4 + 4)

The answers to these problems are:

A. 5

B. 4

C. 12

D. 32

Table 2.2 Order of Operations

Operator	Precedence	Description
( )	First	Parentheses to set precedence
*, /	Second	Multiplication and division
+, −	Third	Addition and subtraction

It's pretty complicated to keep the order of things in mind, especially when you are trying to write a program to solve a math problem for an algebra or calculus class! Table 2.2 lists the basic mathematical operations and the order in which they are evaluated.

Data Types

DB supports many data types, making them available to you for declaring variables in many different ways. Table 2.3 shows the data types you can use in your DB programs.

There's an additional data type not in this list, called *string*. Strings are covered in the next chapter.

BYTE

A byte is made up of 8 bits, meaning a byte can store a number from 0 to 255. Bytes typically store a character because ASCII codes are also represented with 8-bit codes. A byte in DB cannot be a negative. If you're familiar with C++, you can create a *signed byte* with a range of −127 to 128, but DB only supports *unsigned* bytes.

```
byteVar AS BYTE
```

Table 2.3 Numeric Data Types

Data Type	Bit Size	Range
BYTE	8 bits	0 to 255
WORD	16	0 to 65,535
DWORD	32	0 to 4,294,967,295
INTEGER	32	−2,147,483,648 to 2,147,483,647
DOUBLE INTEGER	64	−9,223,372,036,854,775,808 to 9,223,372,036,854,775,807
FLOAT	32	3.4E +/− 38 (7 significant digits)
DOUBLE FLOAT	64	1.7E +/− 308 (15 significant digits)

Table 2.4 Very Large Numbers	
Name	**Size**
Kilo	2^10
Mega	2^20
Giga	2^30
Tera	2^40
Peta	2^50
Exa	2^60
Zetta	2^70
Yotta	2^80

You are probably already familiar with the term "byte" because it's used to describe computer memory. Do you know how far the terminology goes? You've heard of kilobyte, megabyte, and gigabyte, but have you ever heard of a yottabyte hard drive? That would be pretty awesome, wouldn't it? Table 2.4 shows some names for very large numbers.

WORD

A word consists of two bytes, or 16 bits. Due to this increase in bits, a word can store a value up to 65,535. This is a good variable data type to use for keeping track of the score in a game because it doesn't handle negative numbers.

```
wordVar AS WORD
```

DWORD

A DWORD (double word) variable is twice as large as a word, comprised of four bytes, or 32 bits. DWORD has a maximum value of 4,294,967,295. Like a regular word type, the double word cannot store negative numbers so it is known as an unsigned number.

```
dwordVar AS DWORD
```

INTEGER

The INTEGER data type is the same size as a double word (32 bits) but is the signed version of this data type, giving it a range of –2,147,483,648 to 2,147,483,647. The integer data type is a good general-purpose data type for most numeric variables you'll need in a game (I use them more often than any other data type). If you want to improve the performance of a game, though, you should use a data type that closely matches the need because the more bits in a variable, the more time it takes to manipulate that variable.

```
intVar AS INTEGER
```

DOUBLE INTEGER

The DOUBLE INTEGER data type is the king of numbers in DarkBASIC! Double integers are 64-bits wide, which is four times larger than a double word. This data type also supports negative numbers, so it is signed with a staggeringly large range:

–9,223,372,036,854,775,808 to 9,223,372,036,854,775,807 (in the Exa size range). You will probably never need a variable this large, but it's available if you ever do need it.

```
dintVar AS DOUBLE INTEGER
```

FLOAT

The FLOAT data type represents a floating-point number (which is a number that has a decimal point). These types of numbers are called *real numbers* as you'll recall from math class. Floats are 32-bits wide, or four bytes, with a range of 3.4E +/− 38 (with 7 significant digits of precision). What this means is a float rounds off any digits beyond the 7th digit. If you set a float variable to 3.1415926535, it will actually just store 3.1415927.

```
floatVar AS FLOAT
```

DOUBLE FLOAT

A DOUBLE FLOAT is similar to a float, but occupies 64 bits (8 bytes). This additional capacity gives it a much higher range of 1.7E +/− 308 (with 15 significant digits of precision).

```
dfloatVar AS DOUBLE FLOAT
```

Variable Scope

Sometimes when you examine a problem, you need to determine its scope . . . that is, you need to determine how far the problem extends. Variables are similar in the respect that they have a scope. There are two different types of scope that affect variables—global and local.

Global Scope

Global variables are accessible anywhere in the program, including any functions in the program. Information in a global variable is accessible anywhere in the program. Global variables are declared using the GLOBAL keyword followed by the variable name and the data type.

```
GLOBAL myGlobal AS INTEGER
```

Local Variables

Local variables are only visible in the current function in which they reside. I realize we haven't discussed functions yet, but it's important to know about the scope of variables. Just keep this concept in mind for now—functions will be explained in Chapter 4, "Program Logic: Branching Statements, Functions, and Algorithms."

```
function MyFunction()
   firstname AS STRING
   firstname = "John"
endfunction
print "My first name is" + firstname
```

This program will do something strange. Instead of printing out "John" like you might expect, it prints out a blank line. The reason for this is that DB creates a variable when it comes to a new variable in your code that hasn't already been defined. What is essentially happening here is the firstname variable is being created in the main program and the firstname variable that was created in the function is no longer in scope. If you wanted to correct this bug, you would need to declare the variable outside of the function with global scope:

```
GLOBAL firstname AS STRING
function MyFunction()
   firstname = "John"
endfunction
print "My first name is " + firstname
```

This code will print out John just like we expected it would.

Tip

You will learn more about strings in the next chapter, which also covers the advanced subject of user-defined data types.

Assigning Values at Declaration

You can set a value to a variable at the same time that you declare it, either as a global or a local variable. For instance, here is a declaration for a string variable that also sets the variable to a value:

```
myName AS STRING = "Jane Doe"
```

This rule applies to all the data types, such as integers:

```
TheMeaningOfLife AS WORD = 47
```

Note

The old version of DarkBASIC (also known as "DarkBASIC Classic") supported only three data types: integer, float, and string. You had to use special characters for a float (#) and string ($), while a variable without a special character was treated as an integer. Here are some examples:

myInteger = 100

myFloat# = 1.00

myString$ = "Hello"

While you can still declare variables in this manner, it is an obsolete way to write DarkBASIC code and is not recommended.

Summary

This chapter covered a lot of basics in a short amount of time, including a brief course on the basic premise of programming and algorithms (input, process, output) and an overview of video games and what game programming involves. You then learned how to create variables using the different data types supported by DB. If you ever need to refresh your memory about data types, this is a good chapter to refer to in the future, especially if you have a question about the range of the data types (such as 0 to 255 for a byte).

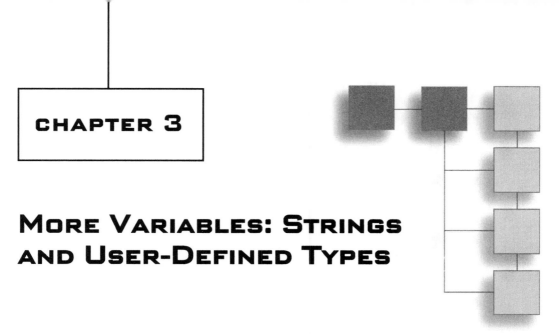

CHAPTER 3

MORE VARIABLES: STRINGS AND USER-DEFINED TYPES

We are now heading into the fascinating subject of strings, which store characters, words, sentences, and any other types of information of which you need to keep track. You can use strings to hold all other data types, which is useful when you need to make sure a user entered the correct type of information (for example, a dollar amount). In this chapter, you will learn how to create, manipulate, and display strings. Computer scientists decided to use the word "string" to represent a series of characters in the computer's memory, used for displaying textual information. In the old days, a printer printed everything out, but today most output is sent to the high-resolution monitor sitting next to your computer. Regardless of the output device, a string is used to store and display text.

This chapter shows you how to do all kinds of things with strings, from converting them to numbers to printing them to the screen using graphical fonts to reading substrings within a string. Strings are the most popular data type that programmers use. Why? String variables are versatile and capable of storing numbers, letters, and punctuation in any combination. One string can store your name, while another string can store how many oranges you have. Here are the key topics you will learn about:

- Strings and text output

- Programming strings

- Displaying text on the screen

- User-defined data types

Programming Strings

Strings are easy to program or define in DarkBASIC. To give you a little perspective, I'll explain how strings work in most languages. They are more or less a collection of characters. A character, of course, is a number, letter, or punctuation mark. In C you can define a string by creating a character array, whereas in C++ you just define a string class. In DarkBASIC it is much, much easier.

Declaring Strings

So how is a string declared? Simply by encasing what you want to store in the string in quotes (" "). For example, "This sentence is a string." The quotes tell DarkBASIC to store the text in the string variable. You can declare a string like so:

```
movie AS STRING
```

Alternately, you may use the dollar sign to signify that a variable is a string by simply setting it to a value, as follows:

```
movie$ = "Primer"
```

However, that is the old way of declaring and using strings and is frowned upon because it makes for messy code (and bugs!). I strongly recommend that you declare all of your variables with a specific data type rather than using shortcut characters. There are some instances when use of the dollar sign shortcut format for a string variable is helpful, such as when you need to create a string and set it to a value in the same line. But you don't want to skimp on writing solid code just to save a line here and there.

Assigning Values to Strings

To assign a string to a variable, you just add an = sign followed by the string. If you wanted to create a string called sentence, containing "One ring to rule them all.", you would type in the following code.

```
phrase AS STRING
phrase = "One ring to rule them all."
```

You can also assign a value to the string at the same time that you declare the string, like this:

```
phrase AS STRING = "One ring to rule them all."
```

Copying Strings

Sometimes declaring a string is just not enough. You might need to copy a string, which is quite simple in DarkBASIC. The following code will copy the string to another and then print it out.

```
jediknight AS STRING = "Mace Windu"
somejedi AS STRING
somejedi = jediknight
PRINT "The name of the Jedi Knight is " + somejedi + "."
```

This code will print out the following line:

```
The name of the Jedi Knight is Mace Windu.
```

Sometimes you will need to add two strings, which will allow you to make more sense of the data you have within your strings. There are two strings in the following code—firstname and lastname. Suppose you want to get the fullname variable from these two. You would just add the strings together like this:

```
firstname as string = "John"
lastname as string = "Smith"
fullname as string
fullname = firstname + lastname
```

When you are running this program, you'll notice that fullname prints out, but there is no space between my first and last name. That does not help you when you are putting my whole name together. You need to add a space between my first and last name. The following code will show you how to do that.

```
firstname AS STRING = "Angus"
lastname AS STRING = "MacGyver"
fullname AS STRING
fullname = firstname + " " + lastname
PRINT fullname
```

String Conversion Commands

Now it's time to do some legwork with strings. You know how to define them, but what's the point of defining them if you can't use them? There are a few commands that will convert strings into useful data; DarkBASIC contains five such commands.

The ASC Command

The ASC command converts a character (one letter) into its corresponding numeric ASCII value. The command will return the ASCII value of the *first* character in the string you input. The syntax is ASC(String), which returns string as an integer.

What is an ASCII value? ASCII stands for American Standard Code for Information Interchange. Computers don't know what characters and words are, but they do understand numbers, and each ASCII character is known by a specific ASCII value. There are 256 ASCII characters. For example, the uppercase A is equal to ASCII value 65. If you need to know an ASCII value for any reason, the ASC command will give you that value.

```
REM This will return the value of 65
AsciiValue AS BYTE
AsciiValue = ASC("A")
REM This will print the number 65
PRINT AsciiValue
```

The VAL Command

The VAL command converts a string into a floating-point number. It only converts strings that contain actual numbers like "123" or "456.00." Thus VAL is useful if you have a number stored in a string and you need to convert it to a real number for use in calculations. The syntax is VAL(String), which returns a float.

```
REM This will return a value of 35
Number AS INTEGER
Number = VAL("35")
```

The CHR$ Command

The CHR$ command converts a decimal number that represents an ASCII character into the single character string. Remember the ASC command? The CHR$ command performs the opposite operation; that is, it converts numbers to characters rather than characters to numbers. The syntax is CHR$(number), where number is the decimal integer of the ASCII value you want converted to a string. This command returns the desired ASCII character as a string.

```
REM this will return the value of "A"
MyString AS STRING
MyString = CHR$(65)
PRINT MyString
```

String Manipulation Commands

Now that you have a basic understanding of strings and what you can do with them, let's take a look at some commands that were designed for manipulating strings in various ways. For instance, there are commands for finding out the length of a string (how many characters it contains), copying a portion of a string, and several more.

The LEN Command

The LEN command returns the number of characters in a string, which is quite useful when used with other string manipulation commands. The LEN command syntax is LEN(String), where String is the string you want to compute the length of. A lot of string manipulation requires you to know how large or small a string is before you manipulate it. If you did not know the length of a string, you could end up going outside the scope of the string and generate an error. For instance, suppose you want to display a message on the *right* side of the screen, but you don't know beforehand how long the string will be. Suppose you are displaying the mouse position like this:

```
MOUSE X/Y = (539,290)
```

Since the mouse could be at (0,0) on the screen, the length of the message will change depending on the mouse position. One way that the LEN command is useful is computing the length of a message right before it is displayed on the screen.

```
REM this will return the value of 17
Number = LEN("This is a string!")
PRINT Number
```

The MID$ Command

The MID$ command lets you retrieve any character from the middle of a string (and also from the start or end of the string as well). All you need to know for this command is the position of the letter in your string. The MID$ command syntax is MID$(String, Number), which returns a string of the character found at the position in the string indicated by number. Here is an example:

```
MyString AS STRING = "Frodo Baggins"
REM this will print F
PRINT MID$(MyString, 1)
REM this will print n
PRINT MID$(MyString, 12)
```

The RIGHT$ Command

The RIGHT$ command returns a string containing the rightmost set of characters in a string. For instance, the last five characters of "Thomas Anderson" is "erson". The RIGHT$ command syntax is RIGHT$(string, number), which returns a string containing the rightmost letters up to the number specified. Here is an example:

```
MyString AS STRING = "Thomas Anderson"
REM this will print "Anderson"
PRINT RIGHT$(MyString,8)
```

The LEFT$ Command

The LEFT$ command is similar to the RIGHT$ command, but it returns characters from the left side of a string. In the string "Agent Smith", the first five characters are "Agent". The LEFT$ command syntax is LEFT$(string, number), which returns a string containing the leftmost letters up to the number specified. Here is an example:

```
MyString AS STRING = "Agent Smith"
REM this will print "Agent"
PRINT LEFT$(MyString,5)
```

The STR$ Command

The STR$ command will convert any numeric variable into a string. This is a good command for converting numbers read in from a file into strings or when printing out strings on the screen. The STR$ command syntax is STR$(integer value), where integer value is returned as a string instead of an integer. Here is an example:

```
REM this will print a "4"
PRINT STR$(4)
REM this will print a "12345.6789"
realNum AS FLOAT = 12345.6789
PRINT STR$(realNum)
```

Printing Text on the Screen

The computer screen is made up of thousands of small picture elements (which is the root phrase for "pixels"). A *pixel* is simply the smallest point on a display screen, comprised of a red, green, and blue element. Each of these elements can be lit independently and to a fine degree of luminosity, providing a large number of colors. The pixels on the screen are arranged in rows and columns. If your screen is set to 1024 × 768, that means there are 1024 pixels from left to right across the screen, and 768 rows of pixels from top to bottom. As you can imagine, that adds up to a *ton* of pixels! To better understand this concept, look at Figure 3.1. Like a sheet of graph paper, the screen is represented by columns and rows described as X and Y, respectively.

The next few commands will help you position strings on the screen. Some commands will simply print text in a pseudo-graphics mode, while others will let you draw text anywhere on the screen.

The PRINT Command

We have already gone over the PRINT command, but it is good to review it. The PRINT command just prints whatever string or series of strings you want on the

Figure 3.1
The display screen is made up of many rows and columns of pixels.

screen. It starts at the top and works its way down to the bottom. The PRINT command syntax is PRINT "something to print" where *something to print* is displayed on the screen. Remember that if you want to print anything other than a variable after a PRINT command, you must enclose it in quotes. For example:

```
heroName AS STRING = "Garnet Til Alexandros 17th"
PRINT "The hero's name is " + heroName
```

The TEXT Command

The TEXT command is similar to the PRINT command, but it allows you to specify exactly where the text string will be printed on the screen at an X and Y position. This allows you to place text anywhere you want on the screen. The syntax for the TEXT command looks like this: TEXT X, Y, String. Here is an example:

```
heroName AS STRING = "Zidane Tribal"
TEXT 500, 300, heroName
```

The CENTER TEXT Command

The CENTER TEXT command is just like the TEXT command but again with a twist. This command centers whatever you wanted to print around the X and Y

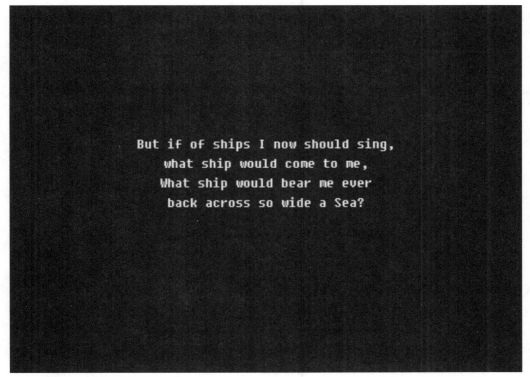

Figure 3.2
Using the CENTER TEXT command to display text centered at an X,Y point.

positions that you entered. If you want to print someone's name on the top of the screen but you do not want to figure out the spacing, this command is for you. The syntax looks like this: CENTER TEXT X, Y, String. The X and Y values must be integers. Here is an example:

```
CENTER TEXT 320, 180, "But if of ships I now should sing,"
CENTER TEXT 320, 200, "what ship would come to me,"
CENTER TEXT 320, 220, "What ship would bear me ever"
CENTER TEXT 320, 240, "back across so wide a Sea?"
REM A poem by J.R.R. Tolkien
```

This short program is shown running in Figure 3.2.

The SET CURSOR Command

The SET CURSOR command places the cursor anywhere you want on the screen. When you use the TEXT command, in fact, DarkBASIC first calls SET CURSOR and then calls the PRINT command—although PRINT only works with the system font (see the section below to learn about changing the font). The syntax of this command is: SET CURSOR X, Y. The X and Y values must be integers.

Font Commands

Now I have covered the basics of displaying text on the screen, but that text is printed in the standard system font by default. In a word processing application, you have a choice of many different fonts, sizes, and styles. Well, DarkBASIC also supports all of the TrueType fonts installed on your Windows system, identified by name. There are many commands to change the appearance, size, and other aspects of any text printed. Something to note about the text font commands: They only work with the TEXT or CENTER TEXT command. They will not work with the PRINT command.

Changing the Text Output Font

The default font used to output text in DarkBASIC is the "system" font, which is monospaced and good for general purpose messages. However, DarkBASIC gives you access to all the fonts installed on your PC, including TrueType fonts such as Times New Roman and Arial. You use the SET TEXT FONT command to change the font. The syntax of the command looks like this:

```
SET TEXT FONT "Font Name"
```

SET TEXT SIZE is a complementary command that is almost always used with SET TEXT FONT, and is used to change the font size. The command sets the point size of the font, with common values of 10, 12, 14, 16, and 18, but you can specify any value you want. Just like in a word processor, this command defines how big the text will appear on the screen. The average font size is usually 12 points. Here is the syntax for this command: SET TEXT SIZE Font_Size. Here's an example:

```
REM Set font to Forte 36
SET TEXT FONT "Forte"
SET TEXT SIZE 36
CENTER TEXT 320,100, "Ere iron was found or tree was hewn, "
CENTER TEXT 320,125, "When young was mountain under moon; "
CENTER TEXT 320,150, "Ere ring was made, or wrought was woe, "
CENTER TEXT 320,175, "It walked the forests long ago."
REM A poem by J.R.R. Tolkien
```

This short program is shown running in Figure 3.3.

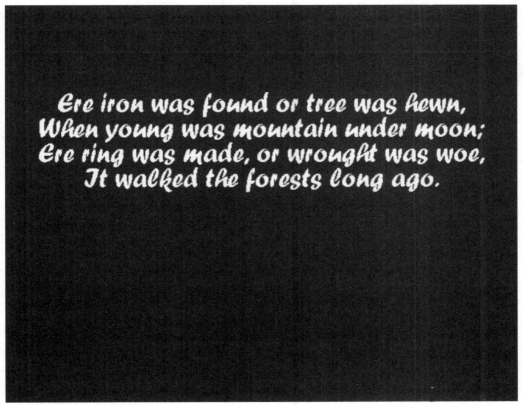

Figure 3.3
Printing text on the screen using a custom font.

Returning the Current Font Name

There might come a situation in which you need to know the name of the current font used for text output. To return the font name as a string, you use the TEXT FONT$ command. Here is a sample snippet of code that shows how you might use this command:

```
FontName as string
FontName = TEXT FONT$()
PRINT "The current font in use is "; FontName
```

Font Size Commands

When you're working on a game using a high-resolution screen, size *does* matter. If the print is too small, no one will be able to read it; if it is too big, it won't fit on the screen. Therefore, you need to define the size of your fonts.

The TEXT SIZE command is like the TEXT FONT$ command. However, instead of returning the name of the font in use, it returns the size of the font as an integer. Here is the syntax of the TEXT SIZE command.

```
Font Size = TEXT SIZE()
```

The following sample snippet of code shows you how you might use the TEXT SIZE command.

```
FontSize = TEXT SIZE()
PRINT "The current font size is "; FontSize
```

The TEXT WIDTH command can be very helpful at times. This command gives you the width of a string in pixels, as it would appear on the screen. Remember, a string is made up of characters. The LEN command tells you how many characters are in a string, but font types and sizes vary widely when printed on the screen. That's where the TEXT WIDTH command is helpful. For example, suppose you want to print a string at the right edge of the screen. Without knowing the exact width of the string, you wouldn't be able to position it at precisely the right location. The syntax for the TEXT WIDTH command looks like this:

```
Width Value = TEXT WIDTH(String)
```

Here is a short program that will print a series of text messages on the right edge of the screen, shown in Figure 3.4.

```
SET TEXT FONT "Forte"
SET TEXT SIZE 32
line1 AS STRING = "Seek for the Sword that was broken,"
line2 AS STRING = "In Imladris it dwells;"
line3 AS STRING = "There shall be counsels taken"
line4 AS STRING = "Stronger than Morgul-spells."
line5 AS STRING = "There shall be shown a token"
line6 AS STRING = "That Doom is near at hand,"
line7 AS STRING = "For Isildur's Bane shall waken,"
line8 AS STRING = "And the Halfling forth shall stand."
REM A poem by J.R.R. Tolkien
TEXT SCREEN WIDTH() - TEXT WIDTH(line1), 100, line1
TEXT SCREEN WIDTH() - TEXT WIDTH(line2), 125, line2
TEXT SCREEN WIDTH() - TEXT WIDTH(line3), 150, line3
TEXT SCREEN WIDTH() - TEXT WIDTH(line4), 175, line4
TEXT SCREEN WIDTH() - TEXT WIDTH(line5), 200, line5
TEXT SCREEN WIDTH() - TEXT WIDTH(line6), 225, line6
TEXT SCREEN WIDTH() - TEXT WIDTH(line7), 250, line7
TEXT SCREEN WIDTH() - TEXT WIDTH(line8), 275, line8
```

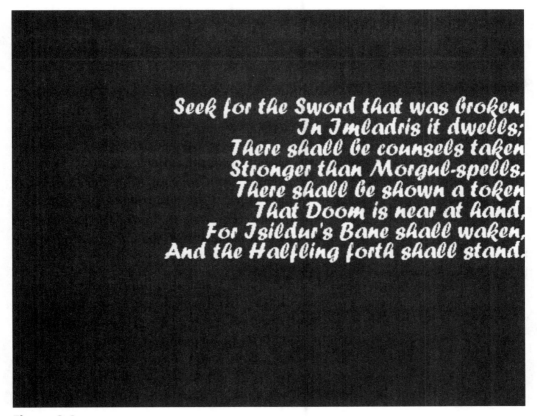

Figure 3.4
Printing text right justified on the screen using the TEXT WIDTH command.

Setting the Text Height

The TEXT HEIGHT command returns the height of the string you want to print in pixels. This gives you the Y size of the text; the TEXT WIDTH command gave you the X size of the text. The syntax for the TEXT HEIGHT command follows.

```
Height Value = TEXT HEIGHT(String)
```

Text Style Commands

Now we come to the fashionable part of the text commands—the text style commands. These commands allow you to alter the appearance of the text once again. You can change the text to bold, italic, or both.

Setting the Font to Normal

The SET TEXT TO NORMAL command sets the font style to normal, which removes any bold or italic font styles in use for the next text output command. Here is a snippet of code that demonstrates how to use this command.

```
SET TEXT FONT "Arial"
SET TEXT TO NORMAL
SET TEXT SIZE 16
TEXT 100,100, "This text is normal"
```

Setting the Font to Italic

The SET TEXT TO ITALIC command sets all the text that follows it to italics. That means your text will not be bold, but it will be in italics. Here is a snippet of code that demonstrates how to use this command.

```
SET TEXT FONT "Arial"
SET TEXT TO ITALIC
SET TEXT SIZE 16
TEXT 100,100, "This text is italic"
```

Setting the Font to Bold

The SET TEXT TO BOLD command sets all the text that follows it to bold. That means your text will not be in italics, but it will be in bold. Here is a snippet of code that demonstrates how to use this command.

```
SET TEXT FONT "Arial"
SET TEXT TO BOLD
SET TEXT SIZE 16
TEXT 100,100, "This text is bold"
```

Setting the Font to Bold-Italic

The SET TEXT TO BOLDITALIC command sets all the text that follows it to italics. That means your text will be in both bold and italics. Here is a snippet of code that demonstrates how to use this command.

```
SET TEXT FONT "Arial"
SET TEXT TO BOLDITALIC
SET TEXT SIZE 16
TEXT 100,100, "This text is bold and italic"
```

Table 3.1 Text Style Values

Return Value	Style
0	Normal
1	Bold
2	Italic
3	Bold and italic

Determining the Current Text Style

The TEXT STYLE command returns an integer indicating the current font style in use (normal, italic, bold, or bold-italic). The command returns a number from 0 to 3, corresponding to the current text style. Table 3.1 describes the four values returned by this command.

Text Transparency

One last thing we need to cover for text appearance is text transparency. That is, what does the background of the text look like? Not the letters per se, but behind the letters. Each letter printed in DarkBASIC is really a square. Anything that is not part of a letter is black or whatever color you specify it to be. However, if you want to put text over a picture, you definitely do not want its background to be black. DarkBASIC has some commands to control transparency.

Definition

> *Transparency* is technically a term that describes an object that is completely see-through. The actual term for partial transparency is *translucency.* A piece of glass is transparent. *Opacity* refers to something that is completely non-transparent, and therefore, opaque.

The SET TEXT OPAQUE command sets the text background to the current color specified in the INK command (which is covered in Chapter 9). If text is printed over any pictures, it will look like a solid rectangle with words in the middle.

```
REM Set the background color to red
CLS RGB(255,0,0)
REM Set the font color to white on black
INK RGB(255,255,255), RGB(0,0,0)
REM Display the opaque text
SET TEXT OPAQUE
TEXT 100,100, "This Text is Opaque"
```

The SET TEXT TRANSPARENT command is the exact opposite of the SET TEXT OPAQUE command. That is, it will set the text background to clear so whatever is behind it can be seen.

```
REM Set the background color to red
CLS RGB(255,0,0)
REM Set the font color to white on black
INK RGB(255,255,255), RGB(0,0,0)
REM Display the transparent text
SET TEXT TRANSPARENT
TEXT 100,100, "This Text is Transparent"
```

The TEXT BACKGROUND TYPE command returns the background type of the current font—either opaque or transparent. Like the TEXT STYLE command, TEXT BACKGROUND TYPE returns an integer. If the background is opaque, a zero is returned; for transparent, a one is returned. Here is the syntax for the command.

```
Background Value = TEXT BACKGROUND TYPE()
```

User-Defined Data Types

A *user-defined type (UDT)* is an advanced data type in DarkBASIC that you can customize for your own needs into a complex structure containing many variables within. A structure of this type greatly reduces the number of global variables you would normally need to use in a complex game.

Defining Your Own UDT

You can define a UDT yourself using the TYPE and ENDTYPE statements, and the result is your own custom data type. Here is an example:

```
TYPE Person
    FirstName AS STRING
    LastName AS STRING
    Age AS INTEGER
ENDTYPE
```

When you're ready to use this type, you can define a variable AS [your type] to create a new variable of the type, like any other variable:

```
padawan AS Person
```

Using a UDT

Voila, now you have a new variable using your custom data type! To use the variables inside a custom data type, you access them using the dot operator (.), like so:

```
padawan.FirstName = "Obi-Wan"
padawan.LastName = "Kenobi"
padawan.Age = 30
```

In future chapters we will be using UDTs extensively, especially when working with 2D sprites and 3D characters that must move around and interact in the game world—which requires a lot of variables. Here is an example of a UDT for keeping track of a sprite:

```
TYPE MY_SPRITE
   x as integer
   y as integer
   speedx as float
   speedy as float
   alive as byte
   spriteType as word
ENDTYPE
```

Creating a new variable using this UDT is then just a matter of declaring it with the new data type:

```
mySprite1 AS MY_SPRITE
```

Nested UDTs

UDTs are really not very difficult to understand and use, as you can see here. We will be using them a lot in future chapters! One of the most interesting aspects of a UDT is that you can declare one UDT inside another UDT. Once you start doing that, things really start to get complicated! By using this feature of DarkBASIC, you can write well-structured code that even has some resemblance to object-oriented code. Here is an example:

```
TYPE ANIMAL_TYPE
   species AS STRING
   numberoflegs AS WORD
ENDTYPE
```

Using this UDT as a basis, we can now define a new one that extends the original:

```
TYPE DOG_TYPE
   animal AS ANIMAL_TYPE
   breed AS STRING
ENDTYPE
```

Now that we have two interesting UDTs, let's declare a variable and see how it looks in code:

```
myDog AS DOG_TYPE
myDog.animal.species = "Canis familiaris"
myDog.animal.numberoflegs = 4
myDog.breed = "German Shepherd"
```

Summary

You learned some very useful new data types and commands in this chapter. Specifically, you learned about the string data type and many of the string manipulation commands such as MID$ and LEN. This chapter also delved into a relatively advanced subject—user-defined types (UDTs), which make it possible for you to create your own custom data types, which may be nested into even more complex structures. These new data types will be very helpful as you start learning to write more complex code in future chapters.

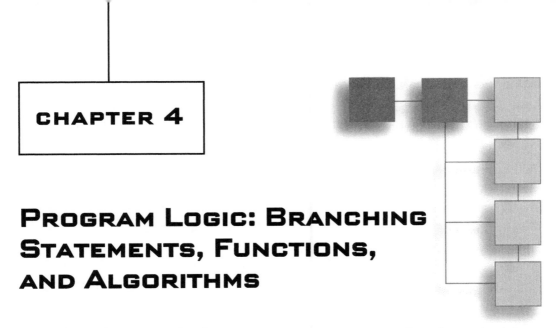

CHAPTER 4

PROGRAM LOGIC: BRANCHING STATEMENTS, FUNCTIONS, AND ALGORITHMS

Regardless of programming language or computer system, there is a point where logic commands reach a roadblock and the program cannot grow any larger without being broken into smaller parts. When the main procedure needs to do something specific, such as check the position of the mouse pointer on the screen, it is better to jump to another part of the program that specifically handles mouse input than to write the mouse code directly in the main procedure's source code. That way other parts of the program can use the mouse, and you don't have to rewrite the mouse commands every time.

This chapter will teach you how to break up a program into smaller parts, called *subroutines*, and how to use branching statements to call upon those subroutines when needed. *Branching* gives a program the logic it needs to perform more than one task based on certain conditions. There are times when you can write small portions of code directly inside a branching statement, but there are other times when that code requires its own space. I'll show you how to create subroutines that perform specific processes in a game, and you will use this in later chapters. Basically, this is one of the most important chapters of the book!

This chapter covers the following topics:

- Introduction to program logic
- Branching statements
- Functions
- Algorithms

Introduction to Program Logic

First I would like to talk about program logic, because you should understand this before you get into subroutines. DarkBASIC calls all subroutines *functions*, but I'll get to that in the second half of the chapter.

What is logic and how does it relate to programming? When I hear the word logic, I think of several descriptions—analysis, deductive reasoning, processing, the rival of intuition. Computers are great at performing logical commands, but how does logic work in DarkBASIC? Most programming languages have a standard set of branching statements that you can use to create the logic in a program. The two branching statements in DarkBASIC are IF ... THEN and IF ... ELSE ... ENDIF. These statements can be more formally described as *conditional statements*. Most programmers will know right away what you are talking about if you mention an "if statement," strange as that may sound at first.

What Is a Branching Statement?

Branching statements, also called *conditional statements*, provide the program with a means to apply rules and tests to variables and then take action based on the results. They are built into programming languages so programmers (like you and I) can process the input and provide the output for a program. Without branching statements, the program would only be able to forward the input directly to the output without any processing. Although this might be something that you want the program to do (perhaps to display a text file on the screen or print a document), it is far more likely that you will need to *do something* with data that has been entered into the program. Branching statements allow you to create complex program logic. You may not be able to create something as complicated as a pattern-recognition neural network like the human brain, but even the human brain works by simple rules. It is just that billions of those small rules are being followed synchronously.

Conditions are factors that limit something within a specific boundary. For example, a football field is a rectangle bordered by white lines that delineate the area in which legal plays can be made. The rules of the game dictate how the game is played, and these rules form a set of conditions that must be met in order to play the game correctly. Who enforces the rules of the game? The referees (and in some cases, the fans!).

The Key to Program Logic

Program logic and logical decisions are at the core of how computers work, providing a means to process data. At the highest level, programs should be designed to accomplish the following three tasks.

1. Receive some input data

2. Process the data

3. Output the result

The goal of any programmer should be to write programs that revolve around these three basic operations. Input, process, and output help to break down a problem into manageable pieces, and you should be able to clearly see how these three concepts apply to every program. When a program doesn't receive input, process data, or output something, then it really isn't a useful program.

Obviously, these operations have a wide range of applications. Input could be from the keyboard, mouse, or joystick, but it could also be a database, text file, serial or infrared port, a network connection, or even a scanner or digital camera. Processing might involve translating, combining, or transforming the data to suit a specific purpose. In the case of a digital camera, processing might involve adjusting the brightness and cropping the photo. Output is the result of the processing, which might involve displaying something on the screen, in a printed report, or possibly to an output file or database. As you can see, input-process-output can be interpreted to mean many things. The important thing is that every program accomplishes at least this basic level of functionality.

Making the Program More Useful

In a computer program, you define a set of conditional statements (or branching commands) that enforce the rules of the program. There are usually many different areas of the program that perform these commands, depending on its state. For instance, a game might check the status of a joystick button. The condition in this case is a rule that if the button is pressed, something will happen (for example, the spaceship will fire a weapon or player will shoot a gun). A more complicated example is reading the keyboard. There are 100 or so keys on a typical AT-101 keyboard. Checking the scan codes (the special codes for each key) involves some logic, as does checking the mouse for input. The point is, without the ability to process input and provide a result, computer programs are not very useful. Imagine a car game in which you just watch the computer drive the cars around. Sound like fun? Obviously, a game needs to interact with the user, and that is my case in point.

Branching Statements: Decisions, Decisions

Decision-making is the first step to adding logic to your program and demonstrates the simplest form of intelligence. Small bugs like beetles have very simple decision-based intelligence of the sort that I am going to describe to you here. But taken to the next level, even a small rodent like a mouse has an exponentially more complex intelligence in the form of a brain comprised of a network of interconnected neuron cells—which is what computer scientists call a *neural network*. If you examine a neural network up close, it is made up of millions or billions of small decision-making neuron cells that perform conditional logic of this form:

IF *condition is true* THEN *do one thing* OTHERWISE *do another thing*

Neurologists and brain research scientists are learning about the complex human brain by studying the brains of small animals like mice. In fact, the most progress made in artificial intelligence research has come from the study of small mammal brains, which are simpler versions of the human brain. Artificial intelligence is, in fact, just a field that seeks to simulate the function of a human brain.

There are two specific branching statements in DarkBASIC: IF ... THEN and IF ... ELSE ... ENDIF. In this section, I'll describe both statements and show you how to use them.

The IF ... THEN Statement

The most common branching statement used in programming languages is the IF ... THEN statement. Following is the general syntax of the statement as it is used in DarkBASIC.

```
IF <condition is true> THEN <do something>
```

Do you see how the entire statement occurs on a single line? This is a *simple* statement, and it can only have one possible action after THEN. There is also a *compound* version of the IF ... THEN statement, which is called IF ... ELSE ... ENDIF.

The IF ... ELSE ... ENDIF Statement

The IF ... ENDIF statement alone is sufficient for most of your logical needs. By using IF and ENDIF, you can have many actions take place as a result of a conditional test. For instance:

```
IF firstname = "John"
   PRINT "Your name is John."
   PRINT "The origin of your name is a Hebrew phrase, 'Yahweh is merciful'."
ENDIF
```

What happens when you need to test more than one condition at a time? You could use multiple IF ... THEN statements, but there is an option in the IF statement, called ELSE, that allows you to respond to the *true* and *false* conditions independently. For example, to test for a true or false condition without the ELSE option, you would have to write code like this:

```
IF age > 17 THEN PRINT "You are an adult."
IF age < 18 THEN PRINT "You are a minor."
```

Following is the general format of the IF ... ELSE ... ENDIF statement.

```
IF <condition is true>
   <do something>
ELSE
   <do something else>
ENDIF
```

By using an ELSE statement, you can rewrite the previous code as follows:

```
IF age > 17
   PRINT "You are an adult."
ELSE
   PRINT "You are a minor."
ENDIF
```

There is one important distinction between the simple and compound statements. The compound IF does not have a trailing THEN when an ENDIF is also used.

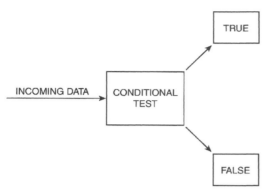

Figure 4.1
Illustration of a branching statement, showing the true or false result.

DarkBASIC identifies the THEN keyword to indicate that the whole statement occurs on a single line, while an IF without a THEN indicates a compound statement. You can use IF ... THEN for simple branching statements when only a single course of action is needed.

The use of the ELSE keyword is equivalent to the following two individual branching statements. Note the use of ENDIF to end each statement.

```
IF<condition is true>
   <perform primary commands>
ENDIF
```

```
IF<condition is false>
   <perform alternate commands>
ENDIF
```

As I mentioned, these two branching statements are equivalent to the IF ... ELSE ... ENDIF statement. The ELSE saves a lot of time! Figure 4.1 shows an illustration of the IF ... ELSE ... ENDIF statement, demonstrating how input is tested for a true or false condition and the program execution is directed down a specific path.

Using Branching Statements

Okay, I don't want to lose you! If you are new to branching statements or to programming in general, this discussion might not have sunk in yet. How about a realistic example? Here is how you might code the branching statement to determine which mouse button has been clicked.

```
IF MOUSECLICK() = 1
   PRINT "Left click"
ELSE
   PRINT "Right click"
ENDIF
```

You could have just as easily written this code using two IF ... THEN statements instead of a single IF ... ELSE ... ENDIF statement, and the result would have been the same.

```
IF MOUSECLICK() = 1
   PRINT "Left click"
ENDIF

IF MOUSECLICK() = 2
   PRINT "Right click"
ENDIF
```

The better solution, of course, is to use the ELSE section instead of the second IF statement, which is relevant when there are one or two possible values to be tested. When there are more than two values that you need to check, you can use compound IF statements as follows.

```
IF MOUSECLICK() = 1
   PRINT "Left click"
ELSE
   IF MOUSECLICK() = 2
      PRINT "Right click"
   ENDIF
ENDIF
```

This type of code is generally not necessary and adds a layer of complexity that is not needed.

Tip

Chapter 6, "Number Crunching: Math Operators and Commands," covers the common relational operators, such as greater than (>), less than (<), and equal to (=), along with mathematical operators such as multiply (*) and divide (/). You can combine this information with what you will learn in this chapter and the next chapter to gain some very useful tools for writing programs.

Dividing and Conquering with Functions

Functions are important for breaking up a large program into smaller, more manageable pieces, leading to better code reuse and legibility. They are also important for creating program logic. Quite often, the conditional statements in a branching statement point to a subroutine to keep the branching statement short. If each case in a branching statement included a page of source code, it would be easy to lose track of the cases! Therefore, functions are essential parts of a programming language. Figure 4.2 illustrates the relationships between the main program and all of its functions, which are broken down into more detail at each level.

What Is a Function?

First, let me clear up something regarding subroutines. A subroutine is a separate sequence of source code within a program that performs a recurring or distinct task. By recurring, I mean something that is repeated over and over. By distinct, I mean something that might be used only once, but for which it makes more sense to put the code in its own subroutine. Functions are meant to help us write better code by breaking up a large program into smaller parts. The entire goal of a function should be the same as that of the overall program: to accept input, perform some processing, and then produce output. Figure 4.3 illustrates the point.

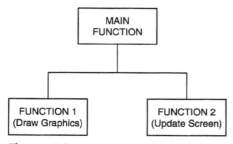

Figure 4.2
Structured programs have a hierarchy of functions from high levels to lower levels of detail.

Figure 4.3
The three steps to programming: input, process, output.

The next thing I want to make clear about subroutines is that you must use the FUNCTION statement to create custom subroutines. For the sake of clarity, I will refer to subroutines and functions interchangeably; they are the same thing. I will use the uppercase FUNCTION when referring to source code and the lowercase "function" when talking about functions in the general sense.

Following is the basic syntax of a function in DarkBASIC.

```
FUNCTION FunctionName([Parameters])
ENDFUNCTION [ReturnValue]
```

Let me explain how this works. You declare a function with a FUNCTION ... ENDFUNCTION block of code. You give it a name and include any parameters that you want to be able to pass to the function, and then you provide an optional return value. Since there really is no easy way to explain this, let me show you a few examples. This first example is a function that displays a message on the screen.

```
FUNCTION PrintHello()
   PRINT "Hello!"
ENDFUNCTION
```

You can simply call this function by name anywhere in the program. The function prints out "Hello!" on the screen any time it is called. Now that is great as a first example, but it isn't very useful. A far more useful function would be one that lets you print out any message you want. Although the PRINT command does this already, it is helpful to demonstrate how parameters work. Here is an example of a function that includes a parameter.

```
FUNCTION PrintHello(Name as string)
   PRINT "Hello, "; Name; "!"
ENDFUNCTION
```

Using Functions

I want you to remember something very important about dealing with string variables. Any time you declare a string parameter, you must use the dollar sign along with the variable name everywhere in the function. If you were to write the previous line without the dollar sign like this (note the variable name in bold):

```
PRINT "Hello, "; Name; "!"
```

the output of the program would be very strange. No matter what text message you send to the PrintHello function, it would always print 0 instead of the text you intended. The rule to follow is this: If you declare a parameter using the dollar sign character instead of the "AS STRING" data type, you must use the dollar sign everywhere you use the variable in the function. DarkBASIC is a very lenient programming language, allowing you to declare variables anywhere.

Divide and Conquer

How about another example to give you a little more practice using parameters? I've written a program called RandomText that uses a custom function called PrintAt. This function prints a string on the screen at a specific location using parameters. Here's the code listing for the RandomText program (shown in Figure 4.4). This program is using several commands you have not really learned

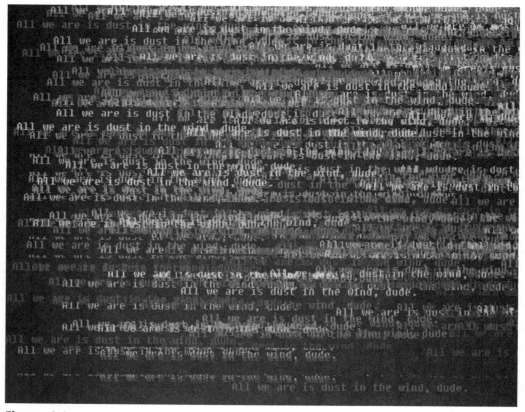

Figure 4.4
Output from the RandomText program.

yet, so just keep them in mind for now and we'll cover them in a more formal basis in due time.

```
DO
    color = RGB(RND(256), RND(256), RND(256))
    INK color, 0
    PrintAt(RND(640), RND(480), "All we are is dust in the wind, dude.")
LOOP
FUNCTION PrintAt(X as integer, Y as integer, Message as string)
    SET CURSOR X, Y
    PRINT Message$
ENDFUNCTION
```

Returning Values

Functions can be used not only to break up lengthy programs with many lines of code and to make code reusable, but also to perform calculations or logic and return a value. This is an important aspect of any programming language. Without the ability to return values from functions, a program would have to use variables for everything, including calculations, and the source code would quickly become unmanageable.

Remember the syntax of a function, which allowed you to return a value? Here's the definition again for reference.

```
FUNCTION FunctionName([Parameters])
ENDFUNCTION [ReturnValue]
```

The return value is added after the ENDFUNCTION keyword when you want the function to return some value. This value can be a string or a number (integer or decimal), derived from a calculation, variable, or by any other means. Following is an example of a function that returns a value.

```
FUNCTION RandomColor()
    Color = RGB(RND(256), RND(256), RND(256))
ENDFUNCTION Color
```

Pay close attention to the use of parentheses after the function name: Random-Color(). When you would like to use this function in your own program, you must include the parentheses at the end, or else DarkBASIC will give you an error message. Some commands do not need the parentheses. Can you think of why some commands might need parentheses, while others do not? The answer is related to the return value. Some commands return a value, and some do not.

You can spot such commands in the source code because they include parentheses at the end. In general, a command that returns a value is called a function. Some languages even use the words "procedure" and "function" so it is easier to tell them apart. DarkBASIC is more flexible, allowing you to decide whether one of your custom functions will return a value or not. Sometimes it is helpful to think of it this way: commands *do* something, while functions *return* something.

Testing Parameters and Return Values: The ReturnValue Program

To demonstrate how to return values from functions, the following program (called ReturnValue) features three functions, two of which were designed to return a value and make the main program easier to read. For example, the custom SetColor function is easier to use than the built-in INK command. Figure 4.5 shows the output from this program.

```
FOR N = 1 TO 20
   color = RandomColor()
   SetColor(color)
   PRINT SPACE$(N); "Line "; N; " - ";
   PRINT "Three cheers for the conquering heroes!"
NEXT N
WAIT KEY
END

FUNCTION RandomColor()
  Color = RGB(RND(256), RND(256), RND(256))
ENDFUNCTION Color

FUNCTION SetColor(Forecolor)
   INK Forecolor, 0
ENDFUNCTION
```

Writing Your Own Functions

You can create any custom function for your programs with your own parameters and return values. As such, you can rewrite much of the DarkBASIC language to fit in with your own ideas of how programs should be written, or you can just combine DarkBASIC commands to perform higher-level processes. For

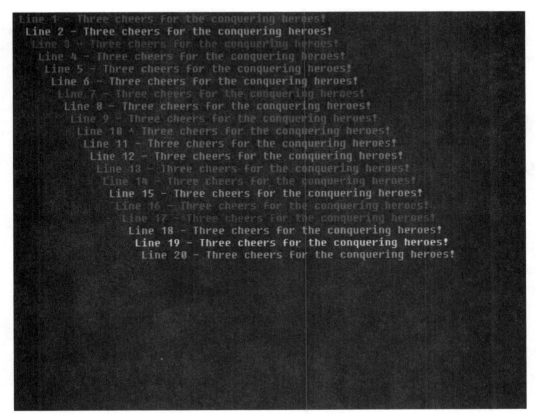

Figure 4.5
Output from the ReturnValue program.

instance, instead of just tracking the mouse, you might write your own function that moves a walking character on the screen based on where the mouse is clicked. Or you might move a spaceship around the screen using the mouse with a custom MoveShip function that you have created. The possibilities are endless, which is what makes programming so much fun! Moreover, once you have a library of functions you can use them for other programs and cut down on your programming time.

Advanced Logic Programming: Algorithms

Once you have mastered the basics of programming, you will develop your own unique programming style using techniques you have found to be useful. One such technique that I often use regularly is to *short circuit* a logic statement by reversing it and then doing away with an ELSE statement in most cases. For example, suppose I want to print a string onto the screen using the TEXT command, but I want to make sure the string contains a value first.

```
IF LEN(message) > 0
   TEXT 100, 100, message
ENDIF
```

Short-Circuit Logic

I like to use the term "short circuit logic" to describe this type of programming, because it is a descriptive term. When you perform a simple test and then exit out of a function when the test fails, you are short circuiting the rest of the logic in the function. Now, assuming this is what you want to do in the first place, a short circuit will speed up your program because none of the remaining logic tests are made when the flow of the program breaks out of the function instead of plodding along through additional logic.

Let me give you an example of a reusable function now to show how short-circuit logic works. This is a bit advanced early on, but good practices are best learned early.

```
FUNCTION PrintText(x as integer, y as integer, message as string, color as integer)
   REM make sure message is not blank
   IF LEN(message$) = 0 THEN EXIT
   REM print the message in specified color
   INK color, 0
   TEXT x, y, message
ENDFUNCTION
```

The PrintText function accepts four parameters (which will be explained later in this chapter). The first two parameters tell the function where to print the message in the specified color. Now let's take a look at another version of this function that is coded with a traditional IF statement instead of short-circuit logic.

```
FUNCTION PrintText(x as integer, y as integer, message as string, color as integer)
   REM make sure message is not blank
   IF LEN(message$) > 0
      REM print the message in specified color
      INK color, 0
      TEXT x, y, message
   ENDIF
ENDFUNCTION
```

These two versions of PrintText are functionally equivalent, so the benefit in the first format is a matter of code readability, but the benefits are more evident when you add more conditions, as you'll see next.

The condition that tests the length of the message is necessary if you have several conditional tests to make in the function, but generally most functions are small like this one, so the short-circuit logic can be a very powerful tool. Why, do you ask? Conditional branching code has a tendency to get ugly if you embed too many nested conditional statements. Instead of writing many IF statements, one inside another, to handle complex logic, it is better to short-circuit the tests by reversing the logic and breaking out of the function when a test fails.

Let's think about a good example to drive the point home. Let's consider the PrintText function and imagine that you want to make sure that all of the parameters passed to it are valid, especially the x and y values. This would require more IF statements. If written in a straightforward manner, the conditions might look like this:

```
FUNCTION PrintText(x as integer, y as integer, message as string, color as
integer)

    REM make sure message is not blank
    IF LEN(message$) > 0
      IF x > 0 AND x < SCREEN WIDTH()
        IF y > 0 and y < SCREEN HEIGHT()
          REM print the message in specified color
          INK color, 0
          TEXT x, y, message
        ENDIF
      ENDIF
    ENDIF
ENDFUNCTION
```

Now, I don't know about you, but I look at this function and think "Yuck." This is some ugly code, even if it does work. After you've been programming for a while, you will get to a point where you no longer have to think very hard about the code you write, as it will flow from your mind as fluidly as you write an e-mail. In fact, I often find myself programming several blocks of code at a time in my mind, and in doing so, I'm able to actually debug the code before it is even typed into the source code file. When I look at the PrintText function above, it actually *looks* ugly to me. The reason is that when you begin to master something, your mind sees larger-scale patterns.

Note

There is actually a system of thought based on this concept called *systems theory*, popularized by Dr. Margaret Wheatley. If you visit her website at http://www.margaretwheatley.com, you will see right away that she sees the world from a very large-scale viewpoint.

Let's rewrite the function using reverse logic.

```
FUNCTION PrintText(x as integer, y as integer, message as string, color as
integer)
    REM make sure parameters are valid
    IF LEN(message$) = 0 THEN EXIT
    IF x < 0 OR x > SCREEN WIDTH() THEN EXIT
    IF y < 0 OR y > SCREEN HEIGHT() THEN EXIT
    REM print the message in specified color
    INK color, 0
    TEXT x, y, message
ENDFUNCTION
```

Now, compare the two versions of the PrintText function and note which one is easier to read, less prone to bugs, and, more importantly, easier to modify. What happens with the first version of the function (with nested conditions) if you want to add *another* condition? You see, the nesting can get ugly. Perhaps the most important result of writing code in this manner is that it helps you to break down a programming problem into smaller parts, each of which performs one small task. After I have put all of this code for printing out a message in a given color into its own function, I don't need to look at the function ever again (unless I need to modify it).

Algorithms

Taken further, short-circuit programming might be thought of as one of many algorithms of good programming practice. There are the more usual types of algorithms as well, which provide solutions to complex problems in a functional way. To help you to understand what an algorithm is, let's consider an example from mathematics. When you were in the first or second grade, you started learning the basics of math: addition, subtraction, and a little multiplication and division. In these early years of your education, you had to do a lot of memorization, and you had to *learn how to learn*. Within a few years, though, you learned that there are ways to get to a solution without using the brute force method.

Counting Apples

For instance, if you have four baskets of apples, each containing five apples, how many apples are there? Multiplication is an algorithm of sorts when compared to simple addition. Instead of counting all 20 apples, you multiply five apples times four baskets. This is an algorithm that can be described as a function in mathematics:

Number of apples = Number of Baskets * Number of Apples per Basket

The algorithm might seem hopelessly simple to you, but then mathematics is a system of complex problems that can be solved with simple tools. Let's reduce the function further:

Number of apples (NA) = Number of Baskets (NB) * Number of Apples per Basket (AB)

NA = NB * AB

Now let's formalize it into a DarkBASIC function:

```
FUNCTION CountApples(Baskets, ApplesPerBasket)
   apples AS INTEGER
   apples = Baskets * ApplesPerBasket
ENDFUNCTION apples
```

Note

If you specify no data type for a function parameter, DarkBASIC assumes it is an integer.

Drawing Circles

Drawing a circle is not an easy task, especially if you want to draw circles *quickly*. You can calculate the points around a circle with a given radius (the distance from the center to the edge) using sine and cosine. But these math functions are extremely slow and they work with floating-point numbers, not integers. The goal of an algorithm is to perform a process either 1) more easily, or 2) more quickly than the brute force method.

Tip

We will cover the FOR loop and all of the other looping statements in the next chapter.

First, let's take a look at some code that draws a circle the slow way using sine and cosine:

```
FUNCTION DrawCircle(startx, starty, radius)
   angle as integer
   x as float
   y as float
   degrees as float
   for angle = 0 to 360 * 58
      degrees = angle * 3.14159 / 180.0
      x = cos(degrees) * radius
      y = sin(degrees) * radius
      dot startx+x, starty+y
   next angle
ENDFUNCTION
```

I've written a program called CircleAlgorithm that demonstrates this function, and the output is shown in Figure 4.6.

One glance at this function and you can see clearly that it will run very slowly. Why? As a general rule, floating-point multiplication and division is much slower than integer math. Now, there are arguments both ways due to the performance of modern processors, but let's just stick with the general assumption that floats are slower than integers. The next thing about this function that jumps out at me is that it draws one-fourth of a circle (that is, one quadrant), and it then goes to great pains to draw the other three quadrants. This is evident in the *360 * 58* and *3.14159/180.0* calculations, which get the pixels moving around the other quadrants. After all, a circle is perfectly symmetrical.

The circle algorithm here works best with just a single quadrant. For instance, by adding another DOT command with mirrored y coordinates, we can draw the circle using 50% of the calculations required before:

```
   for angle = 0 to 360 * 29
      degrees = angle * 3.14159 / 180.0
      x = cos(degrees) * radius
      y = sin(degrees) * radius
      dot startx+x, starty+y
      dot startx+x, starty-y
   next angle
```

Taken to the next step, we can mirror and flip the x coordinate as well, cutting the calculations in half again, resulting in an algorithm that draws circles

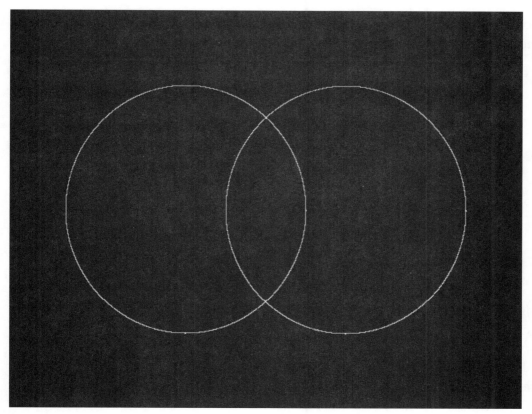

Figure 4.6
The CircleAlgorithm program draws circles the hard way.

four times faster than before:

```
for angle = 0 to 360 * 14.5
   degrees = angle * 3.14159 / 180.0
   x = cos(degrees) * radius
   y = sin(degrees) * radius
   dot startx+x, starty+y
   dot startx+x, starty-y
   dot startx-x, starty+y
   dot startx-x, starty-y
next angle
```

But wait, there are even more optimizations that can be made! Instead of mirroring just to the four quadrants, we can mirror the pixels around the eight *octants* of the circle by reversing the x and y positions for those four DOT commands. This has the effect of filling the screen twice as fast as before—and improving the original brute force algorithm by 800%.

```
for angle = 0 to 360 * 7.25
   degrees = angle * 3.14159 / 180.0
   x = cos(degrees) * radius
   y = sin(degrees) * radius
   dot startx+x, starty+y
   dot startx+x, starty-y
   dot startx-x, starty+y
   dot startx-x, starty-y
   dot startx+y, starty+x
   dot startx+y, starty-x
   dot startx-y, starty+x
   dot startx-y, starty-x
next angle
```

Jack E. Bresenham realized this too. Bresenham came up with his famous line and circle drawing algorithms in the 1960s while working for IBM. Instead of calculating the points around the entire quadrant or octant (45 degrees and 22.5 degrees, respectively), Bresenham's circle algorithm takes the algorithm above and makes it work with integers, but it is otherwise similar to what we have derived with the floating-point code.

Size Versus Speed

Most computer programming algorithms are devised to speed up a process by introducing clever shortcuts into a loop (such as the circle-drawing algorithm). But there is essentially no benefit to writing a complex algorithm that only runs once. The only time you should spend time devising an efficient algorithm is when it will be used repeatedly, which is really the whole point. Of course, with a tool like DarkBASIC, you do not need to reinvent the wheel—or even the circle—when it is already available in the DarkBASIC command library. And you can be sure the commands in DarkBASIC are already highly optimized, given that they're all written in C++. So, no command you write in DarkBASIC will ever be as fast as a built-in command. We'll take a look at all of the vector graphics commands (which means, those graphics commands related to lines and pixels) in Chapter 8, "Introduction to 2D Graphics: Basic Vector Drawing Commands".

Summary

This chapter covered the extremely important subjects of branching and sub-routines, which are both related in functionality. Branching statements allow you to apply rules to a program to keep the program running in a predetermined manner and behaving correctly. In addition, you learned how to use the IF ... ELSE ... ENDIF statement to apply logic and rule enforcement to your programs. This chapter also showed you how to create and use your own functions, complete with parameters and return values. Functions greatly enhance the capabilities of your games, allowing you to extend DarkBASIC beyond what the designers imagined.

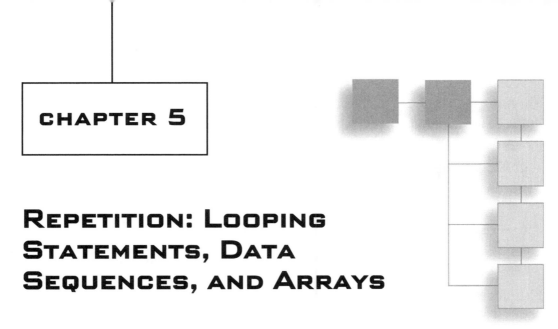

CHAPTER 5

REPETITION: LOOPING STATEMENTS, DATA SEQUENCES, AND ARRAYS

The most common task for a programmer is to automate some process that previously required a great deal of human effort to complete. To automate a process, programmers usually employ loops that run through large lists of transactions and perform tasks depending on the type of data in the list.

Data sequences and arrays are often used with looping statements. You can use a data sequence to add your own information directly into a program without loading that data from a file. For instance, in a shoot-em-up game, you can use a data statement to hold information about the game's levels and then not need any data files. Whereas a complete game might use data files to store information about the objects in the game, this type of data can be inserted into the game right from the start using data sequences.

Also, looping with data sequences allows you to read and apply custom values to your game. For instance, storing monster names along with traits in a data sequence is quick and easy and allows you to make changes to the traits right inside the source code at any time.

This chapter covers the following topics:

- Understanding the importance of looping
- Looping statements
- Introduction to data sequences and arrays
- Data sequences
- Arrays

Understanding Looping Statements

There are four looping statements available in DarkBASIC, and it's important to understand the strengths and weaknesses of each, how they compare with each other, and when each type of loop is preferable. The four looping statements are

- FOR ... NEXT. This loop iterates a specific number of times.

- DO ... LOOP. This loop is endless.

- REPEAT ... UNTIL. This loop repeats *until* a condition is met.

- WHILE ... ENDWHILE. This loop repeats *while* a condition remains true.

I'll explain each of these statements in detail shortly. In the meantime, I'd like to provide you with a little background information.

What Is a Loop?

A *loop* can be defined as anything that repeats something over and over. It has a starting point and an ending point. A loop starts with the first instruction in the loop, and then each command inside the loop is executed until the last instruction has been reached. The loop then jumps back to the first instruction and begins the process again. Figure 5.1 shows a visual representation of a loop.

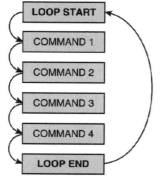

Figure 5.1
Visual representation of a loop.

Loops are about iteration, the ability to repeat something over and over again. A loop in DarkBASIC will help you complete repetitive tasks, such as drawing all of the sprites in your game. A single iteration is complete when you have reached the ending point, where DarkBASIC will decide whether you need to return to the starting point or continue with the program based on the conditions you have set. But an endless loop, such as DO ... LOOP, has no conditions, so it will continue to loop forever—or until you break out of the loop or end the program. For this reason, DO ... LOOP is a good choice for the main loop of a game.

Definition

> *Iteration* is the process of repeating one or more commands until a series has been processed (or completely run).

At this point you might be wondering how looping will help you write a game with DarkBASIC. I'm glad you asked! You might use looping in DarkBASIC to find the solution to a problem. Suppose you write a program that asks the user to type in 10 numbers, which the program will then add. Here's a short example.

```
print "Enter #1: ";
input a
Total = a
print "Enter #2: ";
input a
Total = Total + a
print "Enter #3: ";
input a
Total = Total + a
print "Enter #4: ";
input a
Total = Total + a
print "Enter #5: ";
input a
Total = Total + a
print "Enter #6: ";
input a
Total = Total + a
print "Enter #7: ";
input a
Total = Total + a
print "Enter #8: ";
```

```
input a
Total = Total + a
print "Enter #9: ";
input a
Total = Total + a
print "Enter #10: ";
input a
Total = Total + a
print "Total is " + str$(Total)
wait key
```

After the third or fourth line of code, things started to look familiar, right? This is what we call repetition. Any time you find yourself typing in the same thing two or more times, it's a good hint that a loop will be helpful. This program is made up of about 30 lines of code. Using a loop, that same program can be dramatically shortened. The real advantage of a loop is that it doesn't matter how many repetitions we need to perform, the computer will handle any number of them, quickly and efficiently. Let's learn about the first looping statement so I can show you how to turn this boring, repetitive program into an elegant solution using a loop.

Using Looping Statements

DarkBASIC has several types of loops, each of which has its own unique way of defining the starting and ending points of the loop. Each statement dictates a different starting and ending point for a loop. As I mentioned briefly at the beginning of the chapter, there are four looping statements in DarkBASIC:

- FOR ... NEXT

- DO ... LOOP

- REPEAT ... UNTIL

- WHILE ... ENDWHILE

The main difference among these statements is the condition each one uses to determine when the loop is finished. What is a *condition*? It is a programming statement that resolves to either a true or false answer. Each iteration through a loop is determined by a condition; if the condition is true, then the loop ends and the program continues. Table 5.1 shows the relational operators used to test a condition.

FOR ... NEXT

The first looping statement up to bat is FOR ... NEXT. It's deceptively simple, but it provides predictable results. With the FOR ... NEXT loop, you can define how many times you want the loop to run. A loop that runs forever—in which case, the condition is always false—is called an infinite loop. The starting point of the loop is the FOR statement; the ending point is the NEXT statement. See Figure 5.2 for an example.

Table 5.1 Conditional Symbols

Symbol	Description
=	Equal
<>	Not equal
<	Less than
>	Greater than
<=	Less than or equal
>=	Greater than or equal

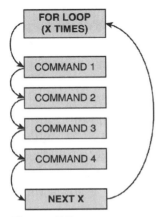

Figure 5.2
Visual representation of a FOR ... NEXT loop.

The command format for the FOR ... NEXT loop is

```
FOR variable = Starting_Value TO Ending_Value
   REM Commands go here
NEXT variable
```

The FOR command initiates the first loop by making the variable equal to the starting number. When DarkBASIC reaches the NEXT command, it returns to the FOR command and adds one to the variable. When the variable reaches the ending value, the NEXT statement does not loop back around again. Instead, it ends the loop.

Using the FOR ... NEXT Statement

Let's use the FOR ... NEXT loop in a practical sense by revisiting the number adding program you saw earlier to see how a loop will improve the program.

```
FOR x = 1 to 10
   print "Enter #" + str$(X) + ": ";
   input a
   Total = Total + a
NEXT x
print "Total is " + str$(Total)
wait key
```

It is pretty simple and yet so very powerful. With a single change of a number, you can make the program add 100 numbers or even 1000 numbers. Try playing with the starting and ending values to see what kind of crazy combinations you can create. Of course, this program is limited in speed to how fast you type in numbers. Most loops do not involve human input in this manner.

Specialty Case: The STEP Option

Sometimes you need to count by something other than one. For example, suppose you want to print every other number between 15 and 33. There is a special command for this, called STEP. It is placed at the end of a FOR statement, and you can specify the increment by which you want to count. For example, if you want to loop between 15 and 33 by increments of 2, the FOR command would be:

```
FOR X = 15 to 33 STEP 2
```

The STEP option is useful because it allows you to loop backward as well as forward! Here is an example program that loops backward.

```
print "Count down to liftoff..."
FOR X = 10 TO 1 STEP -1
   print X
   sleep 300
NEXT x
print "Blast Off!"
wait key
```

DO ... LOOP

Like the FOR loop, DO ... LOOP is another looping statement. The main difference between the two is that DO ... LOOP is an infinite loop, which means that as long as you do not interrupt the loop, it will continue forever (theoretically). Figure 5.3 illustrates the DO ... LOOP.

The format for the DO ... LOOP statement is similar to the format of a FOR loop, except that you do not have to follow the DO or the LOOP with anything.

```
DO
   REM Commands go here
LOOP
```

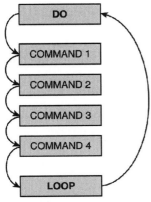

Figure 5.3
A visual representation of a DO ... LOOP statement.

Notice that I indented my source code lines between the DO and the LOOP. This is called *source code formatting*. Indenting makes the source code between the DO and LOOP much easier to read, and it helps you to identify exactly what code is in the loop.

Using the DO ... LOOP Statement

The following program shows you a practical use for the DO ... LOOP statement. To prevent the program from locking up, I've added a line at the end of the loop that breaks out of the loop when the spacebar is pressed. Don't worry about some of the commands you don't recognize. They will be addressed in later chapters. It's a pretty cool program, to bounce whatever you typed around the screen.

```
print "Please type in your name: "
input name$
DO
   cls
   text RND(500),RND(350), name$
   sleep 100
   if SPACEKEY() = 1 then exit
LOOP
print "We're done here, goodbye!"
wait key
```

Breaking Out with EXIT

DO loops are useful if you need to theoretically repeat the loop endlessly. But what if you have reached a certain point in a program and need to quit? For instance, you may need to exit the program when the user chooses to quit. DarkBASIC provides us with the EXIT command, which will break out of any loop immediately. The following program is similar to the previous one you typed in, but with one slight difference. It breaks out after printing your name ten times.

```
print "Please type in your name:"
input name$
REM define a counter variable
count AS WORD = 1

DO
   cls
   text RND(500),RND(350), name$
```

```
    sleep 100
    count = count + 1
    if count > 10 then EXIT
LOOP
wait key
```

REPEAT ... UNTIL

The DO loop is an endless loop, meaning it provides no way to test for a condition in order to exit the loop (which you must code yourself). The EXIT command ensures that you have a way to break out of an endless loop, but what about the times when you want to loop for a while and stop when a condition is met? Welcome to the REPEAT ... UNTIL statement. The REPEAT ... UNTIL statement will *repeat* a series of commands *until* a condition is met. Figure 5.4 shows a visual representation of a REPEAT ... UNTIL loop.

The format of the REPEAT ... UNTIL statement is shown here:

```
REPEAT
    REM Commands go here
UNTIL condition = true
```

An important thing to note about REPEAT ... UNTIL is that the source code inside the loop will always run at least once because the condition is not tested until the end of the loop.

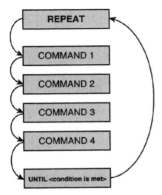

Figure 5.4
Visual representation of a REPEAT ... UNTIL loop.

Using REPEAT ... UNTIL

Now we are going to rewrite the program used previously for the DO loop. This time, though, the code will repeat until you hit the spacebar.

```
print "Please type in your name:"
input name$
REPEAT
   cls
   text RND(500),RND(350), name$
   center text 320,400, "Press Space to quit"
   sleep 100
UNTIL SPACEKEY() = 1
```

EXIT Revisited

Remember the EXIT command used previously in the DO loop? Well, it's back. You can use the EXIT command in the REPEAT ... UNTIL loop as well. Instead of having just one condition to exit the loop, you can create multiple conditions. The following program uses a REPEAT loop with the EXIT command. The program bounces your name around the screen. The program will end either when the spacebar is pressed or after ten iterations, whichever comes first.

```
print "Please type in your name:"
input name$
count AS WORD = 1
REPEAT
   cls
   text RND(500),RND(350), name$
   center text 320,400, "Press Space to quit"
   sleep 100
   count = count + 1
   if count > 10 then EXIT
UNTIL SPACEKEY() = 1
```

WHILE ... ENDWHILE

The last of the looping statements is the WHILE ... ENDWHILE loop. This type of loop is similar to a REPEAT loop, but the condition is tested at the beginning of the loop, rather than at the end. Figure 5.5 shows a visual representation of a WHILE loop.

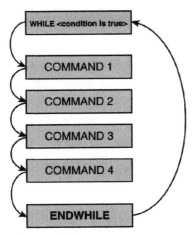

Figure 5.5
Visual representation of a WHILE ... ENDWHILE loop.

The format of the WHILE loop follows:

```
WHILE condition = true
   REM Commands go here
ENDWHILE
```

Using the WHILE ... ENDWHILE Loop

Okay, now it's time to rework the example program again, this time using a WHILE loop. The main difference between this program and the previous version (which used a REPEAT loop) is that it checks for the spacebar before it runs the code. As with the other three looping statements, you can use the EXIT command at any point in the loop to break out.

```
print "Please type in your name:"
input name$
WHILE SPACEKEY() = 0
   cls
   text RND(500),RND(350), name$
   center text 320,400, "Press Space to quit"
   sleep 100
ENDWHILE
```

Introduction to Data Sequences and Arrays

A data sequence can store any data in sequential order. That is, data is read one item at a time, like an assembly line. A *stack* is another way of describing a data sequence. A stack keeps track of data in a first in, last out order (also known as "FILO"). Alternatively, this can be described as last in, first out ("LIFO"). Figure 5.6 illustrates a common example of a stack, in which plates coming from the dishwasher are added to the stack and immediately removed for service. The first plate added to the stack might never even be used if plates continue to be added as fast as they are removed.

Keeping Track of Data

Comparing a data sequence to a stack is not entirely accurate because you can't add new items to the data sequence after the program starts running (during the *runtime*); you can only add new items when you are editing the source code (during the *design time*). However, if you type in the data statements in a data sequence in order, then it does resemble a design-time stack, so I thought this analogy would help you visualize how data sequences work. Another good analogy is that a data statement is like a read-only data file containing infor-mation for a game, such as the game's map or level.

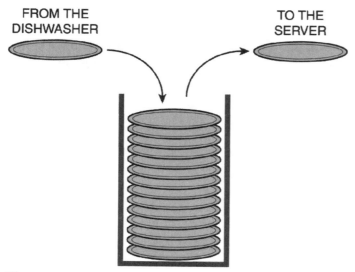

Figure 5.6
A software stack works like a stack of plates, where the last plate added is the first plate removed.

There are two basic types of files—sequential and random-access. Sequential files are like text files that you can edit with Notepad. A program settings file, such as win.ini, is also a sequential text file that you can read with Notepad. Another type of sequential file is a binary file that stores bytes or other types of numbers. Random-access files are structured files that read and write records of data rather than a single character at a time. DarkBASIC does not support structured files, but it does know how to read most game-related files natively (such as 3D Studio Max files, wave files, texture files, and so on).

The difference between a sequential file and a stack is that you must read and interpret a file using number or string variables, and you must keep track of file numbers, filenames, the length of the files, and so on. Data sequences are much easier to use! Just think of a data sequence as a simple kind of sequential file. You will learn more about files in Chapter 7, "Reading and Writing Data: File Input/ Output Commands."

Storing Data Efficiently

All things being equal, data sequences are really only effective for limited amounts of data. When the data in a data sequence becomes too large, it is difficult to maintain the data in your source code file. One way around the problem of lengthy source code listings is to use the #INCLUDE statement to include one or more source code files to your main program file. You can then move the data sequences over to a separate file and keep your main program listing tidier.

What types of data can you imagine storing in a data sequence inside your program? I can think of many:

- Character traits and attributes in a role-playing game

- Spaceship names and traits in a space shooter game

- Weapon names and attack values for a first-person shooter

- Height map data for the 3D terrain in each level of a game

- Power-ups that can be gathered in a game

- Maps and levels for a real-time strategy game

The one drawback to using a data sequence instead of a disk file is that once the game is finished, compiled, and put up for sale or into the public domain, there won't be any way to add new levels and missions or monsters to the game later (unless you recompile and release an update of the game's executable). Mission packs, add-ons, and modifications ("mods") are very popular in the gaming community. If even a simple game supports player-made levels, it will generate a fan following. Players enjoy creating their own levels and add-ons for games and then sharing their work with others. It fosters support for your game by giving players a little fame, a little prestige, and a lot of fun overall.

The tradeoff is really whether you want to go through the additional work required to load data into your program from disk files, rather than just storing the data inside your program. Perhaps one benefit to a data sequence is that it is like a built-in array, so you don't need to use an additional array to use it. Data stored in a file, however, would probably need to be loaded into an array, at which point it would somewhat resemble a data sequence.

Data Sequences

In this section I will show you how to create a data sequence in a DarkBASIC program. Next I'll show you the various commands for reading the data sequence and putting the data to good use. Finally, I'll show you how to reset the data sequence and start reading it from the beginning again. This might be useful when you want to restart the game, for instance.

The DATA Statement

The DATA statement is used to define data in a data sequence. It is specifically called a *sequence* because you can have many DATA statements in your program. In fact, you can insert a DATA command anywhere in your program, but I would recommend keeping all DATA statements at the top of the source code file for clarity. It is very confusing when you have DATA statements strewn all about your program.

One solution that you can employ with multiple data sequences is to label specific data sequences and then jump to specific labels to read a specific data sequence. I'll explain data labels shortly when I cover the RESTORE statement.

The DATA statement supports strings, integer numbers, and decimal numbers. Here is a sample of a data sequence that includes a last name, first name, and age.

```
DATA "Jones", "Bob", 34
DATA "Anderson", "Julie", 19
```

```
DATA "Smith", "John", 26
DATA "Wells", "Joanne", 8
```

See how you can design the data sequence any way you want? This data can accommodate numbers and strings, but there is no way to store binary numbers or bytes—the sort of data you would need to store bitmap pixels, for instance.

The READ Command

The READ command is used to read data stored in a data sequence. The data is read one item at a time (where individual data items are separated by commas) from beginning to end. The READ command is flexible in that it supports integer numbers, decimal numbers, and strings (just like the DATA statement does).

The code to read the data sequence and print out the information looks like the following snippet. Note that this code will use the DATA statements that were shown in the previous section.

```
FOR n = 1 to 4
   READ LastName$, FirstName$, Age
   PRINT FirstName$; ", "; LastName$; ", "; Age
NEXT n
```

Do you see how the variables are printed out in a different order than they are read? When you have read the data, you can do anything you want with it! Take note also of the FOR loop, which performs the READ command four times. Even though there are 12 items in the data sequence, three of them are read each time through the loop: LastName$, FirstName$, and Age.

Testing Data Sequences: The ContactData Program

Now I'll show you a simple program I wrote that uses a data sequence filled with contact information. The data includes the following fields.

- Last name

- First name

- Address

- City

- State

- ▪ Zip

- ▪ Phone

I know you aren't particularly interested in databases, but this simple contact program is a great way to demonstrate how data sequences work. Later I'll show you a more interesting program that uses DATA statements to bounce a ball on the screen.

Writing the Source Code

Now for the source code for the ContactData program. There are four DATA statements that provide the contact information used by the program. There is also a single DATA statement at the beginning of the sequence that provides the number of records that should be read. This is an important thing to remember! Without some sort of total value, you will have to hard-code the total number of data statements into your code, and then it will be more difficult to add new DATA statements later (something that is fairly common when working with information).

For your convenience, this project is located on the CD-ROM in the \Sources\ CH05\ContactData folder.

```
REM Declare the data sequence
DATA 4
DATA "Jones", "Bob", "1234 Somewhere St", "Oblivion", "MD", "10023",
  "916-555-1212"
DATA "Smith", "John", "5678 Super St", "Anchorage", "WY", "33992",
  "414-555-1234"
DATA "Anderson", "Julie", "9293 Prairie Dr", "Orson", "MI", "83923",
  "212-555-8382"
DATA "Wells", "Joanne", "3283 Oak Tree Ln", "Wichita", "KS", "22939",
  "623-555-3928"

REM Declare some variables
NumData AS WORD = 0
FirstName AS STRING
LastName AS STRING
Address AS STRING
City AS STRING
State AS STRING
Zip AS STRING
Phone AS STRING
```

```
REM Read the record count
READ NumData

REM Read and print out the data sequence
FOR n = 1 to NumData
   REM Read the data sequence
   READ LastName, FirstName, Address, City, State, Zip, Phone

   REM Print the contact information
   PRINT "CONTACT   "; n
   PRINT "  NAME   "; FirstName; " "; LastName
   PRINT "  ADDRESS  "; Address; ", ";City; ", "; State; " "; Zip
   PRINT "  PHONE   "; Phone
   PRINT
NEXT n
WAIT KEY
```

Have you noticed that I always include a variable declarations section in the sample programs? Although DarkBASIC doesn't require it, I highly recommend that you include a section at the top of your program for important variables so you can identify them more easily. It can be very confusing when variables are declared at random throughout the source code. This is good programming practice more than a requirement of DarkBASIC. Most programming languages require you to declare variables, so it's a good habit to get into because you might want to learn a highly demanding language like C++ in the near future, and these practices will help you to adapt to the new language more easily.

The RESTORE Command

The RESTORE command moves the internal data sequence position to the beginning of the list where the first DATA statement is located, so the next READ command will pick up the first item of data again. The RESTORE command also supports data labels that allow you to group related items of data.

Command Format

You can call the RESTORE command on its own, in which case the data sequence position will move to the top of the list. If you want to move the position to a data label, just add the name of the label after the RESTORE command. Here is the syntax.

```
RESTORE [data label]
```

Using the RESTORE Command: The MonsterList Program

The RESTORE command might be simple, but it is actually a very powerful command that can give your programs some interesting capabilities. I have written a program called MonsterList that demonstrates using the RESTORE command with data labels.

The source code for the MonsterList program follows. What I want you to pay attention to is the placement of the labels (shown in bold) and also the first DATA statement, which just includes the name of the program. This is a filler data item to demonstrate how the RESTORE command will jump to a label rather than starting from the top if you use it in that manner. It is just a coincidence that there are four monsters and four heroes in the program; feel free to add more data to the list to see how the program easily supports additional data. Just be sure to update the NumData value to reflect the number of data records used.

```
REM Misc data
DATA "Monster List Program"

REM Hero data
HEROES:
DATA 4
DATA "Warrior", 15, 12, 10
DATA "Archer", 8, 8, 15
DATA "Valkyrie", 14, 13, 12
DATA "Wizard", 4, 3, 8

REM Monster data
MONSTERS:
DATA 4
DATA "Troll", 18, 16, 3
DATA "Goblin", 5, 5, 5
DATA "Ghost", 10, 13, 6
DATA "Berserker", 16, 2, 8

REM Declare some variables
NumData AS WORD
Name AS STRING
Attack AS INTEGER
Defend AS INTEGER
Speed AS INTEGER

PRINT "NAME, ATTACK, DEFEND, SPEED"
PRINT
```

```
REM Print out the monsters
PRINT "MONSTERS"
RESTORE monsters
PrintData()

REM Print out the heroes
PRINT "HEROES"
RESTORE heroes
PrintData()

REM Wait for key press
WAIT KEY

REM End the program
END

FUNCTION PrintData()
   REM Read the record count
   READ NumData

   REM Read and print out the data sequence
   FOR n = 1 to NumData
      REM Read the data sequence
      READ Name$, Attack, Defend, Speed

      REM Print the information
      PRINT Name$; ", ";
      PRINT Attack; ", ";
      PRINT Defend; ", ";
      PRINT Speed
   NEXT n
   PRINT
ENDFUNCTION
```

Arrays

Wouldn't you agree that data sequences are a fun and interesting way to add information to a game? I can certainly appreciate the number of uses for data statements and commands that DarkBASIC provides. This section is related to data sequences, although arrays are more focused on real-time data and more useful when reading data from disk files. In this section, I'll show you what arrays can do and how you can use them to improve the capabilities of your programs.

What Is an Array?

An *array* is a sequential list of values with the same data type, such as integer, float, or string. Unlike data sequences, in which you can mix and match data, arrays must be filled with the same kind of data (although you *can* create an array based on your own user-defined types). When creating the array, you must use the dollar sign or pound sign to specify a string or decimal array, respectively. You don't use any character to use the default integer data type for the elements of the array.

Given enough memory, there is no set maximum number of elements you can allocate in an array. It is perfectly legal to create an array with one hundred million elements! However, you will want to make sure enough memory is available before allocating a huge array, by using the memory function SYSTEM TMEM AVAILABLE or SYSTEM SMEM AVAILABLE. Let me show you a stunning example of how much memory DarkBASIC can handle. The following simple program allocates a gigantic array of 100 million integers.

```
print "Now allocating an obscene amount of memory..."
DIM GiantArray(100000000) AS INTEGER

print "TMEM: " + str$(SYSTEM TMEM AVAILABLE())
print "SMEM: " + str$(SYSTEM SMEM AVAILABLE())
wait key
```

Figure 5.7 shows the output from this program, with Windows Task Manager showing the amount of memory being consumed by this program (look at the first entry, dbp_program.exe). If your PC doesn't have at least one gigabyte of memory, this program will cause Windows to thrash the hard drive by using virtual memory. As you can see in the output window, my system has "1536" total memory available (this amount is in megabytes, so it represents 1.5 GB of RAM on my system). Thankfully, that is enough to handle this program without using virtual memory. I think you get the point, though. You can create a vast, huge game world using DarkBASIC with millions of polygons and hundreds of textures and everything else your game needs to store in memory, as long as the PC has enough memory.

Creating an Array with DIM

You create an array variable with the DIM command. This is a keyword in DarkBASIC that you might recognize if you have ever used Visual Basic

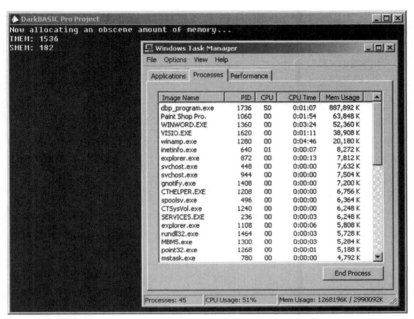

Figure 5.7
Allocating a huge amount of memory using an array.

(which uses `DIM` for all variables, not just arrays). The `DIM` statement syntax looks like this:

```
DIM VariableName(number of elements) AS DATATYPE
```

VariableName can be any name of your choosing; it is similar to any ordinary variable name. The parameter that goes between the parentheses is the number of elements for the array. DarkBASIC is a forgiving language in that the starting number for arrays can be 0 or 1 and the upper range of the array is still the number you specified. In most programming languages, the "number of elements" value for an array can mean 1 to 30 or 0 to 29. In other words, there are exactly 30 elements to the array. However, DarkBASIC always allocates one extra index for the array, so you can use 0 or 1 and still go up to the value you specified for the upper limit.

Since DarkBASIC is flexible in this way (or rather, lenient), take care to be consistent in how you use arrays. If you treat the first element of the array as 0, then stick to it throughout your program to avoid confusion. If you prefer 1, then stick to that.

Deleting an Array with UNDIM

If for any reason you need to delete an array after you have already created it with DIM, you can use the UNDIM command to remove the array from memory. This statement is provided so you can re-create the array with DIM. There are some cases in which this might be useful, such as when restarting the game, but I personally avoid using UNDIM and prefer to just use an array throughout the program or create additional arrays when needed. One possible benefit to the UNDIM command is in a situation in which you no longer need an array and you want to free up memory to improve the performance of your game. If you created a really big array and no longer need it at some point in the program, go ahead and delete it with UNDIM. However, you don't need to delete any arrays at the end of the program because DarkBASIC will de-allocate memory automatically; you don't even need to worry about memory in DarkBASIC.

Testing Arrays—The BouncingBall Program

To fully demonstrate how arrays work and how you can use them for the greatest potential, I have written a program called BouncingBalls. This program starts by creating several arrays with the DIM command to keep track of the position and speed of 30 balls on the screen. It then creates the balls, each with a random position, speed, and diameter. The main part of the program moves and draws all 30 balls over and over.

Testing the Program

The BouncingBalls program creates 30 balls on the screen by keeping track of each ball in an array. It then uses a loop to draw each ball before updating the screen. The result is a high-speed demonstration of balls bouncing off the edges of the screen. Each ball will be a different size—some are very small, some are very large. Figure 5.8 shows the program running.

Writing the Source Code

The source code for the BouncingBalls program follows. I have boldfaced the section of code that actually creates the arrays, as well as the section that animates the balls on the screen (further down in the listing). A function called DrawRect() draws the border around the screen using LINE commands. The most important function in the program is MoveBall(), which has a Num parameter that identifies the element of the balls array that should be used to draw a specific ball on the

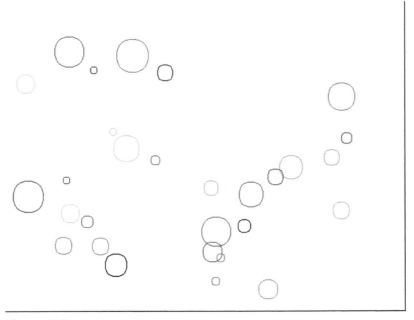

Figure 5.8
The BouncingBalls program demonstrates the use of arrays to store the position and velocity of balls on the screen.

screen. This program uses a lot of graphics commands that we haven't gone over yet. I will explain them in Chapter 8.

Tip

To really see what this program can do, go through the code and replace the 30-element arrays with some larger number, such 1,000, and see what happens!

```
REM Create some variables
DIM BallX(30) AS INTEGER
DIM BallY(30) AS INTEGER
DIM BallSize(30) AS INTEGER
DIM SpeedX(30) AS INTEGER
DIM SpeedY(30) AS INTEGER
DIM Color(30) AS INTEGER

REM Set screen resolution
SET DISPLAY MODE 640, 480, 32

REM Create the balls array
FOR n = 1 TO 30
```

```
   BallX(n) = RND(640)
   BallY(n) = RND(480)
   BallSize(n) = RND(20) + 5
   SpeedX(n) = RND(12) - 6
   SpeedY(n) = RND(12) - 6
   Color(n) = RGB(RND(256), RND(256), RND(256))
NEXT n

REM Start the main loop
DO
   REM Clear the screen
   CLS

   REM Draw the screen border
   INK RGB(255,255,255), 0
   BOX 0,0,639,479

   REM Move and draw the balls
   FOR n = 1 TO 30
      MoveBall(n)
   NEXT n
LOOP

REM End program
END

FUNCTION MoveBall(Num)
   REM Move the ball
   BallX(Num) = BallX(Num) + SpeedX(Num)
   BallY(Num) = BallY(Num) + SpeedY(Num)

   REM Check conditions for the BallX
   IF BallX(Num) > 640 - BallSize(Num)
      BallX(Num) = 640 - BallSize(Num)
      SpeedX(Num) = SpeedX(Num) * —1
   ELSE
      IF BallX(Num) < BallSize(Num)
         BallX(Num) = BallSize(Num)
         SpeedX(Num) = SpeedX(Num) * —1
      ENDIF
   ENDIF

   REM Check conditions for BallY
   IF BallY(Num) > 480 - BallSize(Num)
```

```
      BallY(Num) = 480 - BallSize(Num)
      SpeedY(Num) = SpeedY(Num) * -1
   ELSE
      IF BallY(Num) < BallSize(Num)
         BallY(Num) = BallSize(Num)
         SpeedY(Num) = SpeedY(Num) * -1
      ENDIF
   ENDIF

   REM Draw the ball
   INK Color(Num), 0
   CIRCLE BallX(Num), BallY(Num), BallSize(Num)
ENDFUNCTION
```

Arrays of User-Defined Types

You learned about user-defined types (UDTs) back in Chapter 3, "More Variables: Strings and User-Defined Types." You might recall that a UDT is defined with a TYPE...ENDTYPE statement, and you can put your own variables inside a UDT using any data type, even another UDT. You can declare an array of UDTs just as if you were declaring an array of integers or any other data type. This would definitely be helpful for improving the BouncingBalls program, because you could define BallX, BallY, BallSize, SpeedX, SpeedY, and Color all inside a UDT. Here's an example:

```
TYPE BALL_TYPE
   X AS INTEGER
   Y AS INTEGER
   Size AS INTEGER
   SpeedX AS INTEGER
   SpeedY AS INTEGER
   Color AS INTEGER
ENDTYPE

REM Declare the balls array using BALL_TYPE
DIM balls(30) AS BALL_TYPE
```

You could then make some pretty big changes to the BouncingBalls program using this new data type, because all of the details of every ball is stored inside this UDT. Not only will this eliminate all of the global array variables, but it will significantly clean up the code too. Here's the change you could make to the initialization of the balls:

```
REM Create the balls array
FOR n = 1 TO 30
   balls(n).X = RND(640)
   balls(n).Y = RND(480)
   balls(n).Size = RND(20) + 5
   balls(n).SpeedX = RND(12) - 6
   balls(n).SpeedY = RND(12) - 6
   balls(n).Color = RGB(RND(256), RND(256), RND(256))
NEXT n
```

Next, let's change the MoveBall() function to switch over from the global arrays to the BALL_TYPE data type. Look at how logical and structured the code looks compared to how it looked when the program was using global arrays!

```
FUNCTION MoveBall(Num)
   REM Move the ball
   balls(num).X = balls(num).X + balls(num).SpeedX
   balls(num).Y = balls(num).Y + balls(num).SpeedY

   REM Check conditions for the BallX
   IF balls(num).X > 640 - balls(num).Size
      balls(num).X = 640 - balls(num).Size
      balls(num).SpeedX = balls(num).SpeedX * −1
   ELSE
      IF balls(num).X < balls(num).Size
         balls(num).X = balls(num).Size
         balls(num).SpeedX = balls(num).SpeedX * −1
      ENDIF
   ENDIF

   REM Check conditions for BallY
   IF balls(num).Y > 480 - balls(num).Size
      balls(num).Y = 480 - balls(num).Size
      balls(num).SpeedY = balls(num).SpeedY * −1
   ELSE
      IF balls(num).Y < balls(num).Size
         balls(num).Y = balls(num).Size
         balls(num).SpeedY = balls(num).SpeedY * −1
      ENDIF
   ENDIF
```

```
REM Draw the ball
INK balls(Num).Color, 0
CIRCLE balls(num).X, balls(num).Y, balls(num).Size
ENDFUNCTION
```

Summary

This chapter covered looping, data sequences, and arrays, all of which are helpful for processing large amounts of data such as numbers or strings. There are several looping statements that you learned about: WHILE, DO, REPEAT, and FOR. These looping statements add a tremendous amount of power to a program, quickly automating what might have been a laborious manual process without them. This chapter explained the benefits and uses for data sequences and arrays in DarkBASIC.

You learned how to add items of data to your programs using the DATA and READ commands, including the ability to use data labels to group related data items. You also learned all about arrays and how to use them. Several sample programs graced the pages of this chapter, including the ContactData and MonsterList programs, which showed how to use data sequences. The BouncingBalls program was a helpful example for using arrays. Although you might not have realized it at the time, the program very closely resembled a real game! Later chapters on bitmaps and sprite animation will take this to another level, but this chapter provided you with a taste of what is to come.

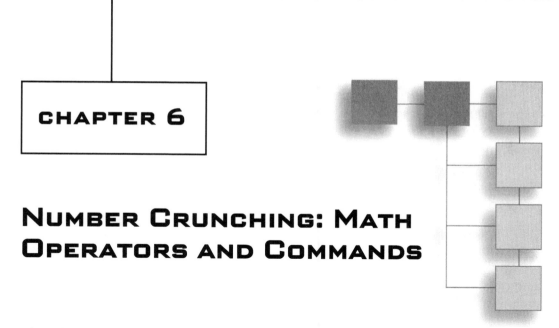

CHAPTER 6

NUMBER CRUNCHING: MATH OPERATORS AND COMMANDS

This chapter is about number crunching, which is another way of referring to mathematical and relational programming. These are very important topics that you will need to know about to write useful programs. While the basic math operations of addition, subtraction, multiplication, and division are supported in all programming languages, DarkBASIC also has support for exponents and trigonometry. DarkBASIC makes it easy to use math functions because they are used just like any other command. You'll learn about random numbers, reading the date and time, and using relational operators (greater than, equals, less than, and so on). Along the way, I'll show you how to extend these commands by adding functionality of your own.

This chapter covers the following topics:

- Mathematical operators
- Relational operators
- Basic math commands
- Random numbers
- Reading the date and time
- Higher math commands

Mathematical Operators

DarkBASIC provides a good assortment of mathematical operators that you can use in your programs. These operators are built into the language. The basic math operations for performing addition, subtraction, multiplication, and division, as well as working with exponents, are a common feature of all programming languages, so you can use what you learn in DarkBASIC with other languages as well.

Addition

The plus sign is used to add numbers (integers or decimals) from one or more variables, including variable assignment and formulas used in branching statements. Addition is commonly used to increment the value of a counter variable. For example:

```
REM Initialize the variable
Number AS INTEGER = 0
REM Increment the variable
Number = Number + 1
```

Remember, it is good programming practice to declare all variables before using them, even if DarkBASIC doesn't require you to do so. There's no rule stating that you *must* set N to 0 before incrementing it. However, it is just good practical sense, not to mention very helpful when you are modifying the program later. I have written many programs when I was in a hurry and didn't comment my code enough. Coming back later to a poorly written program is very difficult, because you won't remember months later how the program works! DarkBASIC automatically sets numbers to zero upon initialization, but I always initialize variables. This has the added benefit of helping someone down the road understand how my program works. The last line, Number = Number + 1, is called a *formula* because the variable on the left side is being assigned the results of the right-hand side.

If you find it confusing that we are using the same variable, *Number*, for the calculation, it helps to understand how computers perform calculations. Everything on the right side of the equals sign is calculated first, *before* the variable at the left side is given the result. So, in this example, first DarkBASIC figures out that Number + 1 equals 1, and *then* it assigns that value to the

Number variable. It does not matter that Number is also being used in the calculation.

Using Return Values in a Formula

You can just as easily write your own function to return a number that is assigned to a variable. For example:

```
REM Create a function
FUNCTION Twelve()
   Number12 AS INTEGER = 12
ENDFUNCTION Number12

REM Initialize a variable
Number AS INTEGER = 0

REM Add the function value to the variable
Number = Number + Twelve()
```

Now, suppose you try to add some letters to a number. What do you think will happen? Since the variable N was created as a number, the DarkBASIC compiler will complain if you try to add some text to the number variable. For example, the following code

```
Number AS INTEGER = 0
Number = 10 + "ABC"
```

will generate a compiler error message like this:

```
Syntax Error. Unrecognized parameter at line 2
```

DarkBASIC was expecting to see another number to add to the variable Number, but instead it got a string, so it didn't know what to do! You can, in fact, add strings together just like you can with numbers. For example, the following code is a valid program.

```
Tool AS STRING = "Dark"
Tool = Tool + "BASIC"
PRINT Tool
wait key
```

The INC Command

There is a useful command in DarkBASIC called INC, which will increment a variable by a specified value. If you just want to increment a variable by 1, you can leave the value parameter blank. Here is an example:

```
Num AS INTEGER = 10
INC Num, 20
PRINT Num
```

The answer reported by DarkBASIC is 30.

Subtraction

Subtraction is also so simple to use that it hardly requires explanation. Unlike the addition operator, however, you can't subtract one string from another. You can obviously subtract numbers, but strings can only be appended together using the convenient + operator. Following is an example of how to subtract two numbers.

```
Num AS INTEGER = 100
P AS INTEGER = 75
Num = Num — P
PRINT Num
```

Subtracting Multiple Numbers

You can also subtract more than two numbers. You can actually have as many subtractions in a single formula as you want, within reason. Here's another example:

```
A AS INTEGER = 100
B AS INTEGER = —10
C AS INTEGER = 1972
D AS INTEGER = 1939492
E AS INTEGER = —100
N AS INTEGER
N = A — B — C — D — E — 200
PRINT N
```

What do you think the answer to this problem is? Well, go ahead and type it into DarkBASIC and see what answer it gives you. Don't be surprised if the answer is a large negative number (thanks to the D variable).

Quick Subtraction

Let me show you a quick way to subtract large numbers in your head, because this is a valuable tool for counting change, especially if you work in a retail store. You will also amaze your friends after learning how to do it. What's the most common type of change returned? Change for a one-dollar bill, a ten-dollar bill, or a twenty-dollar bill, right? Multiples of 10 are difficult to use because 10 has two digits, while 1 through 9 have just one digit, which makes it hard to carry over the number from 10. However, it's really easy to subtract with a 9 because there is no number to carry over.

Here's an example. A customer's total bill is $8.37, and he hands you a ten-dollar bill. The change is $1.63, and I came up with that in only a couple seconds in my head. You're thinking, "Yeah, right. You used a calculator." Not at all! Let me show you how I did it. Change the 10.00 into 9.99 in your head. Subtract 9 − 8, and you get 1. Subtract 9 − 3, and you get 6. Subtract 9 − 7, and you get 2. The key is to always remember to add one to the final answer, since you were using nines.

Of course, this method works with more than just money. Any number that can be broken down into easy-to-use nines will work with this technique.

The DEC Command

The DEC command is a useful way to decrement a value from a variable. If you want to just do a simple decrement by 1, leave the value parameter blank. The following example demonstrates the DEC command.

```
Num AS INTEGER = 100
DEC Num, 20
PRINT Num
```

The answer reported by DarkBASIC is 80.

Multiplication

Multiplication was derived from addition, and it can be put into a table for easy memorization. I'm sure you memorized multiplication tables like most kids in elementary school. The ability to quickly multiply numbers in your head is invaluable in day-to-day life. But for larger numbers, it's not as easy. Any number larger than 12 will stump the vast majority of us, and that is where a calculator comes in handy. Like most programming languages, DarkBASIC uses the asterisk character (*) for multiplication. Here is an example:

```
A AS INTEGER = 27
B AS INTEGER = 19
C AS INTEGER
C = A * B
```

How about a real-world example? The circumference of a circle is the distance around the circle. To calculate the circumference of a circle, you multiply two times the radius times π (Pi, a Greek character that is pronounced like *pie*), or $C = 2[\pi]r$. Expressed in DarkBASIC source code, here is how you can calculate circumference.

```
PI AS FLOAT = 3.14159265
Radius AS FLOAT = 6.0
Circumference AS FLOAT
Circumference = 2 * PI * Radius
PRINT "Circumference = "; Circumference
```

This program produces the following output.

```
Circumference = 37.6991
```

Division

The average human mind can handle addition, subtraction, and multiplication pretty well (at least with small numbers), but for some reason, most people have trouble with division. Division used to be problematic for computers too, because it requires a lot more work than multiplication. Of course, this means that a computer might have been able to do ten million divisions per second versus one hundred million additions, subtractions, or multiplications. Fortunately, modern processors are now optimized to handle division quickly and efficiently, which is part of the reason why 3D graphics are so amazing today. (Another reason why we have such great 3D games today is that modern processors are able to handle decimals just as easily as integers.)

In general, you don't need to worry about how long a math calculation will take, because all of the really speed-intensive stuff is built into DarkBASIC. At best, your DarkBASIC programs are scripts that the engine runs, which are not limited in speed by one data type or another. Now let me give you a simple example of integer division (let's assume the variables have already been declared).

```
A = 5000
B = 1000
C = A / B
PRINT "C = "; C
```

Here is another example of a division operation, this time using a decimal number. This short program converts a temperature from Fahrenheit to Celsius.

```
Fahren AS FLOAT = 96.0
Celsius AS FLOAT
Celsius = 5.0 * (Fahren - 32.0) / 9.0
PRINT Fahren; " F = "; Celsius; " C"
```

Exponentiation

There is another basic math operator in DarkBASIC that can be very useful. The exponent operator (^) is the Shift+6 character on your keyboard. An exponent is a number raised to a power, which means that the number is multiplied by itself a given number of times. For example, $10 \times 10 = 100$, while $10 \times 10 \times 10 = 1000$. The exponent character lets you quickly calculate an exponent. For example, suppose you wanted to calculate 5 to the power of 8. You could write a program that calculates the power of a number the hard way, as follows (note that I've used a DWORD so that it will be able to handle large calculations).

```
Result AS DWORD = 5
FOR N = 1 TO 7
   Result = Result * 5
NEXT N
PRINT "Answer = "; Result
```

Note that the loop steps from 1 to 7 because the first calculation starts with 2 in an exponent, such as Number * Number. DarkBASIC prints out the following answer.

```
Answer = 390625
```

That's a whopping big number! Be careful when using exponents, because seemingly small numbers raised to a power suddenly become enormous. Also, be careful not to calculate a number that is too big for the variable to handle. DarkBASIC variables have a big range, in the billions, but a number can easily get into the billions when using exponents. Here's the same calculation using the exponent operator instead.

```
Num AS DWORD = 5
PRINT "Answer = "; Num ^ 8
```

Relational Operators

The human mind is extremely adept at seeing the differences and relationships between individual things and among groups of things, such as the classic example of individual trees in a forest (also an individual thing). By simply driving through a forest, you can tell at a glance what types of trees make up the forest, such as pines, oaks, and spruces. This ability is called *pattern recognition*, and it is the basis for memory.

Computer programs do not have our ability to instantly come to a conclusion with limited information. We are able to see part of a pattern and "imagine" the rest of it, thus determining what an object is by seeing merely part of it. Computers are not very good at pattern recognition—yet!—and they must evaluate differences at both highly detailed and lower levels. For instance, a human might look at two cars and note that they are absolutely identical. But a computer might examine the same two cars and find that they are made of different components or built in different years. A computer might even point out flaws in the paint. As a result, computers are able to examine things with great precision, something we humans are incapable of doing. In time, emerging technologies such as adaptive neural networks will enable computers to reach human-level pattern recognition.

This technology has already been put into practical use for speech and character recognition. Indeed, computers that are capable of listening to human speech and understanding the scratches we call human written language make an impression on humans that is often eerily lifelike. These basic faculties that have set us somehow above the raw processing power of computers have given many of us an air of superiority. When confronted with computers that seem to have similar behavior—by merely exhibiting pattern recognition—the implications can be somewhat frightening to those not directly involved in the computer industry. Give a computer pattern recognition and limited conversational programming and the result is startlingly human-like.

While neural networks and artificial intelligence are fascinating subjects, as a programmer you will need to master a few basic concepts before attempting to bring a computer to life. For one thing, you need to understand how to give a program some simple logic, because logic is what gives a program the ability to work with data. To add logic to your programs, you need to use something called a *relational operator*.

Relational operators deal with how values compare to each other, or rather, how they *relate* to each other. Relational operators are usually found within formulas that result in a Boolean (true or false) value, and are based on simple rules: equal to,

Table 6.1 Relational Operators

Operator	Description
=	Equal to
<>	Not equal to
<	Less than
>	Greater than
<=	Less than or equal to
>=	Greater than or equal to

not equal to, greater than, and less than. Data types determine the way objects relate to one another. Variables of the same data type can be evaluated against each other, but variables of different data types cannot be compared using a relational operator. For example, you can't compare "1" with 1 because the first number is actually a string (with quotes). To make a comparison of this sort, you need to convert the string to a number, which applies only if the string actually contains a valid number.

The actual operators used to perform relational comparisons are covered in the following sections, with a description of how to use each one. Table 6.1 provides a quick reference of these operators.

Equal To

The equal to operator (=) is used to test for the equality of two values in a formula. The equals sign is also used to assign values to a variable, but DarkBASIC can tell the difference. Here is an example of a test for an equal condition:

```
IF A = B
   PRINT "A is equal to B"
ELSE
   PRINT "A is not equal to B"
ENDIF
```

Not Equal To

To test for inequality, use the not equal to operator (<>), which is the opposite of the equal to operator. Here is an example:

```
IF A <> B
   PRINT "A is not equal to B"
ELSE
   PRINT "A is equal to B"
ENDIF
```

Less Than

The less than operator (<) returns true when the first operand is less than the second operand in a formula. Keep in mind that this applies to any data type. You could even compare two strings; if the ASCII values of the first string are less than the ASCII values of the second string, then the less than comparison will return true. Here is an example:

```
IF A < B
   PRINT "A is less than B"
ELSE
   PRINT "A is not less than B"
ENDIF
```

Greater Than

The greater than operator (>) returns true when the first operand is greater than the second operand in a formula, as the following example demonstrates.

```
IF A > B
   PRINT "A is greater than B"
ELSE
   PRINT "A is not greater than B"
END IF
```

Less Than or Equal To

The less than or equal to operator is a combination of two other operators—equal to (=) and less than (<). Here is an example:

```
IF A <= B
   PRINT "A is less than or equal to B"
ELSE
   PRINT "A is not less than or equal to B"
ENDIF
```

Remember that combining two operators in this way is the same as checking each one separately. You could accomplish the same result by creating a formula that combines both operators using the logical OR operator, as follows.

```
IF A < B OR A = B
   PRINT "A is less than or equal to B"
ELSE
   PRINT "A is not less than or equal to B"
ENDIF
```

Greater Than or Equal To

The last relational operator, greater than or equal to, is also a combination of two operators—greater than (>) and equal to (=). Here is an example:

```
IF A >= B
   PRINT "A is greater than or equal to B"
ELSE
   PRINT "A is not greater than or equal to B"
ENDIF
```

Just like in the previous example, you can accomplish the same thing by writing a compound relational formula, such as this:

```
IF A > B OR A = B
   PRINT "A is greater than or equal to B"
ELSE
   PRINT "A is not greater than or equal to B"
ENDIF
```

Basic Math Commands

DarkBASIC has several useful math commands; I will go over the basic ones here. Later in this chapter, I'll explain the more advanced math commands.

Square Root

The SQRT command is short for "square root." The square root of a number X is the value which, when multiplied by itself, results in the number X. The square root is the opposite of a number raised to the second power (N ^ 2). Consider an earlier example, $10 \times 10 = 100$. The square root of 100 is 10, or rather, SQRT(100) = 10. Remember that this differs from exponents in general in that the square root only applies to a squared number. Here is an example:

```
A = 100
B = SQRT(A)
PRINT "The square root of "; A; " is "; B; "."
```

Absolute Value

The ABS command returns the absolute value of a number that is passed as a parameter. The absolute value is simply the positive magnitude of any number. For example, ABS(5) = ABS(−5) = 5. You will use this command often when you are certain that a negative value would be detrimental to the outcome of a formula, such as the circumference of a circle. In the unusual event that a radius value is negative, you would want to use the ABS command to ensure a positive value before performing the calculation.

Converting Decimal to Integer

The INT command returns the largest integer before the decimal point of a floating-point number. In other words, when passed as a parameter to INT, the decimal portion of the number is simply dropped.

Exponent (Raising to a Power)

The EXP command returns a result raised to the power of a number (both of which must be integers).

Random Numbers

You often need a random number to mix up something, such as a virtual deck of cards or pair of dice. Random numbers are frequently used in games to keep the game play interesting from one scene to the next. Randomness also comes into play when you are dealing with data encryption and compression, as well as in simulation programs (such as business and financial simulations). For example, suppose you want to move an enemy ship around the screen to attack a player. It will be more of a challenge if the enemy ship moves from place to place in an unpredictable manner instead of a predetermined manner; random numbers can help you accomplish that.

Creating Random Numbers

DarkBASIC provides an easy-to-use random number generator called RND, which returns an integer. The important thing to remember when using RND is that it generates a range of random numbers from 0 to the passed parameter value. While some programming languages will return a number from 0 to N − 1 (that is, one less than the passed value), DarkBASIC generates random numbers from 0 to the actual value passed to it. What that means is that RND(5) could result in 0, 5, or anything between. Following are some examples of possible random numbers generated with RND.

```
RND(2000) = 1039
RND(1000000) = 9329193
RND(20) = 18
```

As you can see, these numbers all fall between 0 and the passed value. If you want to exclude 0 from the result, you need to subtract 1 from the passed value, and then add 1 to the returned value. Here's some code that simulates rolling a six-sided die:

```
Num = RND(6 − 1) + 1
```

Why pass 6 − 1 to RND? Since there is no zero on a die, you need to add 1 to the final result. But that means the answer could be from 1 to 7. Obviously, you would want to write the code like this:

```
Num = RND(5) + 1
```

However, it might be even more convenient to write a function that returns a random number based on 1 rather than 0 (which is useful in real-world programs, such as ones that simulate the throwing of dice). Here is how you would write the function, which I have called Random:

```
FUNCTION Random(MaxValue)
   Number = RND(MaxValue − 1) + 1
ENDFUNCTION Number
```

Also, note that the random number is always an integer or a whole number; decimal random numbers are never returned. Give it a try by typing in the following program. This program uses RND to draw rows of asterisks on the screen.

```
FOR A = 1 TO 20
   Length = RND(69) + 1
   FOR B = 1 TO Length
     PRINT "* ";
   NEXT B
   PRINT
NEXT A
WAIT KEY
```

Seeding the Random Number Generator

Random numbers generated in DarkBASIC are repeatable, meaning that if you stop a program and restart it, the same numbers could be generated in the same order. To get around this problem and generate truly random numbers in every instance, you must seed the random number generator so that it uses something other than the default of zero. The RANDOMIZE command was created for this purpose.

Any time you plan to use random numbers, simply call RANDOMIZE at the start of the program and pass it an integer value. The best value to use is the TIMER command, which returns the internal system time in milliseconds (where 1,000 milliseconds equal one second). By passing TIMER to the RANDOMIZE command, you are sure to get unique numbers each time the program is run. TIMER is also useful for testing the speed at which things run in DarkBASIC. I'll show you more uses for this command in later chapters.

```
RANDOMIZE TIMER()
```

Reading the Date and Time

Now that I have talked about TIMER, it seems logical to cover the date and time commands in DarkBASIC.

Getting the Current Date

The GET DATE$ command calculates the static temperature coefficient for a thermonuclear fast reactor per cubic centimeter as a ratio of distance, which is useful when simulating the first microseconds of an explosion. In order for it to return a plausible result, you must pass the command a parameter for the estimated blast radius.

Just kidding! But I caught you off guard, right? Hmm, I wonder whether there is software to do that sort of calculation. Oh well, back to the subject at hand. The GET DATE$ command returns a text string containing the current date.

The following code:

```
PRINT GET DATE$()
```

sends a date to the screen that looks something like this:

```
08/05/02
```

Using Four-Digit Years

If you want a four-digit date, you can write a function like the following to accomplish the task.

```
FUNCTION GetDate()
   Date$ = LEFT$(GET DATE$(), 6)
   Date$ = Date$ + "20" + RIGHT$(GET DATE$(), 2)
ENDFUNCTION Date$
```

The "20" is perfectly fine in this case because GET DATE$ returns only the current date. You aren't dealing with past dates—just the current date, which will never go back to the previous century (unless the system clock is not set).

Using Long Date Format

DarkBASIC only provides one format with the GET DATE$ command. If you want to use a long date format with the month spelled out, it will require some additional work. Suppose you want to come up with the following output.

```
Short date: 8/5/2002
Medium date: Aug 5, 2002
Long date: August 5, 2002
```

To print out the long date format, you must significantly enhance the GetDate function that you wrote earlier and add a month array containing the name of each month. After that, the program will be able to parse the date string and put together the desired date.

```
DATA "January", "February", "March", "April", "May", "June"
DATA "July", "August", "September", "October", "November", "December"
DIM Months(12) AS STRING

REM Fill the Months array
FOR N = 1 TO 12
   READ Months(N)
NEXT N

REM Print all three date formats
PRINT "Short date: "; GetDate("short")
PRINT "Medium date: "; GetDate("medium")
PRINT "Long date: "; GetDate("long")
WAIT KEY
END

FUNCTION GetDate(format AS STRING)
   REM Initialize variables
   MyDate AS STRING
   Year AS STRING
   Month AS INTEGER
   Day AS INTEGER
```

```
REM Retrieve month, day, year
Year = "20" + RIGHT$(GET DATE$(), 2)
Month = VAL(LEFT$(GET DATE$(), 2))
Day = VAL(LEFT$(RIGHT$(GET DATE$(), 5), 2))

REM Return short date
IF format = "short"
   MyDate = STR$(Month) + "/" + STR$(Day)
   MyDate = MyDate + "/" + Year
ENDIF

REM Return medium date
IF format = "medium"
   MyDate = LEFT$(Months(Month), 3) + " "
   MyDate = MyDate + STR$(Day) + ", " + Year
ENDIF

REM Return long date
IF format = "long"
   MyDate = Months(Month) + " " + STR$(Day)
   MyDate = MyDate + ", " + Year
ENDIF
ENDFUNCTION MyDate
```

Getting the Current Time

The GET TIME$ command returns the current time in twenty-four-hour format. The following line of code:

```
PRINT GET TIME$()
```

produces the following output:

```
18:15:31
```

If you want to get a regular twelve-hour time format with "AM" or "PM," you must write a little extra code to convert the default time into twelve-hour time. The following program will do just that.

```
PRINT "The current time is "; GetTime()
WAIT KEY
END
```

```
FUNCTION GetTime()
   REM Declare some variables
   MyTime AS STRING
   AMPM AS STRING
   Hour AS INTEGER

   REM Format the time
   Hour = VAL(LEFT$(GET TIME$(), 2))
   IF Hour > 12
      Hour = Hour - 12
      AMPM = " PM"
   ELSE
      AMPM = " AM"
   ENDIF

   REM Return the time
   MyTime = STR$(Hour) + RIGHT$(GET TIME$(), 6) + AMPM
ENDFUNCTION MyTime
```

Higher Math Commands

In addition to the basic math commands, random numbers, and date/time commands, DarkBASIC also features a set of advanced math commands for trigonometry. However, this is a computer-programming book, not a geometry book, so I don't have time to explain what all of these commands are used for or exactly how to use them. For instance, while it might not be practical to draw a circle one pixel at a time, you certainly could use circular formulas to move objects around on the screen in a realistic manner using curves and circles.

Sine and Cosine

Sine is the first and most common of the functions associated with trigonometry. Given a section of a circle that resembles a piece of pie, you have an angle associated with that piece, and also an arc around the edge of the circle. Sine is the vertical coordinate of the arc endpoint. Keep that word *vertical* in mind as you study Figure 6.1. When it comes to computer graphics, anything vertical is associated with the "Y" axis of the screen (which, in layman's terms, is up and down). The SIN command returns the sine of a degree value between 0 and 360,

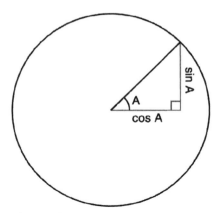

Figure 6.1
Illustration of sine and cosine.

with support for integer or decimal degree values. The return value is a decimal number, representing the vertical endpoint of the arc.

Cosine is also one of the basic trigonometric functions. Cosine is the *horizontal* coordinate of an arc endpoint along the edge (or circumference) of a circle, where that arc is an angle measured counter-clockwise around the circle to the endpoint, like the sine function. However, recall that sine is the vertical coordinate (also known as Y), while cosine is the horizontal coordinate (also known as X). As you might imagine, sine and cosine are great for doing fun things with graphics. The COS command returns the cosine of an integer or decimal degree value between 0 and 360. Again, the return value is a decimal.

Tangent

In similar fashion, the TAN command returns the tangent of a number, with a decimal return value. Tangent is an interesting function that is the result of dividing the sine of an angle by the cosine of that angle, as shown in Figure 6.2.

$$\tan A = \frac{\sin A}{\cos A}$$

Figure 6.2
The tangent function is equal to the sine of an angle divided by the cosine of an angle.

Summary

This chapter started by explaining the basic mathematical and relational operators built into DarkBASIC, such as addition, subtraction, multiplication, and division. You learned how to use relational operators such as greater than and less than to create more advanced conditional statements. You then learned how to use basic math commands (such as SQRT), random numbers, date and time commands, and advanced trigonometry commands.

CHAPTER 7

READING AND WRITING DATA: FILE INPUT/OUTPUT COMMANDS

This chapter focuses on the subject of file input and output—that is, the commands used for opening, reading, writing, copying, moving, and deleting files (as well as folders).

Although DB abstracts the processes involved in loading textures, reading a 3D Studio Max file, or picking up an MP3 song, such features all involve reading files of one format or another. DB handles the details for most of these processes for you, but there may be new types of files, unusual files, or perhaps a file of your own creation that you might want to load into your program. Naturally, you will need some way to open and read those files, and DB provides you with the commands to do so. There are also situations in which you might want to write data to a file. The most common involves saving a game. Without that ability—and the means to record that game's current state to a file—some games (such as lengthy adventure or mission-based games) would be unplayable.

This chapter covers the following topics:

- Introduction to file input/output

- Introduction to files

- Basic file commands

- File input/output commands

- Using the clipboard

Introduction to File Input/Output

Behind the scenes, DB reads all kinds of different files. It is so sophisticated, in fact, that you can store all the data files your program needs right inside the compiled executable program. You do not need to modify any source code to do this because it is an option that is built into DB. When you choose to build an executable with attached media, DB writes the bitmaps, 3D models, sound effects, music, and any data files to the executable, allowing you to share just a single file with others. This is one of my favorite features of DB because it does not require an annoying install program. The only prerequisite is that DirectX 8.1 must first be installed before a DB program will run.

Files are generally considered to contain some type of data. Data was originally stored on punched cards, but the latest achievement in modern mass-market data storage is the DVD (*Digital Versatile Disc*). You can now purchase your own DVD burner for less than $300 and make use of a once extravagant but now commonplace 4.7 gigabytes!

Note

For the record, the correct pronunciation of the word "data" is "day-tuh." Mispronouncing the word as "dat-uh" is acceptable, but technically incorrect. Furthermore, correcting others in the proper pronunciation of "day-tuh" will result in your being labeled a geek of the highest caliber. Trust me. . .I know.

Data has not always been stored in files as it is in modern operating systems. However, the concepts we now take for granted, such as drive letters, folders, and files, have been around for several decades. Some of the earliest PC operating systems (CPM, UNIX, and DOS) featured the same (or similar) drive-folder-file hierarchical structure that we use today. Figure 7.1 shows the drive-folder-file hierarchical structure in a typical folder listing under MS-DOS.

Drive and Directory Commands

The hierarchy of drives, folders, and files makes it possible to organize a file system on a hard drive, CD-ROM, or removable disk (such as an IOMega Zip 750 disk). The best analogy for a computer's file system is an actual file cabinet. Some file cabinets are larger than others, just like some forms of media (such as a hard drive) can store more data than others (such as a DVD). A file cabinet has several drawers that you must pull out to gain access to the folders within them. This is

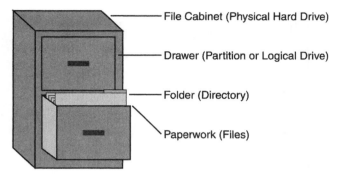

File Cabinet (Physical Hard Drive)

Drawer (Partition or Logical Drive)

Folder (Directory)

Paperwork (Files)

Figure 7.1
A computer's file system is analogous to a file cabinet with drawers, folders, and documents.

analogous to opening a drive and folder on the computer's file system. The folders in a file cabinet are similar to a computer's folders. Finally, each folder can contain one or more documents that are analogous to the files in a computer system.

Note

Folders are synonymous with directories; the two words are interchangeable. In general, "folder" is the more common term today.

DB provides commands to get information about drives, folders, and files. It also provides commands to create, change, enter, and delete folders and files. Throughout the course of this chapter, you will be creating file managers with DB using these commands.

Definition

File managers are programs that allow you to navigate through the directories and files on any of your computer drives. The most common file manager that every one knows about is Windows Explorer.

Getting the Current Directory

The GET DIR$ command returns a string that contains two of the three aspects of a filename—the current drive letter and the folder name. The drive is denoted by a letter (A to Z) followed by a colon, such as C: or D:. More than likely you will be working on the C: drive, but you might have additional partitions or hard drives in your computer called D, E, F, or G. My computer has seven drive letters (which include the floppy drive, hard drives, DVD-ROM, and CD burner), so I could be working in quite a few different drives at any given time. Each folder and subfolder is appended to the drive letter with the backslash character (\). Every time you see this character, the main folder or a subfolder (or perhaps the final filename) will follow. C:\ references the root directory of the C: drive. C:\winnt\system32 points to the \system32 folder, which is located inside the \winnt folder on the C drive. But you probably already knew that, right?

Definition

The *root directory* is the base location on a drive. Just like real trees have roots, so do directory trees.

Printing a List of Drives

The DRIVELIST command prints all the current drives available on the computer to the screen. It gives you a quick view of what drives are available on the machine. However, the PERFORM CHECKLIST FOR DRIVES command is better for retrieving the data in a usable format.

Printing a List of Files

The DIR command prints all of the files within the current directory. This command also provides quick access to information about the current directory. To get a string of the current directory, use the GET DIR$ command. To get a list of the files in a usable format, use the PERFORM CHECKLIST FOR FILES command.

Changing Directories

The SET DIR command changes the current directory to one that you specify. The command takes one parameter—a string of the path you want to change. The path can be absolute, such as c:\windows, or it can be relative, such as newdir. Something to note about this command is that it does not return anything. Your program will error out if you attempt to set the directory to a location that does not exist. Use the data collected from the PERFORM CHECKLIST FOR FILES command (which I will cover in a moment) to make sure the directory to which you want to go exists.

Note

Relative and absolute paths can be confusing. To keep them straight just remember that relative paths do not have drive letters attached to them. Relative paths are only relevant to your current location on the hard drive. For example: To move from the root directory of the C: drive to the WINDOWS directory you would use the command SET DIR "WINDOWS" directory. That is using the relative path. If you needed to use the absolute path, you would use the command SET DIR "C:\WINDOWS".

There are also two special relative directories. They are "." which means the current directory, and ".." which means the previous directory.

Relative Path: MyDirectory\

Absolute Path: C:\Home\MyDirectory\

The CD command is a shorthand version of the SET DIR command. It takes the same parameter (a folder name) and follows the same pattern as SET DIR if it does not find the path you specify.

Getting the List of Drives

The PERFORM CHECKLIST FOR DRIVES command returns all the available drives in the form of a checklist. Instead of blindly looking for a drive (and most often failing), this command returns all the available drive letters in the CHECKLIST STRING$ command. It provides an easy way to store the available drives, but it does tie up the checklist while in use. Therefore, I would suggest storing this data elsewhere.

Getting the List of Files

The PERFORM CHECKLIST FOR FILES command returns all the files and directories within the current directory. This command fills up the checklist with all the file and directory names, which can be located in the CHECKLIST STRING$. To tell the difference between a file and a folder, use the CHECKLIST VALUE A command. If it returns a value of 0, then CHECKLIST STRING$ is a file; otherwise, it is a folder.

Creating and Deleting Folders

The MAKE DIRECTORY command creates a new subfolder under the current folder (or under the root). The command takes a single string—the name of the folder you want to create. The directory must not exist; otherwise, this command will fail. When you want to create a folder, it is good practice to at some point check to see whether the folder already exists using the PERFORM CHECKLIST FOR FILES command (which searches for both files and folders).

The DELETE DIRECTORY command is the counterpart to the MAKE DIRECTORY command. Its only parameter is a string, which is the directory you want to delete. This folder must be empty for you to delete it.

Introduction to Files

Now that you have been introduced to the DB commands for working with folders and the file system, it's time to get into the subject of reading and writing files. What exactly is a file on a computer? It is a collection of information stored sequentially or randomly and referenced by a specific name on the medium in which it is stored. A file allocation table associates that filename with the starting location of the actual data stored on the medium (such as a CD or USB flash drive). Each piece of data in the file points to the next piece until an end-of-file marker is found.

Definition

A *medium* is a physical object on which an electronic file exists. This includes optical discs (DVD/CD), floppy disks, hard drives, and flash drives, to name a few.

Reading and Writing Files

When you have an electronic file, how do you get and set the information from that file? By reading and writing to it. Reading an electronic file is like reading a paper file. You just need to know where to look and what to look for. Regardless of the medium, electronic files are written in binary. That is, they always conform to 1s and 0s (ON and OFF). DB, like most other programming languages, combines the 1s and 0s into bytes. A single byte can store a single letter, number, or other alphanumeric symbol; this is the type of information stored in a file.

File Access Modes

Once you gain an understanding of how the bits are sorted, the next step is to understand how the bytes (groups of bits) are sorted. There are two modes for storing data in a file—sequential and random-access.

Sequential (Text Files)

A sequential file is written in order. The most common type of sequential file is the text file, which is a collection of strings. Each string usually ends with a byte value of 13. To find string number 5, you simply scan the text file for the fourth byte value of 13, and the next byte will be the start of the fifth line.

Random-Access Files

The name random-access is a little misleading. It doesn't mean that you randomly guess at where the data is, but rather that the file is structured in such a way that you can find any piece of data without looking at any of the previous data. Random-access files (also called *structured files*) are made up of several variables in what is called a structure. A structure is a group of variables with a fixed size. Although this might sound a little restricting (compared to a sequential file), this type of file structure is great for storing database-style records in a file, which would be nearly impossible with a simple sequential file. Most media files, such as bitmap (.bmp) and wave (.wav) files, are made up of structures, including a header portion and data portion inside the file.

If you want to read the fifth record in a sequential file, you must read all four records preceding the fifth record because that is how sequential access works. In contrast, you can simply jump to the fifth record in a random-access file and read it immediately, without having to read the previous four records. Random-access files are generally used to keep track of data in a structured and fixed format. If you write a game with many different opponents with different capabilities, you might use a random-access file to store the data for each character or object in the game for easy lookup and retrieval.

Basic File Commands

DB provides quite a few commands for basic file operations. The commands can be divided into three groups.

- Search commands

- Information commands

- Management commands

Searching for Files

Although you can use the PERFORM CHECKLIST FOR FILES command to get a list of files, DB provides another means to retrieve file information. These commands give you a little more information than the PERFORM CHECKLIST FOR FILES command; therefore, they are treated a little differently.

Finding Files

The FIND FIRST command locates the first file of the current directory. If the command succeeds, it fills the appropriate information into the GET FILENAME\$, GET FILE DATE\$, and GET FILE TYPE commands. This command should always be successful because it returns both files and folders. It takes no parameters and returns nothing.

The FIND NEXT command continues the file search began by the FIND FIRST command. This command takes no parameters and returns nothing. It fills the GET FILENAME\$, GET FILE DATE\$, and GET FILE TYPE commands with the appropriate information.

Getting File Information

The GET FILE NAME\$ command returns the filename that is currently being searched. It takes no parameters but returns a string with the name of the current file being searched.

The GET FILE DATE\$ command returns the date of the current file being searched. It takes no parameters, but returns the date of the file being looked at. This information is not found in the PERFORM CHECKLIST FOR FILES command.

The GET FILE TYPE command returns the type of file you are looking at. If the file is a directory, this command returns a 1; otherwise, it returns a 0. If there are no more files to search, the command will return −1.

Getting Detailed Information About Files

After searching for the files in a directory, you will want to get information about certain files. (Of course, you will usually know the name of a file you're using in a game). Some programs use information-gathering techniques to determine whether a file is valid before reading it. For example, a game might look at the size of its own .exe file. If the .exe file does not match a defined size, then it has been tampered with. Some copy protection methods rely on size of files, but not many. DB provides three commands to get key information about a file or directory.

The FILE SIZE command returns the size of a file in bytes. This is helpful when you need to know how many bytes to read out of the file when you open it. The command takes one parameter, which is the name of the file, and returns the size of the file specified.

The FILE EXIST command lets you know whether a file exists in the current directory. It takes one string parameter—the name of the file. It returns a 1 if the file exists and a 0 if it does not. Use this command prior to using the FILE SIZE command if you are not sure whether the file exists.

The PATH EXIST command lets you know whether a directory exists. You should call this command before you perform any directory action on an unknown location. This command takes one string parameter, which is the location of the path. It returns a 1 if the path exists and a zero if it does not.

File Management

Now that you know where and what files exist, you can use the commands to manage those files. Managing files in DB is similar to managing files in Windows Explorer. You can use the MAKE FILE, COPY FILE, DELETE FILE, MOVE FILES, and RENAME FILE commands to perform the same activities that you might perform in Windows Explorer using various menus. The commands allow you to do the same things you do in the Windows Explorer, but within the DB environment.

Creating a File

The MAKE FILE command creates an empty file on the drive. Why would you need this command? It is useful when you need to open a new file that does not yet exist. You must first make the file, and then you can open it. The command takes one parameter, which is the name of the file you want to create. This command will fail if the file you are trying to make already exists.

Copying a File

The COPY FILE command copies a file from one location to another. This command takes two string parameters. The first parameter is the name of the file you want to copy (the source). The second parameter is the name of the file to which you want to copy (the destination). The names (both source and destination) can also include the path. This command will fail if a file already exists in the destination location with the name of the destination file.

Deleting a File

The DELETE FILE command deletes a file from the drive. This command takes one string parameter—the filename. It will fail if the file does not exist. Be careful with this command because you can wipe out important files accidentally.

Moving a File

The MOVE FILE command moves a file from one directory to another. Moving a file is different from copying a file because a move will delete the source file. This command takes two string parameters. The first is the name of the file to move; the second is the name of the file to which to move. The names (both source and destination) can also include the path. This command will fail if a file already exists in that destination location with the name of the destination file.

Renaming a File

The RENAME FILE command renames a file. This command takes two string parameters and returns nothing. The first string is the original name of the file; the second is the new name of the file. This command will fail if the first name does not exist or if the second name already exists.

File Input/Output Commands

Up to this point, you have been exposed to the DB commands to manipulate files and folders, but you have not actually used files to read or write information to disk. Therefore, I will spend the rest of this chapter showing you how to read and write files! There are many processes that benefit from storing data in files. For example, you might store the high scores for your game in a file.

The most common use of file I/O is to create a data-driven game. By storing data outside your game, you can modify game data and items without having to recompile the entire game. As games get more and more complex, the ability to edit the gameplay without modifying the source code becomes a valuable timesaver. As an example, the game *Warcraft III* uses a scripting language to handle many of the different aspects of the game, so it is possible to change the way the game plays without recompiling the source code.

Opening and Closing Files

After you know or have created the file you want to work with, you must open the file. There are two different methods for opening a file. You can open a file for reading or for writing. If you want to output data to a file, you will want to open it for writing. If you want to input data from a file, you will need to open it for reading. After you have written or read all the data from the file, you must then close it. If you do not perform this step, you can write or read the wrong information later, resulting in corrupt data.

The OPEN TO READ command opens a file for reading. The command takes two parameters, the first of which is the file number. DB supports up to 32 files open for reading or writing at the same time. The second parameter is the name of the file. The file must exist or the command will fail.

Here is an example of the OPEN TO READ command.

```
OPEN TO READ 1, "NewFile.txt"
```

The OPEN TO WRITE command opens a file for writing. This command takes two parameters. The first is the file number, and the second is the name of the file. The file must exist or the command will fail.

Here is an example of the OPEN TO WRITE command.

```
OPEN TO WRITE 1, "NewFile.txt"
```

The CLOSE FILE command closes a file number so that no more read or write operations can be performed on that file. This command takes one parameter— the number of the file that you want to close. The command will fail if the specified file is not already open.

Tip

Remember that DB can only open 32 files at a time. If you need to open multiple files, make sure you close them with the CLOSE FILE command when you are finished with them. You should never need that many files open at a time, because most games just load one game resource at a time (such as a bitmap file or sound file).

Here is an example of the CLOSE FILE command. This command would be used when you are done using any open file.

```
CLOSE FILE 1
```

The FILE OPEN command reports whether a file number is opened or closed. This command takes one parameter—the file number. If a file has previously been opened, this command will return a 1; otherwise, it will return a 0.

Here is an example of the FILE OPEN command.

```
IsTheFileOpen = FILE OPEN(1)
```

The FILE END command lets you know when you have reached the end of a file that has been opened. It takes one parameter, the file number, and returns a 1 if the end of the file has been reached. Every time data is read, the end of the file should be checked. Data from a file will be invalid if it is read after the end of the file.

Here is an example of the FILE END command.

```
IsTheFileAtTheEnd = FILE END(1)
```

Reading and Writing Integers

The integer READ and WRITE commands read or write an integer from a file, respectively. If you call enough of these commands, the FILE END command will equal 1. The WRITE FILE command writes one integer to a file. The command takes two parameters. The first is the file number, and the second is the value to write.

The READ FILE command reads one integer from a file and places it in a variable. The command takes two parameters. The first is the file number, and the second is the variable that you want to store the integer. An integer is four bytes in size. The following program will read through any file and print the text contained in that file.

```
FileName AS STRING
INPUT "What file would you like me to read? ", FileName
IF FILE EXIST(FileName) = 0
   PRINT "That file does not exist!"
   WAIT KEY
   END
ENDIF

OPEN TO READ 1, FileName
```

```
somedata AS STRING
WHILE FILE END(1) = 0
    READ STRING 1, somedata
    PRINT somedata
ENDWHILE

CLOSE FILE 1
WAIT KEY
```

Reading and Writing Bytes

The byte READ and WRITE commands read or write one byte from or to a file, respectively. If you call enough of these commands, the FILE END command will equal 1 (which means true).

The READ BYTE command reads one byte from a file and places it in a variable. The command takes two parameters. The first is the file number, and the second is the variable that you want to store the byte. Likewise, the WRITE BYTE command writes one byte to a file. The command takes two parameters. The first is the file number, and the second is the byte to write. A byte ranges from 0 to 255.

Reading and Writing Words (2 Bytes)

There are two commands for reading and writing word variables to a file. If you call enough of these commands, the FILE END command will equal 1. A word variable is equal to two bytes.

The READ WORD command reads one word from a file and places it in a variable. The command takes two parameters. The first is the file number, and the second is the variable that you want to store the number. The WRITE WORD command writes one word number to a file. The command takes two parameters. The first is the file number, and the second is the variable to write. A word ranges from 0 to 65,535.

Reading and Writing Longs (4 Bytes)

The long number READ and WRITE commands read or write one long number to a file, respectively. These commands function similarly to the READ FILE and WRITE FILE commands. If you call enough of them, the FILE END command will equal 1. A long is equal to four bytes.

The READ LONG command reads one long number from a file and places it in a variable. The command takes two parameters. The first is the file number, and the second is the variable that you want to store the number. The WRITE LONG command writes one word-sized number to a file. The command takes two parameters. The first is the file number, and the second is the word number to write. A byte ranges from 0 to 4,294,967,295.

Reading and Writing Floats

The floating-point number READ and WRITE commands read or write one number to a file, respectively. If you call enough of these commands, the FILE END command will equal 1. A FLOAT is the size of 4 bytes.

The READ FLOAT command reads one floating-point number from a file and places it in a variable. The command takes two parameters. The first is the file number, and the second is the variable that you want to store the number. The WRITE FLOAT command writes one floating-point number to a file. The command takes two parameters. The first is the file number, and the second is the number to write.

Reading and Writing Strings

The string READ and WRITE commands read or write one string from or to a file, respectively. If you call enough of these commands, the FILE END command will equal 1.

The READ STRING command reads one string from a file and places it in a variable. The command takes two parameters. The first is the file number, and the second is the variable that you want to store the string. A newline (ASCII 13) character separates strings in a file. The WRITE STRING command writes a string to a file. The command takes two parameters. The first is the file number, and the second is the string to write.

Writing Your Own File

The following section of code will create a file and will write to the file whatever text you type in to the requested prompts for input, and then it will re-open and print out the contents of the file.

```
REM declare some variables
MyName AS STRING
```

```
MyColor AS STRING
MyMovie AS STRING

PRINT "This program demonstrates how to use the"
PRINT "DarkBASIC file read and write commands."
PRINT "To Start off I need some information from you."
PRINT
INPUT "What is your name? ", MyName
INPUT "What is your favorite color? ", MyColor
INPUT "What is your favorite movie? ", MyMovie
PRINT

IF FILE EXIST("MyTextFile.txt") = 1
   DELETE FILE "MyTextFile.txt"
ENDIF

OPEN TO WRITE 1, "MyTextFile.txt"
WRITE STRING 1, MyName
WRITE STRING 1, MyColor
WRITE STRING 1, MyMovie
CLOSE FILE 1

PRINT "Ok, I have written the file."
PRINT "Now I am clearing the Variables"
MyName = ""
MyColor = ""
MyMovie = ""
PRINT
PRINT "Variables are cleared!"
PRINT "Press any key..."
WAIT KEY
PRINT "Now reading the data from the file."
PRINT

OPEN TO READ 1, "MyTextFile.txt"
READ STRING 1, MyName
READ STRING 1, MyColor
READ STRING 1, MyMovie

PRINT "Your name is " + MyName
PRINT "Your favorite color is " + MyColor
PRINT "Your favorite movie is " + MyMovie

WAIT KEY
```

Using the Clipboard

The Clipboard is memory that Windows has set aside to store and retrieve data. The Clipboard is like a file, but you do not have to open or close it. Almost any program has access to this memory through a copy to clipboard, cut to clipboard, or paste from clipboard command. It is filled with text from a program that gives access to the Windows clipboard. DB gives you access to the Clipboard anytime you want.

Reading from the Clipboard

If you want to read the clipboard, you can use the GET CLIPBOARD$ command, which is the DB equivalent of pasting text in a word processor, e-mail software, or other program that supports copy and paste functions. The command takes no parameters, but it returns a string containing the content of the clipboard.

Saving to the Clipboard

Any time you need to save information to the Clipboard, you can use the WRITE TO CLIPBOARD command to store a string. This is the DB equivalent of the copy feature in a copy and paste operation (such as in a word processor). The command takes one parameter—the string you want to save to the Clipboard.

Summary

You have now covered the exhaustive concepts of file system management and file input and output programming in DB. This chapter provided an introduction to the commands you will need to tackle these important subjects in your own game projects. When you have access to the file system, you can literally write any type of application or utility that you set your mind to. For example, you can use the file input/output commands to write your own game editors, such as a level design tool or character editor that stores game data in files.

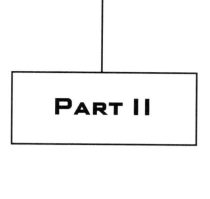

PART II

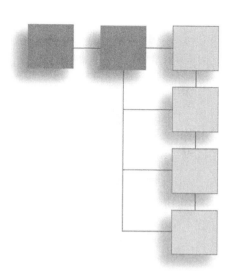

2D GAME PROGRAMMING

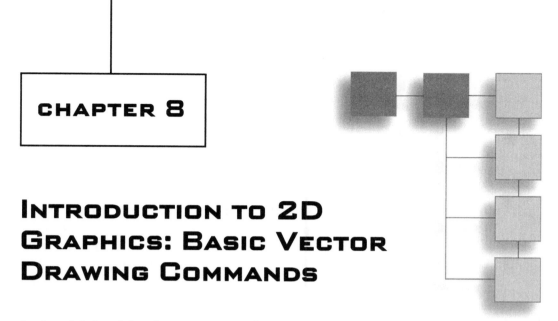

CHAPTER 8

INTRODUCTION TO 2D GRAPHICS: BASIC VECTOR DRAWING COMMANDS

So far, this book has been a primer for computer programming with the BASIC language. My goal so far has been to teach you the fundamentals of programming. There is a lot of prerequisite information required that most established game programmers take for granted, but it can be intimidating to someone who has never written a program before, let alone a game! This chapter provides an introduction to graphics in general, followed by the specific commands in DarkBASIC for programming your own graphics programs.

As you know, some folks learn quickly, while others take a little longer to catch on. That's why the book has kept a leisurely pace up to this point. But this chapter, and in particular the next two chapters, will quicken the pace dramatically. I'm sure you will be pleasantly surprised by all the amazing features that are built into DarkBASIC!

This chapter covers the following topics:

- Graphics in abundance

- System and video card commands

- Display mode commands

- Basic graphics programming

Graphics in Abundance!

The first step to writing a game on any platform—for example, Windows, Mac, Linux, or Game Boy Advance—is to learn the language, which you have now done. The language on many platforms is called the SDK (*Software Development Kit*). In the early days of Windows—circa 1992 and Windows 3.0— programmers had to use Microsoft C and the Windows SDK to write programs. This was before the invention of Visual Basic, which made Windows programming easy. In that regard, DarkBASIC has made it even easier (although DB was designed just for making games). DB is absolutely loaded with graphics commands! If you love graphics, then you've found a great tool for working with them. I'll go over the graphics commands built into DB soon. First, I'd like to explore some of the finer features that DB provides to enhance the graphics for a game.

Behind the Magic

What behind-the-scenes magic causes graphics to be displayed on a monitor? Every PC has a video card of one type or another that sends output to the monitor. The capabilities of the video card determine how the graphics will look. See Figure 8.1 for a sample illustration.

As a foregone conclusion, the better the video card, the better the graphics will look. The problem is that competition in the video card industry has been absolutely insane in recent years. The two top contenders, Nvidia and ATI, constantly leapfrog each other with each new generation of 3D chip. In general, you will do well to buy a new video card every two years. It doesn't have to be the

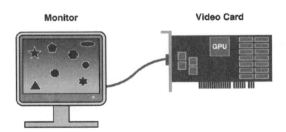

Figure 8.1
Graphics commands are routed to the video card, which prepares and sends the display screen to the monitor.

latest, greatest, top-of-the-line, expensive card. I personally prefer features to raw graphics power. For instance, I usually prefer a video card with video input and output ports, for doing video capture and also output to a big-screen TV. Some video cards even have a built-in TV tuner so that you can watch and record programs on your PC or digitize home movies.

Pixels and Resolution

The key to all graphics is the pixel, which is short for *picture element*. The display screen is made up of many thousands or millions of pixels, especially in the case of extremely high resolutions. For example, a resolution of 1600×1200, which is usually the upper limit for most monitors, is actually comprised of 1,920,000 pixels. This means that everything on the screen is made up of individual little point lights that are almost too small to see with the unaided eye. Screen resolution is measured by the number of pixels that make up the screen. Take a look at Figure 8.2, which shows a 640×480 screen.

Figure 8.2 shows that there are 640 horizontal pixels (from left to right) and 480 vertical pixels (from top to bottom). To get the total number of pixels for the screen, just multiply the horizontal resolution by the vertical resolution. In the case of a 640×480 screen, there are 307,200 pixels, which is very few

Figure 8.2
The display screen is made up of pixels that define the resolution.

compared to a 1600×1200 screen. Even though 1600×1200 is three times as large as 640×480, there are actually more than six times as many pixels at the higher resolution.

Resolutions

While a low-end video card might run great at 640×480, it would choke at 1600×1200. It takes a lot of processing power to push two million pixels through the monitor cable and out the screen at 60 frames per second (fps) or more! Just do the math. At 640×480 and 307,200 pixels, a game running at 60 fps will need to process 18,432,000 pixels every second! Take it to the high resolution, and it will be a startling revelation. At 1600×1200 and 1,920,000 pixels, a game running at 60 fps will need to process a whopping 115,200,000 pixels every second. That is a phenomenal number of pixels, to put it mildly. But that's only half the story.

Colors

Each pixel on the screen is capable of displaying any one of a possible 16.7 million colors in 32-bit color mode, or any one of around 64,000 colors in 16-bit color mode. 32-bit images are made up of red, green, blue, and alpha parts, each with eight bits of information. 16-bit images are a little more complicated, with five red, five blue, and either five or six green bits. Figure 8.3 shows how a pixel is physically displayed on a monitor.

As Figure 8.3 shows, each pixel is actually made up of three electron streams of red, green, and blue. By varying the intensity of an electron stream, the pixel displays a desired color. So, a 32-bit display actually requires four bytes of memory for every single pixel on the screen (since eight bits equal one byte).

Note

In a 32-bit display, only 24 bits are needed for each pixel. The remaining 8 bits make up what is called the *alpha* byte, and it is used for translucent and transparent effects.

Now you start to see why a powerful graphics accelerator is required to process all the pixels that make up a game screen. Without a graphics processor (such as the Nvidia GeForce 7800), the CPU would have a hard time drawing all those pixels

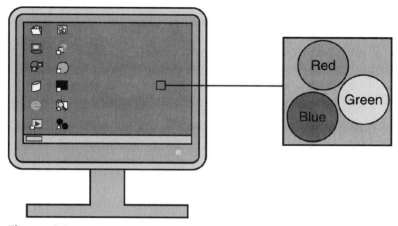

Figure 8.3
The display screen is made up of pixels. Each pixel is made up of red, green, and blue electron streams.

and doing other things in the computer at the same time. Just to give you an idea of the raw pixel fill rate of a modern graphics processor without getting into the subject of polygons and 3D graphics (which make even more demands of the graphics chip), a 1600×1200 32-bit display needs to move 460,800,000 bytes every second just to fill the screen.

Bits, Bytes, and . . . Polygons?

If you are an avid video game player (like I am), then you are probably familiar with consoles such as the Xbox 360, PlayStation 3, and Nintendo Wii. The video game industry prefers to deal with bits instead of bytes because graphics hardware is fiercely competitive. Console makers will avidly market their machines' capabilities by the data bus or processors inside, which can be 32-bit, 64-bit, 128-bit, or 256-bit. Keep in mind that 8 bits make up a single byte.

The ATI graphics chip inside the Xbox 360, for example, is capable of pushing a theoretical resolution of 1920×1440 in 32-bit color (which requires a very expensive HDTV set). Now if only the game developers would make better use of the HDTV capabilities! Of course, video game consoles are now rated with 3D performance, instead of the bytes or bits that make up a pixel, as was the case with previous consoles. They are rated in millions of polygons per second. A polygon is a 2D shape that is made up of three or more points which are referred to as vertices (see Figure 8.4).

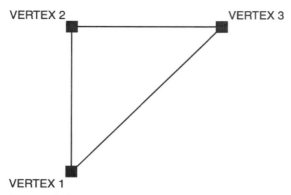

Figure 8.4
Polygons are made up of three or more vertices.

I will hold off on any more details about 3D graphics for now because 3D is a huge subject that I will cover in later chapters. I just want you to understand that 3D graphics are measured differently from the raw pixels involved in drawing 2D graphics.

Double Buffering

New programmers tend to want to just jump in and start writing a game using the best skills available. I remember when I started learning to write programs. At the time, I was learning Microsoft BASIC, which was frequently distributed with MS-DOS under the name of GW-BASIC. I remember trying desperately to make a Pac-Man game without any flicker. The problem is that once you learn how to draw things on the screen, they tend to leave a trail behind them as they move (unless you know some more advanced tricks). The solution to that problem is to erase an object on the screen, and then redraw it in a new location. This gets rid of the trails behind the object, which result from the object not being erased before it is moved.

If you've ever written a program in BASIC, then you are likely familiar with screen flicker. It is caused when an image on the screen is erased, moved, and redrawn in a new location—the basis for animation. Unfortunately, I neither

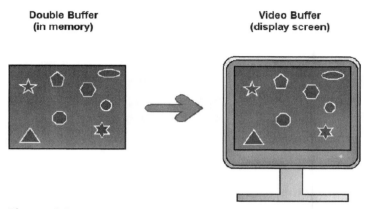

Double Buffer
(in memory)

Video Buffer
(display screen)

Figure 8.5
A double buffer eliminates flicker and provides for smooth, high-speed animation.

had the skill nor the know-how at the time to create a double buffer to reduce flicker.

What Is a Double Buffer?

What is a double buffer, you might ask? It is kind of a copy of the display screen in memory. You perform all drawing commands on that memory screen first, and then draw the memory screen to the real screen (see Figure 8.5).

Definition

A *double buffer* is a mirror image of the screen, located in high-speed memory. Instead of drawing directly to the screen, graphics commands are pointed to the double buffer. Once all drawing for a frame has been finished, the entire double buffer is quickly drawn to the screen, thus eliminating flicker.

Built-In Double Buffering

Double buffers are somewhat irrelevant because DB handles that aspect of programming automatically. Double buffers are so common that it is no wonder that the creators of DB put in that functionality by design. In the past, game programming books have spent dozens of pages on this topic alone, so it's great that DB handles this difficult programming problem in the background. In fact, there are ways to control the speed of the double buffer updates using the SYNC command, but that is a topic for the next chapter.

Drawing Commands

DB includes all the graphics commands you need to write a game. The best part is that you don't need a special library to make use of DirectX, which is completely integrated and abstracted inside DB. When you write a command such as CIRCLE, DB draws a circle on the full-screen DirectX display. You need not know anything about DirectX to make it work, which is something of a key to understanding what makes DB tick: It just works.

When you are working with DB, there are no header files to include, no library files to link, no DLLs to reference, no runtime to install. It just works. Best of all, you do not need an installer, because programs that have been compiled with DB are standalone executables with no dependencies. Most languages require at least some runtime library or a list of external definitions to use DirectX. Not so with DB.

DB has numerous vector graphics commands—that is, commands that deal with points and lines—in addition to sprite blitting commands. If you have never heard the terms "sprite" and "blitting" before, don't worry; I'll get into those subjects in the next two chapters.

DirectDraw versus Direct3D

Did you know that DB programs use DirectX? That's right—when you write a program with DB, you are writing DirectX programs without any effort! Possibly the most difficult aspect of DirectX programming is initializing DirectX components, such as Direct3D. DB actually utilizes Direct3D for all graphics output. Direct3D handles all the 3D graphics such as textures and polygons, but it also handles all 2D output as well. DB uses 3D mode for everything—including 2D graphics commands. This might be part of the reason why DB is considered a 3D programming language. Although DB has many 2D graphics commands built in, it was clearly designed for rendering 3D graphics. This might sound amazing, but DB may be able to draw a textured polygon faster than it is able to draw a simple line on the screen!

System and Video Card Commands

Now that you have had an introduction to the graphics commands available in DB, let's get into some initialization and management commands that will be useful as you begin to explore the more advanced features of DB. There is a sample program at the end of this section called CheckSystem, which runs through these commands, showing you how to use them and the resulting values returned by them.

Graphics Card Commands

The graphics card commands are helpful when you want to know the name of the primary video card or retrieve a list of cards in a multiple-monitor system.

Getting the Name of Your Video Card

The CURRENT GRAHICS CARD$() command returns a string with the name of the primary video card installed on the system. Unfortunately, this command doesn't return the actual name of the video card, just the name of the driver reported by DirectX.

Tip

> Important reminder: Commands that return a value must include empty parentheses at the end because that is how DB differentiates between regular functions and those that return a value.

Detecting Multiple Video Cards

The PERFORM CHECKLIST FOR GRAPHICS CARDS command is possibly the longest command in the entire DB language! However, it does perform a useful service by providing a list of video cards that are installed on your PC. This will usually just reference the single video card installed on most systems, but there are some cases in which multiple video cards are being used (such as in dual-monitor systems). In such cases, you might want to allow the user to select the correct video card before running the game. Most of the time you will just initialize the primary video card and not bother with multiple displays. There is an option in the DirectX driver options that allows the user to select the default video card, so you can ignore this feature if you want.

The SET GRAPHICS CARD command is used in conjunction with PERFORM CHECKLIST FOR GRAPHICS CARDS to select a specific video card in a multiple-display system. As I mentioned previously, this is probably not something that you will need to worry about, because the end user has the ability to select the primary display by setting a DirectX driver option.

Transform and Lighting Commands

The transform and lighting (T&L) commands are applicable for systems with a video card capable of offloading matrix transformations and hardware lighting from the main processor to the graphics processor (which is now old technology). When a video card supports T&L, it frees the main processor from these mathematically demanding computations, particularly when such video cards are optimized for handling T&L. Figure 8.6 shows the relationships between DB, DirectX, and the video display driver.

The TNL AVAILABLE() command returns the value 1 if transform and lighting is supported by the primary video card. If your game uses many 3D objects that are visible on the screen at once, or if you use hardware lighting, you might want to check to see whether T&L is available to ensure that a suitable video card is installed before allowing the game to run. This is an extreme case, and it is not likely to be an issue. In general, you will want the user to play the game no matter what the performance will be like. If the user's PC is out of date, then your game might be what convinces the user to upgrade to a faster processor or video card.

This command has become obsolete since DB now supports shaders. When you use a shader to render 3D graphics, this overrides the transform and lighting

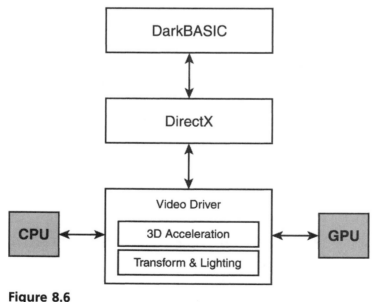

Figure 8.6
The video driver handles advanced features such as T&L and 3D acceleration, providing DirectX programs with a consistent interface regardless of differences among the various video cards.

engine in a video chip. For the most part, this process is entirely transparent to you as the programmer. You don't need to use shaders to write a 3D game, but you do have the ability to use this technology if you want.

Memory Commands

This section includes some system commands for retrieving the memory available, including system memory and video memory. These commands are useful if you are allocating a lot of memory and you want to make sure that you don't allocate beyond the memory that is available—meaning, of course, that Windows will use the swap file and virtual memory. The resulting performance hit is akin to killing a game.

Getting the Amount of Video RAM

The SYSTEM DMEM AVAILABLE() command returns the amount of free display memory. Generally, this value will return the total amount of installed display memory on the video card when your DB program first starts running, given that you haven't allocated any textures or 3D objects.

Getting the Amount of System RAM

The SYSTEM SMEM AVAILABLE() command returns the amount of free system memory. This is generally referred to as RAM (*Random Access Memory*), although this particular command returns just the amount of free memory, not the total installed memory. Therefore, this command might be useful if you are allocating large blocks of memory and you want to make sure that there is enough memory to hold the objects you are trying to allocate.

Getting the Total System RAM (Including Virtual RAM)

The SYSTEM TMEM AVAILABLE() command returns the amount of total system memory that is available to programs. This differs from the SMEM command in that it takes into account the virtual memory in use on the system (in the form of a swap file). This value usually will be very large, depending on the default size of your swap file. For this reason, this command is not very useful in the course of writing a game because you will likely just be interested in the amount of free memory that the SMEM command provides.

The CheckSystem Program

Okay, how would you like to put all this newfound knowledge to use in a real program? The CheckSystem program displays the primary video card, the available features, and the amount of free memory in your computer system. Before you begin, I want to start a new trend. It's time to replace the REM statement with something more convenient. From this chapter forward, I will use the apostrophe instead of the REM statement. The apostrophe character, which is located to the left of the 1 key on most keyboards, is an alternative way to start a comment line in DB. Notice how I have used the apostrophe instead of REM in the listing for the CheckSystem program. The comment lines are less imposing, making the source code easier to read.

```
'Check for installed video cards
PERFORM CHECKLIST FOR GRAPHICS CARDS
VideoCards = CHECKLIST QUANTITY()
IF VideoCards > 1
   PRINT "There are ",VideoCards, " installed video cards. "
   FOR Index = 1 TO VideoCards
      PRINT " ", Index, " - ", CHECKLIST STRING$(Index)
   NEXT Index
ELSE
   PRINT "There is one installed video card. "
ENDIF

'Display current video driver
PRINT "Video driver: ", CURRENT GRAPHICS CARD$()

'Check for transform and lighting
IF TNL AVAILABLE() = 1
   PRINT "Transform and lighting supported. "
ELSE
   PRINT "No transform and lighting. "
ENDIF

'Display memory available
PRINT "Total video memory: ", SYSTEM DMEM AVAILABLE()
PRINT "System memory free: ", SYSTEM SMEM AVAILABLE()
PRINT "Total memory free: ", SYSTEM TMEM AVAILABLE()

'Wait for user to press a key
WAIT KEY
```

```
'Delete checklist array from memory
EMPTY CHECKLIST

'End the program
END
```

Display Mode Commands

DB includes a number of useful utility commands for retrieving a list of display modes supported by your video card. The default resolution that DB uses is 640×480×16, but there are many more display modes available, all the way up to the maximum resolution supported by your video card. This section shows you how to retrieve and use the list of display modes.

Reading and Setting the Display Modes

This section includes the commands for reading the list of display modes, as well as setting and checking them.

Getting the List of Available Video Modes

PERFORM CHECKLIST FOR DISPLAY MODES is a very long command, but it provides a useful list of the modes supported by your video card, filling in the CHECKLIST STRING$ array with the values returned. The CHECKLIST QUANTITY() command returns the number of display modes returned by the PERFORM CHECKLIST FOR DISPLAY MODES command. You can use this value to loop through the display modes. Once you know how many video modes that are available, you can retrieve them by number. The CHECKLIST STRING$() command accepts a single parameter—the display mode number—and returns the name of the display mode, such as 1024×768×16 or 1600×1200×16.

Getting the Video Mode Values

The CHECKLIST VALUE A() command grabs the first part of the display mode name returned by the CHECKLIST STRING$() command. Since the display mode is returned in the format of 640×480×16, this command returns the 640 part, which is the horizontal resolution of the display. The CHECKLIST VALUE B() command grabs the second part of the display mode name returned by the CHECKLIST STRING$() command. Since the display mode is returned in the format of 640×480×16, this command returns the 480 part, which is the vertical resolution of the display. The third part of the video mode is the color depth of the screen. The CHECKLIST VALUE C() command grabs the third part of the display mode. Since the display mode is returned in the format of 640×480×16, this command returns the 16 part.

Setting the Video Mode

The SET DISPLAY MODE command accepts three parameters to change the display mode—horizontal resolution, vertical resolution, and color depth. For example:

```
SET DISPLAY MODE 640, 480, 16
```

Note that DB Pro still supports this command, but it is recommended that you set the video mode from the project settings rather than from source code, due to the way DB Pro compiles the source code and adds bitmaps and other media files to the executable.

The CHECK DISPLAY MODE() command checks the display mode passed as parameter values to see if it is available on the system. If the display mode is invalid, this command returns a value of 0. For example:

```
Value = CHECK DISPLAY MODE(640, 480, 16)
```

Display Mode Properties

Let's take a look at some commands that are useful for getting information about the specific video mode currently in use. The SCREEN TYPE() command determines whether 2D hardware acceleration is supported by the video card. A return value of 0 means that hardware acceleration is not available. The SCREEN WIDTH() command returns the horizontal resolution of the current display mode in pixels. For example, if the display mode is 1280×960×32, the SCREEN WIDTH() command returns a value of 1280. Likewise, the SCREEN HEIGHT() command returns the vertical resolution of the current display mode in pixels.

The SCREEN DEPTH() command returns the color depth of the current display mode in bits per pixels (BPP). For example, if the display mode is 1280×960×32, the SCREEN DEPTH() command returns a value of 32.

Another useful command that is related to the video system is one that returns the frame rate. The SCREEN FPS() command is a useful command. It reports the performance of the video card in frames per second. Depending on the video card this value will vary widely, but it generally won't go above 100 FPS.

The DisplayModes Program

The DisplayModes program will help you learn the various video modes supported by the video card on your PC. This program will also show you how to return the list of supported modes and how to set a particular video mode using the code you have learned so far in this section. The DisplayModes program draws several boxes on the screen to represent each display resolution, so you can see how the video modes compare. Allow me to give you a tour of the program. DB programs default to the display mode of 640×480×16 unless you specify otherwise. Here's a program that demonstrates:

```
' Get the list of video modes
PERFORM CHECKLIST FOR DISPLAY MODES
SET DISPLAY MODE 640, 480, 32

DO
   ' Draw gray resolution markers
   CLS
   INK RGB(120,120,120),0
   BOX 0,0,1599,1199
   INK RGB(100,100,100),0
   BOX 0,0,1279,959
   INK RGB(80,80,80),0
   BOX 0,0,1023,767
   INK RGB(60,60,60),0
   BOX 0,0,799,599
   INK RGB(30,30,30),0
   BOX 0,0,639,479

   ' Display the list of video modes
   INK RGB(255,255,255),0
   modes = CHECKLIST QUANTITY()
   FOR t = 1 TO modes / 2
      ' First column of resolutions
      SET CURSOR 0,t * 16
      PRINT t; " ";CHECKLIST STRING$(t);
      ' Second column of resolutions
```

```
        SET CURSOR 200,t * 16
        index = modes / 2 + t
        PRINT index; " ";CHECKLIST STRING$(index)
    NEXT t

    ' Ask user to select a video mode
    INPUT "Select mode: ";position

    ' Rip the values out of the modes array
    width=CHECKLIST VALUE A(position)
    height=CHECKLIST VALUE B(position)
    depth=CHECKLIST VALUE C(position)

    ' Change the display mode
    SET DISPLAY MODE width, height, depth
LOOP
```

Basic Graphics Programming

This section of the chapter involves some actual commands for drawing objects on the screen, unlike the previous sections, which dealt only with initializing and reading information about the video card.

Changing the Drawing Color

By default, DB uses white for graphics and text output. If you want to change the color, you can use the INK command in conjunction with RGB, as explained next.

The INK command changes the foreground and background colors used for graphics and text drawing commands. INK accepts two parameters—foreground color and background color—which must be integer values. Normally, you will use the RGB command to generate them. For example:

```
Forecolor = RGB(120, 120, 120)
Backcolor = RGB(255, 0, 0)
INK Forecolor, Backcolor
```

The RGB command, as you have already seen, uses the parameters that you pass to the command and returns an integer containing the red, green, and blue parts that make up a color.

Clearing the Screen

One of the most overlooked commands for keeping the display clean and attractive involves a simple screen clear. The CLS command clears the display screen using the current background color that was set using the INK command, as shown in the following code.

```
' Set the background color to green
INK 0, RGB(0, 255, 0)
CLS
```

Note that you can simply pass an integer to the INK command, which is useful when you want to set a color to black, which is the value 0. The CLS command uses the background color previously set with INK. To show how the INK and CLS commands work together, I've written a short program called ClearScreen. Here is the source code for the ClearScreen program. Feel free to experiment by changing the display mode to some other resolutions.

```
' Initialize the program
SET DISPLAY MODE 640, 480, 16
' Start the main loop
DO
   ' Set a random color
   bcolor = RGB(RND(255),RND(255),RND(255))
   INK 0,bcolor
   ' Clear the screen
   CLS
LOOP
```

Reading and Setting Pixels

You can read the basic picture elements (pixels) that make up the screen individually using the DOT and POINT commands.

The DOT command does just what it sounds like—it draws a dot on the screen in the form of a single pixel. Before calling the DOT command, you will want to set the color of the pixel using the INK command. DOT accepts two parameters—the horizontal and vertical positions of the pixel, usually referenced as X and Y coordinates.

To help demonstrate drawing pixels, I've written a short program called RandomPixels that quickly draws pixels in random locations on the screen. Here is the source code for the RandomPixels program. This program is fun to experiment with, so feel free to change the resolution and the color settings to see what happens.

```
' Initialize the program
SET DISPLAY MODE 640, 480, 16
CLS

' Start the main loop
DO
   ' Pick a random color
   fcolor = RGB(RND(255),RND(255),RND(255))
   INK fcolor, RGB(0,0,255)
   ' Draw the pixel
   DOT RND(640),RND(480)
LOOP
```

The converse of DOT is the POINT command. POINT reads the color value of the pixel referenced by the two parameters that are passed (X and Y). The returned value is an integer like the one returned by RGB. This command is somewhat slow, so you wouldn't want to use it to scan the entire screen (for whatever reason) because it would slow down the program.

Drawing Lines

Pixels are interesting, but the action really begins when you learn to draw lines in DB. As you might already know, 3D graphics utilize lines more than pixels because polygons are made up of lines (although lines are comprised of pixels . . . but you get the idea). The LINE command draws a line on the screen using the current color set with the INK command. There are four parameters passed to the LINE command, representing the left, top, right, and bottom points of the line.

To demonstrate how the LINE command works, I've written a program called RandomLines that quickly draws random lines on the screen, as shown in Figure 8.7. The source code for the RandomLines program follows.

```
' Initialize the program
SET DISPLAY MODE 640, 480, 16
CLS
```

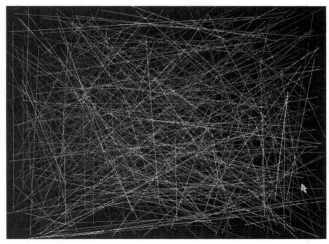

Figure 8.7
The RandomLines program uses the LINE command to draw lines at random locations.

```
' Start the main loop
DO
   ' Pick a random color
   fcolor = RGB(RND(255),RND(255),RND(255))
   INK fcolor, RGB(0,0,0)
   ' Draw the line
   LINE RND(640), RND(480), RND(640), RND(480)
LOOP
```

Drawing Rectangles

A rectangle is comprised of four lines that make up the edges. However, rectangles are treated just like lines as far as the parameters for drawing are concerned. The BOX command is used to draw rectangles. Like the other graphics drawing commands, BOX depends on the color set previously with the INK command. There are four parameters for the BOX command, just like those for the LINE command—left, top, right, and bottom. To demonstrate the BOX command, I've written a program called RandomBoxes that draws random rectangles on the screen using random colors (see Figure 8.8). The source code follows.

```
' Initialize the program
SET DISPLAY MODE 640, 480, 32
CLS
```

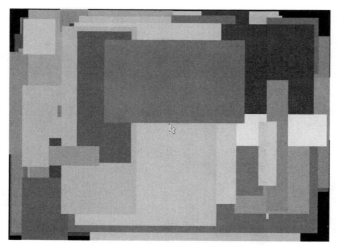

Figure 8.8
The RandomBoxes program uses the BOX command to draw filled rectangles at random locations.

```
' Start the main loop
DO
    ' Set a random color
    fcolor = RGB(RND(255),RND(255),RND(255))
    INK fcolor,0
    ' Draw the rectangle
    BOX RND(640), RND(480), RND(640), RND(480)
LOOP
```

Drawing Circles

Circles are quite a bit different from pixels, lines, and rectangles, which sort of build upon each other. Circles must be drawn using a special algorithm that draws pixels using the mathematical sine and cosine functions. Suffice it to say, it's not as fast or easy to draw a circle as it is to draw a line. Fortunately, DB handles the difficulty of drawing circles for you.

The CIRCLE Command

The CIRCLE command draws circles in DB. There are three parameters for this command—X, Y, and radius. Radius determines the size of the circle. Just remember that the radius only represents half the width of the circle. The diameter of a circle is made up of two radii.

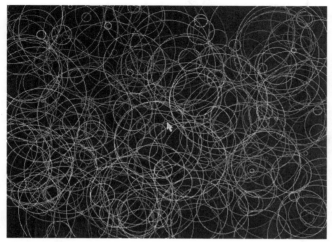

Figure 8.9
The RandomCircles program uses the CIRCLE command to draw circles at random locations.

The RandomCircles program demonstrates how to use the CIRCLE command to draw random circles on the screen, as shown in Figure 8.9. The source code follows.

```
' Initialize the program
SET DISPLAY MODE 640, 480, 16
CLS

' Start the main loop
DO
    ' Set a random color
    fcolor = RGB(RND(255),RND(255),RND(255))
    INK fcolor,0
    ' Draw the circle
    CIRCLE RND(640), RND(480), RND(100)
LOOP
```

Drawing a Circle, One Pixel at a Time

Do circles intrigue you at all after seeing the RandomCircles program run? I remember the first time I drew a circle using BASIC—I was fascinated by it! Let me show you an interesting little variant of the RandomCircles program. This new program, called DrawCircle, actually plots each of the pixels that make up a circle, so you can see how circles are created. Take a look at Figure 8.10 to see the program running.

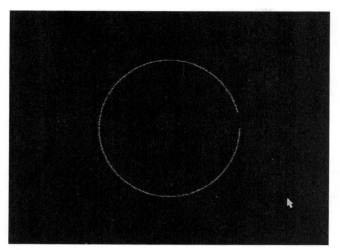

Figure 8.10
The DrawCircle program uses the DOT command to draw each pixel that makes up a circle.

Following is the source code for the DrawCircle program. The core of this program is the two lines that call the COS() and SIN() functions to position the current pointer around the circumference of the circle (which has a random size). You can use this circle-drawing code for all kinds of cool things! In later chapters, I'll show you how to load bitmaps and sprites and animate them on the screen. One of the most impressive features of animation is the ability to move a sprite around a curve; the code for drawing a circle really helps in that department, as I'll show you in upcoming chapters.

```
' Initialize the program
SET DISPLAY MODE 640, 480, 16
CLS
v = 0
size = RND(100) + 100

' Start the main loop
DO
    ' Set a random color
    fcolor = RGB(RND(255),RND(255),RND(255))
    INK fcolor,0

    ' Move the point around the circle
    ox = COS(v) * size
    oy = SIN(v) * size
    v = v + 1
```

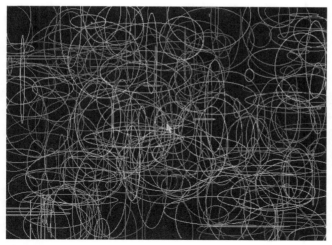

Figure 8.11
The RandomEllipses program uses the `ELLIPSE` command to draw ellipses at random locations.

```
   ' Draw the point
   DOT 320 + ox, 240 + oy
LOOP
```

Drawing Ellipses

Ellipses are related to circles but are not equidistant in radius, meaning that the distance from the center of an ellipse to the edge is not always the same around its circumference. The `ELLIPSE` command draws ellipses. It takes four parameters—X, Y, X-radius, and Y-radius. The first two parameters are obvious, but what about the last two? X-radius determines the radius from left to right, and Y-radius determines the radius from top to bottom.

The RandomEllipses program demonstrates how to use the `ELLIPSE` command (see Figure 8.11). This program is similar to the RandomCircles program, so you can adapt that program rather than rewrite it, if you like.

```
' Initialize the program
SET DISPLAY MODE 640, 480, 16
CLS
' Start the main loop
DO
   ' Pick a random color
   fcolor = RGB(RND(255),RND(255),RND(255))
   INK fcolor,0
```

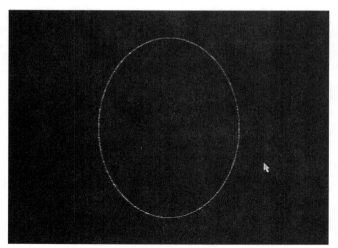

Figure 8.12
The DrawEllipse program uses the DOT command to draw each pixel that makes up an ellipse.

```
    ' Draw the ellipse
    ELLIPSE RND(640), RND(480), RND(100), RND(100)
LOOP
```

Drawing an Ellipse the Hard Way

To further enhance your understanding of circles and ellipses, I have adapted the DrawCircle program to use ellipses. In this program, instead of using just a single size variable for the radius of the circle to be drawn, there are hsize and vsize variables to represent the radius of the X and Y radii of the ellipse (see Figure 8.12).

```
' Initialize the program
SET DISPLAY MODE 640, 480, 16
CLS
v = 0
hsize = RND(100) + 100
vsize = RND(100) + 100

' Start the main loop
DO
    ' Pick a random color
    fcolor = RGB(RND(255),RND(255),RND(255))
    INK fcolor,0
```

```
   ' Move the point around the circle
   ox = COS(v) * hsize
   oy = SIN(v) * vsize
   v = v + 1

   ' Draw the point
   DOT 320 + ox, 240 + oy
LOOP
```

Summary

This chapter provided an introduction to graphics programming in DB. The language provides many useful commands for drawing points, lines, circles, and other shapes. There are also commands for setting the foreground and background colors and for clearing the screen. In this chapter you learned to identify the video card, the available 2D and 3D graphics capabilities, and the display modes provided by the video card, as well as how to change the screen resolution.

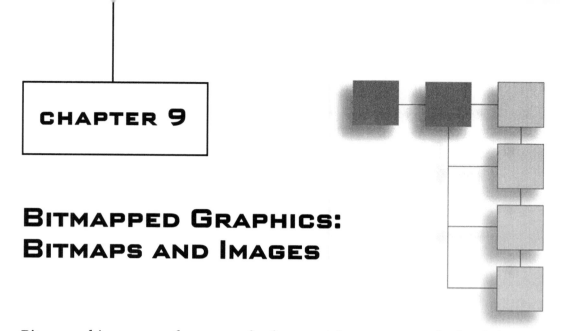

CHAPTER 9

BITMAPPED GRAPHICS:
BITMAPS AND IMAGES

Bitmapped images are the core and substance of every game, whether it is a 2D vertical scrolling arcade game like the classic *Heavy Barrel,* a war simulation like *Battlefield 2,* a first person shooter like *Doom III,* or a real-time strategy game like *Warcraft III: Reign of Chaos.* None of these games would amount to anything without the ability to load, manipulate, and display bitmap images in one form or another. So when you learn how to use bitmaps, you are really getting down to the core of what it takes to make a game. This chapter covers the subject of handling bitmaps in great detail, showing you how to load, create, and display bitmap files in a variety of formats that DarkBASIC supports. This chapter will be a helpful introduction to the more advanced subject of sprites, which is covered in the next chapter. Here are the key subjects in this chapter:

- Introduction to bitmaps

- Creating and loading bitmaps

- Bitmap information commands

- Basic bitmap commands

- Special effects commands

Introduction to Bitmaps

The phrase *bitmapped graphics files*, in the truest sense, refers to any file format used to store pictures, such as those taken from digital cameras or scanners, downloaded off the Internet, or even hand-drawn artwork. The term *bitmap* refers to the way bits in the image are encoded in the image file or in the memory prior to being displayed.

Tip

Recall that 8 bits = 1 byte, and a 32-bit video card requires 4 bytes for every pixel.

The bit format of the display screen (your monitor) is not always the same as the bit format of a picture in memory or in a disk file, but Windows and DirectX (which powers DB) are able to handle the task of converting pictures from disk to a format that is supported by your video card.

Bitmaps range from simple letters to complex pictures and anything in between. Early game consoles such as the Nintendo or Sega relied almost solely on small bitmaps for the graphics in video games. (In contrast, most current games run in 3D and use polygons with textures, which are bitmaps, too.)

What Is a Bitmap?

So what exactly is a bitmap? It might help if you first had an inkling of what bitmaps are useful for, but I'll get to that shortly. A bitmap is a collection of bytes (where each byte equals 8 bits) that represents a picture or graphic image. The simplest form of a bitmap would be a black and white picture: All white pixels are represented as 0, and all black pixels are represented by 1. Figure 9.1 shows an example of a bitmap image. This picture of a car was taken with a digital camera

Figure 9.1
A typical bitmap image—in this case, it's a digital photo.

that stored the image in a bitmap file. These digital images are the same sort of images we use in a game. The difference is that game artwork is drawn by hand using a graphic editor program like Photoshop, Paint Shop Pro, or Pro Motion.

Bitmap File Formats

There are many bitmap file formats, but they are all based on the premise that a pixel of color can be represented by a numeric value. DB handles the details of converting a bitmap file to a format required for a game. If you can start to imagine the difficulties involved in converting an 8-bit image to a 32-bit image, you will develop considerable respect for the amount of work that DB does for you. DB uses the Windows Bitmap (.bmp) file format natively. Although there are other popular formats such as Tagged Image File Format (.tiff), Joint Photographic Group Format (.jpg), Graphical Interchange Format (.gif), and Picture Exchange (.pcx), it is easier to simply use the format natively supported by DB.

The most important factor to consider when working with bitmaps is color depth. The most common color depths include 8, 16, 24, and 32 bits. The number of colors in an image is often referred to as *bit depth* because the number is representative of the bits, not the number of colors. To figure out how many colors are supported by a color depth (also referred to as *bits per pixel*, or BPP), use the following formula:

```
Total Colors = 2 ^ (Bit Depth)
```

This formula takes 2 to the power of the bit depth of the image (or video display). Table 9.1 shows the common bit depths, along with the total number of colors associated with each.

You'll notice that the number of colors increases with the higher color depth. That is because the computer has more bits to represent colors. In a monochrome

Table 9.1 Bitmap Color Depths

Bit Depth	Number of Colors
8	256
12	4,096
16	65,536
24	16,777,216
32	4,294,967,296

bitmap there are just 2 bits per pixel, black and white. In a 16-bit image, you have a total of 65,535 combinations from which to choose.

Creating Bitmaps

You might be curious at this point about how to load a bitmap from a file and draw it on the screen. I'll show you how to do that soon enough. First, I want to explain something important before you jump in and start using bitmaps in DB. So, how do you create a bitmap? I guess that would be a good place to start, especially if you are not familiar with paint programs. First, you can create a bitmap using DB code with some of the built-in commands. Second, you can use a graphic editor such as Paint Shop Pro (shown in Figure 9.2) to create some interesting graphics and then load them into your DB program. To create a bitmap that will be loaded by DB, you need a graphic editor. My favorite graphic editor is the aforementioned Paint Shop Pro, by Jasc Software (which is now

Figure 9.2
Paint Shop Pro is a powerful graphic editor. Shown here is one of the skybox images from SkyMATTER, available at http://www.thegamecreators.com.

owned by Corel). You can download a trial version of this program from http://www.jasc.com or http://www.corel.com.

This program has all the tools you need to create a bitmap file for use in DB. Paint Shop Pro has many image editing tools, and a zoom feature that is useful for editing your graphics with precision. Editing and manipulating game graphics is a serious subject, and a serious career choice for many who find employment in the graphic arts, advertising, and even games industries, and is beyond the scope of this book. If you are interested solely in 3D graphics, you will still want to know how to create 2D graphics, because 3D textures are created with programs like Paint Shop Pro.

Another favorite tool that I frequently use is Pro Motion, created by Cosmigo and available for download from http://www.cosmigo.com. The trial edition of Pro Motion 5.1 is found on the book's CD-ROM. This fantastic program (shown in Figure 9.3) is an ideal choice for working with animated sprites, and we will begin to use it in the next chapter.

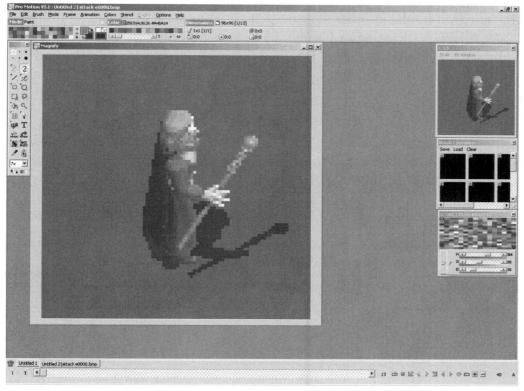

Figure 9.3
Cosmigo's excellent Pro Motion 2D animation software.

Uses for Bitmaps

So what kinds of uses are there for bitmaps? There are plenty of things you can do with them. You can create beautiful backgrounds or use smaller bitmaps to display score lines and statistics. Instead of drawing your pictures pixel by pixel or line by line, bitmaps allow you to stamp the entire image on the screen. I have found quite a few uses for bitmaps in the years I have been programming. I have used them to create fonts (for text on the screen) and textures (for skins of models), and even for height mapping to create a realistic landscape. We will learn how to use bitmaps in a game later in this chapter and how to create sprites out of bitmaps in the next chapter.

Creating and Loading Bitmaps

First I will cover the series of commands to load and create bitmaps. These commands are useful for loading a picture you create with your favorite graphic editor or creating your own pictures within DB.

DB has a limit on the number of bitmaps it can support at one time. This limit is 32, which means that you can only load or create 32 bitmaps at one time. This might seem like a small number, but you can be creative and get around any problems related to the small number of bitmaps. Usually, you won't be using more than five or six bitmaps at a time, because most of the work in a 2D game is handled by sprites, which are stored separately from bitmaps.

Each bitmap is addressed like an array. That is to say, each bitmap has a number attached to it, ranging from 0 to 31. Bitmap 0 is special in that it is the bitmap that will be displayed on the screen by default. Therefore, if you load a graphic into bitmap 0, it will be displayed on the screen.

Note

> Bitmap 0 is an important bitmap. This bitmap is a bitmap reserved for the screen. Any bitmap image copied onto bitmap 0 will appear directly on the screen.

Loading a Bitmap File

The LOAD BITMAP command is the first of the important bitmap commands. The command format is LOAD BITMAP *Filename, Bitmap Number*. The first parameter is the name of the file to load; the second parameter is the bitmap number (between 0 and 31) into which to load the image. In DB, there are no bitmap variables; instead, there is a built-in array of bitmaps that you can use. In other languages, such as C++, Visual Basic, and Delphi, you would have to create a variable and then load the bitmap into memory, after which you would be able to draw it on the screen. In DB, though, you can just load a bitmap into the bitmap array.

Creating a New Bitmap in Memory

The CREATE BITMAP command is the second of the important bitmap commands. Whereas LOAD BITMAP loaded a bitmap from disk and displayed it on the screen, CREATE BITMAP creates a blank bitmap with whatever dimensions you want. This is the command you would use to create bitmaps on which to draw within DB. The syntax for this command is CREATE BITMAP *Bitmap Number, Width, Height*.

Unlike the LOAD BITMAP command that has a *Bitmap Number* parameter, when you call the CREATE BITMAP command, all drawing operations (such as LINE or CIRCLE) then take place on that new bitmap by default. So, if you create a new bitmap and then perform some drawing commands, those operations will not go to the screen, but instead to the new bitmap! Be mindful of this situation; when things do not appear on the screen as you expected, you might want to make sure that you have first called SET CURRENT BITMAP 0 in order to set the current output to the screen.

CREATE BITMAP takes three parameters and requires all three parameters to work (meaning, none are optional). The first parameter is the number of the bitmap you want to create. This parameter will take anything between 1 and 31. You cannot use 0 in this parameter because 0 is the screen. Technically, there are only 31 bitmaps that may be loaded at a time in DB, although the screen acts like a bitmap as well. Also, you cannot use a bitmap number that has already been used (either via CREATE BITMAP or LOAD BITMAP) without first deleting the bitmap.

The second and third parameters are the width and height of the bitmap. These do not have to match the screen's width and height. You can make a bitmap 100×100 pixels, or you can make it 1600×1200 pixels, although I can't imagine why you would need one that big!

The following program, which is called CreateBitmap, creates a bitmap and displays circles on the new bitmap. This program is located on the CD-ROM in \sources\chapter09\CreateBitmap.

```
' create a new bitmap
PRINT "Creating the bitmap... "
CREATE BITMAP 1, 640, 480

' display message on the screen
SET CURRENT BITMAP 0
PRINT "Drawing circles... "

' draw some circles on the bitmap surface
SET CURRENT BITMAP 1
FOR N = 1 TO 100
   INK RGB(RND(255), RND(255), RND(255)), 0
   CIRCLE RND(540)+50, RND(380)+50, RND(40)
NEXT N

SET CURRENT BITMAP 0
PRINT "Press a key to display the bitmap... "
WAIT KEY

' copy bitmap 1 to the screen
COPY BITMAP 1, 0

WAIT KEY
END
```

Checking the Status of a Bitmap

Creating and loading bitmaps can be complicated, especially if you don't know whether a bitmap has been created or loaded already. The BITMAP EXIST command can help you there. The command format is BITMAP EXIST(*Bitmap Number*). This command takes one parameter—the bitmap number—and tells you whether that bitmap has been created or loaded. It returns a 0 if the bitmap does not exist and a 1 if it does exist. These two numbers are standard in most languages, where true = 1 and false = 0. I find it easier to remember that false always equals zero, rather than trying to remember both.

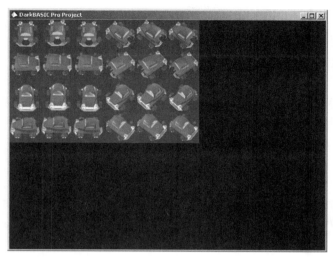

Figure 9.4
The LoadBitmap program.

Loading a Bitmap

You can load a bitmap file using the LOAD BITMAP command, which accepts two parameters—the filename and the bitmap number. For example:

```
LOAD BITMAP "bitmap.bmp", 1
```

Let's try it out. Figure 9.4 shows the output of the LoadBitmap program, which is listed next. This program is small because DB does all the work of loading and drawing the bitmap for us. In the next chapter, you'll learn how to copy a portion of a bitmap image to use as a sprite.

```
LOAD BITMAP "jeep.bmp", 1
COPY BITMAP 1, 0
WAIT KEY
```

Bitmap Information Commands

Now that you know how to load and create bitmaps, it is time to move on to some other important commands. Each bitmap has information specific to it. There are three things that every bitmap has—width, height, and depth. The width and height are pretty self-explanatory. The depth is the color depth of a bitmap. DB provides you with commands to find these properties.

Determining the Width, Height, and Color Depth

The BITMAP WIDTH command returns the width of a bitmap. It takes one parameter—the bitmap number. The BITMAP WIDTH command syntax is BITMAP WIDTH (*bitmap number*) which returns the height in pixels of the bitmap whose number matches the bitmap number. The BitmapInfo program will demonstrate the use of the BITMAP WIDTH command.

The BITMAP HEIGHT command returns the height of the bitmap. It takes one parameter, just like the BITMAP WIDTH command. In fact, it is the same parameter. The BITMAP HEIGHT command is BITMAP HEIGHT (*bitmap number*) which returns the height in pixels of the bitmap whose number matches the bitmap number. The BitmapInfo program will demonstrate the use of the BITMAP HEIGHT command.

The BITMAP DEPTH command returns the color depth of the bitmap. It has one parameter as well—the bitmap number. The command is BITMAP DEPTH (*bitmap number*). It returns a bit depth value shown in Table 9.1, not the number of colors. The BitmapInfo program will demonstrate how to use the BITMAP DEPTH command.

The BitmapInfo Program

The BitmapInfo program (which is located on the CD-ROM under \sources\chapter09\BitmapInfo) loads a bitmap file and then displays the width, height, and depth of the bitmap. Figure 9.5 shows the output of the program.

Figure 9.5
The BitmapInfo program demonstrates how to read the width, height, and color depth of a bitmap.

```
' load the bitmap file
LOAD BITMAP "earth.bmp", 1

' display the bitmap file
COPY BITMAP 1, 0

' display information about the bitmap
SET CURRENT BITMAP 0

TEXT 460, 0, "WIDTH: " + STR$(BITMAP WIDTH(1))
TEXT 460, 20, "HEIGHT: " + STR$(BITMAP HEIGHT(1))
TEXT 460, 40, "COLOR DEPTH: " + STR$(BITMAP DEPTH(1)) + " bits"

' delete the bitmap from memory
DELETE BITMAP 1
WAIT KEY
END
```

Basic Bitmap Commands

Now that you know the commands to create and measure bitmaps, it's time to manipulate them. This is not as hard as it sounds. All the commands required to manipulate bitmaps are included in DB. What you will need to keep track of is where each bitmap is located in the bitmap array. Remember how I told you that DB supports 32 bitmaps (0–31)? The next set of commands will allow you to manipulate those different bitmaps.

Copying One Bitmap to Another

Here is a command that you have been using throughout the examples. Finally, the COPY BITMAP command is explained! This is one of the more complicated commands because it can take two different sets of parameters. If you want to copy the contents of an entire bitmap from one bitmap to another, the format is COPY BITMAP *From Bitmap, To Bitmap*, where the entire bitmap in the "from bitmap" is copied to the "to bitmap".

You use the slightly more complicated version of the command when you want to copy only part of a bitmap. Then the COPY BITMAP command takes 10 parameters. The command format is COPY BITMAP *From Bitmap, Left, Top, Right, Bottom, To Bitmap, Left, Top, Right, Bottom*. The "from bitmap" and "to bitmap" parameters are the same as the first command. The "left", "top", "right", and "bottom" parameters on both sides specify what pixels to copy and to where.

There is a catch to the ten-parameter COPY BITMAP command of which you should be aware. When copying pixels from one bitmap to another, the COPY BITMAP command uses 0,0 as the upper-left corner. This means that when you copy to or from a bitmap, the furthest right you should copy is BITMAP WIDTH −1, and the furthest down you should copy is BITMAP HEIGHT −1.

Changing the Current Bitmap

SET CURRENT BITMAP is the most common command for programming bitmaps because it changes the bitmap number to which drawing commands are directed. If you use the CIRCLE command, the normal output is to the screen, which is bitmap 0 in the array. The TEXT command works the same way, drawing to the current bitmap. The SET CURRENT BITMAP command allows you to change the current bitmap. The command format is SET CURRENT BITMAP *Bitmap Number*. When you use this command, you can draw to any bitmap, not just to the screen.

Likewise, the CURRENT BITMAP command returns the number of the currently active bitmap. The command format is *Return Value* = CURRENT BITMAP() (meaning that this command has no parameters). This is a useful command to help you keep track of which bitmap you are using.

Saving a Bitmap to a File

Sometimes you will want to save the work that you do or take a screenshot of your game while it's running. DB provides a command for that—the SAVE BITMAP command. It has two different sets of commands. If you want to save the contents of the screen, the command is SAVE BITMAP *Filename*. If you want to save the contents of a specific bitmap number, the command is SAVE BITMAP *Filename*, *Bitmap Number*.

Deleting a Bitmap

Now comes a very useful command called DELETE BITMAP. Remember how I told you that you can only have 32 bitmaps at a time? The DELETE BITMAP command helps you manage those 32 bitmaps by allowing you to delete the ones that are no longer in use. After you are done with a bitmap, it is a good habit to delete it so the bitmap will be available elsewhere in the program. When a DB program ends, all the bitmaps are deleted automatically, but it is good programming practice to delete things when you no longer need them—and before a program ends.

Note

Remember bitmap 0 is a special bitmap. This bitmap points to the screen. So you really have 31 bitmaps you can delete. You cannot delete bitmap 0.

Special Effects Commands

DB comes with some interesting special effects commands for bitmaps. There are five types of special effects you can use with bitmaps: MIRROR, FLIP, FADE, BLUR, and SET GAMMA. These commands are easy to use and can be a lot of fun.

The Bitmap Mirror Effect

Just like looking in a mirror, the MIRROR effect will flip your bitmap horizontally. If the image has writing on it, the writing will appear backward. The MIRROR BITMAP command takes one parameter—the bitmap number. The format is MIRROR BITMAP *Bitmap Number*.

How can you tell if a bitmap has been mirrored? By using the BITMAP MIRRORED command, of course. This command takes one parameter—the bitmap number. It returns a 0 if the bitmap is mirrored or a 1 if it is not. The command format is BITMAP MIRRORED (*Bitmap Number*) where bitmap number is the bitmap you are checking.

The Bitmap Flip Effect

The flip effect is the opposite of the mirror command. Instead of inverting the bitmap horizontally, it inverts the bitmap vertically. The FLIP BITMAP command is similar to the MIRROR command, but it works vertically rather than horizontally. This command takes one parameter—the bitmap number. The command format is FLIP BITMAP *Bitmap Number*.

Whereas the FLIP BITMAP command actually vertically inverts a bitmap, the BITMAP FLIPPED command determines whether the bitmap has actually been flipped. This command is similar to the BITMAP MIRRORED command in that it returns 1 if the bitmap is flipped or 0 if it is not flipped. The syntax is BITMAP FLIPPED(*Bitmap Number*).

The Bitmap Fade Effect

The FADE BITMAP command fades the contents of a bitmap by a percentage of darkness. The command takes two parameters—the bitmap number and fade value. The fade value ranges from 0 (blackness) to 100 (no fading). The syntax is FADE BITMAP *Bitmap Number, Fade Value*. When you have run the FADE BITMAP command, the effects are permanent until you create or load the bitmap again.

The Bitmap Blur Effect

The BLUR BITMAP command blurs a bitmap, which makes it look fuzzy and indistinct. This command takes two parameters, like the FADE BITMAP command—bitmap number and blur value. The blur value ranges between 1 (a beer) to 6 (a bottle of vodka). The command format is BLUR BITMAP *Bitmap Number, Blur Value*. Just like the FADE BITMAP command, BLUR BITMAP is also permanent.

The Bitmap Gamma Effect

The SET GAMMA command is the last of the special effects commands. The command takes three parameters and adjusts the gamma display, which is related to the brightness of an image. The three parameters are red, green, and blue. Each value ranges from 0 to 511, with 255 being the middle value. For instance, you can remove all the red from a bitmap by setting Red = 0. The syntax is SET GAMMA *Red, Green, Blue*. There is a caveat that comes with this command: Some graphics cards do not support the SET GAMMA command.

ImageShuffle: A Complete Bitmap-Based Game

This chapter project is a fun game. Do you remember the old plastic tile shuffling games? The ones that had tiles numbered 1 through 15, and you had to get the numbers in the correct order? The chapter project mimics that game. Click a tile to move it into the blank space. Figure 9.6 shows what the ImageShuffle game looks like when it first starts, and Figure 9.7 shows the game screen after the puzzle has been won.

This is your first complete game project! As a complete game, it utilizes all of the things you have learned in the last nine chapters, and it even goes into some things that you haven't learned yet so you are sure to find some items in the

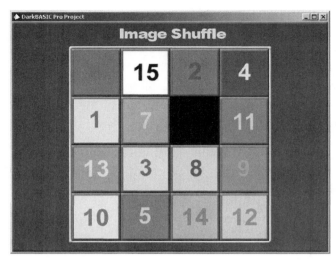

Figure 9.6
The ImageShuffle game in action.

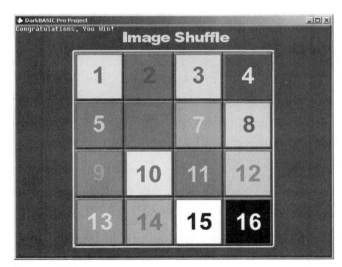

Figure 9.7
The ImageShuffle game has been completed!

source code that will interest you. This program is also the largest amount of source code you've seen so far. This is very typical of a complete game, because there are a lot of things you have to keep track of in a game—even a simple puzzle game like ImageShuffle.

```
' Tile position data for calculating valid moves
DATA 2,5,0,0
DATA 1,3,6,0
DATA 2,4,7,0
DATA 3,8,0,0
DATA 1,6,9,0
DATA 2,5,7,10
DATA 3,6,8,11
DATA 4,7,12,0
DATA 5,10,13,0
DATA 6,9,11,14
DATA 7,10,12,15
DATA 8,11,16,0
DATA 9,14,0,0
DATA 13,10,15,0
DATA 14,16,11,0
DATA 12,15,0,0

' Declare some variables
DIM Tiles(17) as integer
DIM MovingMatrix(64) as integer
DIM Selected(2) as integer
DIM MoveIt(4) as integer
TempX as integer = 0
TempY as integer = 0
done as integer = 0
Width as integer = 0
Height as integer = 0

' Initialize the display
SYNC ON

' Load the game graphics
LOAD BITMAP "mainback.bmp", 17
LOAD BITMAP "tiles.bmp", 18

' Create the tile bitmaps
FOR x = 1 TO 16
   CREATE BITMAP x, 100, 100
NEXT x

' Copy the tile bitmaps
FOR y = 0 TO 3
```

```
      FOR x = 0 TO 3
         pos = (y * 4 + x) + 1
         TX = x * 100
         TY = y * 100
         COPY BITMAP 18,TX,TY,TX + 99,TY + 99,pos,0,0,99,99
      NEXT x
   NEXT y

   ' Set the moving matrix
   FOR x = 1 TO 64
      READ a
      MovingMatrix(x) = a
   NEXT x

   ' Initialize the game
   SET CURRENT BITMAP 0
   ShuffleTiles()
   DisplayBoard()
   Selected(1) = 0
   Selected(2) = 0

   ' Main game loop
   REPEAT
      SYNC
      IF MOUSECLICK()=1
         ' Wait for mouse button to be released
         WHILE MOUSECLICK()=1
         ENDWHILE
         ' Figure out which tile was clicked
         bitmap = BitmapNumber(MOUSEX(), MOUSEY())
         b2 = CheckValid(bitmap)

         ' Swap the clicked tile and the blank tile
         IF b2 <> 0
            SwapTiles(bitmap, b2)
            DisplayBoard()
            done = CheckForWin()
         ENDIF
      ENDIF
   UNTIL done = 1

   ' Game over
   PRINT "Congratulations, You Win! "
   SYNC
```

```
' Delete the tile bitmaps from memory
FOR x = 1    TO 16
   DELETE BITMAP x
NEXT x

' End the game
WAIT KEY
END

' This function will randomize the tiles
FUNCTION ShuffleTiles
   FOR count = 1 TO 16
      Tiles(count) = count
      IF count = 16 THEN Tiles(count) = -1
   NEXT count
   RandomMoves = RND(50) + 100
   FOR count = 1 TO RandomMoves
      MoveTheSpace()
   NEXT count
ENDFUNCTION

' This function displays the tiles on the screen
FUNCTION DisplayBoard
   COPY BITMAP 17,0
   FOR y = 0 TO 3
      FOR x = 0 TO 3
         pos = (y * 4 + x) + 1
         IF Tiles(pos) >= 0
            TX = x * 100
            TY = y * 100
            W = TX + 99 + 120
            H = TY + 99 + 56
            COPY BITMAP Tiles(pos),0,0,99,99,0,TX+120,TY+56,W,H
         ENDIF
      NEXT x
   NEXT y
   SYNC
ENDFUNCTION

' This function checks the coordinates for a valid tile
FUNCTION CheckValid(rx)
   IF rx = -1 THEN EXITFUNCTION 0
   IF Tiles(rx) = -1 THEN EXITFUNCTION 0
```

```
    FOR x= 1 TO 16
       ptr = ((x - 1) * 4) + 1
       IF rx = x
          a1 = MovingMatrix(ptr)
          a2 = MovingMatrix(ptr + 1)
          a3 = MovingMatrix(ptr + 2)
          a4 = MovingMatrix(ptr + 3)
          IF a1 <> 0 and Tiles(a1) = -1 THEN EXITFUNCTION a1
          IF a2 <> 0 and Tiles(a2) = -1 THEN EXITFUNCTION a2
          IF a3 <> 0 and Tiles(a3) = -1 THEN EXITFUNCTION a3
          IF a4 <> 0 and Tiles(a4) = -1 THEN EXITFUNCTION a4
       ENDIF
    NEXT x
ENDFUNCTION 0

' This function returns the value of the bitmap located at x,y
FUNCTION BitmapNumber(x, y)
   dx = x - 120
   dy = y - 56

   IF dx < 0 or dy < 0 THEN EXITFUNCTION -1

   dx = dx / 100
   dy = dy / 100

   pos = ((dy * 4) + dx) + 1

   IF pos > 16 THEN pos = -1
   IF pos < 0 THEN pos = -1
ENDFUNCTION pos

' This function swaps two tiles in the Tiles array
FUNCTION SwapTiles(c1, c2)
   temp = Tiles(c1)
   Tiles(c1) = Tiles(c2)
   Tiles(c2) = temp
ENDFUNCTION

' This function moves the empty tile
FUNCTION MoveTheSpace
   spt = 0
   FOR x = 1    TO 16
      IF Tiles(x) = -1 THEN spt = x
   NEXT x
```

```
   IF spt = 0 THEN EXITFUNCTION

   FOR x= 1    TO 16
      ptr = ((x-1)*4)+1
      IF spt = x
         MoveIt(1) = MovingMatrix(ptr)
         MoveIt(2) = MovingMatrix(ptr + 1)
         MoveIt(3) = MovingMatrix(ptr + 2)
         MoveIt(4) = MovingMatrix(ptr + 3)

         movenum = RND(3)+1
         WHILE MoveIt(movenum) = 0
            movenum = RND(3)+1
         ENDWHILE
         c1 = spt
         c2 = MoveIt(movenum)
         SwapTiles(c1,c2)
      ENDIF
   NEXT x
ENDFUNCTION

' This function scans the tiles for a win
FUNCTION CheckForWin
   FOR x = 1 TO 15
      IF Tiles(x) <> x THEN EXITFUNCTION 0
   NEXT x
   Tiles(16) = 16
   DisplayBoard()
   SLEEP 1000
   EXITFUNCTION 1
ENDFUNCTION 0
```

This is a simple yet fun puzzle game—which is the best type of game to work on when you're learning a new programming language! However, there are still some things that you can add to make this game even more fun. Here are some suggestions for improving the ImageShuffle game.

- **High Score.** Keep track of how many clicks it takes to solve the puzzle.

- **New Tilesets.** Create new tilesets and choose one randomly.

- **Board Size.** Increase the board size to 8×8 tiles.

- **Special Effects.** Add a special effect when the tiles move (such as sliding or fading).

Summary

Bitmaps are the key to writing 2D games in DB, and this introductory chapter merely scratched the surface of what DB can do. There are many different commands that you can use with bitmaps, such as the special effects commands covered in this chapter. The next chapter will take bitmaps to another level entirely, combining the bitmap image with transparency using a technique called *sprite animation.*

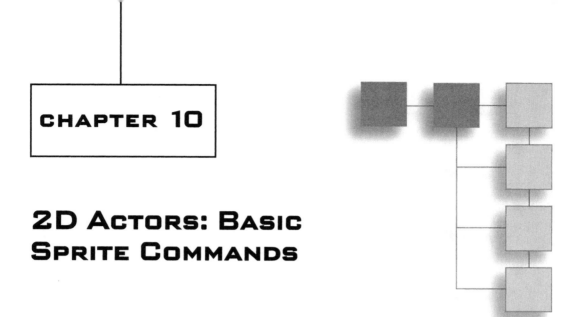

CHAPTER 10

2D Actors: Basic Sprite Commands

In the old days, before video games ran in 3D, all game graphics were hand-drawn and displayed on the screen as static, non-moving objects or as animated sprites. While it might seem like the subject of sprites is dated and irrelevant today, the truth is quite contrary. Numerous commercial games are released each year that run in 2D using graphics very much like the sprites used in classic arcade games such as *Heavy Barrel* and *Akari Warriors*. Consider Sid Meier's *Civilization III*, for instance. That game has some fantastic 3D models in it, but the models are all pre-rendered and stored as snapshots to be drawn on the screen as sprites. The game is designed as an isometric turn-based strategy game, and simply does not need to run in 3D mode. Yet despite the fact that this game is 2D, it is a phenomenal best-selling game. The latest in the series, *Civilization IV*, did go entirely to 3D, using an engine called Gamebryo. After learning about the basics of sprite programming, later in this chapter you will begin work on a complete game called Darkanoid that will span the next four chapters. We will hold off on animation until next chapter.

Here are the key topics you will learn about in this chapter:

- Introduction to sprites
- Creating and loading sprites
- Sprite properties
- Drawing and moving sprites
- The all-powerful game loop
- Getting started on the Darkanoid game

213

Introduction to Sprites

Why do you suppose anyone would develop a 2D game in today's world of advanced 3D video cards? The argument might be made that games have not been able to tap the potential of the latest generation of video cards, and yet new graphics chips are developed every six to twelve months, often doubling the performance of the previous chip. The reason is not that 2D games are easier to program or that 3D models are difficult to design. In fact, *Civilization III* uses 3D models in a 2D fashion. It is usually a matter of gameplay. Even after moving to 3D, *Civilization IV* is still just as compelling as (and maybe even better than) its predecessor.

A *sprite* is a small, two-dimensional bitmap that is drawn to the screen at a specified position and usually with transparency. There are many ways to create a sprite and many ways to program its functionality. Will a particular sprite be a solid image or will it have transparent pixels? Will the sprite automatically move in a specified way on the screen, or will it respond interactively with the player? Before these questions even arise, however, how do you create a sprite and load the graphic image (or images) it uses?

Civilization III is a good example of a modern 2D game—something that is unusual in today's world of advanced 3D accelerators. *Civilization III* is a turn-based strategy game that does not use any real-time 3D effects or animation. The remarkable thing about *Civilization III* is that it is such an engrossing game despite the somewhat limited graphics. Now, don't get me wrong— *Civilization III* looks very good, but the game simply does not push the limits of graphics technology. Given the lack of real-time effects in a turn-based game, why is *Civilization III* so much fun and so utterly mesmerizing? In a word, gameplay. *Civilization III* puts the player in control of an entire civilization of people in competition with the other civilizations of the world. The core aspects of the game, such as researching technology, improving the quality of life, and developing weapons and defenses, all take time to develop over a period of turns. It is this progression of development that makes *Civilization III* such an addictive game.

Transparency

Transparency in a sprite is defined by pixels in the source bitmap that are set to a certain color. When the sprite is drawn on the screen, any pixels with that

Sprite with Transparency

Figure 10.1
The dark circle represents the pixels used by the sprite, and the lighter color around the circle represents the transparent pixels.

transparent color are not drawn, which results in the background showing through the sprite in those places. Figure 10.1 illustrates this concept.

If you were to load this particular sprite and draw it transparently, the transparent pixels around the ball would not be drawn, so you would only see the ball. However, if you were to draw the sprite *without* transparency, then all the pixels in the sprite's bitmap image would be drawn, as shown in Figure 10.2.

Indeed, transparency is the key to drawing sprites, and is essential for any decent 2D game. Without transparency, there really is no possible way to write a game. When you get into the 3D realm, transparency takes on a whole new meaning, but when it comes to 2D games, transparency is the single-most important factor.

Transparency was the primary bottleneck in video game design in the past, and it was often the most highly optimized piece of code in a game (in the very early days of the video game industry). Sprites are drawn to the screen using a technique called *bit-block transfer*, or BITBLT. The most common shorthand is "blit" or "blitting." This term means that blocks of memory are copied from one location to another as quickly as possible, often using a high-speed loop written in assembly language (the closest thing to machine language). Although reusable sprite libraries were available for various platforms (Atari, IBM PC,

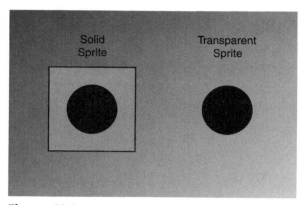

Figure 10.2
When a sprite is drawn over a background image on the screen, it becomes clear how helpful transparency can be for displaying the sprite properly.

Amiga, and Mac), most programmers had their own optimized blitters and improved the code for each new game project.

Take a gander at Figure 10.3, which shows a tank sprite with animated treads.

In recent years, however, a single sprite library has been used more than any other for the Windows platform (the world's primary gaming platform). This library is called DirectDraw, and it was available in DirectX up through version 7.0 (which is what DarkBASIC supports, although DarkBASIC Pro uses DirectX 8.1). Since most of the work in a game in past years involved writing the blitters, sound mixers, and so on, the advent of DirectX has significantly improved the quality and reusability of game code, allowing programmers to focus on higher-level game functionality such as physics and more intelligent computer players.

Figure 10.3
This animated tank sprite has eight frames.

Creating and Loading Sprites

DarkBASIC has built-in sprite support, so there is no need to write any custom code for loading or drawing sprites or testing collisions (more on that later). For starters, you need to load the source image that will be used by the sprite. An image is like a bitmap in memory. To load a bitmap into a sprite, you must first load a source file into an image and then copy it to the sprite.

Grabbing Sprites Out of a Bitmap

There are two ways to load a sprite.

The first step to drawing a sprite on the screen is to use the LOAD BITMAP command to load the image in a bitmap file into a DarkBASIC bitmap (any number from 0 to 32). It should be noted again that the first bitmap, number 0, references the display screen. You can load a bitmap and display it on the screen in a single command by loading the bitmap directly into bitmap 0. The syntax of the command is LOAD BITMAP *Filename*, *Bitmap Number*.

This command works well when you want to load a bitmap file containing many sprites and then copy sprites out of the large "sprite sheet" into individual images. Typically you will use an image instead of a bitmap when working on a sprite-based game.

The GET IMAGE command grabs a piece of a bitmap for use in a sprite, and is most useful for ripping out bitmap tiles that are laid out in sequence for an animated sprite. This command is used along with LOAD BITMAP and the SPRITE command to animate a sprite on the screen. The syntax of the command is GET IMAGE *Image Number*, *Left*, *Top*, *Right*, *Bottom*.

Loading a Sprite Image Directly

There is another way to load a sprite without using LOAD BITMAP and GET IMAGE. This process works great if you have a bunch of sprites on a large bitmap image, and want to grab a single sprite out of that large image. This is the hard way to do it, though. A far easier way to load game graphics is to store a sprite in its own bitmap file (either single frame or animated).

Instead, you can use the LOAD IMAGE command to accomplish the same thing as the previous two commands combined, because a sprite graphic is stored in an image. The syntax is LOAD IMAGE *Filename*, *Image Number*.

Drawing a Sprite

The SPRITE command draws a sprite on the screen (or the current bitmap surface) using a specified position and image. When it has been drawn, the properties of this sprite are applied to the specified sprite number. The syntax of the command is SPRITE *Sprite Number, X, Y, Image Number*. This command also moves the sprite to that location, for use in sprite collision testing with the sprite collision command.

Sprite Properties

There are some useful commands that return information about a sprite, such as the image number, width, and height. In addition, several commands allow you to manipulate the way in which a sprite is drawn to the screen.

The SPRITE IMAGE command returns the image number used by the specified sprite. The syntax of the command is Return Value = SPRITE IMAGE (*Sprite Number*).

The SPRITE WIDTH command returns the width of the image currently in use by the specified sprite. The syntax of the command is Return Value = SPRITE WIDTH (*Sprite Number*).

The SPRITE HEIGHT command returns the height of the image currently in use by the specified sprite. The syntax of the command is Return Value = SPRITE HEIGHT (*Sprite Number*).

The SPRITE EXIST command returns a 1 if the specified sprite (passed as a parameter) was previously created with the SPRITE command. If the sprite does not exist, it returns a 0. The syntax for the command is Return Value = SPRITE EXIST (*Sprite Number*).

The OFFSET SPRITE command changes the horizontal and vertical offset of a sprite's origin. The default origin is the top-left corner of the image, but this command allows you to change the offset so that the sprite draws from the center point or from some other corner of the sprite.

The SPRITE OFFSET X command returns the horizontal offset or shift value of the sprite referenced by the sprite number that is passed as a parameter to the command. The syntax for the command is Return Value = SPRITE OFFSET X (*Sprite Number*).

The SPRITE OFFSET Y command returns the vertical offset or shift value of the sprite referenced by the sprite number that is passed as a parameter to the command. The syntax for the command is `Return Value = SPRITE OFFSET Y` (*Sprite Number*).

Drawing and Moving Sprites

When dealing with sprites, the most important commands involve moving and drawing them. Rather than provide separate commands for these functions, DarkBASIC combines the two in a single command called SPRITE. There are SHOW SPRITE, HIDE SPRITE, and several other useful sprite commands that I'll go over in this section.

Drawing a Sprite

The SPRITE command, which bears mentioning again, draws a sprite using the specified position and image number and stores the settings for that sprite number. The syntax of the command is SPRITE *Sprite Number, X, Y, Image Number*.

The SPRITE command simultaneously moves and draws a sprite using a specified image number, but once the sprite has been drawn, how do you determine its position? This is important when you are dealing with sprite collision (more on that later).

The SPRITE X command returns the current horizontal position of the sprite referenced by the passed sprite number. The command syntax is `Return Value = SPRITE X` (*Sprite Number*). The SPRITE Y command returns the current vertical position of the sprite referenced by the passed sprite number. The command syntax is `Return Value = SPRITE Y` (*Sprite Number*).

Setting Sprite Rendering Properties

The SET SPRITE command is very important because it lets you change both the background restoration and the transparency properties of the sprite. The default for these values is 1, which means that the background is saved and restored when the sprite is moved, and transparency is enabled so that black pixels are not displayed with the sprite. Setting the background parameter to 0 will disable the background-saving property, which means that the sprite will "smear" across the screen, and it is up to you to restore the area under the sprite. The syntax of the command is SET SPRITE *Sprite Number*, BackSave State, *Transparency State*. This command is not usually needed.

Making Sprites Visible or Invisible

The following commands are used to make a sprite visible or invisible, and apply to the normal sprite-drawing commands.

The SHOW SPRITE command shows the specified sprite (passed as the sprite number parameter) that was previously hidden using the HIDE SPRITE command. This command does not change the position of the sprite, but simply draws it at the current X and Y position using the current sprite properties. The syntax for the command is SHOW SPRITE *Sprite Number*. The HIDE SPRITE command makes a specified sprite invisible so that it is not drawn with the other sprites on the screen. The syntax for the command is HIDE SPRITE *Sprite Number*.

This command might be useful in a game in which you want to add special effects to a sprite without changing its image. For example, suppose you have a space combat game with power-ups, and when the player's ship gets a forcefield power-up, a small outline appears around the ship, showing the player that the power-up is active. Rather than drawing a whole new image for every power-up that the ship can take on, you could draw the forcefield outline (and any other special effects) as a separate image. Then you simply move the special effects sprites along with the spaceship and make them visible when needed.

The SHOW ALL SPRITES command universally draws all sprites that were previously set to invisible, setting them all to visible. The HIDE ALL SPRITES command universally sets all sprites to invisible so they no longer appear on the screen when draw commands are issued.

The All-Powerful Game Loop

The key to real-time animation, which is the goal of most games (even turn-based games), is the game loop. The game loop repeats over and over as quickly as possible, and it is essentially what has come to be known as the *game engine*. Granted, there are some powerful 3D game engines out there—often referred to by the games that they were first used to create. Table 10.1 presents a list of game engines in use today.

Oddly enough, some game engines were created out of existing game engines, so there is a strange hierarchy or family tree of games. For example, *Half-Life* was based on the Quake engine by id software, and was then used to create several more games, all of which have a family heritage with *Quake*.

Table 10.1 Game Engines

Game Engine	Developer	Games That Use It
Wolfenstein 3D	id software	*Spear of Destiny*
Half-Life	Sierra Studios	*Counter-Strike, Opposing Force*
Gamebryo	Emergent	*Civilization IV*
Quake III	id software	*Quake III Arena, Voyager: Elite Force*
Torque	Garage Games	*Tribes 2*
Doom III	id software	*Quake IV*
Unreal Warfare	Epic Games	*America's Army, Unreal Tournament 2004*

Now, I don't want you to think that all there is to a game engine is a game loop. Obviously, there's a lot more to it than that. Usually a game engine includes 3D special effects such as shadows, lighting, support for level files and character files, multiplayer support, computer-controlled players, game physics, weapon trajectories, and countless other factors. But at the core of all this functionality is a real-time game loop.

Creating a Game Loop

You have already seen a game loop in operation in previous chapters, although I didn't mention it at the time. A game loop is usually set to run indefinitely. When a condition for ending the game has been met, you can use the EXIT command to break out of the loop. To create a game loop, you can use any one of the following looping commands:

- DO . . . LOOP

- REPEAT . . . UNTIL

- WHILE . . . ENDWHILE

The DO loop is probably the most obvious choice because it doesn't use a condition for ending (although you can use the EXIT command to break out of the loop). Figure 10.4 illustrates what usually takes place in a game loop.

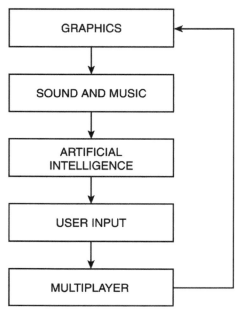

Figure 10.4
The usual game loop calls subroutines that handle graphics, sound effects, music, artificial intelligence, user input, and multiplayer functionality.

Using REPEAT . . . UNTIL for a Game Loop

The REPEAT and WHILE loops are also suitable for a game loop that uses a condition. For example, you could create a variable called Running and create a REPEAT loop, as shown in the following code.

```
Running = 1
REPEAT
   IF MOUSECLICK() = 1
      Running = 0
   ENDIF
UNTIL Running <> 1
```

Using WHILE . . . ENDWHILE for a Game Loop

The WHILE loop is similar to the REPEAT loop, but the condition is checked at the beginning of the loop rather than at the end.

```
Running = 1
WHILE Running = 1
   IF MOUSECLICK() = 1
      Running = 0
   ENDIF
ENDWHILE
```

Using DO . . . LOOP for a Game Loop

The DO loop is my preferred way of writing a game loop because there is no condition in the loop statement itself. Instead, I prefer to handle the condition myself, inside the loop.

```
DO
  IF MOUSECLICK() = 1
    EXIT
  ENDIF
LOOP
```

Game Timing Commands

The sample game loops I just showed you run as fast as possible with no timing. Although DarkBASIC handles frame rate and screen refresh automatically, it doesn't perform timing, so that is something you have to include in a high-speed game loop yourself. I'll explain some of the timing and screen refresh commands, and then I'll show you a new and improved game loop in the following pages.

The SLEEP command pauses the program for a specified number of milliseconds (where 1,000 milliseconds equal one second). The WAIT command performs the exact same function as SLEEP and is simply an alternative command. Use whichever command is more intuitive to you. For example, you might use SLEEP inside a game loop for short-duration timing, and use the WAIT command elsewhere for longer-duration timing (which seems intuitive to me). The syntax of these commands looks like this:

```
SLEEP Duration
WAIT Duration
```

Getting the System Time

The TIMER command returns the internal system time in milliseconds. The system timer is updated 1,000 times per second, so it is a good way to set the speed of your program to a specific rate (not to be confused with the frame rate). The meaning of speed in this context is the amount of work done by the program every second, such as moving sprites, determining collisions, and so on.

The TIMER command is also an excellent tool for profiling a game. Suppose you have written a high-speed game that has a bottleneck somewhere in the code, but you can't find out what is slowing things down. The best way to find the bottleneck is to check the system time before and after a section of code, and then display the amount of time that the code took to run. Following is an example of timing a section of code.

```
StartTime = TIMER()
' update the screen
SYNC
EndTime = TIMER()
PRINT "Sync time = "; EndTime - StartTime
```

Refreshing the Screen

Next to timing, the most important aspect of a game loop is the screen refresh. Regardless of how fast a game loop is running, DarkBASIC can only refresh the screen at a specified frame rate. DarkBASIC tries to keep the screen updated as best that it can, but in a high-speed game loop, you want to take control of the screen update yourself. This involves the SYNC command.

The SYNC Command

As the timing example showed, SYNC is one of the key commands you will use in a game loop, and it is absolutely critical to keeping a game running at top speed. If you let DarkBASIC handle the screen refresh for you, it will run much too slowly for a decent game. The SYNC command performs a screen refresh manually, which is what you need to insert into your game loop after all drawing has been completed.

DarkBASIC maintains a hidden copy of the screen called the back buffer (using an old technique called *double buffering*), which gets all of your drawing commands. Drawing directly to the screen is too slow, so to speed things up, DarkBASIC uses this double buffer for all drawing commands and then quickly copies the double buffer to the screen in one fell swoop. In case you haven't guessed it yet, the SYNC command is what copies the double buffer to the screen.

The SYNC OFF Command

The SYNC OFF command turns on the automatic screen refresh in DarkBASIC (which is the default) and might be useful if you are at a point in the program where you no longer want to manually perform a screen refresh and you would like DarkBASIC to take over. You can always call SYNC ON again if you need to resume manual screen refresh with the SYNC command.

The SYNC ON Command

To manually use the SYNC command in your game loop, you first need to call SYNC ON to turn off DarkBASIC's automatic screen refresh. After you have called SYNC ON somewhere at the start of the program, it is up to you to call SYNC to update the screen; otherwise, nothing will be displayed and the screen will remain blank.

The SYNC RATE Command

The SYNC RATE command is applicable when DarkBASIC is handling the screen refresh automatically; it sets the frame rate of the display. By default, DarkBASIC tries to maintain a frame rate of 40. However, by using the SYNC RATE command, you can override this default and set the screen refresh to any value. Again, just remember that this is not relevant if you are using SYNC to maintain the screen refresh yourself (which is the preferred method).

Tip

If you want your DarkBASIC program to run as fast as possible with no timing whatsoever, call SYNC RATE 0.

Starting Work on Darkanoid (Your First Complete Game Project)

You have come a long way in your study of DarkBASIC as we are now nearing the end of Chapter 10. It's time to put all of the knowledge gained in the last ten chapters to work in a complete game. Rather than build this game entirely in one chapter, we will just get started on it for now, and you will see the game expand and develop over the next four chapters. This game was inspired by classics such as *Breakout* and *Arkanoid,* and is known as a typical "ball-and-paddle" style game. Figure 10.5 shows the first step taken in this chapter toward building this complete game.

Current Development Goals

Our first goal for the game is to get the basic gameplay in place without any of the bells or whistles. Here are our immediate goals:

1. To create or acquire the artwork used in the game.

2. To draw the background onto the screen.

3. To draw blocks in a certain predefined arrangement.

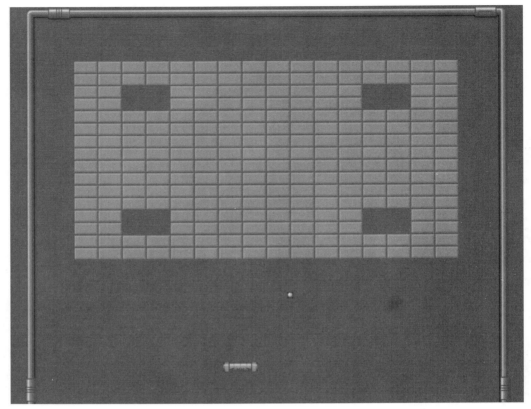

Figure 10.5
The groundwork for the Darkanoid game is put together in this chapter.

4. To move and draw the ball and deflect it from the walls.

5. To move and draw the paddle based on player input.

The first goal we can tackle by borrowing some artwork from a free sprite library that is available at http://www.flyingyogi.com. Ari Feldman's SpriteLib contains a complete set of graphics suitable for this type of game. Figure 10.6 shows the three bitmap images currently needed along with the background (which was also created using images from SpriteLib). The remaining four goals are accomplished in the source code of the game.

The game will only be using images at this point. Although you have learned how to use simple sprites in this chapter, I want to focus more on the gameplay in Darkanoid rather than on sprite code. So, all of the graphics in the game are

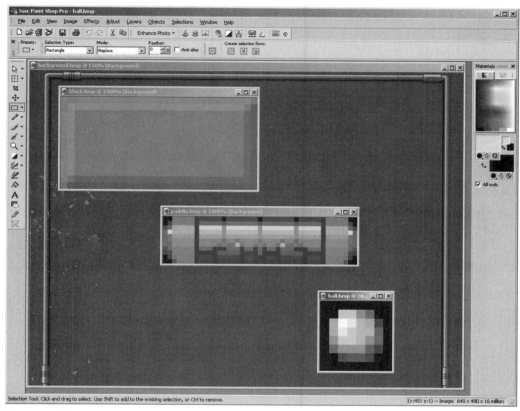

Figure 10.6
The artwork in Darkanoid so far includes a background, a block, a ball, and a paddle.

drawn using the PASTE IMAGE command. The reason for this will be clearer in the next chapter when you learn about animated sprites. We will explore some seriously advanced sprite code in the next chapter!

The Source Code

The source code for Darkanoid will start off quite meager compared to what the sources for the complete game will look like several chapters from now. At this point, we just want to get our bearings as far as what this game is supposed to do, and get some simple graphics up on the screen. Having the paddle move based on player input (using the mouse) is a bonus at this point, because you haven't learned about device input yet—but you will soon.

So let's get started on this new project. If you haven't done so already, run DarkBASIC and create a new project. If you aren't sure how to create a new project, you can refer back to Chapter 1 for a detailed explanation. You can name this project "Darkanoid". I have highlighted all key lines of code related to bitmaps and sprites so that they will stand out and be more visible as you are reading the code.

Variable Definitions

The first portion of code for the game adds the block layout and all of the variables used in the game (which are all globals).

```
remstart
  Project: DARKANOID GAME
  Source: Chapter 10
  Date:   May, 2006
remend

data 1,1,1,1,1,1,1,1,1,1,1,1,1,1,1,1
data 1,1,1,1,1,1,1,1,1,1,1,1,1,1,1,1
data 1,1,0,0,1,1,1,1,1,1,1,1,0,0,1,1
data 1,1,0,0,1,1,1,1,1,1,1,1,0,0,1,1
data 1,1,1,1,1,1,1,1,1,1,1,1,1,1,1,1
data 1,1,1,1,1,1,1,1,1,1,1,1,1,1,1,1
data 1,1,1,1,1,1,1,1,1,1,1,1,1,1,1,1
data 1,1,1,1,1,1,1,1,1,1,1,1,1,1,1,1
data 1,1,1,1,1,1,1,1,1,1,1,1,1,1,1,1
data 1,1,1,1,1,1,1,1,1,1,1,1,1,1,1,1
data 1,1,1,1,1,1,1,1,1,1,1,1,1,1,1,1
data 1,1,1,1,1,1,1,1,1,1,1,1,1,1,1,1
data 1,1,0,0,1,1,1,1,1,1,1,1,0,0,1,1
data 1,1,0,0,1,1,1,1,1,1,1,1,0,0,1,1
data 1,1,1,1,1,1,1,1,1,1,1,1,1,1,1,1
data 1,1,1,1,1,1,1,1,1,1,1,1,1,1,1,1
' image constants

global IMG_BACKGROUND as word = 1
global IMG_BALL as word = 2
global IMG_PADDLE as word = 5
global IMG_BLOCK as word = 10

' paddle position variables
global paddleX as integer
global paddleY as integer
```

```
' ball position variables
global ballX as integer = 400
global ballY as integer = 400
global ballSpeedX as integer = 2
global ballSpeedY as integer = -2

' grid of blocks
dim blockData(20,20) as byte
```

Calling Functions

The next portion of code is quite small, comprised of just three lines of code and a comment. This code is just organizational in nature, to simplify the code into two support functions. Init_Game loads the bitmap files and initializes variables. Run_Game contains the actual game loop that runs the game.

```
' start game running
Init_Game()
Run_Game()
End
```

Initializing the Game

The Init_Game function gets the game started. This function loads all of the bitmap files containing the graphics used in the game, and it fills the blockData array using the data statements you saw earlier in the program that defined what the wall of blocks would look like.

```
function Init_Game()
  sync on
  sync rate 40
  hide mouse
  randomize timer()

  ' load background
  load image ''background.bmp", IMG_BACKGROUND

  ' load paddle
  load image ''paddle.bmp", IMG_PADDLE
  paddleX = SCREEN WIDTH() / 2
  paddleY = SCREEN HEIGHT() - 50

  ' load the ball
  load image ''ball.bmp", IMG_BALL
```

```
' load the blocks
load image ''block.bmp", IMG_BLOCK

' read the data statements for the blocks
for y = 1 to 16
  for x = 1 to 16
    read blockData(x,y)
  next x
next y
endfunction
```

The Game Loop

The Run_Game function contains the game loop. This is a DO loop that causes the game to run by repeatedly calling on several support functions and updating the screen. In due time, this function will become more complex to accommodate all of the improvements that will be made to the game in the next few chapters.

```
function Run_Game()
  do

    ' draw background
    paste image IMG_BACKGROUND, 0, 0

    ' draw the blocks
    Draw_Blocks()

    ' move and draw the ball
    Move_Ball()
    ' move the paddle with the mouse
    Move_Paddle()

    ' refresh the screen
    sync
    if escapekey() = 1 then exit
  loop

endfunction
```

Drawing the Blocks

The blocks in this type of game are what the game is all about. You move your paddle along the bottom of the screen and bounce the ball upwards to destroy the blocks while preventing the ball from hitting the bottom (in which case, you lose). The blocks must be defined ahead of time. In this game, I've defined the blocks using data statements. This data is then stored in an array and the appropriate block is drawn at each position on the screen. This early in the game's development, we're only going to use a single block. But you will learn how to add additional blocks to the game in the next chapter.

```
function Draw_Blocks()
  blockCount = 0
  for x = 1 to 16
    for y = 1 to 16
      if blockData(x,y) > 0
        inc blockCount
        ' now draw this block
        dx = 50 + 30 * x
        dy = 50 + 15 * y
        paste image IMG_BLOCK, dx, dy
      endif
    next x
  next y
endfunction
```

Moving the Ball

The Move_Ball function is tasked with moving and drawing the ball on the screen. Most of the code in this function deals with keeping the ball inside the boundary of the screen. If the ball reaches an edge of the screen, it is bounced off that edge (top, right, left, or bottom).

```
function Move_Ball()
  ' move the ball in the X direction
  ballX = ballX + ballSpeedX

  ' bounce the ball off the right and left edges
  if ballX < 30
    ballX = 30
    ballSpeedX = ballSpeedX * -1
  endif
  if ballX > screen width() - 35
    ballX = screen width() - 35
```

```
      ballSpeedX = ballSpeedX * -1
    endif

    ' move the ball in the Y direction
    ballY = ballY + ballSpeedY

    ' bounce the ball off the top and bottom
    if ballY < 20
      ballY = 20
      ballSpeedY = ballSpeedY * -1
    endif
    if ballY > screen height() - 6
      ballY = screen height() - 6
      ballSpeedY = ballSpeedY * -1
    endif

    ' draw the ball
    paste image IMG_BALL, ballX, ballY
endfunction
```

Moving the Paddle

The Move_Paddle function moves and draws the paddle based on player input (using the mouse). The paddle is limited to moving only left or right, and cannot move beyond the edge of the screen.

```
function Move_Paddle()
  ' get mouse movement value
  m = mousemovex()
  if m <> 0
    paddleX = paddleX + m
  endif

  ' move the paddle based on mouse movement
  if paddleX < 30 then paddleX = 30
  if paddleX > screen width() - 75
    paddleX = screen width() - 75
  endif

  ' draw the paddle
  paste image IMG_PADDLE, paddleX, paddleY
endfunction
```

Summary

This chapter covered one of the most important subjects in the field of gaming—sprites. Sprites are usually small, animated objects on the screen that give a game its graphics. Although there are many 3D games now, and 3D is the preferred realm for commercial games today, there is still plenty of room for 2D games. Thankfully, DarkBASIC excels at handling sprites, as you have learned in this chapter. In addition to learning how to create and manipulate sprites on the screen, you also learned about transparency and got started on a large game project that will be continued in the next chapter.

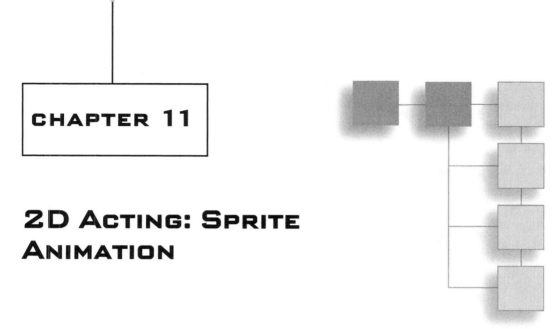

CHAPTER 11

2D Acting: Sprite Animation

The previous chapter introduced you to sprite programming as an extension of working with bitmap images. This chapter continues the lesson by exploring sprite animation programming. You will learn how to load and draw animated sprites, and how to rotate and scale sprites as well. Along the way, you'll learn how to create and edit sprite sheets using a powerful animation program called Pro Motion. Here are the key concepts to cover:

- Drawing animated sprites

- Creating and editing sprites

- Manipulating sprites with rotation and scaling

- Using pre-made sprite sheets

- Updating the Darkanoid game

Animated Sprites

Let's go over the key concepts of sprite programming that you learned in the last chapter. The term "sprite" is an old-school game programming concept that dates back to the early '80s. Modern game designers call them "actors." In a sense this is a good term to use since game sprites really are playing a role in the game. "Sprite" was coined within the game industry. In the old days, before video games ran in 3D, all game graphics were hand-drawn and displayed on the screen as static, non-moving objects—or as animated sprites. The term "actor" may have originated in an early version of Macromedia Director.

While it might seem like the subject of sprites is dated and irrelevant today, the truth is quite contrary. Numerous commercial games are released each year that run in 2D using graphics very much like the sprites used in classic arcade games. A *sprite* is a small, two-dimensional bitmap that is drawn to the screen at a specified position and usually with transparency. Transparency in a sprite is defined by pixels in the source bitmap that are set to a certain color. When the sprite is drawn on the screen, any pixels with that transparent color are not drawn, which results in the background showing through the sprite in those places.

You will normally use three basic commands to draw a sprite:

```
LOAD BITMAP Filename, Bitmap #
GET IMAGE Image #, Left, Top, Right, Bottom
SPRITE Sprite #, X, Y, Image #
```

The SPRITE command draws a sprite onto the screen (or rather, the current bitmap) using a specified position and image. These commands work fine for many types of games where just a static (non-animating) image will suffice. But DarkBASIC also provides us with commands for loading an animated sprite and drawing it on the screen with just a few commands.

Drawing Animated Sprites the Hard Way

DarkBASIC has very solid support for animated sprites that does not require very much work on the part of the programmer. But before I show you the *easy way* to do this, I want to first show you how to load and animate a sprite using just the static sprite commands you learned about in the previous chapter. "What's the point?" you may ask. That's a good question, sort of like the question you ponder in algebra class about whether you'll actually ever need to know any algebra to get through life. I've actually been surprised by how well a basic understanding of algebra has served me in life, which reinforces my belief that a good breadth of knowledge can be very helpful for solving unusual problems. We will learn how to draw an animated sprite the "hard way" (whether anything in DarkBASIC is truly *hard* is another matter) first, and then learn how DarkBASIC provides help for working with animated sprites. So, let's first learn how to create an animated sprite using just a series of static sprites.

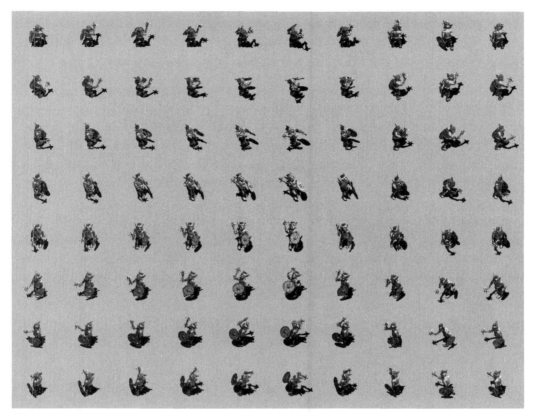

Figure 11.1
The 80 frames of animation for this ogre sprite are just for attacking, nothing else.

Figure 11.1 shows the source artwork that I will use to demonstrate sprite animation here shortly. In this bitmap file, there are 80 frames of animation, with 10 frames for each direction:

- North
- Northeast
- Southeast
- South
- Southwest
- West
- Northwest

The Ogre-Attack file is an example of the incredibly high quality artwork you'll find at Reiner's Tileset (http://www.reinerstileset.de), and it is royalty free, meaning you can use the artwork in your own games as long as you give Reiner Prokein the credit in your game.

The big question is this: How do you draw these frames of animation in an actual game? The amateur game programmer will load each one of these animation "cells" from individual bitmap files and store them in memory using an array of images. But this is a sloppy way to handle an animated sprite. For one thing, how do you keep track of so many images? In this first example, we have 80 frames of animation just to allow this *one character* to attack in all eight directions. What about walking? Or running? Or any other actions that the character might take? As you can imagine, a game becomes a resource management nightmare because so much work will have to be put into the logistics of dealing with all those images. I've tried to create games in this manner, and it's not a pretty picture.

Here's a good example: take a look at Figure 11.2. This figure shows a very nice-looking tank sprite that has been rotated in 32 directions. This tank will look very

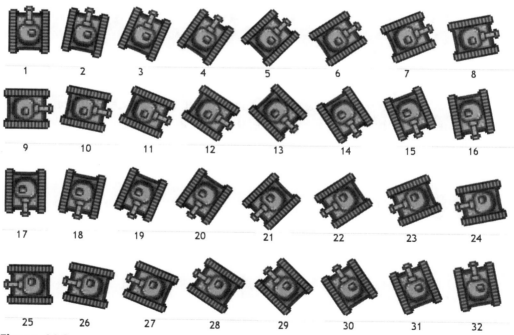

Figure 11.2
This tank sprite can rotate in 32 directions.

Figure 11.3
An animation sequence for the tank sprite.

smooth when rotating on the screen, but there's just one flaw: this tank has no animation. How would you deal with each direction like this image shows if each direction is supposed to be animated as well?

If you'll take a look at the next figure, shown in Figure 11.3, you'll see one possible animation sequence for the tank sprite. The treads are animated here, so that the tank will actually look like it's moving when the frames of this animation are drawn in sequence. You could rotate each of these frames of animation and save them in one large bitmap image, or you could just load this single animation and rotate the sprite when the game is running (sprite rotation is covered in the next section of this chapter).

A far better way to deal with animation is to just leave the frames alone in the tiled bitmap file, and draw them directly out of that large tiled image. By doing it this way, you have just *one image* to deal with instead of 80 (not to mention walking and other actions).

DarkBASIC can handle large numbers of animation frames using images, which can be drawn using the SPRITE command. The first step is to load the bitmap image containing your animation frames, which have all been placed inside a single bitmap file. The next step is to grab a portion of the image representing each frame of animation and drawing just the frame that's needed, one at a time.

Tip

If you'd like to convert animations with frames stored in individual bitmap files (which is the case with Reiner's Tilesets, for instance), then I recommend you use a program called Pro Motion. The trial edition of Pro Motion is available on the book's CD-ROM. This is a fantastic programmer's tool as it allows you to manipulate sprite animations and save them as a single tiled image.

If you'll look again at the animated ogre sprite, you'll notice that there are 10 frames for each animation, which is duplicated for all 8 directions. These sprite frames were actually rendered with a 3D modeling program called Caligari

TrueSpace, so you can't merely rotate a high-quality sprite like this that has been rendered out with shadows and is in an isometric perspective (in other words, the sprite is not in a simple top or side view orientation).

These frames of animation will allow you to show the ogre creature attacking in all 8 directions. The key is learning how to draw a single frame at a time. You can grab each frame out of the large bitmap and copy it into a smaller image using the GET IMAGE command. This process is a little difficult to handle if you have a lot of sprites in your game, but it does work. Basically, you just need to follow the same process you did for drawing a static sprite for each frame of the animation. Along the way, you have to tell GET IMAGE where each frame is located in the large tiled image, which means you need to know the size of each frame.

Let's write a short program to demonstrate the process. The AnimationTest program source code follows, and the output is shown in Figure 11.4.

Figure 11.4
Output from the AnimationTest program showing the animated ogre sprite.

```
sync on
sync rate 30
hide mouse

'set transparent color to pink
set image colorkey 255, 0, 255

'load the ogre sprite
load bitmap ''ogre_attack.bmp'', 1

'copy each frame out of the larger image
for n = 0 to 9
  get image 10+n, n * 128, 128*5, n * 128 + 128, 128*6
next n

set current bitmap 0
frame = 0
do
  frame = frame + 1
  if frame > 9 then frame = 0
  sprite 1, 200, 200, 10+frame
  sync
loop
```

Drawing Animated Sprites the Easy Way

DarkBASIC provides a better, easier way to handle sprite animation. Instead of loading an animation using images, DarkBASIC has a command that will do all of the work of loading and managing an animation for you. The CREATE ANIMATED SPRITE command loads a bitmap, grabs the frames out of it (sort of), and handles animation in a single step. After you have loaded the sprite animation sequence, you can use the PLAY SPRITE command to update the animation frame each time through your game loop. You can then use the PASTE SPRITE or SPRITE command to draw the current sprite frame to the screen.

The PLAY SPRITE command is very interesting. When you load a sprite sheet using the CREATE ANIMATED SPRITE command, DarkBASIC keeps track of the specifications for the sprite and then uses that information to draw any single frame out of that sprite sheet, so that you don't have to do it yourself (which can get a bit complicated).

Figure 11.5
Output from the CreateAnimatedSprite program showing the animated raptor sprite.

Let's write a test program to demonstrate this powerful and useful command. The CreateAnimatedSprite program code listing follows, and the output is shown in Figure 11.5.

```
'set screen to manual update
sync on
sync rate 40
hide mouse

'set transparent color to pink
set image colorkey 255, 0, 255

'load the animated sprite from a single bitmap file
create animated sprite 1, ''raptor_attack.bmp'', 13, 8, 5

'make sure all drawing now goes to the screen
set current bitmap 0
```

```
do
   'update the sprite frame each time thru the game loop
   play sprite 1, 1, 104, 50

   'draw the current sprite frame at X,Y
   sprite 1, 200, 200, 5

   sync
loop
```

Creating and Editing Sprites Using Pro Motion

We've been moving along pretty quickly through this subject of sprite animation, and I've just been showing you examples of animated sprites. But where do they come from? Now that you understand how to *program* sprites, I think it would be beneficial to go over a quick tutorial on *creating and editing* sprites as well.

I use a powerful sprite editing program called Pro Motion, which was developed by a company called Cosmigo (http://www.cosmigo.com). You can purchase a licensed copy of Pro Motion directly from Cosmigo, or you can buy it from The Game Creators' website at http://www.thegamecreators.com. In case you've forgotten, these are the folks who created DarkBASIC, and they have a very nice online store that puts software you've purchased into your own library archive so that you can return and download your products at any time. There are also some package deals that include Pro Motion, so it's worth a look.

The main window of Pro Motion is shown in Figure 11.6. I'm going to show you how to load an animation sequence from multiple bitmap files and then save the animation back as a sprite sheet.

I'm assuming you are using some of the same animated sprites that I'm using, because many of them have been provided on the book's CD-ROM. I'm going to focus my attention in this tutorial on an animated flying wasp sprite. You can find the wasp sprite on the CD-ROM in the \sources\chapter11 folder, if you'd like to use it while following along here. Okay, now, open the File menu, choose Animation, and select the Load/Append as Single Images option, as shown in Figure 11.7.

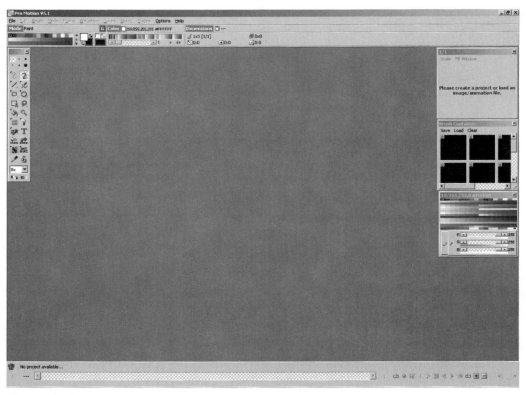

Figure 11.6
Pro Motion is a powerful sprite animation editor by Cosmigo.

This brings up the Load Animation as Single Images dialog box, which is shown in Figure 11.8. Using this dialog box, browse for the folder containing your animation images and then use the Shift key to select one or more files from the list (as shown in Figure 11.9).

Before you click the Open button, you need to configure the color depth of the animation sequence; otherwise, Pro Motion will dither the images and that adds all kinds of artifacts to the images. On the bottom-left corner of the Load Animation dialog is a 24bit Images button. Clicking this button brings up the Quantize Colors dialog. Make sure the Nearest Color option is selected, as shown in Figure 11.10.

When you click the Open button, a Please Confirm dialog box will appear to notify you that a new project is about to be created with the specified settings (see Figure 11.11). Click Yes.

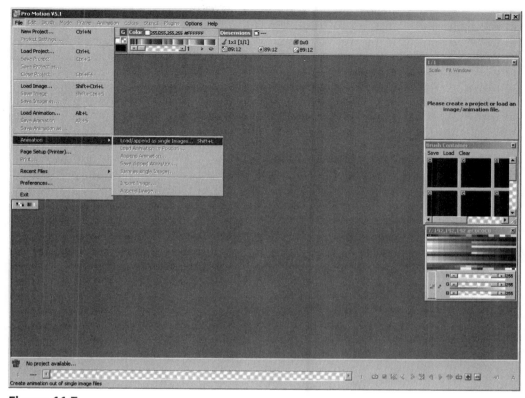

Figure 11.7
Pro Motion makes it easy to load animation sequences from individual bitmap files.

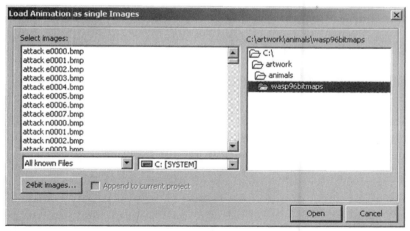

Figure 11.8
Selecting the bitmap files containing the individual sprite animation frames.

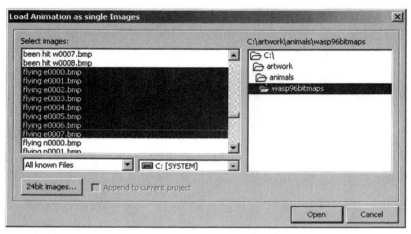

Figure 11.9
You can use the mouse to select image files. Hold down the Shift key to select multiple files.

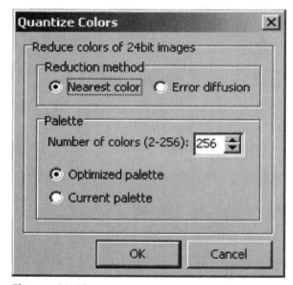

Figure 11.10
Selecting the proper color depth for a sprite sheet.

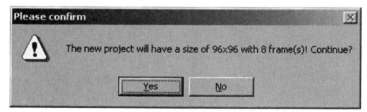

Figure 11.11
Confirming that you want to create a new project with the given specifications.

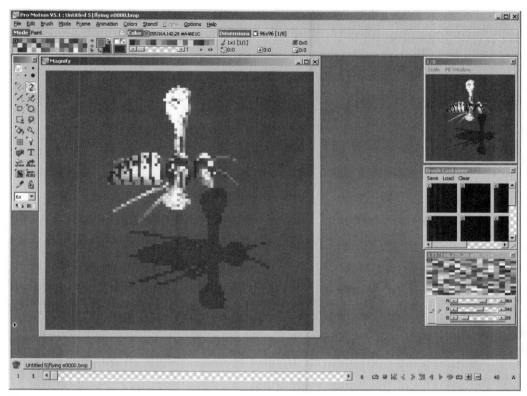

Figure 11.12
The animation has been imported into Pro Motion and can be edited or saved as a sprite sheet.

After you have successfully imported the animation sequence, Pro Motion is ready for editing. Figure 11.12 shows the program with the new wasp sprite loaded, currently with only eight frames.

At this point you can edit the animation frames if you want. I want to simply save the animation out as a sprite sheet. To do this, open the File menu and select Save Animation As (shown in Figure 11.13). This is by far the most common task I perform with Pro Motion—converting individual animations into sprite sheets. I don't do very much pixel-level editing.

This brings up the Save Animation dialog. You can type in a filename for the new bitmap file and select the type of animation to save. As you can see in Figure 11.14, I have chosen "AnimStrip as BMP" from the list of choices. This is equivalent to a sprite sheet.

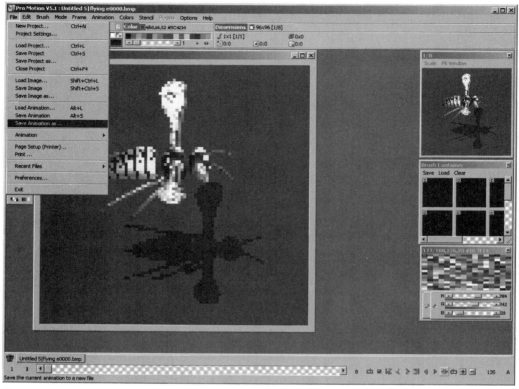

Figure 11.13
Preparing to save the animation sequence to a sprite sheet.

Next, Pro Motion brings up the AnimStrip layout dialog box shown in Figure 11.15. Since this animated wasp sprite only has eight frames of animation, it's a simple choice to go with an "8 × 1" layout.

But this is not usually the case. Most of the time, your sprites will have dozens (if not hundreds) of frames, which makes this an important decision. You want to save the sprite so that each row of the image contains an entire animation sequence for one direction. So, in this case, I'm going to just choose one row with eight columns. But if I were to append the remaining directions to this animation (for north, northwest, west, and so on), then I would want to save out each direction in one complete row of eight frames. At any rate, Figure 11.16 shows the bitmap file that Pro Motion saved.

Once you have learned how to do this much, you can easily manipulate sprite animation sequences to suit your own needs. For instance, suppose I want to save

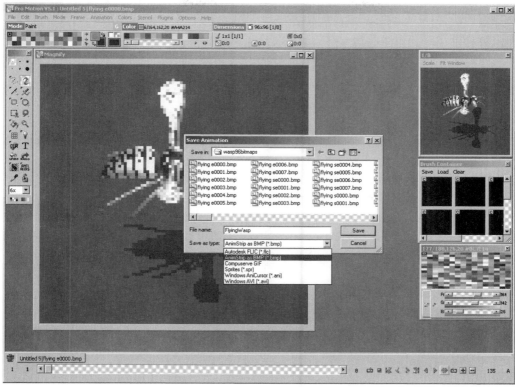

Figure 11.14
The Save Animation dialog box.

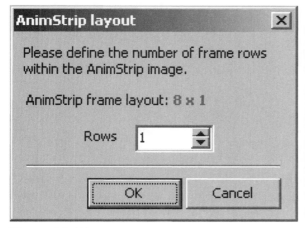

Figure 11.15
The AnimStrip layout dialog box.

Figure 11.16
Animated flying wasp sprite.

all eight directions that have been rendered out for this wasp sprite (courtesy of Reiner Prokein). First, I need to decide which direction to start with. When dealing with multiple directions for a sprite, it's best to choose one starting direction and stick with it throughout all your artwork. I'll start with north-facing images and follow around the circle in a clockwise direction. When you want to add another set of frames to a Pro Motion animation, you must start at the last frame, because Pro Motion inserts new frames wherever the current

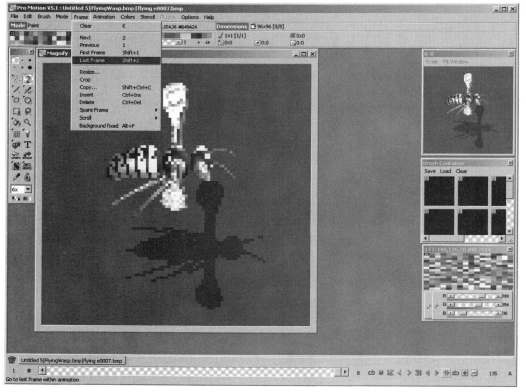

Figure 11.17
Moving to the last frame of the animation in Pro Motion.

frame pointer (so to speak) is located within the animation. Open the Frame menu (shown in Figure 11.17) and select the Last Frame option to jump to the last frame.

Now you can append another animation set to the current animation. To do this, open the File menu, go to Animation, and choose the Load/Append as Single Images option again. This time, take a look at the Append to Current Project checkbox option near the bottom of the dialog. Make sure this checkbox is selected, and then any new frames you add to the project will be appended. If you don't check this option, new frames will be added to a new project. Figure 11.18 shows Pro Motion with all 64 frames of this animation of a wasp flying in eight directions. Note the frame count at the bottom-left corner of the window. You must be certain that there are an even number of frames because all rows must have exactly the same number of frames or Pro Motion won't let you save it.

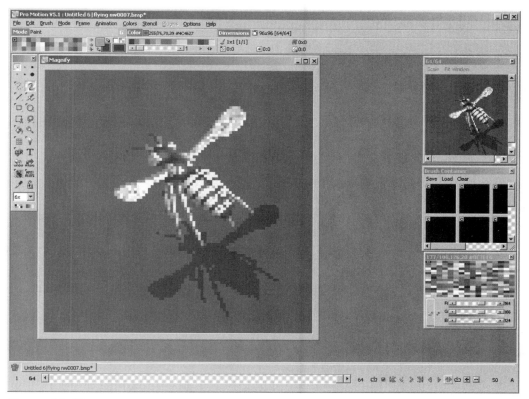

Figure 11.18
A complete 64-frame animation sequence that will be saved as a sprite sheet.

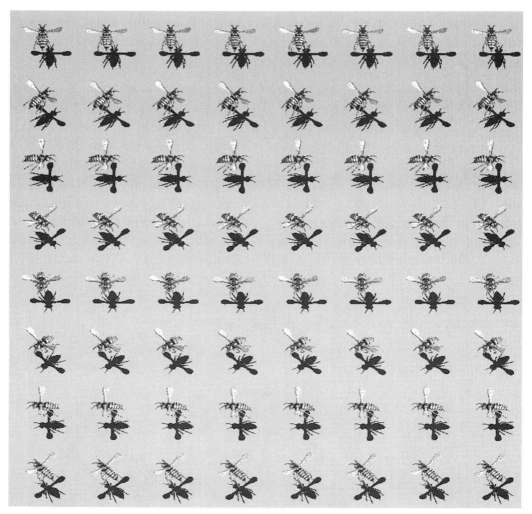

Figure 11.19
The 64-frames animated wasp has been saved to a single bitmap as a sprite sheet.

I'll choose File, Save Animation As, and save the sprite sheet using the AnimStrip as BMP file type, which was explained earlier. The resulting sprite sheet is shown in Figure 11.19.

Manipulating Sprites: Rotation and Scaling

DarkBASIC has a fairly good sprite rotation command that rotates a sprite using an algorithm that retains a high level of quality in the resulting sprite image. Most sprite rotation is done in a graphic editor by an artist because this is a time-consuming procedure in the middle of a high-speed game, and also for more obvious quality issues. The last thing you want slowing your game down is a sprite rotation occurring while you are rendering your sprites. However, what about rotating and rendering your sprites at game startup and then using the resulting bitmaps as a sprite array? That way, sprite rotation is provided at runtime, and you only need to draw the first image of a sprite (such as a tank) facing north, and then rotate all of the angles you need for the game. This is just one solution, and I will explain both of them to you so you'll have a complete picture of the possibilities.

Using Pre-Rotated Sprite Sheets

A sprite sheet is a bitmap image containing all of the frames for an animation sequence, arranged in a tiled manner on the image. In a professional game studio, the artists prepare these sprite sheets and give them to the programmers to insert into a game. But most of us are not working in a game shop with artists who are creating original artwork for a game (but wouldn't that be great!).

For some programmers this is a wonderful and welcome feature because many of us are terrible artists. Chances are, if you are a good artist, you aren't a game programmer, and vice versa. In reality, you will probably want a rotation scheme that generates 8, 16, or 32 rotation frames for each sprite. I've never seen a game that needed more than 32 frames for a full rotation. A highly spatial 2D shooter such as Atari's classic *Blasteroids* probably used 16 frames at most.

8-Direction Sprite Rotation

Take a look at Figure 11.20 for an example of a tank sprite comprised of eight rotation frames. When you want to generate eight frames, rotate each frame by 45 degrees more than the last one. This presumes that you are talking about a graphic editor, such as Paint Shop Pro, that is able to rotate images by any angle. The following table provides a rundown of the eight-frame rotation angles. For an 8-way game, each direction is 45 degrees from the previous one. See Table 11.1.

16-Direction Sprite Rotation

A 16-way sprite is comprised of frames that are each incremented 22.5 degrees from the previous frame. Using this value, you can calculate the angles for an

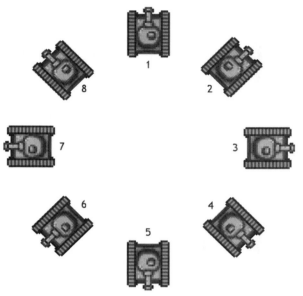

Figure 11.20
The tank sprite rotated so that it can move in eight directions.

Table 11.1 8-Way Rotation Angles

Frame	Angle
1	0
2	45
3	90
4	135
5	180
6	225
7	270
8	315

entire 16-way sprite, shown in Figure 11.21. Table 11.2 shows the angle used for each direction, with the original eight angles highlighted in bold. When you add new rotation angles you are simply adding more detail. I should point out that it's usually better to base all of your game's lists and arrays on 0, rather than 1. This is what we call "zero-based" programming, rather than "one-based".

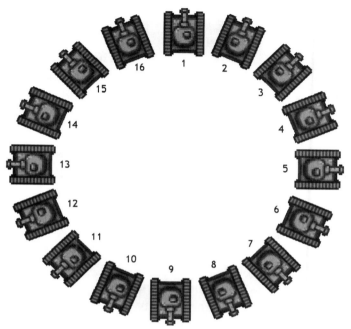

Figure 11.21
This tank sprite has been rotated so that it can move in 16 directions.

Table 11.2 16-Way Rotation Angles

Frame	Angle
1	**0**
2	22.5
3	**45**
4	67.5
5	**90**
6	112.5
7	**135**
8	157.5
9	**180**
10	202.5
11	**225**
12	247.5
13	**270**
14	292.5
15	**315**
16	337.5

Zero-based programming makes more sense because the computer always performs calculations with a zero base. In the view of the computer, zero is the first number, rather than one. But DarkBASIC is flexible, so if you prefer to work in a one-based world, you can still do so, but in a lot of my code you'll see that I use zero base. So, for example, the zero base for a 16-way rotation would be 0 to 15 rather than 1 to 16.

32-Direction Sprite Rotation

It's certainly a great goal to try for 24 or 32 frames of rotation in a 2D game (especially for a game with a top-down view), but each new set of frames added to the previous dimension of rotation adds a whole new complexity to the game. Remember, you need to calculate how the gun will fire in all of these directions! If your tank (or other sprite) needs to shoot in 32 directions, then you will have to calculate how that projectile will travel for each of those directions, too! To put it mildly, this is not easy to do. Combine that with the fact that the whole point of using higher rotations is simply to improve the quality of the game, and you might want to scale back to 16 if it becomes too difficult. Figure 11.22 shows a 32-frame rotation for the tank.

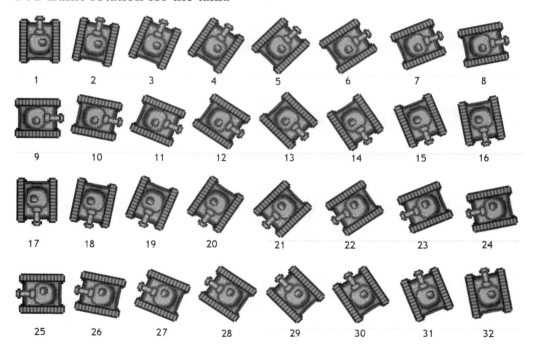

Figure 11.22
The tank sprite rotated so that it can move in 32 directions.

A sprite with this large number of directions can be difficult to program. For one thing, what happens when you need to fire a shot at an enemy tank? You would have to figure out how to move the bullet based on the angle that the tank is facing—no simple task. I have actually written games using this technique, before I saw the light and changed my ways. This is the most logical way to write a game for most programmers, so it's natural to follow a progression from simple static sprites to animated sprites (using a sprite sheet—a bitmap filled with frames of animation). But there is a better, easier way to accomplish the same thing, and get better results as well.

Rotating Sprites on the Fly

DarkBASIC has a command for rotating a sprite on the fly, so that you only need to provide it with a single sprite image. This is a very time-saving feature, but it has not been widely used in the game industry. The first reason is that dynamic sprite rotation takes up processor cycles (in other words, it places a load on the processor). Not too many years ago, 2D game programmers had a hard time coaxing cycles out of a processor because video cards were so slow. Today, that is no longer a problem, so we can rotate sprites dynamically without thinking twice about it. I don't want to suggest that dynamic rotation is *always* better than using pre-rendered sprites. There is definitely a noticeable loss of quality unless the rotation algorithm does a good job of keeping pixels positioned, and you will get a better result using larger sprites, as smaller ones (say, 16 × 16 or so) tend to have more noticeable artifacts (misplaced pixels).

This is one reason why I will never allow myself to be transported in the future when teleporters are invented—because of chaos theory, it's impossible to make a perfect copy of a complex structure, and you would have to be *destroyed* in order to be re-created at the destination. I don't know about you, but I just can't grasp the concept of having my body annihilated and then re-created somewhere else. However, that is essentially what you are doing when you write a sprite-based game—you are annihilating sprites and re-creating them in a new location! When you clear the screen in your game loop, that annihilates the sprites in your game, and the game then re-creates them in new locations, often with the next frame of animation. This is a form of teleportation. I'll bet you didn't think about that!

To rotate a sprite in DarkBASIC, you use the ROTATE SPRITE command. This command takes just two parameters: the sprite number and the angle of rotation

Figure 11.23
The tank sprite is rotating—but not from the center.

(which is an absolute, not additive, from 0 to 359). Let's write a short program to demonstrate how this new command works. Figure 11.23 shows the output from the program.

```
global angle as integer = 0

sync on
sync rate 40
hide mouse

'load the tank sprite and draw it
set image colorkey 255, 0, 255
create animated sprite 1, ''tank.bmp'', 8, 1, 1
sprite 1, screen width()/2, screen height()/2, 1
```

```
repeat
  'left/right keys rotate the tank
  if leftkey() then angle = wrapvalue(angle - 1)
  if rightkey() then angle = wrapvalue(angle + 1)
  rotate sprite 1, angle

  sync

until (ESCAPEKEY() = 1)
```

There's one major flaw in this program. The sprite is rotating, but not around its center. Instead, the sprite is rotating around the upper-left corner. To correct this problem, DarkBASIC provides a command called OFFSET SPRITE that allows you to specify where exactly in the sprite image the rotation should take place, to the pixel. Below is the new line of code that fixes the program (shown in bold), and the new output shown in Figure 11.24 now shows that the tank is rotating around its center.

Figure 11.24
The tank sprite is now rotating correctly from the center.

```
'load the tank sprite and draw it
set image colorkey 255, 0, 255
create animated sprite 1, "tank.bmp", 8, 1, 1
sprite 1, screen width()/2, screen height()/2, 1

'set rotation origin to center of sprite
offset sprite 1, 32, 32
```

Resizing Sprites on the Fly

DarkBASIC also makes it possible to resize—or *scale*—a sprite, dynamically. The command of interest here is SCALE SPRITE (surprised?). This command takes two parameters: the sprite number, and the scale factor as an integer. The scale factor is essentially treated as a percentage. Passing a value of 100 to SCALE SPRITE gives you the original scale (a full gallon). Passing 50 gives you a two-quart sprite. On the other hand, a value of 200 gives you two gallons. Or, something like that. Let's just see how the SCALE SPRITE command works. The ScaleSprite program code listing follows, and the output is shown in Figure 11.25.

```
global scale as integer = 100

sync on
sync rate 40
hide mouse

'load the sprite and draw it
set image colorkey 255, 0, 255
load image "wasp.bmp", 1
sprite 1, 100, 100, 1

repeat

    'left/right keys scale the sprite
    if leftkey() then scale = scale - 1
    if rightkey() then scale = scale + 1

    scale sprite 1, scale

    sync

until (ESCAPEKEY() = 1)
```

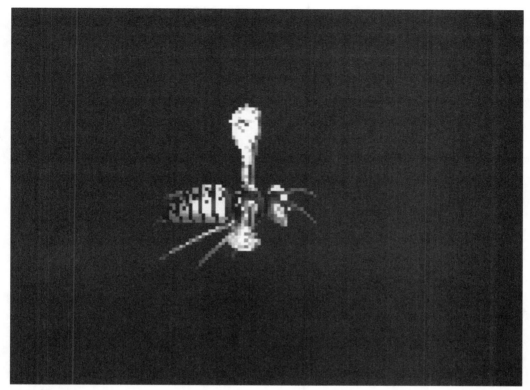

Figure 11.25
The ScaleSprite program resizes a sprite when you press the arrow keys.

Tip

You can't change the scale of an animated sprite created using the CREATE ANIMATED SPRITE command, because DarkBASIC looks at the source image to determine how to scale a sprite, and the source of an animation is a large sprite sheet. If you want to change the scale of an animated sprite, you can use GET IMAGE to draw each frame of the animation individually while applying a scale factor.

Darkanoid: The Continuing Saga

One might argue that Darkanoid was started a bit too early in the last chapter since you had not learned about the powerful new commands available for doing sprite animation. I think it's a far better argument to say that you could have written a complete game just after reading the first ten chapters, even though we haven't covered sound or input yet. Nevertheless, work continues on the Dar-kanoid game, and I think you will like the new version presented in this chapter.

Darkanoid will eventually be a complete game with a lot of animation and collision testing and sound effects. But I don't want to take it too fast too soon. So, let's take a look at the next version of the game that benefits from the new information you learned about in this chapter, regarding animated sprites. The most significant change in this new version of the game is that all drawing code has been upgraded to use real sprites instead of just images. You might recall in the last chapter the game just used PASTE IMAGE for all output. This code has been replaced and now all the objects in the game are being drawn using the SPRITE command. In addition, the game now uses the features of animated sprites to draw the blocks on the screen using a simple algorithm. Figure 11.26 shows what the game looks like at this point.

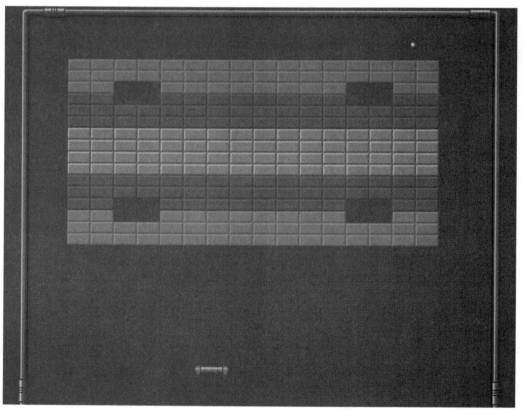

Figure 11.26
The new version of Darkanoid now displays many different blocks.

Updating the Level Data

The level data is stored in data statements, just like in the last chapter, but now there are many numbers in the data statements instead of just 1s and 0s (which previously just represented a block or no block).

```
remstart
   Project: DARKANOID GAME
   Source: Chapter 11
   Date:   May, 2006
remend

data 5,5,5,5,5,5,5,5,5,5,5,5,5,5,5,5
data 5,5,5,5,5,5,5,5,5,5,5,5,5,5,5,5
data 5,5,0,0,5,5,5,5,5,5,5,5,0,0,5,5
data 6,6,0,0,6,6,6,6,6,6,6,6,0,0,6,6
data 6,6,6,6,6,6,6,6,6,6,6,6,6,6,6,6
data 6,6,6,6,6,6,6,6,6,6,6,6,6,6,6,6
data 4,4,4,4,4,4,4,4,4,4,4,4,4,4,4,4
data 4,4,4,4,4,4,4,4,4,4,4,4,4,4,4,4
data 4,4,4,4,4,4,4,4,4,4,4,4,4,4,4,4
data 4,4,4,4,4,4,4,4,4,4,4,4,4,4,4,4
data 6,6,6,6,6,6,6,6,6,6,6,6,6,6,6,6
data 6,6,6,6,6,6,6,6,6,6,6,6,6,6,6,6
data 6,6,0,0,6,6,6,6,6,6,6,6,0,0,6,6
data 5,5,0,0,5,5,5,5,5,5,5,5,0,0,5,5
data 5,5,5,5,5,5,5,5,5,5,5,5,5,5,5,5
data 5,5,5,5,5,5,5,5,5,5,5,5,5,5,5,5
```

New Sprite Constants

Since we want to make the game's source code easier to read, it's helpful to use global "constant" variables to represent the image and sprite numbers used in the game. These are not true *constants* in the sense that they are unchangeable (which is the case with constants in some languages like C++), but we can treat them as constants for the purpose of writing clean code. The lines in bold need to be added to the source code.

```
'image and sprite constants
global IMG_BACKGROUND as word = 1
global IMG_BALL as word = 2
global IMG_PADDLE as word = 5
global IMG_BLOCK as word = 10
```

```
global SPR_BALL as word = 2
global SPR_PADDLE as word = 5
global SPR_BLOCKS as word = 10
```

Creating the Paddle, Ball, and Block Sprites

Moving along down through the source code of Darkanoid, look for the Init_Game function, as shown below. You will need to add the lines of code marked in bold to create the new paddle, ball, and block sprites. They were just bitmaps in the previous chapter, but now we're upgrading these game objects to full-blown sprites. As you can see, only a few additional lines of code are needed.

You are probably wondering why I've started off the sprites at X = 999 and Y = 999, right? Well, this is often necessary just so you can start working with a sprite, but you aren't quite ready to draw it yet. So, you can tell DarkBASIC to draw the sprite at a location that is off the screen in order to initialize the sprite.

```
function Init_Game()
  sync on
  sync rate 60
  hide mouse
  randomize timer()

  'load background
  load image "background.bmp", IMG_BACKGROUND

  'load paddle
  load image "paddle.bmp", IMG_PADDLE
  sprite SPR_PADDLE, 999, 999, IMG_PADDLE
  paddleX = SCREEN WIDTH() / 2
  paddleY = SCREEN HEIGHT() - 50

  'load the ball
  load image "ball.bmp", IMG_BALL
  sprite SPR_BALL, 999, 999, IMG_BALL
```

In the next few lines of code, note that you need to comment out the original line that loaded block.bmp as a bitmap image, because the file is loaded with a new sprite function called create animated sprite.

```
  'load the blocks
  'load image ''block.bmp'', IMG_BLOCK
  create animated sprite SPR_BLOCKS, ''blocks.bmp'', 4, 2, IMG_BLOCK
  set sprite frame IMG_BLOCK, 1
```

```
'load level data into an array
for y = 1 to 16
  for x = 1 to 16
    read blockData(x,y)
  next x
next y
endfunction
```

Drawing the Blocks

We need to make some minor changes to the Draw_Blocks function so that it looks at the width and height of each sprite. Previously, this function used hard-coded values for the width and height, which is not versatile (if you change the size of your block images, then the game would no longer work properly). I have highlighted the *old* lines of code that must be commented out (or deleted) using an italic font. The new lines of code that need to be added are shown in bold.

```
function Draw_Blocks()
  for x = 1 to 16
    for y = 1 to 16
      if blockData(x,y) > 0
        ' dx = 50 + 30 * x
        ' dy = 50 + 15 * y
        ' paste image IMG_BLOCK, dx, dy
        dx = 50 + sprite width(SPR_BLOCKS) * x
        dy = 50 + sprite height(SPR_BLOCKS) * y
        set sprite frame SPR_BLOCKS, blockData(x,y)
        paste sprite SPR_BLOCKS, dx, dy
      endif
    next x
  next y
endfunction
```

Moving the Ball

There is a small change that needs to be made to the Move_Ball function to convert it from drawing the ball image to drawing the ball sprite instead. There is a single line that needs to be removed (shown in italics), and a single line that is added (shown in bold).

```
function Move_Ball()
  'bounce the ball off the right/left
  ballX = ballX + ballSpeedX
```

```
  if ballX < 30 or ballX > screen width() - 35
    ballSpeedX = ballSpeedX * -1
    ballX = ballX + ballSpeedX
  endif

  'bounce the ball off the top edge
  ballY = ballY + ballSpeedY
  if ballY < 20 or ballY > screen height()
    ballSpeedY = ballSpeedY * -1
    ballY = ballY + ballSpeedY
  endif

  'draw the ball sprite
  ' paste image IMG_BALL, ballX, ballY
  sprite SPR_BALL, ballX, ballY, IMG_BALL
endfunction
```

Moving the Paddle

There's one more change needed in the game to convert it over to sprites. The final change to make is in the Move_Paddle function, and it involves replacing a hard-coded value for the paddle's width (75) with a function call to sprite width() to calculate the actual width. This function also needs to draw the sprite instead of the old paddle image. Obsolete lines that must be removed are in italics, while new lines of code are shown in bold.

```
function Move_Paddle()
  'get mouse movement value
  m = mousemovex()
  if m <> 0
    paddleX = paddleX + m
  endif

  'move the paddle based on mouse movement
  if paddleX < 30 then paddleX = 30
  ' if paddleX > screen width() - 75
  if paddleX > screen width() - sprite width(SPR_PADDLE) - 30
    ' paddleX = screen width() - 75
    paddleX = screen width() - sprite width(SPR_PADDLE) - 30
  endif

  'draw the paddle
  ' paste image IMG_PADDLE, paddleX, paddleY
  sprite SPR_PADDLE, paddleX, paddleY, IMG_PADDLE
endfunction
```

Summary

This has been one of the most challenging chapters yet, with extensive coverage of animated sprites and sprite special effects such as rotation and scaling. At this point, you definitely have enough information to create many complete games. All that remains is an understanding of DarkBASIC's device input and sound and music support, which are coming up in the next three chapters. The next chapter covers the very important subject of collision testing, which will allow Darkanoid to actually destroy blocks when the ball hits them!

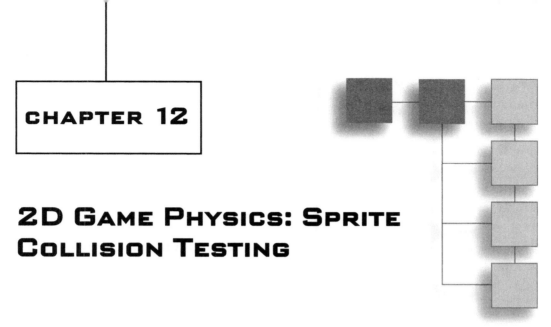

CHAPTER 12

2D GAME PHYSICS: SPRITE COLLISION TESTING

Collision testing, also called collision detection, allows the objects in a game to interact with each other. This occurs whenever two objects (or rather, sprites) hit each other on the screen. DarkBasic has two different ways to detect a collision between two sprites, and that is essentially what you will learn to do in this chapter. You'll then put this powerful new game voodoo to work in the Darkanoid game to make it actually do something useful other than move the ball around. In this chapter, the following topics will be covered:

- Detecting sprite collisions

- Testing for collisions

- Improving the Darkanoid game

Detecting Sprite Collisions

Have you ever wondered how to make a missile blow up an alien ship in a game? Or how about when an enemy plane crashes into yours in games like *1943*? Although it seems like a simple feat to check when two sprites crash into each other, the details are actually not so simple. The technical term for this is *collision detection*, which means that the position of one sprite is compared to the position of another sprite, and if any of the visible pixels intersect, then the sprites have collided!

Types of Collisions

There are three types of collisions (or lack thereof) for which your program should check.

- Bounding rectangle collision

- Impact collision

- No collision

Okay, technically the third option is not a type of collision, but it is important to consider the no-collision event because it helps to illustrate the other two events (see Figure 12.1).

NO COLLISION

Figure 12.1
The first example of collision detection shows a complete miss.

Transparent Pixels

Bounding Rectangle

Sprite Pixels

Figure 12.2
A typical sprite with an imaginary bounding rectangle.

Bounding Rectangle Collision

The first real type of collision that I want you to consider is bounding rectangle. This describes a process where a rectangular shape that completely encompasses the sprite is used to test for collisions. Because a rectangle only has four points, it becomes an easy algorithm to compare two rectangles to see if they are overlapping. Figure 12.2 shows an example of a sprite with a bounding rectangle around it. The bounding rectangle is usually just the border of the image that is the basis for the sprite.

When two sprites overlap each other, we say that they have collided. Take a look at Figure 12.3, which shows an example of bounding rectangle collision detection. As you can see from Figure 12.3, the missile has clearly *not* hit the fighter plane, and yet bounding rectangle would call this a hit. Why is that helpful, do you suppose? Although this method is not entirely accurate in every case, it is sufficient to narrow down the list of suspect collisions so a more detailed comparison can be made.

When there are dozens or even hundreds of sprites in a game, it can be very time consuming to check for a collision between every single one because each sprite must be compared to *every other sprite* in the game! So, if there are 100 sprites in a game, a collision detection procedure would have to make 10,000 comparisons just to see which sprites have collided! Thankfully, bounding rectangle is a quick way of checking for collisions, so it shouldn't slow down the game. Now on to a more specific method.

BOUNDING RECTANGLE COLLISION

Figure 12.3
Bounding rectangle collision detection uses the bounding rectangles of two sprites to check for a collision.

Impact Collision Detection

Impact collision detection is a precise method of checking for sprite collisions that involves comparing the actual pixels of each sprite to see whether any sprites overlap (the *damage zone*). Using this method, you can have a tiny sprite with a relatively large bounding rectangle still return an accurate result (see Figure 12.4).

DarkBASIC provides both types of collision so you can keep the game running at a good speed while still allowing for precision in collision checking (which results in a better game). After a bounding rectangle collision occurs, the program can then perform an impact comparison to see whether it was just a near miss or an actual hit. Impact collision detection is also called *pixel perfect* collision detection because it compares the actual pixels of two sprites to determine if they are overlapping. You would not want to do impact collision detection *all the time*, only to narrow down a precise hit *after* bounding rectangle has narrowed down the most probable collisions first. In most cases, bounding rectangle works fine.

Collision Commands

DarkBASIC provides two commands for detecting collisions. (Obviously, you don't need a command to check for no collision!) The two commands are SPRITE COLLISION and SPRITE HIT.

IMPACT COLLISION

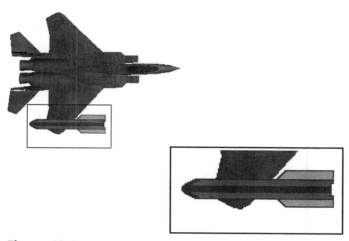

Figure 12.4
Impact collision (also called *pixel-perfect collision*) detection compares the non-transparent pixels of two sprites for overlap.

The SPRITE COLLISION command uses the bounding rectangle collision detection method to check whether two sprites are overlapping. The key word to remember with the SPRITE COLLISION command is *overlap*. If the bounding boxes of two sprites are overlapping even a little bit, this command will return a 1 (otherwise, it will return a 0).

The SPRITE HIT collision command is more specific and determines whether two sprites have actually hit each other using the more precise impact collision method. This command determines an impact by looking at the actual pixels in each sprite and comparing whether any pixels in one sprite are overlapping the pixels in the other.

The CollisionTest Program

To give you some idea about what collision testing makes possible in a game, I've written a short simulation program called CollisionTest. This program draws ten random balls on the screen, which are animated and which bounce off the edges of the screen (so they stay on the screen at all times). The twist to this program is that one of the balls is a vampire which sucks the life out of the other balls whenever it collides with them. Figure 12.5 shows the program shortly after it has started running.

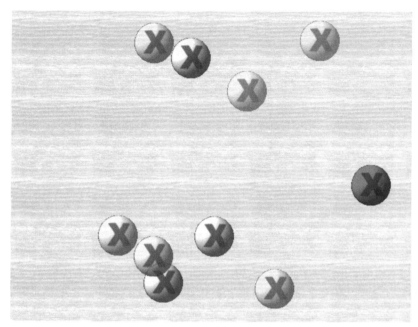

Figure 12.5
The CollisionTest program demonstrates sprite collision with an interesting simulation.

As you can see from this figure, the vampire ball has already started to glow blue, which reflects its energy level (consumed from other balls). Over time, the vampire ball becomes a darker tint of blue while the rest of the balls in the simulation gradually fade away into nothingness. (Actually, their alpha value is decreased every time a collision occurs with the vampire ball). Figure 12.6 shows the simulation after it has been running for a few minutes. Note how the vampire ball is now a dark blue while several of the other balls have already been consumed, and those that remain are already fading.

Let's go over the source code for CollisionTest line by line so you'll gain a full understanding of how it works. First up is a new sprite structure that cuts down on the number of global variables that would otherwise be required in the program.

```
'define the sprite structure
type SPRITET
   x as integer
   y as integer
   speedx as integer
```

Figure 12.6
The blue ball is the vampire, sucking the life out of the other balls (which are fading away).

```
    speedy as integer
    alpha as integer
endtype
```

Next, let's declare the ball array that is based on the new sprite structure.

```
global NUM as integer = 10
dim ball(NUM) as SPRITET
```

Next up is the screen refresh settings and a couple other useful initializations.

```
sync on
sync rate 40
hide mouse
randomize timer()
```

Now we get to the image loading code. Here the program loads the background image (a woodgrain texture) and creates a new animated sprite out of the ball.bmp image. Figure 12.7 shows the ball sprite sheet. Then the ball sprite is cloned to create duplicate ball sprites.

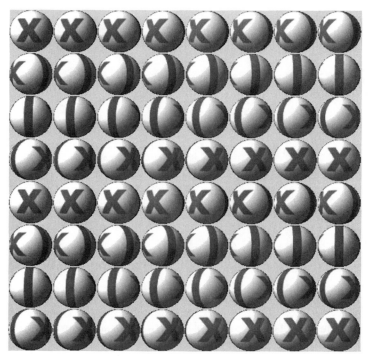

Figure 12.7
The animated ball has 64 frames and was rendered using a 3D modeling tool.

```
'load the background image
load image "woodgrain.bmp", 100

'load the animated ball
set image colorkey 255, 0, 255
create animated sprite 1, "ball.bmp", 8, 8, 1

'clone the additional sprites
for n = 2 to NUM
   clone sprite 1, n
next n
```

Now we can get the animated balls started off with some random values for the position and speed of each ball.

```
'randomize the balls
for n = 1 to NUM
   ball(n).x = rnd(screen width() - sprite width(1))
   ball(n).y = rnd(screen height() - sprite height(1))
```

```
    ball(n).speedx = rnd(4) + 2
    ball(n).speedy = rnd(4) + 2
    ball(n).alpha = 255
next n
```

The first sprite, which I have called the "vampire" ball (because it sucks the life out of the other balls during collisions), is fixed to a certain speed so it's easier to identify it on the screen; the other balls move at random speeds.

```
'slow down the first sprite
ball(1).speedx = 2
ball(1).speedy = 2
```

Next up is the main loop. The first thing to do is draw the background image.

```
'main loop
repeat
    'draw the background
    paste image 100, 0, 0
```

At this point, you can add the code to move the ball sprites. This code is a bit lengthy because it also checks the bounds to keep the sprites inside the screen (bouncing off the screen edges).

```
'move the balls
for n = 1 to NUM
    'update the ball's X position
    w = screen width() - sprite width(1)
    ball(n).x = ball(n).x + ball(n).speedx
    if ball(n).x > w or ball(n).x < 0
        ball(n).speedx = ball(n).speedx * -1
        ball(n).x = ball(n).x + ball(n).speedx
    endif

    'update the ball's Y position
    h = screen height() - sprite height(1)
    ball(n).y = ball(n).y + ball(n).speedy
    if ball(n).y > h or ball(n).y < 0
        ball(n).speedy = ball(n).speedy * -1
        ball(n).y = ball(n).y + ball(n).speedy
    endif
next n
```

Now that all the sprites have moved, you can perform some collision testing to see if any have hit the vampire sprite. If that happens, then the blue hue of the vampire sprite is increased by one and the alpha channel (translucency) of the target sprite is reduced. Eventually, all of the sprites but one will disappear.

```
'perform collision testing with sprite 1
for n = 2 to NUM
  if sprite hit(1, n)
    'suck the life out of this poor ball!
    ball(n).x = ball(n).x + ball(n).speedx * 2
    ball(n).y = ball(n).y + ball(n).speedy * 2
    ball(n).alpha = ball(n).alpha - 1
    if ball(n).alpha < 0 then ball(n).alpha = 0
    set sprite alpha n, ball(n).alpha

    'give more life to the vampire ball
    ball(1).alpha = ball(1).alpha - 1
    if ball(1).alpha > 0 then ball(1).alpha = 0
    set sprite diffuse 1, ball(n).alpha, ball(n).alpha, 255
  endif
next n
```

The last tidbit of code actually draws all of the sprites on the screen. After that, all you have to do is call sync to update the screen.

```
'draw the balls
for n = 1 to NUM
  play sprite n, 1, 64, 30
  sprite n, ball(n).x, ball(n).y, n
next n

sync
until (escapekey() = 1)
```

And that's it for the CollisionTest program. Any questions? No? Okay, good, then lets get cracking on the Darkanoid game again.

Darkanoid Revisited

Let's add some more features to the Darkanoid game. Now that you've learned how collision testing works and have seen some example code, I think you'll be able to add this new capability to Darkanoid very easily. The new collision code in the game will make it possible to deflect the ball using the paddle (although

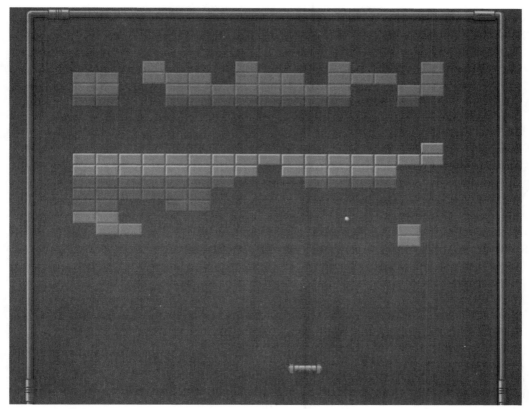

Figure 12.8
The latest improvements to Darkanoid add collision testing to the game.

you still can't "lose" by missing the ball—yet). The ball also hits blocks and makes them disappear. This is done by simply setting the blockData array value to zero whenever a block is destroyed. Then, next time through the game loop, that particular block is not drawn. The new changes definitely help this game feel more functional, as you can see in Figure 12.8.

Adding a New Sprite Structure

Let's get started modifying the game. You'll want to open the project that you've been building up to this point, up to where we left off in the previous chapter. Up near the top of the program, add the following type definition called SPRITET. This new structure will make it easier to work with sprites and avoid using so many global variables. This is just a rudimentary structure, containing only the sprite properties needed up to this point. In time, it will grow to add new properties in future chapters.

```
'define the sprite structure
type SPRITET
   x as integer
   y as integer
   speedx as integer
   speedy as integer
endtype
```

Modifying the Global Variables

Now that you have a new sprite structure available, you'll need to remove the old global variables and replace them with new sprite definitions. In the code below, I have highlighted in italics the code that should be removed, and provided the new lines of code in bold as a replacement.

```
'paddle position variables
'global paddleX as integer
'global paddleY as integer

'ball position variables
'global ballX as integer = 400
'global ballY as integer = 300
'global ballSpeedX as integer = 2
'global ballSpeedY as integer = -2
```

Now for the code to replace what you have just removed from the source code listing.

```
'paddle position variables
global paddle as SPRITET

'ball position variables
global ball as SPRITET
ball.x = 400
ball.y = 400
ball.speedx = 2
ball.speedy = -3
```

Building Blocks

Next up is the Draw_Blocks() function, which needs a slight overhaul due to the changes introduced in the global variables. This is also where the collision testing code will be added so that the game will determine when the ball hits a block. I've shown the new lines of code in bold text.

```
function Draw_Blocks()
    for x = 1 to 16
        for y = 1 to 16
            if blockData(x,y) > 0
                'figure out where this block is located
                dx = 50 + sprite width(SPR_BLOCKS) * x
                dy = 50 + sprite height(SPR_BLOCKS) * y
                'position and draw the current block
                sprite SPR_BLOCKS, dx, dy, IMG_BLOCKS
                set sprite frame SPR_BLOCKS, blockData(x,y)
                paste sprite SPR_BLOCKS, dx, dy

                'check for collision with ball
                if sprite collision(SPR_BLOCKS,SPR_BALL) = 1
                    blockData(x,y) = 0
                    ball.speedy = ball.speedy * -1
                endif
            endif
        next x
    next y
endfunction
```

Moving the Ball

Next, you'll need to modify the Move_Ball() function. The only change being made here is to convert the global variables to use the new sprite structure and its properties. All that's involved is the addition of a period at several places, which are highlighted in bold.

```
function Move_Ball()
    'bounce the ball off the right/left
    ball.x = ball.x + ball.speedx
    if ball.x < 30 or ball.x > screen width() - 35
        ball.speedx = ball.speedx * -1
        ball.x = ball.x + ball.speedx
    endif

    'bounce the ball off the top edge
    ball.y = ball.y + ball.speedy
```

```
   if ball.y < 20 or ball.y > screen height()
      ball.speedy = ball.speedy * -1
      ball.y = ball.y + ball.speedy
   endif

   'draw the ball sprite
   sprite SPR_BALL, ball.x, ball.y, IMG_BALL
   'check for collisions
   if sprite hit(SPR_BALL, SPR_PADDLE)
      ball.speedy = ball.speedy * -1
   endif
endfunction
```

Moving the Paddle

Likewise, you need to make a few minor changes to Move_Paddle() so that it will use the new sprite structure instead of the old global variables. Changes have been highlighted in bold.

```
function Move_Paddle()
   'get mouse movement value
   m = mousemovex()
   if m <> 0
      paddle.x = paddle.x + m
   endif

   'move the paddle based on mouse movement
   if paddle.x < 30 then paddle.x = 30
   if paddle.x > screen width() - sprite width(SPR_PADDLE) - 30
      paddle.x = screen width() - sprite width(SPR_PADDLE) - 30
   endif

   'draw the paddle
   sprite SPR_PADDLE, paddle.x, paddle.y, IMG_PADDLE
endfunction
```

Summary

You have learned a very important new skill of game development by learning about collision detection. You saw how DarkBasic implements collision testing and put it to work in a new version of Darkanoid. The game is really taking shape now! The next chapter will formally introduce you to the mouse input commands you've been using off and on up to this point, and show you how the keyboard and joystick interface works as well.

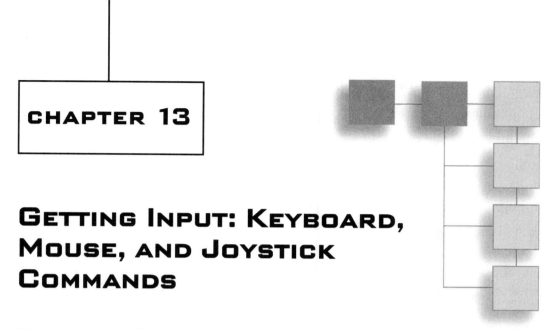

CHAPTER 13

GETTING INPUT: KEYBOARD, MOUSE, AND JOYSTICK COMMANDS

This chapter is dedicated to the subject of input—specifically, taking control of the computer's input devices with DarkBASIC. DarkBASIC includes numerous commands for handling input events from the keyboard, mouse, and joystick. It also includes features such as force feedback that are available with many joysticks.

This chapter covers the following topics:

- Introduction to user input
- Keyboard commands
- Mouse commands
- Joystick commands
- Defining control devices
- Force feedback

Introduction to User Input

Every device, from a TV to a microwave oven, requires some sort of control device to use it. A TV requires a remote to change channels, and a microwave has a front control panel for programming the temperature and time to cook a meal.

In fact, most consumer electronics devices require some sort of user input. User input is what makes the difference between a technical demo and a game. Reading the input from a control allows the game to ascertain what the player would like to do, and then perform that task.

Every game console, from the Atari 2600 to the Xbox, has some form of user input. The user input is relayed to the console via some form of controller. DB uses the DirectInput library to get all of its input. If you are familiar with DirectInput, you will recognize some of the functions within DB, as well as how they correspond to their DirectInput counterparts.

DB supports three different basic types of controllers—the keyboard, mouse, and joystick. Most PC users have one or more of these devices. These days, it is hard to imagine a computer without at least a keyboard and a mouse. However, it was not long ago that PC gamers only had one type of input—the keyboard.

Keyboard Basics

The keyboard is the most basic form of user input to which you will have access. Every computer has a keyboard. However, this was not always the case. The keyboard itself has been around since 1868, when an inventor by the name of Christopher Lathem Sholes took out a patent on the first typewriter. Computers in their present form were not even then. And in fact, some of the earliest computers did not use keyboards; they used punch cards, on which the computer instructions were punched and then fed into the computer.

In 1964, MIT, Bell Labs, and General Electric designed the first computer that used a keyboard. It was called the Mutlics. It was nothing more than a collection of monitors and keyboards (called *dumb terminals*) hooked up to a larger system, but since that moment every computer has used a keyboard.

A keyboard has many different keys, but most keyboards are laid out in the QWERTY format. The QWERTY format, also invented by Christopher Lathem Sholes, specifies the layout of the keys on the keyboard. Q, W, E, R, T, and Y are the first six letters in the top row of letter keys on the QWERTY keyboard.

Many keyboards have 101 to 104 keys. Most of the older keyboards have 101 keys, and the newer keyboards have 104 or more keys. To help visualize the keyboard as a control device, you must view each key as a button (like on a joystick, which I will cover later, in the "Joystick Commands" section). Each button has three different states: UP, DOWN, and PRESSED. Although it might seem a little odd that there are three different states, it's really quite simple. If a key has not been pressed, it is in the UP state. If a key is being pressed currently, it is in the DOWN state. If a key is currently in the UP state but was previously in the DOWN state, it is in the PRESSED state.

Most game applications use four main keys for movement. They traditionally are the up, down, left, and right arrows. The AWSD keys are sometimes used for movement, but this is rather uncommon. In that case, W is used for up, A is used for left, S is used for down, and D is used for right. Generally, there is one key used for fire in a game; this is usually the Ctrl key. Other common keys used in games are the Enter key, the Alt key, and the spacebar.

Although the keyboard is the largest control that is hooked up to the computer, it is not the only common controller. Almost all computers have a mouse attached to them; at $10 for a cheap mouse, who can't afford one?

Mouse Basics

It is hard to imagine a computer without a mouse; they feel unusable without one. However, the mouse has not always been part of the computer. In 1964, a man by the name of Douglas C. Engelbart created the first mouse. He patented this mouse as an X-Y position indicator, but nicknamed it the "mouse" because it had a tail coming out the back of it. His original mouse was nothing more than a wooden box with two roller balls inside. In 1998, Douglas Engelbart was inducted into the National Inventors Hall of Fame. I think he most richly deserves that induction, since he invented the most well loved and oft-used input device since the keyboard.

Mouse devices come in all different shapes and sizes, from a traditional ball-and-wheel mouse to a more complex optical mouse to a trackball. Each mouse, though unique in style, has the same basic function—to indicate an X-Y position. In the Windows and Macintosh operating systems, you have a cursor that is controlled by the mouse. In DB you may have a cursor that looks slightly different but serves the same function as the Windows or Macintosh cursor. You might be wondering about games such as *Quake 3* or *Doom 2*. They don't have a cursor, right? You are correct, but they still read the mouse information and convert the X-Y position into useful user control.

The mouse has one other feature that makes it a popular gaming control—buttons. Most mouse devices have two or more buttons (unless you have a Macintosh mouse, in which case you only have one button). These buttons can each be assigned to a different aspect of a program. Windows uses the buttons to select, execute, and control different files. Just as the keyboard keys have different states, so do the mouse buttons. However, there are four different states for a mouse button—UP, DOWN, CLICKED, and DOUBLE CLICKED.

The UP state is just like the keyboard UP state—the mouse button has not been clicked. The DOWN state is just like the keyboard DOWN state, but with one unique difference. In most applications, the mouse button DOWN state is used to drag a box around a collection of items. This is the most common use of the DOWN state, but it does not always have to be the case. The CLICKED state is the same as the keyboard PRESSED state. The new DOUBLE CLICKED state is nothing more than the mouse being in the CLICKED state twice in a row.

There is one more aspect of the mouse that I need to cover. Most new mouse devices have a wheel, but not all do. This wheel allows the user to scroll up and down. It is usually used to scroll between weapons in a game or to scroll up and down on a webpage without using the side scroll bar.

Although the mouse is a wildly popular input device for PC games (I would almost venture to say that it is *the* most popular for PC games), it is not the only gaming input device. There is also the joystick, which is nearly as popular as the mouse for most computer or console-based games.

Joystick Basics

The joystick is the most common user input device for any console or console-based game. The Atari 2600 had a basic one-button controller, while the GameCube has a more complex control. They all serve the same function: To allow human input into a game in the most convenient manner possible.

Although I cannot pinpoint the exact inventor of the joystick, I know that joysticks have been hooked to computers since 1964, when the first computer game (*Space War*) was written. The standard for joystick connection to the PC did not come until much later, however. The game port is the most common type of connection for a joystick. Also known as the joystick port, the game port is generally connected like a traditional mouse and is found on most sound cards. You can use a Y splitter to connect up to two joysticks at one time to a game port.

The USB port is becoming a wildly popular connection for the joystick. I think this is a great idea because USB ports support faster communications between the joystick and the computer, which allows greater precision in the joystick.

Definition

Precision is the accuracy of a controller. The more precise a joystick or mouse is, the better the input the game will receive from it.

The joystick is a lot like the mouse in that it is an X-Y indicator. Most joysticks have some form of X and Y input. What makes a joystick different than a mouse is that the X and Y input can be separated on a joystick, whereas they cannot on the mouse. A prime example of this is a driving wheel. The wheel portion of the joystick is the X input, and the pedals are considered the Y input.

Just like the keyboard and mouse, the joystick also has buttons. (This seems to be a common theme among controllers, doesn't it? Joysticks generally have between two and ten buttons, a mouse usually has two to five buttons, and a keyboard has approximately 104 buttons.) Each button again has three different states—UP, DOWN, and PRESSED. The UP state is just like the UP state for the mouse and keyboard—the button has not been pressed. The DOWN state is the same as well, but most games use the DOWN state for rapid-fire functions. The PRESSED state is also the same as the keyboard and mouse, and it is usually used for single fire.

Now that you have covered the three major input devices for a PC game, it is time to cover them in detail, from concepts to commands. Each device has a unique set of commands assigned to it to make it function with DB. I will start with the keyboard, and you will work your way through the mouse and the joystick.

Keyboard Commands

The keyboard commands in DB are pretty easy to use. There are commands for reading entire strings as well as for reading one character. You have used many of the commands in previous chapters without knowing exactly what they are or what they do.

Reading Text Input

The most fundamental requirement of basic input commands is reading a string or number input. You need to read a string to gather information such as the player's name or his favorite color. Although you can create your own string input routine with the key press commands, DB provides a command to read strings for you.

The INPUT command is one of the oldest commands in any BASIC language. In fact, it is as old and widely used as the PRINT command. The INPUT command can take two forms. The first format of the command is a simple INPUT *string$*, where keyboard keys are read and the keys are stored in string$. The second format of the INPUT command is INPUT string$, *variable$*, where the keyboard input is read and placed in string$ and variable$ is printed on the string. This form is a little more useful because it will print something right before the location where the user will input text.

I must tell you about one important drawback to the INPUT command. Although it is a useful command for reading entire strings, it might not always be the best command for game programming because it is a blocking command, which will not allow any other commands to run until it is finished. INPUT is a good command to use only if you do not need to process anything else while waiting for the user to type something. At the end of the keyboard section, I will show you how to write a non-blocking INPUT command.

Reading Key Presses

The INPUT command is not the only keyboard command that DB supports. DB can also use the keyboard as a series of buttons. Remember, the keyboard has three states for its keys: UP, DOWN, and PRESSED. The following commands will help you determine these states accurately.

Waiting for a Keypress

The WAIT KEY command waits for any key to be pressed. This command takes no parameters. Like INPUT, it is a blocking command. This command is good for holding title screens and winning screens. The SUSPEND FOR KEY command performs the same function. These commands will wait for any key to be put in the PRESSED state before continuing.

The INKEY$() Command

The INKEY$() command is one my favorites of the keyboard commands. It tells you which key is currently being pressed. It is a non-blocking command, so you can use it in loops without stalling the program. The INKEY$() command takes no parameters, but it returns a single character that represents the key that is currently being pressed. Note that INKEY$() only returns one letter (or chr$). You can only read one key at a time in the DOWN state with this command.

You can use INKEY$() to detect the three different states of each key on the keyboard. To detect the DOWN state of a key, just check to see whether INKEY$() is equal to the value of that key. To detect the UP state, check to see whether INKEY$() is not equal to value of that key. To detect the PRESSED state, check to see whether INKEY$() is equal to, and then not equal to, the value of that key.

There are two other things to note about the INKEY$() command. First, INKEY$() will detect the difference between uppercase and lowercase letters. So the p and P keys are two different things in the INKEY$() command. When detecting whether the P key is pressed, you should look for the P key as well as the p key. You can also take the input of INKEY$() and pass it to the UPPER$ command to convert it to uppercase automatically.

Second, the INKEY$() command can return more then just the letters on the keyboard. It can also return the ASCII value of whatever key is currently pressed. Remember the CHR$(value) command? This is where it comes in handy, because you can now detect different keys being pressed. For example, to detect whether the Enter key has been pressed, check to see whether INKEY$() = CHR$(13). Table 13.1 shows some of the most common keys and their ASCII values.

Reading Special Keys

In addition to reading any key with the INKEY$() command, DB also supports the reading of special keys such as the up, down, left, and right arrows. There are a total of nine special keys that DB exclusively reads. There are nine special key

Table 13.1 Commonly Used ASCII Codes

Code	Key
8	Tab
9	Backspace
13	Enter
27	Esc
32	Spacebar

Table 13.2 Special Key Commands

Command	Key
UPKEY	Up arrow
DOWNKEY	Down arrow
LEFTKEY	Left arrow
RIGHTKEY	Right arrow
CONTROLKEY	Control (sometimes labeled Ctrl)
SHIFTKEY	Shift
SPACEKEY	Spacebar
RETURNKEY	Enter (not the number pad Enter)
ESCAPEKEY	Escape (sometimes labeled Esc)

commands for the common keys used in a game. DB uses a different set of commands for reading the rest of the keys on the keyboard simultaneously, as you will see in the next section. Table 13.2 sums up the nine special key commands.

Let's go over all of the special key input commands. The UPKEY() command reads whether the up arrow is in the up or down state. It takes no parameters and returns a 0 if the up arrow is in the up state and a 1 if it is in the down state. To detect whether the up arrow is in the PRESSED state, look for it to be in the down state (1), and then in the up state (0). The up arrow is most commonly used to move a character upward in a keyboard-based game.

The DOWNKEY() command reads whether the down arrow is in the up or down state. It returns a 0 if the down arrow is in the up state and a 1 if it is in the down state. The down arrow is most commonly used for moving a character downward in a keyboard-based game.

The LEFTKEY() command reads whether the left arrow is in the up or down state. It returns a 0 if the left arrow is in the up state and a 1 if it is in the down state. The left arrow is most commonly used for moving a character left in a keyboard-based game.

The RIGHTKEY() command reads whether the right arrow is in the up or down state. It returns a 0 if the right arrow is in the up state and a 1 if it is in the down state. The right arrow is most commonly used for moving a character right in a keyboard-based game.

The CONTROLKEY() command reads whether the Control key is in the up or down state. (The Control key is usually labeled Ctrl on a keyboard.) This command returns a 0 if the Ctrl key is in the up state and a 1 if it is in the down state. The Ctrl key is most commonly used for firing weapons in a keyboard-based game. This command does not tell you whether the left or right Ctrl key was hit; it just lets you know that one was hit.

The SHIFTKEY() command reads whether the Shift key is in the up or down state. It returns a 0 if the Shift key is in the up state and a 1 if it is in the down state. This command does not tell you whether the left or right Shift key was hit; it just lets you know that one was hit.

The SPACEKEY() command reads whether the spacebar is in the up or down state. It returns a 0 if the spacebar is in the up state and a 1 if it is in the down state. The spacebar is most commonly used for either firing or jumping in a keyboard-based game.

The RETURNKEY() command reads whether the Return key is in the up or down state. The Return key is generally labeled Enter on the keyboard; it can be found above the right Shift key. This key should not be confused with the Return key on the number pad (which is sometimes labeled Enter as well). Although the Return key by the number pad returns the same ASCII value in INKEY$() as the Enter key above the Shift key, the RETURNKEY() command only detects the Enter key above the Shift key. It returns a 0 if the Enter key is in the up state and a 1 if it is in the down state. The Enter key is most commonly used for performing an action in a keyboard-based game, which can range from opening a door to talking to another character.

The ESCAPEKEY command returns whether the Escape key is in the up or down state. The Escape key is generally labeled Esc on the keyboard. This command returns a 0 if the Esc key is in the up state and a 1 if it is in the down state. The Esc key is most commonly used for quitting a game.

Reading Multiple Keys and Scan Codes

Sometimes reading one key is just not enough. There are times when you need to read multiple keys. Although you can use all of the special functions at the same time, sometimes that is not enough. For example, you might want to move upward while firing your guns at the same time. This works fine if the fire command is attached to the Ctrl key and the up command is attached to the up arrow. But what if the fire command is attached to the P key and the up command is attached to the W key?

DB provides a few commands that will detect whether multiple keys are pressed. To detect multiple key presses, you must understand scan codes, which are different from ASCII values. A scan code is the raw number that the keyboard assigned to a key before sending it to the computer. Usually scan codes are assigned from the upper left of the keyboard to the lower right.

Definition

A *scan code* is the value assigned by the keyboard (not Windows, ASCII, or anyone else) to a specific key. The keyboard actually has a small microcontroller inside of it that handles all the key presses and complexities of the keyboard's operation. This controller is programmed with a standard set of scan codes for PC-AT 101 keyboards and is the ultimate source of keyboard information to the computer.

The SCANCODE Command

Although it only returns the value of one key, the SCANCODE() command is useful in determining what scan code is assigned to each key. This command takes no parameters, but it returns the scan code of the key currently being pressed.

The KEYSTATE Command

The KEYSTATE() command takes one parameter—the scan code of the key you are looking for—and returns whether the key is up or down. The UP state of the key returns a 0, and the DOWN state returns a 1.

Non-Blocking Input

DB has two commands that make non-blocking input a simple task. They are the ENTRY$() and the CLEAR ENTRY BUFFER commands. These two commands use the windows keyboard buffer to keep track of what has been typed on the keyboard without having to keep track of every key (as would be the case with an INKEY$() based non-blocking input).

The ENTRY$() command reads whatever string is stored in the Windows keyboard buffer at the time it is called. The Windows keyboard buffer stores every key typed on the keyboard until the CLEAR ENTRY BUFFER is called. The CLEAR ENTRY BUFFER command clears the Windows keyboard buffer so a new string can be read.

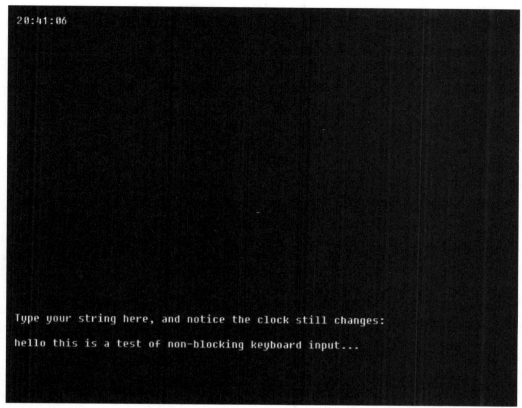

Figure 13.1
Example of non-blocking keyboard input.

The following source code shows you how to use the ENTRY$() and CLEAR ENTRY BUFFER command in conjunction with the INKEY$() command to keep track of input while other processes are running. There is a clock in the upper left-hand corner. Watch it change as you are typing in your text. Change the program to use INPUT$ instead and notice the difference. Figure 13.1 also shows the output of the non-blocking example.

```
sync on

InputString as string
StaticString as string
charhit as string
newlen as integer
```

```
repeat
  cls
  ink rgb(255,255,255), rgb(0,0,0)
  text 10,10, get time$()
  text 10,370, "Type your string here, and notice the time keeps ticking:"

  charhit = inkey$()
  if charhit = chr$(8)
     StaticString = StaticString + entry$()
     NewLen = len(StaticString)-1
     StaticString = left$(StaticString, NewLen)
     clear entry buffer
  endif

  InputString = StaticString + entry$()
  text 10,400, InputString
  sync
until escapekey() = 1
```

Mouse Commands

Next to the keyboard, the mouse is the most popular input device for the PC. Almost any program requires a mouse. Mouse devices come in all shapes, colors, and sizes. However, they all have one thing in common: They move that thing on the screen called the cursor. There are ten different DB commands that control the mouse.

Hiding and Showing the Mouse

The HIDE MOUSE command gets rid of that pesky mouse cursor. The mouse cursor is cute, but sometimes it can be annoying when it follows your mouse. The two most annoying examples I can think of are in a flight-simulator-type game, where the mouse cursor should not be seen, and in a game where you need a custom mouse cursor, such as a targeting game. The command takes no parameters and returns nothing.

The SHOW MOUSE command does just the opposite of the HIDE MOUSE command. It returns the cute, lovable mouse cursor. The command takes no parameters and returns nothing.

Mouse Position

Perhaps the most important data received from the mouse is the cursor's X and Y position on the screen. A game programmer translates this information into useful data for movement of characters, sprites, or 3D objects. The X and Y positions of a mouse start from the upper-left corner of the screen and work toward the lower-right corner. The mouse cursor moves further right the more positive the X value is, and further down the more positive the Y value is.

There is a third position of the mouse that DB reads—the Z position. It is hard to visualize a mouse with three positions, because there is only a left-right, up-down orientation on a mouse pad. Most often, the Z position of the mouse refers to the wheel located in the center of the mouse. It is a little misleading, but it makes sense after you have used it.

Reading the Three Mouse Axes

The MOUSEX() command returns the X position of the mouse cursor on the screen. This command takes no parameters but returns the X value of the cursor, which is between 0 and the width of the screen in pixels −1. The maximum value is the screen width −1 because the minimum position starts at 0.

The MOUSEY() command returns the Y position of the mouse cursor on the screen. It takes no parameters but returns the Y value of the cursor, which is between 0 and the height of the screen in pixels −1. The maximum value is the screen height −1 because the minimum position starts at 0.

The MOUSEZ() command returns the value of the mouse wheel. It takes no parameters but returns the value of the mouse wheel, which ranges between 0 and 100.

Positioning the Mouse Cursor

The POSITION MOUSE command positions the mouse cursor on the screen. It takes two parameters (X position and Y position) and returns nothing. The Mouse-Position program demonstrates the uses of the mouse input commands. It displays the X, Y, and Z positions of the mouse on the screen and shows the mouse cursor. It also uses the keyboard to move the mouse using the POSITION MOUSE command. Figure 13.2 shows the results of this program.

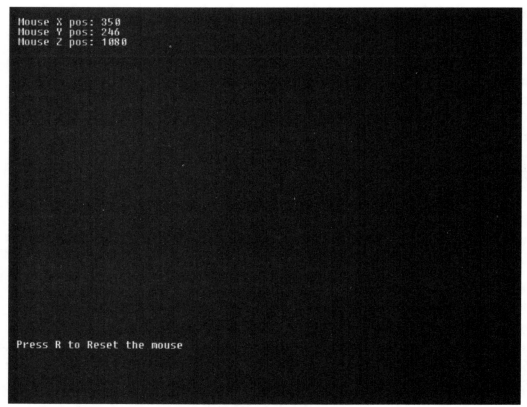

Figure 13.2
The MousePosition program demonstrates the use of the mouse commands

```
SYNC ON
White = RGB(255,255,255)
Black = RGB(0,0,0)
WHILE ESCAPEKEY()=0
    INK 0,0
    BOX 0,0,639,479
    INK White,Black
    tempstring$ = "Mouse X pos: "+STR$(MOUSEX())
    TEXT 10,10, tempstring$
    tempstring$ = "Mouse Y pos: "+STR$(MOUSEY())
    TEXT 10,22, tempstring$
    tempstring$ = "Mouse Z pos: "+STR$(MOUSEZ())
    TEXT 10,34, tempstring$
    tempstring$ = "Press R to Reset the mouse"
    TEXT 10,400, tempstring$
```

```
IF INKEY$()="R" OR INKEY$()="r"
   POSITION MOUSE 0,0
ENDIF
SYNC
ENDWHILE
```

Mouse Movement

Now that you know how to use the mouse position commands, you can read the difference between the mouse positions. The oldest way of knowing how far the mouse moved is by using the following formulas: $dx = x2-x1$, $dy = y2-y1$, $dz = z2-z1$. dx, dy, and dz are all delta values. In other words, they are the difference between the last mouse position and the current mouse position. DB provides some mouse movement commands so that calculating dx, dy, and dz is not necessary.

Mouse Motion Commands

The MOUSEMOVEX command tells you the distance between the current MOUSEX() and the last MOUSEX(). It is the same as the $dx = x2 - x1$ formula. This command takes no parameters and returns the distance in the X position.

The MOUSEMOVEY command tells you the distance between the current MOUSEY() and the last MOUSEY(). It is the same as the $dy = y2 - y1$ formula. This command takes no parameters and returns the distance in the Y position.

The MOUSEMOVEZ command tells you the distance between the current MOUSEZ() and the last MOUSEZ(). It is the same as the $dz = z2 - z1$ formula. This command takes no parameters and returns the distance the mouse wheel has moved.

Using the Mouse Motion Commands

The MouseMove program demonstrates the uses of the mouse movement commands. It scales a bitmap based on the movement of the mouse. To quit the program, just press the Esc key. Figure 13.3 shows the output of the mouse movement example.

```
HIDE MOUSE
SYNC ON
SYNC RATE 30

SIZEX = 100
SIZEY = 100
```

Move the mouse to scale the picture

Figure 13.3
The MouseMove program demonstrates a use of the mouse moving commands.

```
LOAD BITMAP "mustang.bmp", 1

SET CURRENT BITMAP 0
WHILE ESCAPEKEY()=0
  cls
  sizex = sizex + (MOUSEMOVEX()/10)
  IF sizex > 100 THEN sizex = 100
  IF sizex < 1 THEN sizex = 0
  sizey = sizey + (MOUSEMOVEY()/10)
  IF sizey > 100 THEN sizey = 100
  IF sizey < 1 THEN sizey = 0

  x2 = (bitmap width(1) * sizex) / 100
  y2 = (bitmap height(1) * sizey) / 100
```

```
COPY BITMAP 1,0,0,bitmap width(1),bitmap height(1),0,0,0,x2,y2
TEXT 10,460,"Move the mouse to scale the picture"
SYNC
ENDWHILE
```

Mouse Buttons

Now that you can determine the position and movement of the mouse, there is one more item that must be read—the state of the mouse button. A given mouse button has four states: up, down, clicked, and double clicked. The clicked and double clicked states are derived from the up and down states.

The MOUSECLICK() command returns which button on the mouse is currently pressed. This command takes no input but returns a value that indicates which button is being pressed.

The left mouse button is a value of 1; the right mouse button is a value of 2. If there are more than two buttons, the third and fourth buttons are valued at 4 and 8, respectively. This way, you can determine which buttons are being pressed at one time. The MOUSECLICK() command will add the values of the buttons that are being clicked, so if the left and right mouse buttons are pressed, the value is 3. Table 13.3 shows the return values for MOUSECLICK() and what they mean.

Table 13.3 Return Values of MOUSECLICK

Value	Buttons Pressed
0	None
1	Left
2	Right
3	Left and right
4	Third
5	Third and left
6	Third and right
7	Third, left, and right
8	Fourth
9	Fourth and left
10	Fourth and right
11	Fourth, left, and right
12	Fourth and third
13	Fourth, third, and left
14	Fourth, third, and right
15	Fourth, third, left, and right

Determining clicked and double clicked states is not that hard. For the clicked state, you simply detect when the button is pressed. At that point, you wait until the mouse button is up: MOUSECLICK() = 0. You now have a button in a clicked state. The double clicked state is a little trickier. You must determine that the button is in a clicked state two times within a given timeframe.

The Mouse Handler

The mouse handler is a concept that works well with game programming. It is nothing more than a function that is created to handle all mouse-related input. Every stage of a game can contain a different mouse handler, but placing all of the mouse-related input into a function will make it easier to control items with the mouse. The following source code is for a simple shooting gallery game. It uses most of the mouse commands that I have covered in this chapter. The mouse handler is clearly defined. To destroy the targets, move the cursor over the target and left-click on it. Figure 13.4 shows the output of the ShootingGallery program.

```
SYNC ON
SYNC RATE 30
DIM SpriteHit(20)
DIM SpriteTimer(1)
HIDE MOUSE
SpriteTimer(1) = 0
LOAD IMAGE "crosshair.bmp",25
LoadTargetAnims()
' Initialize all the sprites
FOR x = 2 TO 20
    SPRITE X,-100,68,5
    SET SPRITE x,1,1
    SpriteHit(x) = 0
NEXT X
' Set the mouse cursor sprite
SPRITE 1,320,240,25
SET SPRITE 1,1,1
' Setting up the lines in the background
SET CURRENT BITMAP 0
Green = RGB(0,255,0)
Red = RGB(255,0,0)
Black = RGB(0,0,0)
White = RGB(255,255,255)
```

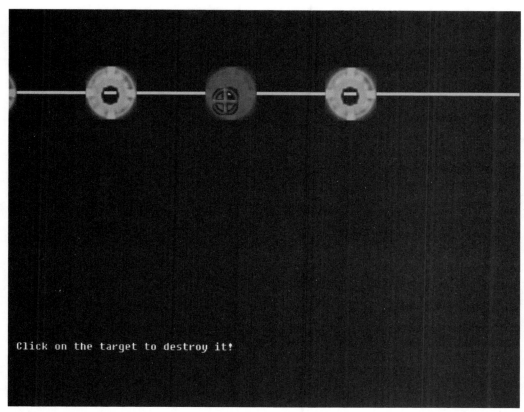

Figure 13.4
Output of the ShootingGallery program

```
INK Green,Black
BOX 0,98,639,102
INK Red,Black
BOX 0,100,639,100
INK White,Black
inum = 5
TEXT 10,400,"Click on the target to destroy it!"
' Play the game until the Escape key is hit.
WHILE ESCAPEKEY()=0
    ProcessSprites()
    ControllerHandler()
    SYNC
ENDWHILE
END
```

```
' This moves the crosshairs to where the mouse is.
FUNCTION ControllerHandler()
   SPRITE 1, MOUSEX(), MOUSEY(), 25
   IF MOUSECLICK()=1
     FOR X = 2 TO 20
       IF SPRITE COLLISION(1,X)
          SpriteHit(X) = 1
       ENDIF
     NEXT X
   ENDIF
ENDFUNCTION

' This does all the Sprite Collision processing.
FUNCTION ProcessSprites()
   SpriteTimer(1) = SpriteTimer(1) - 1
   IF SpriteTimer(1) <= 0 THEN MoveNewSprite()
   FOR X = 2 TO 20
     IF SPRITE X(X) > 704
        SPRITE X,-100,68,5
     ENDIF
     IF SpriteHit(X)
        SPRITE X,SPRITE X(x)+5,SPRITE Y(X), SPRITE IMAGE(X)+1
        IF SPRITE IMAGE(X) >= 15
           SPRITE X,-100,68,5
           SpriteHit(X) = 0
        ENDIF
     ELSE
        IF SPRITE X(X) >= -64
           SPRITE X,SPRITE X(x)+5,SPRITE Y(X), 5
        ENDIF
     ENDIF
   NEXT X
ENDFUNCTION

' Moves out a new sprite
FUNCTION MoveNewSprite()
   FOR X = 2 TO 20
     IF SPRITE X(X) <= -100
        SPRITE X , -64, SPRITE Y(X), 5
        X = 21
     ENDIF
   NEXT X
   SpriteTimer(1) = 30
ENDFUNCTION
```

```
' Loads are the Target Animations.
FUNCTION LoadTargetAnims()
   LOAD BITMAP "target.bmp",1
   inum = 5
   fadestep = 100
   SET CURRENT BITMAP 1
   FOR X = 0 TO 10
      FADE BITMAP 1,90
      GET IMAGE inum,0,0,64,64
      inum = inum + 1
   NEXT X
   DELETE BITMAP 1
   SET CURRENT BITMAP 0
ENDFUNCTION
```

Joystick Commands

What do all gaming consoles have in common? A controller! From the Atari 2600 to the modern PC, the joystick (or controller) is the preferred input device for most video games. (Anyone who prefers W-A-S-D on a keyboard is delusional.) DB has a good selection of commands to control the joystick.

Analog versus Digital Input

Before you go on into the wonderful world of DB joystick commands, you need a little understanding of how a joystick works. There are two different types of joysticks—digital and analog. Each type works with a PC, but they generate the data in completely different ways.

An analog joystick is like most old-school mouse devices. It consists of two rollers that, when moved, calculate the distance that they are moved and report the information to the computer. All older joysticks generate this analog input. When the input is generated, it is converted to a digital signal for the computer to use. The problem with analog input is that the joystick has a tendency to drift because of slight movements.

Digital joysticks read differently than analog joysticks do. Instead of having two rollers to read the distance between movements, digital joysticks use an optical or light sensor that converts user movements into a digital signal. This gives you a much more accurate reading of the user input without the drifting problems. A common digital joystick (the one I use) is the Microsoft Sidewinder 3D.

Joystick Position

Like the mouse, the joystick has two common positions—X and Y. Unlike the mouse, however, you do not have to move the joystick around a large pad to get your X and Y position readings. You just move your hand up while holding the joystick, and the Y position decreases. Move your hand left to decrease the X position.

Some joysticks also contain a third position—the Z position. This is very much like the mouse wheel.

Reading the Joystick's Position

The JOYSTICK X() command returns the X position of the joystick, which ranges between −1000 and +1000. The joystick is in the center of the X axis when the X position is equal to 0.

The JOYSTICK Y() command returns the Y position of the joystick, which also ranges between −1000 and +1000. The joystick is in the center on the Y axis when the Y position is equal to 0.

The JOYSTICK Z() command returns the Z position of the joystick, which also ranges between −1000 and +1000. The joystick is in the center on the Z axis when the Z position is equal to 0.

Enhancing a Familiar Program

To demonstrate the X, Y, and Z joystick commands, I have rewritten the mouse movement command to read the joystick. Notice that there is no joystick position command because you cannot reposition the joystick.

```
SYNC ON
White = RGB(255,255,255)
Black = RGB(0,0,0)

WHILE ESCAPEKEY()=0
   INK 0,0
   BOX 0,0,639,479
   INK White,Black
   TEXT 10,10, "Joystick X pos: "+STR$(JOYSTICK X())
   TEXT 10,22, "Joystick Y pos: "+STR$(JOYSTICK Y())
   TEXT 10,34, "Joystick Z pos: "+STR$(JOYSTICK Z())
   SYNC
ENDWHILE
```

Joystick Movement

The joystick movement commands are not like the mouse movement commands. They do not give you the distance that the joystick moves, but rather they tell you what direction the joystick is moving.

Detecting Joystick Motion

The JOYSTICK UP() command tells you whether the joystick is moving upward. This command takes no parameters and returns a 1 if the joystick is moving in the up position. If the joystick is moving downward, this command returns a 0.

The JOYSTICK DOWN() command tells you whether the joystick is moving downward. This command takes no parameters and returns a 1 if the joystick is moving in the down position. If the joystick is moving upward, this command returns a 0.

The JOYSTICK LEFT() command tells you whether the joystick is moving left. This command takes no parameters and returns a 1 if the joystick is moving to the left. If the joystick is moving right, this command returns a 0.

The JOYSTICK RIGHT() command tells you whether the joystick is moving right. This command takes no parameters and returns a 1 if the joystick is moving to the right. If the joystick is moving left, this command returns a 0.

Testing Joystick Input

The mouse movement program scaled a bitmap with the mouse. Notice that the JOYSTICK UP() value is subtracted from the scalex value, and JOYSTICK DOWN() is added. This is different from the mouse code, in which you just added one value, because neither JOYSTICK UP() nor JOYSTICK DOWN() returns a negative number. So, you just create the negative value. The same is true with JOYSTICK LEFT() and JOYSTICK RIGHT().

```
HIDE MOUSE
SYNC ON
SYNC RATE 30
White = RGB(255,255,255)
Black = RGB(0,0,0)
SIZEX = 100
SIZEY = 100
LOAD BITMAP "graphic.bmp", 1
```

```
SET CURRENT BITMAP 0
' Scales with Joystick movement
' until the escape key is pressed
WHILE ESCAPEKEY()=0
  INK 0,0
  BOX 0,0,639,479
  INK White,Black
  sizex = sizex - JOYSTICK UP()
  sizex = sizex + JOYSTICK DOWN()
  sizey = sizey - JOYSTICK LEFT()
  sizey = sizey + JOYSTICK RIGHT()
  IF sizex > 100 THEN sizex = 100
  IF sizex < 1 THEN sizex = 0

  IF sizey > 100 THEN sizey = 100
  IF sizey < 1 THEN sizey = 0
  x1 = 0
  x2 = (638*sizex)/100+1
  y1 = 0
  y2 = (478*sizey)/100+1
  COPY BITMAP 1,0,0,639,479,0,x1,y1,x2,y2
  tempstring$ = "Move the JoyStick to scale the picture"
  TEXT 10,460,tempstring$
  SYNC
ENDWHILE
```

Joystick Buttons

Just like the mouse, the joystick has buttons. Some joysticks have lots of buttons (such as for the Xbox, GameCube, and PlayStation 2), while other joysticks have one button (such as the Atari 2600). However, each button has one thing in common—it provides a game with user input. Each button is assigned to a specific action or series of actions. In *Super Mario Brothers*, for example, one button is used to jump, and the other button is used to fire. DB provides commands to read these buttons from the joystick and use them in your game.

The JOYSTICK FIRE A() command lets you know when the primary button on the joystick has been pressed. This is most commonly used for firing at objects in most first-person shooters. The command takes no parameters, but it returns a 0 if the primary button is in the UP state and 1 if it is in the DOWN state.

The JOYSTICK FIRE B() command lets you know when the secondary button on the joystick has been pressed. This is most commonly used for a secondary firing function in most first-person shooters. The command takes no parameters, but it returns a 0 if the secondary button is in the UP state and 1 if it is in the DOWN state.

The JOYSTICK FIRE C() command lets you know when the third button on the joystick has been pressed. This is most commonly used for checking status or performing actions in some first-person shooters. The command takes no parameters, but it returns a 0 if the third button is in the UP state and 1 if it is in the DOWN state.

The JOYSTICK FIRE D() command lets you know when the fourth button on the joystick has been pressed. This is not commonly used in first-person shooters, but it can be assigned to change things in the display. The command takes no parameters, but it returns a 0 if the fourth button is in the UP state and 1 if it is in the DOWN state.

Joystick Sliders

Some joysticks, both analog and digital, have sliders on them, much like you would see in the cockpit of a spaceship or on the top of a soundboard. DB provides a means to read these sliders as well.

The JOYSTICK SLIDER A() command returns the value of the primary slider on a joystick. I usually use this slider for controlling my thrust in a space flight simulation. The command takes no input, but returns a value between 0 and 65535. This is much more precise than JOYSTICK X() and JOYSTICK Y(), so you can get more precision out of a slider.

Note

The number 65535 will show up frequently when you are programming devices. This is because it has 16 bits and is a computer friendly number (based on a power of 2).

The JOYSTICK SLIDER B() command returns the value of a secondary slider on a joystick. The command also takes no inputs, but returns a value between 0 and 65535. I have never had a joystick with two sliders before, but I'm sure it is a great combination of control and style.

Joystick Hat and Twist Commands

There are four other joystick commands that I need to address. These commands cover some of the unconventional aspects of a joystick. However, DB would not be complete without them. Not every joystick has a hat or twist

Table 13.4 Hat Directions

Direction	Angles (1/10 degrees)
North	0
East	900
South	1800
West	2700

ability, but DB provides support for them in case you would like to support these features.

The JOYSTICK TWIST X() command reads the twist of the X position of the joystick. It takes no parameters but returns the value of the joystick twisted in the X direction. This value is between 0 and 65535.

The JOYSTICK TWIST Y() command reads the twist of the Y position of the joystick. It takes no parameters but returns the value of the joystick twisted in the Y direction. This value is between 0 and 65535.

The JOYSTICK TWIST Z() command reads the twist of the Z position of the joystick. It takes no parameters but returns the value of the joystick twisted in the Z direction. This value is between 0 and 65535.

The JOYSTICK HAT ANGLE command returns the degrees of the hat controller on your joystick. Some joysticks have more than one hat, so this command takes one parameter—the number of the hat. It supports up to four different hats, and returns the angle at which the hat is pointing in tenths of a degree. The value of the angle will range from 0 to 3600. Table 13.4 lists the most common directions of the hat.

Definition

A *hat* is a multidirectional button on a joystick. You simply press down most buttons, but you press a hat button in a direction.

Revisiting the Shooting Gallery Program

Now that you know all the joystick commands, it is time to revisit the ShootingGallery program. This time you will replace the mouse commands with joystick commands. Because of the way the program was written, you only need to change one function—the mouse handler. The following source code lists the changes you need to make to enable the ShootingGallery program to use the joystick. You can find the full source code for the JoystickShootingGallery program on the CD in \sources\chapter13.

Place the following source code after the SYNC command in the original ShootingGallery program.

```
DIM XPos(1)
DIM YPos(1)
XPos(1) = SCREEN WIDTH() /2
YPos(1) = SCREEN HEIGHT() /2
```

Now replace the ControllerHandler() section with this new section, which uses the JOYSTICK commands.

```
FUNCTION ControllerHandler()
   IF JOYSTICK UP() = 1 THEN YPos(1) = YPos(1) - 3
   IF JOYSTICK DOWN() = 1 THEN YPos(1) = YPos(1) + 3
   IF JOYSTICK LEFT() = 1 THEN XPos(1) = XPos(1) - 3
   IF JOYSTICK RIGHT() = 1 THEN XPos(1) = XPos(1) + 3
   IF XPos(1) < 0 THEN XPos(1) = 0
   IF YPos(1) < 0 THEN YPos(1) = 0
   IF XPos(1) > SCREEN WIDTH()-1 THEN XPos(1) = SCREEN WIDTH()-1
   IF YPos(1) > SCREEN HEIGHT()-1 THEN YPos(1) = SCREEN HEIGHT()-1
   SPRITE 1, XPos(1), YPos(1) , 25
   IF JOYSTICK FIRE A()=1
     FOR X = 2 TO 20
        IF SPRITE COLLISION(1,X)
           SPRITEHIT(X) = 1
        ENDIF
     NEXT X
   ENDIF
ENDFUNCTION
```

Defining Control Devices

Before you move on to the final capabilities of the joystick, you will need to take a side trip. This trip takes you down the path of control devices. Some computers have more than one control device, which can be just about any human input device. Some examples are joysticks, head-mounted trackers, and driving wheels. The next set of commands tells DB which one of those control devices to use and sets the default control devices.

Getting a List of Joysticks

The PERFORM CHECKLIST FOR CONTROL DEVICES command will fill up the checklist information with all the available control devices. Each device gets its own space within the checklist. The name of the device is returned in CHECKLIST STRING$(). If the device supports force feedback, CHECKLIST VALUE A() returns a 1; otherwise, it returns a 0.

Setting the Control Device

Once you have listed the control devices, you will need to set the default control device using the SET CONTROL DEVICE command. This command takes one parameter, which is a string with the name of the device. If PERFORM CHECKLIST FOR CONTROL DEVICES returns more than one control device, you should ask the user which device to use and then pass the string for that device to this command.

The CONTROL DEVICE NAME$ command returns the string name of the control device. This is very useful because you will not have to keep track of the current control device; you can just read its name from CONTROL DEVICE NAME$. This command takes no parameters, but returns a string with the control device's name.

Control Device Position

The CONTROL DEVICE X command returns the X value of the current controller. This is exactly like the JOYSTICK X() command, but it works for any control device specified.

The CONTROL DEVICE Y command returns the Y value of the current controller. This is exactly like the JOYSTICK Y() command, but it works for any control device specified.

The CONTROL DEVICE Z command returns the Z value of the current controller. This is exactly like the JOYSTICK Z() command, but it works for any control device specified.

Force Feedback

Now that you have learned about the control devices, I will cover force feedback, which includes more than just the standard joystick. Driving wheels and other control devices (including some mouse devices) also support force feedback.

What is force feedback? It is a tactile sensation returned to the gamer from the control device they are using. An example would be a gamer playing a boxing game. In real boxing, when your opponent hits you, you feel the hit on your face. In the gaming world, you really don't want to be hit in the face, but you would like some other feedback to let you know you've been hit. Thus your joystick will rumble or move to one side as your opponent strikes you. That is why it is called force feedback—the joystick is forcing you to feel some feedback. The joystick or input device accomplishes this with small motors that are built into the device.

Programming Force Feedback

Programming force feedback in DB does not take a rocket scientist. When I finish explaining the command, you will add some source code to the ShootingGallery program to add force feedback.

Before activating any of the force-feedback commands, you must first determine whether the device supports it. Remember that the checklist created by PERFORM CHECKLIST FOR CONTROL DEVICES stores a value of 1 in CHECKLIST VALUE A() if the device supports force feedback. Your program will fail if you attempt to use force feedback on a device that does not support it.

You can split the force-feedback commands into two groups—the standard commands and the special commands. Each group of commands takes similar input. At least one of their parameters (unless otherwise specified) takes a magnitude value.

Definition

> *Magnitude value* is the extent of the force-feedback effect. This value ranges from 0 to 100, where 0 is no effect and 100 is the largest possible effect.

Standard Force-Feedback Commands

The standard force-feedback commands allow you to create your own force-feedback effects. They give you the ability to move the joystick in any direction you want. Let's go over the force feedback commands.

FORCE ANGLE is the most versatile of the standard force-feedback commands. It takes three parameters and returns none. The first parameter is the magnitude of the force. The second value is the angle at which you want to put the force-feedback device. The third value is the time for which you want to leave the device at that angle, measured in milliseconds.

The FORCE UP command forces the joystick into the up position. It provides resistance if you are trying to pull down on the joystick. The command takes one parameter, which is the magnitude of the force, and returns nothing. The FORCE DOWN command forces the joystick into the down position. It provides resistance if you are trying to pull up on the joystick. The command takes one parameter, which is the magnitude of the force, and returns nothing.

The FORCE LEFT command forces the joystick into the left position. It provides resistance if you are trying to pull the joystick right. The command takes one parameter, which is the magnitude of the force, and returns nothing. The FORCE RIGHT command forces the joystick into the right position. It provides resistance if you are trying to pull the joystick left. The command takes one parameter, which is the magnitude of the force, and returns nothing.

The FORCE AUTO CENTER ON command forces the joystick to always return to the center. Instead of forcing left, right, up, or down, it returns the joystick straight to the center. This command is great for stiffing the joystick. It takes no parameter, and it returns nothing. The FORCE AUTO CENTER OFF command frees the joystick to stay in whatever position it is. This command is great for loosening the joystick. It takes no parameter, and it returns nothing.

The FORCE NO EFFECT command is the last of the standard commands, and it affects both the standard and the special force-feedback commands. This command cancels all force feedback applied to the joystick. It takes no parameters and returns nothing.

Special Force-Feedback Commands

Sometimes just moving the joystick up, down, left, and right is not enough. DB provides commands to do more than just standard stuff. These are special case commands that perform more complex actions. Let's go over these unusual commands.

The FORCE CHAINSAW command creates a chainsaw effect within the control device. Imagine revving up a chainsaw and keeping it running. That's what this command simulates. It takes two parameters. The first is the magnitude value, and the second is the duration of the effect. Like all force-feedback effect commands, the duration is measured in milliseconds.

The FORCE SHOOT command emulates the kickback from a pistol. The kickback occurs when you pull the trigger of a pistol. You'll notice that your hand moves back and the bullet moves forward. This command takes two parameters. The first is the magnitude value, and the second is the duration value.

The FORCE IMPACT command is probably the most versatile of the special force-feedback commands. It can be used for hitting walls, hitting people, or getting hit. I think this might be my favorite special force-feedback command. It takes two parameters. The first is the magnitude value, and the second is the duration value.

FORCE WATER EFFECT is an interesting command. It creates the sensation of walking through water. This command takes two parameters. The first is the magnitude value, and the second is the duration value.

Using the Force

This is your last visit to the ShootingGallery program. This time you will add special force-feedback commands to the program. You will add two new commands, change the control handler, and modify the main portion of the program. You can find the full source code for this program on the CD in the Chapter 13 directory, under ForceShootingGallery.

First, add the following source code after the SYNC RATE 30 section. This code checks the force-feedback capabilities of the joystick. You will enter SETCONTROL-DEVICE() in a little while.

```
DIM SupportsForceFeedBack(1)
SupportsForceFeedBack(1) = 0
SetControlDevice()
```

Add the following source code after inum = 5. These are the instructions to activate the force-feedback commands if the joystick supports them.

```
IF SupportsForceFeedBack(1) = 1
    TEXT 10,292,"C - Chain Saw Effect"
    TEXT 10,304,"V - Water Effect"
    TEXT 10,316,"W - Force UP"
    TEXT 10,328,"S - Force DOWN"
    TEXT 10,340,"A - Force LEFT"
    TEXT 10,352,"D - Force RIGHT"
```

```
   TEXT 10,364,"O - Auto Center On"
   TEXT 10,376,"P - Auto Center Off"
ENDIF
```

Add the following line of code after `ControllerHandler()`. This processes the other force-feedback effects.

```
   DoOtherEffects()
```

Next, replace the `ControllerHandler()` function with the following `ControllerHandler()` function.

```
FUNCTION ControllerHandler()
   IF JOYSTICK UP() = 1 THEN YPos(1) = YPos(1) - 3
   IF JOYSTICK DOWN() = 1 THEN YPos(1) = YPos(1) + 3
   IF JOYSTICK LEFT() = 1 THEN XPos(1) = XPos(1) - 3
   IF JOYSTICK RIGHT() = 1 THEN XPos(1) = XPos(1) + 3
   IF XPos(1) < 0 THEN XPos(1) = 0
   IF YPos(1) < 0 THEN YPos(1) = 0
   IF XPos(1) > SCREEN WIDTH()-1 THEN XPos(1) = SCREEN WIDTH()-1
   IF YPos(1) > SCREEN HEIGHT()-1 THEN YPos(1) = SCREEN HEIGHT()-1
   SPRITE 1, XPos(1), YPos(1) , 25
   IF JOYSTICK FIRE A()=1
     IF SupportsForceFeedBack(1) <> 0 THEN FORCE SHOOT 50,25
       FOR x = 2 TO 20
         IF SPRITE COLLISION(1,x)
           IF SupportsForceFeedBack(1) <> 0
             FORCE IMPACT 50,25
           ENDIF
           SpriteHit(x) = 1
         ENDIF
       NEXT x
   ENDIF
ENDFUNCTION
```

Now add the following two functions to the end of your program, and you will have force-feedback capability in your ShootingGallery program.

```
FUNCTION SetControlDevice()
   PERFORM CHECKLIST FOR CONTROL DEVICES
   IF CHECKLIST QUANTITY() = 0
     EXITFUNCTION "NONE"
   ENDIF
```

```
   IF CHECKLIST QUANTITY() = 1
      SET CONTROL DEVICE CHECKLIST STRING$(1)
      SupportsForceFeedBack(1) = CHECKLIST VALUE A(1)
      EXITFUNCTION CHECKLIST STRING$(1)
   ENDIF
   CLS
   PRINT "Please Select Control Device"
   FOR x = 1 TO CHECKLIST QUANTITY()
      tempstring$ = STR$(x)+": "+CHECKLIST STRING$(x)
      PRINT tempstring$
   NEXT X
   INPUT ConDev
   SupportsForceFeedBack(1) = CHECKLIST VALUE A(X)
   SET CONTROL DEVICE CHECKLIST STRING$(ConDev)
ENDFUNCTION CHECKLIST STRING$(ConDev)

FUNCTION DoOtherEffects()
   IF SupportsForceFeedBack(1) =0 THEN EXITFUNCTION
   KeyPress$ = UPPER$(INKEY$())
   IF KeyPress$ = "" THEN EXITFUNCTION
   IF KeyPress$ = "C" THEN FORCE CHAINSAW 50,1000
   IF KeyPress$ = "V" THEN FORCE WATER EFFECT 50,1000
   IF KeyPress$ = "W" THEN FORCE UP 50
   IF KeyPress$ = "S" THEN FORCE DOWN 50
   IF KeyPress$ = "A" THEN FORCE LEFT 50
   IF KeyPress$ = "D" THEN FORCE RIGHT 50
   IF KeyPress$ = "O" THEN FORCE AUTO CENTER ON
   IF KeyPress$ = "P" THEN FORCE AUTO CENTER OFF
ENDFUNCTION
```

Summary

Wow, there are a lot of commands to pick from to take control of input devices. This chapter explained all of the commands and how to execute them. User input devices are what change a technical demo to a game. The ShootingGallery program is an excellent example of using input devices. How about if you enhance the game yourself? All it needs is for someone to take the game and add sound effects, a high score, and plenty of bells and whistles. That being said, we didn't do anything with Darkanoid in this chapter! Are you bummed? Well, the game already has basic mouse input so there isn't much more you can do with it, unless you want a ball-and-paddle game with force feedback. The game will be wrapped up in the next chapter.

CHAPTER 14

GAME AUDIO: SOUND EFFECTS AND MUSIC

Sounds surround us every day and are transmitted through the air, through water, through solid objects, and as vibrations. Before the invention of the television, radio highlighted many family evenings. There were no spectacular visual effects, so it relied on something else—sound effects. The creaking door in "The Shadow" let you know that a house was haunted and the Shadow character was in danger.

This chapter will introduce you to the commands built into DarkBASIC to create ear popping sound effects and music. It will give you a tour of loading, playing, and positioning sound and music files. You will learn all about 3D positional sound effects. Background music is used in many forms of entertainment to affect an audience's mood. Specifically, this chapter will show you how to load and play WAV, MIDI, and MP3 files. Here are the main points of the chapter:

- Creating and loading sounds
- Playing sounds
- Panning and volume control
- Sound properties
- Positional sound commands
- Loading music files
- Playing background music
- Music playback properties
- Updating Darkanoid

Sound Effects

Picture a world without sound. It's not hard to do. Just watch TV sometime and hit the mute button. What a difference! Imagine watching the big screen without the thunderous speaker systems in a theater. The show might be watchable, but the whole experience is changed without audio. The ear is a marvelous part of the body. It can pick up a wide range of sound and then translate sound waves into signals that the brain can understand. From a bass violin in an orchestra to a hot rod squealing its tires, there is a huge range of possible sounds, and the human ear can hear wide ranges of those audio frequencies. Surprisingly, that is also how computers read sound. Audio is stored in a file as a digital recording from an analog sound signal, recorded with a simple microphone or by other means.

Can you see a sound? No, because sound is just a vibration of air molecules. Sound travels as a wave that hits your ear drum and vibrates it. The effect is similar to how a speaker vibrates up and down to produce sound, only in reverse. Your ear drum picks up sound vibrations from the air. These particles are vibrated in a pattern, so observing this pattern will allow you to see the sound. The patterns generated by sounds can be represented by sine waves. No matter how simple or how complex the sound, it can always be described as a series of sine waves of varying amplitudes and frequencies. Figure 14.1 shows an example of a sine wave.

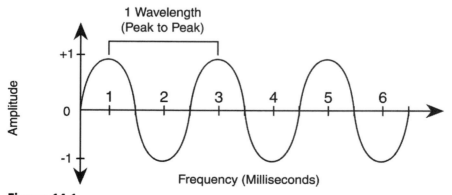

Figure 14.1
An illustration of a common sound effect in the form of a sine wave.

Definition

The *frequency* is the number of times that a sound wave rises and falls over a period of time, usually measured in Hertz (Hz). The *amplitude* is the height and depth of a single sound wave.

Sampling Rate

Sound in the analog wave format presents a problem for the computer. The computer only knows how to represent data in terms of 1s and 0s. A sound wave has more than two states attached to it. So the sound wave must be digitized. The mechanics of digitizing the sound waves from analog to digital are done via your sound card. A sound card takes "snapshots" of the sound wave at different intervals. The process of taking these "snapshots" is called sampling. Unlike a video camera which takes between 24 and 30 pictures a second, the sound card samples a sound at many thousand times a second. The frequency of the sound wave is the number of times the sound wave rises and falls over a period of time. The sampling rate of a sound wave is also called frequency because it samples the sound at a specific number of times per second. A CD-quality sound is sampled at 44 Hz (samples per second).

When sampling a sound, a bit rate is established. A bit rate is the amount of bits used to describe a single sample of sound. Because every sound varies in amplitude, a bit rate needs to be established to represent the height (or depth) of the amplitude. Bit rates are generally referred to by the number of bits each sample contains. A CD-quality sound has a bit rate of 16 bits. That means every sample in the sound has a total of 16 bits of data to it.

The Wave Sound Format

A wave file is one file type that contains a digital representation of a sound wave. Usually with the extension of .wav, a wave file contains all the samplings of an analog sound file. There are many such file formats, but wav is the sound format used most for sound effects. Other sound formats include Mpeg Layer 3 (.MP3), Audio format (.AU), and Real Audio (.RA).

A wave file can be created in many different ways. Windows comes with a program called Sound Recorder that uses a microphone to create waves. A more professional approach would be to use Cool Edit 2000 or some other wave editing software. You can also download pre-recorded sound effect wave files from many different Internet websites. Some of the easiest sound effects are those you can make with your mouth. By using a microphone and your imagination, you can make cows moo and dogs bark.

Loading Sound Files

Loading sounds in DarkBASIC is very simple. There is no need to create a sound device, set the parameters, set up buffers, and cross your fingers. It takes one command to load a sound. DarkBASIC does all the hard work for you. DarkBASIC stores all sound effects in buffers, which are addressed by an integer number. It is a good idea to keep track of what buffer goes with what sound effect at the top of your file or on a separate notepad. You do not want to play the "game won" sound effect when the player just lost all their points.

Loading a Sound File

The LOAD SOUND command is the most basic sound-loading command. Here is the syntax for this command:

```
LOAD SOUND "file name", sound number
```

Here are some examples of using the LOAD SOUND command.

```
LOAD SOUND "yeah.wav", 13
LOAD SOUND "bummer.wav", 14
```

The LOAD 3DSOUND command is similar to the LOAD SOUND command, but with a twist. The LOAD 3DSOUND command marks the buffer sound number into which it is loaded with a special flag that denotes it as a 3D sound. Here is the syntax for this command:

```
LOAD 3DSOUND "file name", sound number
```

Here are some examples of using the LOAD 3DSOUND command.

```
LOAD 3DSOUND " meow.wav", 1
LOAD 3DSOUND " bark.wav", 1
```

How do you know whether a sound has been loaded? By using the SOUND EXIST command. This command returns a 0 if the sound does not exist and a 1 if it does. The syntax for this command is

SOUND EXIST (*sound number*)

Note the sound number is surrounded by parentheses.

Cloning a Sound Buffer

The CLONE SOUND command clones a sound into a specified sound buffer. The advantage to using clone sound is that you can play more than one copy of a sound with one set of sound data, saving valuable memory for other things. The format for this command follows.

CLONE SOUND *destination sound number, source sound number*

Here is an example of the CLONE SOUND command.

CLONE SOUND 4,114

Deleting a Sound Buffer

Another memory-saving technique is to use the DELETE SOUND command when you no longer need a sound. This also allows you to reuse a sound buffer for another sound effect. Just like a bitmap, you can load a sound over another sound, but it's always wise to delete a sound buffer before reusing it. The DELETE SOUND command syntax looks like this:

DELETE SOUND *Sound Number*

Here are some examples of the DELETE SOUND command.

DELETE SOUND 13
DELETE SOUND 14

Playing Sound Files

Boom! The enemy ship just exploded and you can hear it. Now you get to program the playing of the sounds. After the sounds are loaded, you can use them in the game. Playing back sounds is just as easy as loading them. No need to know the frequency of the sound or the timing of the sound card; just a simple command and presto, you hear the firepower of your awesome ship blasting away another alien scumbag. The sound playback commands use the same integer buffers as the load commands. They also give you a few more options for playback control. It only takes one command to play back a sound.

Playing and Looping a Sound Buffer

The PLAY SOUND command is the most basic sound playback command. You can specify an optional start position in bytes that tells DarkBASIC to start the sample at that position. The command looks like this:

```
PLAY SOUND sound number, start position
```

Here are some examples of the PLAY SOUND command.

```
PLAY SOUND 5
PLAY SOUND 5, 30000
```

The LOOP SOUND command allows you to repeat a sound. It is handy so you do not have keep using the PLAY SOUND command. This command also allows you to specify a starting position in bytes, as well as an ending position and an initial position. The ending position is where the sound will stop and start over at the starting position. The initial position lets you specify where you want the first loop to start. This command has the following format.

```
LOOP SOUND sound number, start position, end position, initial position
```

Here are some examples of the LOOP SOUND command.

```
LOOP SOUND 5
LOOP SOUND 5,3000
LOOP SOUND 5,3000,5000
LOOP SOUND 5,3000,5000,2500
```

Interrupting Sound Playback

The STOP SOUND command does just that—stops a sound. You can use this feature on looping sounds or non-looping sounds. The syntax for this command follows.

```
STOP SOUND sound number
```

Here are a few examples of the STOP SOUND command.

```
STOP SOUND 5
STOP SOUND 1
```

The PAUSE SOUND command pauses a sound while it is playing or looping. It is used in conjunction with the RESUME SOUND command. This command has this format:

```
PAUSE SOUND sound number
```

Here are a few examples of the PAUSE SOUND command.

```
PAUSE SOUND 1
PAUSE SOUND 5
```

The RESUME SOUND command starts playing a sound at that point where it was last paused. This command must be used in conjunction with the PAUSE command, and it can provide some interesting effects. The command has this format:

```
RESUME SOUND sound number
```

Panning and Volume Control

Zoom! Did you just see that car go past? It sounded like it was going 190 miles per hour. Wow! The sounds you hear in everyday life move from left to right and change volume all the time. That is how you can tell where the sound is coming from and where it is going.

Definition

Panning represents the amount of sound coming from the left and right speakers. Something panned left will come completely out of the left speaker.

Playing with the panning, speed, and volume in DarkBASIC is very easy. A simple command and the sound's panning is set. Another command allows you to speed up the sound. Let's have some fun playing with sound effects.

Panning a Sound Left or Right

The SET SOUND PAN command places a sound effect somewhere between the two speakers. The values for SET SOUND PAN range from −100 to 100. −100 locates a sound effect on the left speaker; 100 locates it on the right speaker. Anywhere between −100 and 100 locates a sound effect on both the left and right speakers. This command has the following format.

```
SET SOUND PAN Sound Number, Pan Value
```

Here are a few examples of the SET SOUND PAN command.

```
SET SOUND PAN 5, 100
SET SOUND PAN 1, -50
```

The GET SOUND PAN command returns the current pan value. This lets you know where in the speakers your sound is playing. The syntax for this command follows.

```
GET SOUND PAN(Sound Number)
```

Changing a Sound's Playback Frequency

The SET SOUND SPEED command changes a sound's playback frequency. Just like when you play a micro cassette recorder and speed up the playback, SET SOUND SPEED allows you to adjust the speed of a sound effect. My favorite effect is to turn my voice into that of the Chipmunks. This command has the following format.

```
SET SOUND SPEED sound number, frequency value
```

Here are a few examples of the SET SOUND SPEED command.

```
SET SOUND SPEED 5 , 75000
SET SOUND SPEED 5 , 45000
SET SOUND SPEED 5 , 15000
```

The GET SOUND SPEED command returns the current playback speed of a sound, which lets you know how fast your sound is playing back. The syntax for this command follows.

```
GET SOUND SPEED(Sound Number)
```

Setting a Sound's Volume

The SET SOUND VOLUME command adjusts the volume of a sound effect. Volume is a very powerful thing. It can be used to tell how hard a punch was or the caliber of a shot fired. The SET SOUND VOLUME command is DarkBASIC's volume control knob. The value to be set is between 0 and 100 percent. This command has the following format.

```
SET SOUND VOLUME sound number, volume value
```

Here are a few examples of the SET SOUND VOLUME command.

```
SET SOUND VOLUME 3 , 75
SET SOUND VOLUME 4 , 50
SET SOUND VOLUME 5 , 100
```

The GET SOUND VOLUME command returns the volume of a sound effect, which you can use to determine the strength of a punch. The syntax for this command follows.

```
GET SOUND VOLUME (Sound Number)
```

Sound Buffer Properties

Now you come to one of the more interesting parts of sound management—sound properties. These tell you the type of sound you are listening to and whether it is playing or paused. Retrieving sound properties is a snap in Dark-BASIC. All of the commands return a 1 or a 0 to let you know the information for which you are looking.

The SOUND TYPE command reports the type of sound that is loaded in the buffer. There are two different types of sounds that can be loaded—normal sounds and 3D sounds. If SOUND TYPE returns a 0, the sound effect in question is a normal sound; if it returns a 1, the sound effect in question is a 3D sound. The syntax for this command is

```
SOUND TYPE (Sound Number)
```

Here are some examples of the SOUND TYPE command.

```
SoundType = SOUND TYPE(5)
SoundType = SOUND TYPE(6)
```

The SOUND PLAYING command reports whether a sound is playing. This can be useful when a sound needs to be played completely through before continuing. Here is the syntax for this command:

```
SOUND PLAYING (Sound Number)
```

Here are a few examples of the SOUND PLAYING command.

```
IsSoundPlaying = SOUND PLAYING(5)
IsSoundPlaying = SOUND PLAYING(6)
```

The SOUND PAUSED command reports whether a sound is paused. This will allow complete control over the playback of the sound. You will know whether a sound is playing or paused. The command looks like this:

```
SOUND PAUSED(Sound Number)
```

Here are a few examples of the SOUND PAUSED command.

```
SoundIsPaused = SOUND PAUSED(5)
SoundIsPaused = SOUND PAUSED(6)
```

3D Positional Sound Playback

My first experience with good positional sound was while watching the first *Jurassic Park* movie, which was a pioneer effort in digital sound. I remember being engrossed in the action of the movie when I noticed something. Rain—it sounded as though it was raining outside. It shouldn't be raining in the middle of the summer. Then I realized that it was the movie. The rain completely permeated the room so that it sounded like it was raining outside the theater! What an amazing feeling that was, listening to the sounds around me and being completely fooled like that.

Positional sound is known by many names, including Dolby Digital, DTS, and Surround Sound. LucasFilm developed a standard for high-quality sound production with the THX standard, but THX is related to recording technology, not playback equipment.

Tip

An interesting anecdote: George Lucas named his company's THX sound standard after his first movie as a film student, *THX 1138*. This was a strange "indie" film released in 1971, and from the few clips I've seen, it reminds me a little bit of the more recent movie *The Island*, starring Ewan McGregor, although I've heard some compare it to George Orwell's *1984*.

Positional sound is any sound that incorporates more than two directional sound (left and right). Can you have sound with just two speakers? Using panning, speed, and volume tricks, two speakers can make a sound seem to be behind you or in front of you—so yes, even two speakers can reproduce positional sound.

DarkBASIC incorporates some of the latest technology available with the DirectSound library to use positional sound. DirectSound3D sounds will work on anything from two speakers to a full-blown Dolby Digital system. Direct-Sound allows you to position sound effects anywhere in a virtual room. That's not all, though—it also lets you position the user in the room. So you can sit in your chair and be moved in a whirlwind effect around a room of sound. Planning is key in positional sound. You must keep track of where you are and where your sound is in the virtual room. Confusion will set in if you're hit in the front left of the virtual room, and the sound comes from the back right.

Setting the Source Position

Positioning a sound is a simple process in DarkBASIC. First you load a sound effect as a 3D sound, and then you use the POSITION SOUND command to position it. Finally, you play the sound effect. POSITION SOUND is the most important command for the 3D positioning of a sound effect. It takes a sound effect and positions it in a 3D room. For more information on the fundamentals of 3D, read Chapter 18. Here is the syntax for this command:

```
POSITION SOUND Sound Number, X position, Y position, Z position
```

Here are a few examples of the POSITION SOUND command.

```
POSITION SOUND 5, 700,50,500
POSITION SOUND 6, -20,45,-40
```

The SOUND POSITION X command returns the location of the sound effect on the X plane. The command looks like this:

SOUND POSITION X(Sound Number)

Here are a few examples of the SOUND POSITION X command.

```
tempstring$ = "X pos = "+STR$(SOUND POSITION X(5))
xpos = SOUND POSITION X(6)
```

The SOUND POSITION Y command returns the location of the sound effect on the Y plane. This command has the following format.

SOUND POSITION Y(Sound Number)

Here are a few examples of the SOUND POSITION Y command.

```
tempstring$ = "Y pos = "+STR$(SOUND POSITION Y(5))
ypos = SOUND POSITION Y(6)
```

The SOUND POSITION Z command returns the location of the sound effect on the Z plane. The syntax for this command follows.

SOUND POSITION Z(Sound Number)

The following example shows how to use the POSITION SOUND, SOUND POSITION X, SOUND POSITION Y, and SOUND POSITION Z commands.

Changing the "Listener" Position

The sound effects are now placed in the room. Who is listening to them? What if this listener turns around? Would that reposition all the sound effects? Not really. The sound effects would be in the same locations as they were before, but the orientation of the listener would be different. In DarkBASIC, it is just as easy to orient the listener as it is to move all the sounds. There are two key commands to orient the listener to the positions of the sounds. I recommend trying to place the sounds in the room as if the listener were in the center of the room, facing forward, and then rotating the listener rather than all of the sound sources in the virtual room.

Setting the Listener's Position

The POSITION LISTENER command places the listener somewhere in the virtual room. This affects the audible location of the sound based on where the listener is located. Here is the syntax for this command:

```
POSITION LISTENER X position, Y position, Z position
```

Here are a few examples of the POSITION LISTENER command.

```
POSITION LISTENER 300,0,10
POSITION LISTENER 40,-50,-3
```

Getting the Listener's Position

The LISTENER POSITION X command returns the listener's X position. The syntax for this command follows.

```
LISTENER POSITION X()
```

Here are a few examples of the LISTENER POSITION X command.

```
tempstring$ = "Listener X pos = "+STR$(LISTENER POSITION X())
ListenerX = LISTENER POSITION X()
```

The LISTENER POSITION Y command returns the listener's Y position. This command has the following format.

```
LISTENER POSITION Y()
```

Here are a few examples of the LISTENER POSITION Y command.

```
temptring$ = "Listener Y pos = "+STR$(LISTENER POSITION Y())
ListenerY = LISTENER POSITION Y()
```

The LISTENER POSITION Z command returns the listener's Z position. The command looks like this:

```
LISTENER POSITION Z()
```

Rotating the Listener

The ROTATE LISTENER command faces the listener in the correct direction. This also affects the audible location of the sounds. The sound might be to the right of the listener, but if the listener is facing the sound, it is then in front of him. Here is the syntax for this command:

```
ROTATE LISTENER X angle, Y angle, Z angle
```

Here are a few examples of the ROTATE LISTENER command.

```
ROTATE LISTENER 0,0,45
ROTATE LISTENER 30,15,15
```

Getting the Listener's Rotation Value

The LISTENER ANGLE X command returns the X angle of the listener direction. The command looks like this:

```
LISTENER ANGLE X()
```

Here are a few examples of the LISTENER ANGLE X command.

```
temptring$ = "Listener X angle = "+STR$(LISTENER ANGLE X())
xangle = LISTENER ANGLE X()
```

The LISTENER ANGLE Y command returns the Y angle of the listener direction. This command has the following format.

```
LISTENER ANGLE Y()
```

Here are a few examples of the LISTENER ANGLE Y command.

```
tempstring$ = "Listener Y angle = "+STR$(LISTENER ANGLE Y())
yangle = LISTENER ANGLE Y()
```

The LISTENER ANGLE Z command returns the Z angle of the listener direction. The syntax for this command follows.

```
LISTENER ANGLE Z()
```

The following example shows how to use the ROTATE LISTENER, LISTENER ANGLE X, LISTENER ANGLE Y, and LISTENER ANGLE Z commands.

Music

Take your mind's eye back to one of your favorite TV shows. What sticks out the most about that show? Most people would tend to say that it was funny or had a good story line, but rarely do you hear people mention the background music. The background music, however, is a key component to any form of entertainment. Background music definitely helps you visualize another place and time with a concept called *suspension of disbelief,* in which, for a short time, you are fully immersed in a game (or a TV show or movie, as the case may be). If you are able to accomplish this esoteric manipulation of another person's mind using your own imagination, then you have succeeded in making a great game. A video game without music misses the key opportunity to influence the player's emotions with sound.

Setting the Mood for the Game

Background music can set a mood. Just like a window with light coming through it sets a lighter tone than a room with no windows, background music helps to set the feeling in a game. If a player is being chased by an evil alien, the game music should probably be something fast-paced to get the heart pumping. Or, if the character falls in love with another character, the music should reflect a romantic mood.

How do you choose what mood you want to set for a game? This is simple, but hard at the same time. If your game were full of alien bad guys that you are shooting out of the sky, your mood would be panic. If you were writing an adventure between two star-crossed lovers, your mood would be romantic. The best way to decide a mood is by looking at the overall picture you are producing. Once you've decided that, picking the music is pretty easy. Trust your tastes in music. If the music makes you feel energized, put it in an action-packed part of your game.

Loading Music Files

All this talk about music has probably made you wonder, "Okay, how do I add music to my game?" DarkBASIC supports two key music file formats: MIDI and MP3.

MIDI (*Musical Instrument Direct Interface*) is a synthesized format of music playback. A MIDI song is a collection of music notes stored in a file that are rendered by your computer's sound card. In other words, MIDI is not digital in the sense that music has been recorded. Instead, a MIDI song is played based on the notes for a song. The normal extension of a MIDI file is .mid. MIDIs are generally created using a combination of software and hardware.

A good piece of professional software is a program like Cakewalk's Sonar. A good piece of professional hardware is a Yamaha synthesizer. Most people, however, cannot afford such high-grade stuff, so there are alternatives. You can find many low-cost software alternatives by searching the Internet for MIDI software. You can also find a good sound card and a cheap synthesizer to handle the hardware side. I use a Casio keyboard with the Sound Blaster Live audio card in my computer. You can also find MIDIs on the Internet. You don't have to generate the songs yourself to get good songs; just doing a search of the Internet can be fruitful.

MIDI and MP3

MIDIs are smaller than MP3s. This is because there is no digital sound stored in a MIDI. A MIDI song is more like a piece of sheet music than an actual digital recording. So depending on your sound card, MIDIs can sound really good or really bad. In the old days (early to mid 1990s) sound cards would synthesize (or generate) the instruments in a MIDI. A modern Sound Blaster card now makes MIDIs sound really good because it uses digitized instruments instead of synthesized instruments. They have prerecorded wave files on the sound card that represent each instrument.

MP3s are more popular today than MIDI because they are a highly compressed digital sound format. MP3s with good compressed sound can run near CD quality music at about 1 MB per minute (44KHz, 16 bit). MP3s can be found all over the Internet, in most offices, or even on some of your favorite games (*Age of Empires 2* is one example).

Why use one format over the other? Well, if you are concerned about space in your game, a good way to save some room is to use a MIDI instead of an MP3. A MIDI (using a good quality sound card) will be about 30 kilobytes for a 3 minute song, whereas the same song in MP3 format will be about 3 MB. However, because MIDI is more sheet music like, it may not be suitable for all situations. Any instrument that is not loaded into the sound card will not play. So if you need instruments not readily available via MIDI, your best bet would be to use the MP3 format.

Loading a Music File

The LOAD MUSIC command loads a MIDI file or an MP3 file into a specific music slot in the memory. The song number must be an integer. There can be a maximum of 32 songs loaded into memory at one time. Here is the syntax for this command:

LOAD MUSIC *Filename, Music Number*

Note

> You can never have more then 32 songs loaded into memory at any one time. Keep this in mind when creating music tracks. Normally you will only use one song at a time, but DarkBASIC gives you the ability to load more than one track into memory.

Deleting a Previously Loaded Song

The DELETE MUSIC command removes a MIDI file from a specific music number. This is useful when you are trying to conserve memory because it frees up a music number. The format for this command follows.

DELETE MUSIC *Music Number*

Playing Music

Now you will attack the most important background music commands—the playback commands. These commands are pretty simple, yet very powerful. They give you control over the state of the background music.

The PLAY MUSIC command starts a music number playing. This command always starts at the beginning of the music and plays to the end. The command looks like this:

PLAY MUSIC *Music Number*

Here is an example of how to use the PLAY MUSIC command:

```
LOAD MUSIC "TitleMusic.mid", 20
PLAY MUSIC 20
```

The LOOP MUSIC command starts a music number playing and looping. This command always starts at the beginning of the music, plays to the end, and loops back to the beginning. This command has the following format.

LOOP MUSIC *Music Number*

The STOP MUSIC command stops any music number that is playing or looping. Once a music number is stopped, it will only play from the beginning again. The syntax for this command follows.

```
STOP MUSIC Music number
```

The PAUSE MUSIC command pauses any music at the point at which it is playing. This command has this format:

```
PAUSE MUSIC Music Number
```

Following is a short snippet of code that demonstrates how to use the PAUSE MUSIC command.

```
LOAD MUSIC "TitleMusic.mid", 20
PLAY MUSIC 20
SLEEP 1000
PAUSE MUSIC 20
```

The RESUME MUSIC command resumes playback of a song from the position where it was previously paused. The command has this format:

```
RESUME MUSIC Music Number
```

Here is an example of the RESUME MUSIC command:

```
LOAD MUSIC "TitleMusic.mid",20
PLAY MUSIC 20
SLEEP 1000
PAUSE MUSIC 20
SLEEP 1000
RESUME MUSIC 20
```

Music Playback Properties

Some of the most important commands in music playback are the music playback properties. These give you limited control over what music is playing and when. They are useful when you are trying to determine the status of the music.

Checking the Validity of a Song

The MUSIC EXIST command determines whether a song has been loaded into memory in the music slot specified by the *Music Number* parameter. The command returns a 1 if the song exists, or a 0 if it does not. The syntax for this command is

```
Value = MUSIC EXIST( Music Number )
```

Determining when a Song Is Playing

The MUSIC PLAYING command lets you know whether a music number is currently playing. There can only be one background music number playing at a time. This command returns 0 if the music number is not playing and 1 if it is. Here is the syntax for this command:

```
Value = MUSIC PLAYING( Music Number )
```

Here is a snippet of code that demonstrates how to use the MUSIC PLAYING command:

```
LOAD MUSIC "TitleMusic.mid",20
PLAY MUSIC (20)
While MUSIC PLAYING(20) = 1
Endwhile
STOP MUSIC (20)
```

Checking Playback Flags

The MUSIC LOOPING command lets you know whether a music number is looping. This is different from checking whether a music number is playing because a loop will play the number continuously. This command returns a 0 if the music number is not playing and a 1 if it is. The format for this command follows.

```
Value = MUSIC LOOPING( Music Number )
```

The MUSIC PAUSED command lets you know whether the music number is paused. Pausing music can be a good dramatic effect. The command looks like this:

```
Value = MUSIC PAUSED( Music Number )
```

Here is an example of how to use the MUSIC PAUSED command:

```
LOAD MUSIC "TitleMusic.mid",20
PLAY MUSIC 20
SLEEP 1000
PAUSE MUSIC 20
```

```
WHILE MUSIC PAUSED(20) = 1
   IF(MOUSEKEY() = 1) THEN RESUME MUSIC 20
ENDWHILE
```

Enhancing Darkanoid

Well, it's time to put the final touches on our Darkanoid game. It's been in development for a long time now, since way back in Chapter 10, so I'm going to miss it! But we have bigger and better games to write in future chapters so it's time to wrap up this game and move on. Since this is the final chapter for work on Darkanoid, I want to finish it off with a bang, so there are a lot of changes to put into the game. Even so, the possibilities for this game are endless, and I've had to scrap a lot of features that I wanted to put into the game for the sake of time. Here are the new features that you will find in the game this chapter:

- Improved collision code

- Added scoring

- Added game state

- Added "lives"

- Added powerups

- Added explosions

- Added sound effects and music

- Added auto play mode

Originally, I had many more powerups than you will see in the game at this point, but I've had to cut back to just four powerups. One of the interesting powerups that I wanted to see in the game was a roaming animated eyeball that did not collide with the paddle or blocks—just the ball. So it would roam around on the screen until the ball hits it, at which point you would get a huge bonus added to your score. However, I feel that there is enough of a framework in the game at this point that you will be able to add features such as this on your own.

Another feature that I would have liked to add is a special effect that draws a shadow under every sprite in the game. At present, the blocks, paddle, and other objects look nice, but a shadow underneath them would dramatically improve the appearance of the game. I would use the set sprite alpha command to draw a darker version of each sprite slightly offset before drawing the regular image, and that would simulate a shadow image.

Multiple Game Levels

One of the biggest changes in the game now is that it supports multiple levels of tiles. When you clear the tiles in level 1, the game loads up level 2 and you can continue playing rather than just repeating the same level over and over. Figure 14.2 shows the first level of the game.

Since the game levels are stored inside the source code using data statements, I've moved them into a separate source code file called levels.dba. You can add as many source code files to your DB project as you want by clicking the Files button at the bottom-right corner of the IDE, as shown in Figure 14.3.

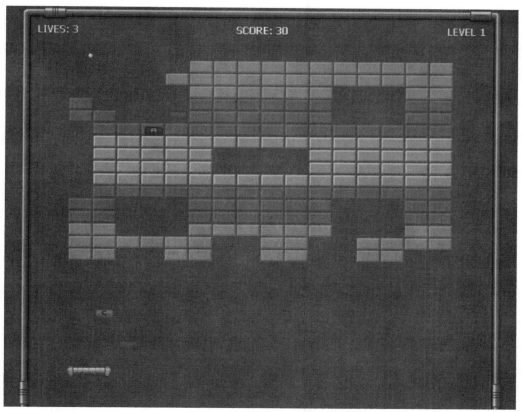

Figure 14.2
The first level of Darkanoid.

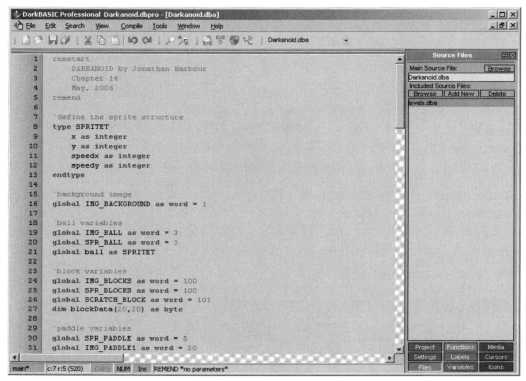

Figure 14.3
The list of source code files in the project. Note the highlighted Files button at the bottom right.

Tip

If your DB is still in tutorial mode, which shows the help system at the right instead of the project manager mode, then you will need to switch to PM mode. First, click the small "X" at the top right corner of the tutorial mode window. You will be told that the project must be closed and re-opened. Go ahead and save your project and then switch to PM mode and re-open your project. DB will be in PM mode from now on. Tutorial mode might be good for beginners, but at a certain point you will need to take control of the project settings, files, and so on.

If you look in the list of Source Files in Figure 14.3, you'll notice that Darkanoid.dba is not in the list. That is because the main source code file for your project is always open and is *assumed* to be in the project already. Think of the Source Files list as a list of *additional* files in your project.

Click the Add New button at the top of the list to add a new file called levels.dba. Here are the first three levels of the game as I have designed them. Feel free to change the levels to your liking, and you may also add new levels too. To add a new level, just add one to the NUM_LEVELS data entry at the top and then add another level to the bottom with the appropriate label. For instance, to add the 4th level to the game, you can copy the entire level 3 data and paste it at the bottom of the code listing, and then rename it to LEVEL4. It's easier to modify an existing level than to create one from scratch. By following this technique, you can add as many new levels to the game as you want. Just remember that there are only eight tiles available, unless you add more tile images yourself.

After adding a couple more levels you'll see why I chose to move the level data to another source code file, because it can get really long, which would make it harder to browse through the source listing of the main program. In the same manner, if you have written some functions that don't need to be modified very often, go ahead and move them to another source code file in the project to clean up your main source listing. When a game starts to get really large, organizing your code is a time saver because scrolling through hundreds or thousands of lines of code is difficult. Figure 14.4 shows level 2 of the game.

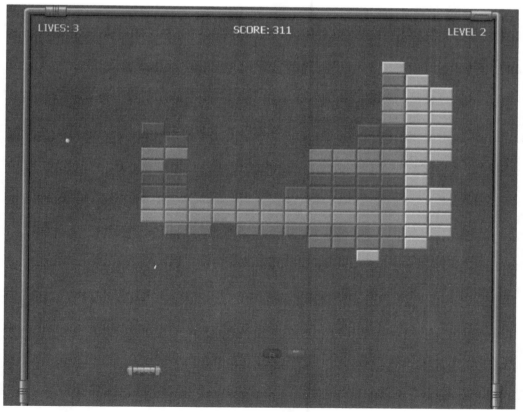

Figure 14.4
Level 2 of Darkanoid.

Tip

DarkBASIC combines all of the source code files in your project into a single, long source file before it is compiled. So, you may put any code you want in separate source files and all of your code will be visible to all of your other code. For instance, you can put reusable functions in a separate file, and call them from your main program file.

```
NUM_LEVELS:
data 3

LEVEL1:
data 5,5,5,5,5,5,5,5,5,5,5,5,5,5,5,5
data 5,5,5,5,5,5,5,5,5,5,5,5,5,5,5,5
data 5,5,0,0,0,5,5,5,5,5,5,0,0,0,5,5
data 6,6,0,0,0,6,6,6,6,6,6,0,0,0,6,6
data 6,6,0,0,0,6,6,6,6,6,6,0,0,0,6,6
data 6,6,6,6,6,6,6,6,6,6,6,6,6,6,6,6
data 4,4,4,4,4,4,4,4,4,4,4,4,4,4,4,4
data 4,4,4,4,4,4,0,0,0,0,4,4,4,4,4,4
data 4,4,4,4,4,4,0,0,0,0,4,4,4,4,4,4
data 4,4,4,4,4,4,4,4,4,4,4,4,4,4,4,4
data 6,6,6,6,6,6,6,6,6,6,6,6,6,6,6,6
data 6,6,0,0,0,6,6,6,6,6,6,0,0,0,6,6
data 6,6,0,0,0,6,6,6,6,6,6,0,0,0,6,6
data 5,5,0,0,0,5,5,5,5,5,5,0,0,0,5,5
data 5,5,5,5,5,5,5,5,5,5,5,5,5,5,5,5
data 5,5,5,5,5,5,5,5,5,5,5,5,5,5,5,5

LEVEL2:
data 1,1,1,1,1,1,1,1,1,1,1,1,1,1,1,1
data 1,1,2,2,2,2,2,2,2,2,2,2,2,2,1,1
data 1,1,2,2,2,2,2,2,2,2,2,2,2,2,1,1
data 1,1,3,3,3,3,3,3,3,3,3,3,3,3,1,1
data 1,1,3,3,3,3,3,3,3,3,3,3,3,3,1,1
data 1,1,7,7,7,7,7,7,7,7,7,7,7,7,1,1
data 1,1,7,7,7,7,7,7,7,7,7,7,7,7,1,1
data 1,1,8,8,8,8,8,8,8,8,8,8,8,8,1,1
data 1,1,8,8,8,8,8,8,8,8,8,8,8,8,1,1
data 1,1,7,7,7,7,7,7,7,7,7,7,7,7,1,1
data 1,1,7,7,7,7,7,7,7,7,7,7,7,7,1,1
data 1,1,3,3,3,3,3,3,3,3,3,3,3,3,1,1
data 1,1,3,3,3,3,3,3,3,3,3,3,3,3,1,1
data 1,1,2,2,2,2,2,2,2,2,2,2,2,2,1,1
data 1,1,2,2,2,2,2,2,2,2,2,2,2,2,1,1
data 1,1,1,1,1,1,1,1,1,1,1,1,1,1,1,1
```

```
LEVEL3:
data 5,5,5,5,5,5,5,5,5,5,5,5,5,5,5,5
data 5,5,5,5,5,5,5,5,5,5,5,5,5,5,5,5
data 5,5,0,0,0,5,5,5,5,5,5,0,0,0,5,5
data 6,6,0,0,0,6,6,6,6,6,6,0,0,0,6,6
data 6,6,0,0,0,6,6,6,6,6,6,0,0,0,6,6
data 6,6,6,6,6,6,6,6,6,6,6,6,6,6,6,6
data 4,4,4,4,4,4,4,4,4,4,4,4,4,4,4,4
data 4,4,4,4,4,4,0,0,0,0,4,4,4,4,4,4
data 4,4,4,4,4,4,0,0,0,0,4,4,4,4,4,4
data 4,4,4,4,4,4,4,4,4,4,4,4,4,4,4,4
data 6,6,6,6,6,6,6,6,6,6,6,6,6,6,6,6
data 6,6,0,0,0,6,6,6,6,6,6,0,0,0,6,6
data 6,6,0,0,0,6,6,6,6,6,6,0,0,0,6,6
data 5,5,0,0,0,5,5,5,5,5,5,0,0,0,5,5
data 5,5,5,5,5,5,5,5,5,5,5,5,5,5,5,5
data 5,5,5,5,5,5,5,5,5,5,5,5,5,5,5,5
```

Variable Declarations

At the top of the main source code file, the LEVEL1 data statements have been moved to the levels.dba file, so that is the first casualty in the new regime of the game. Now let's go over the changes and additions to the variables and constants used in the game. If you would prefer to just open up the completed game for this chapter, you will find it on the CD-ROM under \sources\chapter14. Since so many dramatic changes have been made to the game, I will just go over the complete listing. You will see a lot of familiar code from Chapter 12, but it would be too difficult to point out all of the changes, so I'll go over the entire game with you.

The variable declarations section at the top of the program defines not just variables but also many constant values used throughout the game. By using constants (such as SPR_BALL) it is much easier to modify the code, whereas using literals (such as 3) makes the code harder to read. You just have to be careful about spelling since DB does not enforce variable names, and a misspelled variable is a very hard bug to track down.

```
remstart
   Project: DARKANOID GAME
   Source: Chapter 14
   Date:   May, 2006
remend
```

```
'define the sprite structure
type SPRITET
   x as integer
   y as integer
   speedx as integer
   speedy as integer
endtype

'background image
global IMG_BACKGROUND as word = 1

'ball variables
global IMG_BALL as word = 3
global SPR_BALL as word = 3
global ball as SPRITET

'block variables
global IMG_BLOCKS as word = 100
global SPR_BLOCKS as word = 100
global SCRATCH_BLOCK as word = 101
dim blockData(20,20) as byte

'paddle variables
global SPR_PADDLE as word = 5
global IMG_PADDLE1 as word = 20
global IMG_PADDLE2 as word = 21
global IMG_PADDLE3 as word = 22
global paddle as SPRITET
global paddleImage as word = IMG_PADDLE1

'game state variables
global gameState as byte = 2
global autoPlay as byte = 0
global score as dword = 0
global level as word = 0
global maxlevels as word
global lives as byte = 3

'powerup states
global SPR_POWERUP as word = 10
global SCRATCH_POWERUP as word = 14
dim powerups(4) as byte
dim powerupImage(4) as byte
```

```
'for blowing stuff up
global SPR_EXPLOSION as word = 15
dim explosionTimer(4) as byte
dim explosions(4) as byte

'sound effects
global SND_PADDLE as byte = 1
global SND_BLOCK as byte = 2
global SND_WIN as byte = 3
global SND_GONG as byte = 4
global SND_POWERUP2 as byte = 5
global SND_POWERUP1 as byte = 6
global SND_POWERUP3 as byte = 7
global SND_POWERUP4 as byte = 8
```

The few lines after the variable declarations section get the game moving. First, Init_Game() initializes all of the variables, loads the graphics and sounds, and prepares the game to run. Secondly, the Run_Game() function is called, and this function contains the game loop which does all of the real work. Finally, the game is shut down by calling the end command, which comes up when you hit the Esc key to exit out of Run_Game().

```
'start game running
Init_Game()
Run_Game()
END
```

Initializing the Game

The Init_Game() function initializes all of the variables, loads the game resources, and gets the ball rolling, so to speak. You will notice a lot of familiar code, but it has changed significantly since the last version of the game.

```
function Init_Game()
    sync on
    sync rate 40
    hide mouse
    randomize timer()
    'load background
    load image "background.bmp", IMG_BACKGROUND
```

```
'load paddle
load image "paddle1.bmp", IMG_PADDLE1
sprite SPR_PADDLE, 999, 999, IMG_PADDLE1
paddle.X = SCREEN WIDTH() / 2 - SPRITE WIDTH(SPR_PADDLE) / 2
paddle.Y = SCREEN HEIGHT() - 50
load image "paddle2.bmp", IMG_PADDLE2
load image "paddle3.bmp", IMG_PADDLE3

'load the ball
load image "ball.bmp", IMG_BALL
sprite SPR_BALL, 999, 999, IMG_BALL
ball.speedx = 1
ball.SpeedY = -1

'load the blocks
create animated sprite SPR_BLOCKS, "blocks.bmp", 4, 2, IMG_BLOCKS
set sprite frame SPR_BLOCKS, 1
sprite SPR_BLOCKS, 999, 999, IMG_BLOCKS
load image "block_outline.bmp", SCRATCH_BLOCK
sprite SCRATCH_BLOCK, 999, 999, SCRATCH_BLOCK
Load_Level()

'load explosion animation
create animated sprite SPR_EXPLOSION, "explosion.bmp", 7, 1, SPR_EXPLOSION
for n = 1 to 3
   clone sprite SPR_EXPLOSION, SPR_EXPLOSION + n
next n

'load the powerup animations
powerups(0) = 0
powerups(1) = 0
powerups(2) = 0
powerups(3) = 0
create animated sprite SPR_POWERUP, "powerupa.bmp", 1, 7, SPR_POWERUP
create animated sprite SPR_POWERUP+1, "powerupb.bmp", 1, 7, SPR_POWERUP+1
create animated sprite SPR_POWERUP+2, "powerupc.bmp", 1, 7, SPR_POWERUP+2
create animated sprite SPR_POWERUP+3, "powerupd.bmp", 1, 7, SPR_POWERUP+3
load image "powerup_outline.bmp", SCRATCH_POWERUP
sprite SCRATCH_POWERUP, 999, 999, SCRATCH_POWERUP

'load sound effects
load sound "paddle.wav", SND_PADDLE
load sound "block.wav", SND_BLOCK
```

```
load sound "medal.wav", SND_WIN
load sound "cork.wav", SND_POWERUP1
load sound "boing.wav", SND_POWERUP2
load sound "axe.wav", SND_POWERUP3
load sound "crush.wav", SND_POWERUP4
load sound "gong.wav", SND_GONG
play sound SND_GONG

'*** uncomment and insert your own favorite MP3 song here ***
'load music "music.mp3", 1
'loop music 1
'set music volume 1, 40

rem Setup nice font
set text font "Tahoma"
set text size 14
set text to bold
endfunction
```

The Game Loop

The main function that contains the game loop is Run_Game(). This function takes into account the game state, which determines what is currently happening in the game. Game state 1 is the normal gameplay mode. When you miss the ball, then you lose a life and the game state goes into state 2, where the ball follows the paddle and waits for the player to launch it with the mouse button. Game state 3 occurs when you have lost all lives and the game has ended. Clicking the mouse button at this point will restart the game from the beginning. Study this function well, because it is the heart of the game.

```
function Run_Game()
    rem Main loop
    do
        'draw background
        paste image IMG_BACKGROUND, 0, 0

        'move the paddle with the mouse
        Move_Paddle()

        'move the ball based on game state
        SELECT gameState
            'normal gameplay state
```

```
      case 1:
         Draw_Blocks()
         Move_Ball()
         Check_Collision()
         Move_Powerups()
         Draw_Explosions()
         endcase
      'lost a life-ball following paddle state

      CASE 2:
         Draw_Blocks()
         Move_Powerups()
         Track_Ball()
         if mouseclick() = 1 then gameState = 1
         endcase
      'game over state

      CASE 3:
         'hide all sprites
         center text screen width() / 2, screen height() / 2, "GAME OVER"
         lives = 3
         if mouseclick() = 1
            autoPlay = 1
            gameState = 2
            score = 0
            level = 0
            Load_Level()
            wait 1000
         endif
         endcase
   endselect

   'print number of lives left
   ink rgb(0,255,128), 0
   text 40, 20, "LIVES: " + str$(lives)

   'print the score
   ink rgb(255,255,0),0
   center text screen width()/2,20, "SCORE: " + str$(score)

   'print the current level
   ink rgb(128,255,128), 0
```

```
    temp as string
    temp = "LEVEL " + str$(level)
    text screen width() - text width(temp) - 40, 20, temp

    sync

    if inkey$() = "a" then autoPlay = 1
    if escapekey() = 1 then exit
  loop
endfunction
```

Drawing the Blocks

The Draw_Blocks() function draws the blocks that are visible based on the blockData array. This array has room for 20 blocks across, and 20 blocks down, but only 16 are used in each direction. You could fill in more of the screen by using 18 or 20 blocks, but then you would need to change the starting location for the first block, which is drawn at pixel location (50,50). If you add more blocks, you will need to modify the Load_Level() function and modify the level data as well. I prefer to have an empty region around the edges of the blocks so the ball can get up there to do some damage. But classic games like *Arkanoid* usually give you a solid mass of blocks and you have to clear a path up to the top. The neat thing about getting the ball up to the top of the screen is that it will usually bounce around up there for a long time, wiping out scads of blocks in the process and quickly clearing the level.

In addition to drawing, this function also performs collision testing to determine when the ball hits a block. Normally, this would have gone into the Test_Collision() function, but it was easier to put the collision test here while the blocks are being drawn. Since the two for loops are already in place for going through the blockData array to do the drawing, it's a convenient place to test for collision as well. The SCRATCH_BLOCK constant represents a temporary block that is used for collision testing, because the real block image is a sprite sheet with a much larger width and height, so that would mess up the collision result.

Lastly, this function determines when the entire level has been cleared. When all the blocks have been destroyed, the player gets a huge bonus added to the score, the next level is loaded, and the game waits for the player to launch the ball again (game state 2).

```
function Draw_Blocks()
   w = sprite width(SCRATCH_BLOCK) + 1
   h = sprite height(SCRATCH_BLOCK) + 1
   blockCount = 0
   for x = 1 to 16
     for y = 1 to 16
       if blockData(x,y) > 0
          inc blockCount

          'set temporary sprite to test for collision
          sprite SCRATCH_BLOCK, 50 + w * x, 50 + h * y, SCRATCH_BLOCK
          hide sprite SCRATCH_BLOCK

          'draw the block
          dx = 50 + w * x
          dy = 50 + h * y
          set sprite frame SPR_BLOCKS, blockData(x,y)
          paste sprite SPR_BLOCKS, dx, dy

          'check for collision with ball
          if sprite collision(SCRATCH_BLOCK, SPR_BALL) = 1
             play sound SND_BLOCK
             blockData(x,y) = 0
             score = score + 1
             Bounce_Off_Block()
             if rnd(10) < 4 then Launch_Powerup(dx,dy)
          endif

       endif
     next y
   next x

   'check for cleared blocks
   if blockCount = 0
      play sound SND_WIN
      gameState = 2     'launch mode
      score = score + 500
      powerups(0) = 0
      powerups(1) = 0
      powerups(2) = 0
      powerups(3) = 0
      ball.x = paddle.x
      Load_Level()
   endif
endfunction
```

Loading the Levels

The Load_Level() function supports more than one level (where the levels are defined as data statements). The first data statement in the program should be the total number of levels, which is read first. This value is used to determine when the game should loop around back to level 1 after the last level has been completed. Figure 14.5 shows level 3 of the game.

```
function Load_Level()
    'read the number of levels
    restore
    read maxlevel

    'go to the next level
    level = level + 1
```

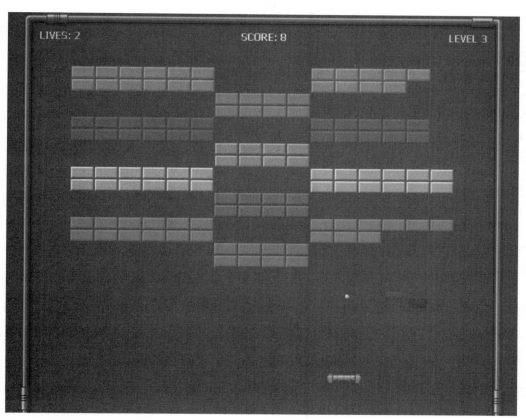

Figure 14.5
Level 3 of Darkanoid.

```
    if level > maxlevel then level = 1

    'jump to the start of the level data
    select level
       case 1: restore LEVEL1: endcase
       case 2: restore LEVEL2: endcase
       case 3: restore LEVEL3: endcase

       'add more levels here
    endselect

    'read the level data
    for y = 1 to 16
       for x = 1 to 16
          read blockData(x,y)
       next x
    next y
endfunction
```

Rebounding the Ball Realistically

The most important aspect of a ball-and-paddle game like this is making sure the ball bounces off the paddle and blocks realistically—or rather, fairly. This genre of game was epitomized by *Arkanoid* and *Breakout*, which set a standard that I have followed here for moving the ball. When you move the paddle so that the ball hits it in the center, the ball will just bounce back up at the same rate. But if you hit the ball from the right or left side of the paddle, it will add "English" to the ball (a term borrowed from Snooker and Billiards), causing the ball to move more in that direction. This feature allows you to rebound the ball in the direction you want in order to hit certain blocks.

```
function Bounce_Off_Paddle()
   'get the ball center
   ax = sprite x(SPR_BALL) + sprite width(SPR_BALL) / 2
   ay = sprite y(SPR_BALL) + sprite height(SPR_BALL) / 2

   'get the paddle center
   bx = sprite x(SPR_PADDLE) + sprite width(SPR_PADDLE) / 2
   by = sprite y(SPR_PADDLE) + sprite height(SPR_PADDLE) / 2

   'get paddle edges
   left = sprite x(SPR_PADDLE)
   right = sprite x(SPR_PADDLE) + sprite width(SPR_PADDLE)
```

```
'ball hits left edge of paddle
if ax < left + 6
   ball.speedx = 0 - rnd(4) - 4
else
   if ax < left + 12
      ball.speedx = 0 - rnd(2) - 2
   endif
endif

'ball hits right edge of paddle
if ax > right - 6
   ball.speedx = rnd(4) + 4
else
   if ax > right - 12
      ball.speedx = rnd(2) + 2
   endif
endif

'set ball y direction to up
ball.speedy = 0 - rnd(4) - 4

endfunction
```

Rebounding off the Blocks

The code to rebound off the blocks should not be quite as *intelligent* as the paddle rebound code, because we really don't want any "English" with the blocks. Instead, the ball should just rebound off all four edges of a block as realistically as possible, without hitting any other blocks at the same time.

```
function Bounce_Off_Block()
   'get the ball center
   ax = sprite x(SPR_BALL) + sprite width(SPR_BALL) / 2
   ay = sprite y(SPR_BALL) + sprite height(SPR_BALL) / 2

   'get the block center
   bx = sprite x(SCRATCH_BLOCK) + sprite width(SCRATCH_BLOCK) / 2
   by = sprite y(SCRATCH_BLOCK) + sprite height(SCRATCH_BLOCK) / 2

   'get block edges
   left = sprite x(SCRATCH_BLOCK)
   right = sprite x(SCRATCH_BLOCK) + sprite width(SCRATCH_BLOCK)
```

```
'if ball hits the far left edge, treat it as a left edge hit
if ax < left + 1
  ball.speedx = abs(ball.speedx) * -1
else

  'if ball hits the far right edge, treat it as a right edge hit
  if ax > right - 1
    ball.speedx = abs(ball.speedx)
  else

    'now just handle top or bottom edge hits normally
    if ay < by
      ball.speedy = abs(ball.speedy) * -1
    else
      ball.speedy = abs(ball.speedy)
    endif

  endif
endif

endfunction
```

Drawing Explosions

The code to draw explosions comes next. This function just updates the explosion animation for any active explosions, which occur when the paddle hits a powerup.

```
function Draw_Explosions()
  'draw any explosions currently in process
  for n = 0 to 3
    if explosions(n) = 1
      num = SPR_EXPLOSION + n
      if timer() > explosionTimer(n) + 400
        explosions(n) = 0
        hide sprite num
      endif
      play sprite num, 1, 7, 40
      paste sprite num, sprite x(num), sprite y(num)
    endif
  next n
endfunction
```

Moving the Ball

The code to move the ball is just a simple screen bouncing behavior that keeps the ball inside the screen. The last section of code just checks to see if the ball dropped past the paddle, at which point the player loses a life and has to launch the ball again.

```
function Move_Ball()
   'move the ball in the X direction
   ball.x = ball.x + ball.speedx

   'bounce the ball off the right and left edges
   if ball.x < 30
     ball.x = 30
     ball.speedx = ball.speedx * -1
   endif
   if ball.x > screen width() - 35
     ball.x = screen width() - 35
     ball.speedx = ball.speedx * -1
   endif

   'move the ball in the Y direction
   ball.y = ball.y + ball.speedy

   'bounce the ball off the top edge
   if ball.y < 20
     ball.y = 20
     ball.speedy = ball.speedy * -1
   endif

   'hit the bottom edge...you lose!
   if ball.y > screen height() - 6
     lives = lives - 1
     if lives < 1
       gameState = 3
     else
       gameState = 2
     endif
   endif

   'draw the ball
   sprite SPR_BALL, ball.x, ball.y, IMG_BALL
endfunction
```

Tracking the Ball in Pause Mode

Whenever the game is in state 2, the ball follows the paddle as it prepares to be launched by the player (using the mouse button). This state occurs at the start of the program, whenever you lose a life, and when the game is over.

```
function Track_Ball()
   'attach the ball to the top of the paddle
   ball.X = paddle.X + sprite width(SPR_PADDLE) / 2 - sprite width(SPR_BALL) / 2
   ball.Y = paddle.y - 10
   ball.speedx = rnd(2) + 1
   ball.speedy = rnd(2) - 6
   'draw the ball
   sprite SPR_BALL, ball.x, ball.y, IMG_BALL
endfunction
```

Moving the Paddle

The code to move the paddle just causes the paddle to move left or right based on mouse motion information. The Move_Paddle() function also makes it possible to use the "auto play" feature (which is invoked by pressing the "a" key). In auto play mode, the paddle will automatically follow the ball. The rest of the code keeps the paddle inside the screen boundary.

```
function Move_Paddle()
   'get mouse movement value
   m = mousemovex()
   if m <> 0
      paddle.X = paddle.X + m
      autoPlay = 0
   endif

   'autoplay mode?
   if autoPlay = 1
      centerx = paddle.x + sprite width(SPR_PADDLE)/2
      if ball.x < centerx - 2 then dec paddle.x, 6
      if ball.x > centerx + 2 then inc paddle.x, 6
   endif

   'move the paddle based on mouse movement
   if paddle.x < 30 then paddle.x = 30
   right = screen width() - sprite width(SPR_PADDLE) - 30
```

```
  if paddle.x > right
     paddle.x = right
  endif

  'draw the paddle
  sprite SPR_PADDLE, paddle.x, paddle.y, paddleImage
endfunction
```

Checking for Collisions

The Check_Collision() function tests for collisions between the paddle and the ball, and the paddle and powerups. The collision testing for ball and blocks occurs in the Draw_Blocks() function (where it is more convenient). Depending on the type of powerup, different things happen, which accounts for the large size of this function. You can add new powerups to the game using the basic template provided here for dealing with a certain powerup number.

```
function Check_Collision()
   'hit ball?
   if sprite collision(SPR_PADDLE, SPR_BALL) = 1
      Bounce_Off_Paddle()
      play sound SND_PADDLE
   endif

   'powerup 1 makes paddle small
   if powerups(0) = 1
    if sprite collision(SPR_PADDLE, SPR_POWERUP)
      play sound SND_POWERUP1
      Explode(sprite x(SPR_POWERUP), sprite y(SPR_POWERUP))
      powerups(0) = 0
      paddleImage = IMG_PADDLE1
      hide sprite SPR_POWERUP
    endif
   endif

  'powerup 2 makes paddle medium
  if powerups(1) = 1
     if sprite collision(SPR_PADDLE, SPR_POWERUP+1)
        play sound SND_POWERUP2
        Explode(sprite x(SPR_POWERUP+1), sprite y(SPR_POWERUP+1))
        powerups(1) = 0
        paddleImage = IMG_PADDLE2
```

```
            hide sprite SPR_POWERUP+1
        endif
    endif

    'powerup 3 makes paddle big
    if powerups(2) = 1
        if sprite collision(SPR_PADDLE, SPR_POWERUP+2)
            play sound SND_POWERUP3
            Explode(sprite x(SPR_POWERUP+2), sprite y(SPR_POWERUP+2))
            powerups(2) = 0
            paddleImage = IMG_PADDLE3
            hide sprite SPR_POWERUP+2
        endif
    endif

    'powerup 4 gains extra life and 50 points
    if powerups(3) = 1
        if sprite collision(SPR_PADDLE, SPR_POWERUP+3)
            play sound SND_POWERUP4
            lives = lives + 1
            score = score + 50
            Explode(sprite x(SPR_POWERUP+3), sprite y(SPR_POWERUP+3))
            powerups(3) = 0
            hide sprite SPR_POWERUP+3
        endif
    endif
endfunction
```

Launching Powerups

Any time the ball destroys a block, there is a 40% chance that it will generate a powerup. This is a small animated object that "rolls" down the screen toward the bottom. If you grab a powerup with the paddle, then you have various things happen in the game. I have defined four powerups in the game so far. The first three powerups change the paddle size to small, medium (normal), or large. The fourth powerup gives the player an extra life and 50 bonus points. Launch_Powerup() just creates a new powerup based on the current powerups in use. The function doesn't create a *random* powerup, but simply launches the *next* powerup that is available. If all four powerups are already in use, then nothing happens.

```
function Launch_Powerup(x as word, y as word)
    for n = 0 to 3
```

```
      if (powerups(n) = 0)
         powerups(n) = 1
         sprite SPR_POWERUP+n, x, y, 10
         exit
      endif
   next n
endfunction
```

Moving the Powerups

The function to update the position and animation frame of the powerups is called Move_Powerups(). This function looks at all four powerups to determine which ones are currently active, and then updates them.

```
function Move_Powerups()
   for n = 0 to 3
      if powerups(n) = 1
         num = SPR_POWERUP + n
         x = sprite x(num)
         y = sprite y(num) + 2
         'draw powerup image
         sprite num, x, y, SPR_POWERUP
         play sprite num, 1, 7, 50 + rnd(5)
         paste sprite num, x, y
         if sprite y(num) > screen height() - 10 then powerups(n) = 0
      else
         hide sprite n+10
      endif

   next n
endfunction
```

Creating Explosions

To spice up the game a little, there is an explosion whenever the player catches a powerup. This is just a small effect, but the result is worth the effort because the quick explosions really highlight the fact that the player has caught a powerup. The Explode() function accepts two parameters, x and y, that determine where the new explosion should occur. There are only four explosions available, and if they are all being used, then nothing happens.

```
function Explode(x,y)
   for n = 0 to 3
      if explosions(n) = 0
         explosions(n) = 1
         sprite SPR_EXPLOSION + n, x, y, SPR_EXPLOSION + n
         explosionTimer(n) = Timer()
      endif
   next n
endfunction
```

Summary

Well, that was certainly a lot of changes to the Darkanoid game, but it is now finished! The game is complete according to the goals I set out for it back in Chapter 10. The end result is a fun game that is not too complicated so you can add new features and tweak the gameplay without wading through too much source code.

Before getting into the final Darkanoid project here, this chapter covered all of the sound effects and music commands in DarkBASIC. Sound effects are essential in creating games that have dynamic output, because sound helps the player become immersed in the game. Good sound effects significantly improve the overall game experience. Along with nice-looking graphics, well-considered sound effects and music are essential for setting the mood of a game.

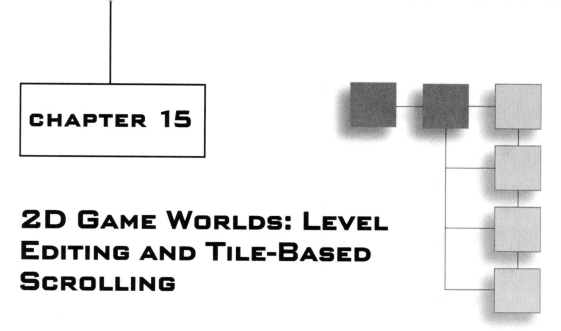

CHAPTER 15

2D GAME WORLDS: LEVEL EDITING AND TILE-BASED SCROLLING

Tile-based scrolling arcade games have a history that goes way back to the 1980s, when games like *Akari Warriors* and *Contra* ruled the arcades and game systems. While IBM PC users were stuck playing text adventures and ASCII role-playing games (in which your player was represented by @ or P), most gamers using Atari and Amiga computers were playing with tile-based scrolling, hardware-accelerated sprites, and digital sound. Back in the old days, the technique presented in this chapter to scroll a background was a necessity because system memory was so limited. We take for granted a gigabyte of memory today, but that figure was unbelievable in the 1980s and 90s. Virtual screen buffers were very limited because they were designed for video cards with 256 to 1024 KB of video memory. You were lucky to have a 320 × 240 screen and a back buffer for smooth animation, let alone enough memory for a large scrolling world. This chapter focuses on creating tile-based backgrounds with scrolling using tiles just like they did *in the old days*. It turns out that even today this is still the easiest way to do a scrolling game world. DB has no built-in scrolling functionality, but that has never stopped us before so we'll just learn how to do it ourselves in this chapter. Here is what you'll learn in this chapter:

- Scrolling

- Working with tile-based backgrounds

Introduction to Scrolling

What is scrolling? In today's gaming world, where 3D is the focus of everyone's attention, it's not surprising to find gamers and programmers who have never heard of scrolling. What a shame! The heritage of modern games is a long and fascinating one that is still relevant today, even if it is not understood or appreciated. The console industry puts great effort and value into scrolling, particularly on handheld systems, such as the Game Boy Advance.

Definition

Scrolling is the process of displaying a small portion (or window) of a larger virtual game world that would not otherwise fit entirely on the screen.

A Limited View of the World

The key to scrolling is actually having something in the virtual game world to display in the scroll window. Also, I should point out that the entire screen need not be used as the scroll window. It is common to use the entire screen in scrolling-shooter games, but role-playing games often use a smaller window on the screen for scrolling, using the rest of the screen for gameplay (combat, inventory, and so on) and player/party information. You could display one huge bitmap image in the virtual game world representing the current level of the game, and then copy (blit) a portion of that virtual world onto the screen. This is the simplest form of scrolling. Another method uses tiles to create the game world, which I'll cover shortly. First, you'll write a short program to demonstrate how to use bitmap scrolling.

Scrolling the Screen

I have written a program called ScrollScreen that I will show you. The \bitmaps folder on the CD-ROM contains the bigbg.bmp file used in this program. Although I encourage you to write the program yourself, feel free to open the project located on the CD-ROM in \sources\chapter15\ScrollScreen. Figure 15.1 shows the bigbg.bmp file.

When you run the program, the program will load the bigbg.bmp image into the virtual buffer and display the upper-left corner in the 640 × 480 screen. You can change the resolution if you want, and I also encourage you to try running the program in full-screen mode using several different resolutions. The program detects when the mouse is moving and adjusts the X and Y variables accordingly.

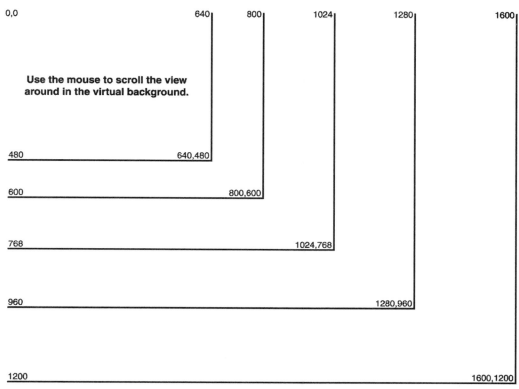

Figure 15.1
The bigbg.bmp file is loaded into the virtual memory buffer for scrolling.

Displaying the correct view is then a simple matter of drawing the portion of the image based on the X and Y scroll values. Figure 15.2 shows the output from the ScrollScreen program.

```
'position variables
x as integer = 0
y as integer = 0

'load the large bitmap image
load bitmap "bigbg.bmp", 5

sync on
sync rate 40
hide mouse

width = screen width()-1
height = screen height()-1
```

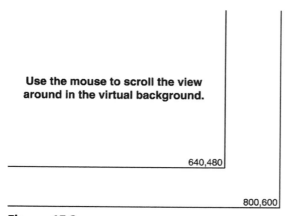

Figure 15.2
The ScrollScreen program demonstrates how to perform virtual buffer scrolling.

```
repeat
    movex = mousemovex()
    movey = mousemovey()

    'check left/right movement
    if movex <> 0
        x = x + movex
        if x < 0 then x = 0
        if x > bitmap width(5) - width
            x = bitmap width(5) - width
        endif
    endif

    'check up/down movement
    if movey <> 0
        y = y + movey
        if y < 0 then y = 0
        if y > bitmap height(5) - height
            y = bitmap height(5) - height
        endif
    endif

    'draw the scroll window portion of the virtual buffer
    copy bitmap 5, x, y, x+WIDTH, y+HEIGHT, 0, 0, 0, WIDTH, HEIGHT

    sync
until escapekey() = 1
```

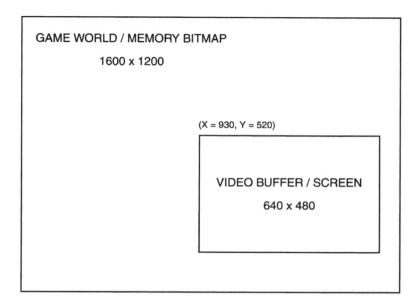

Figure 15.3
A single large scroll buffer contains the image of the entire game world all at once.

The key to this program is the line shown in bold. By using the copy bitmap command, you can copy a portion of the large bitmap image onto the screen. The trick, then, is to figure out where on that source image you want to copy a screen full of pixels. By keeping track of the X and Y scroll values, you can do just that. Figure 15.3 shows an illustration of how a single large bitmap is used as the scroll buffer in the ScrollScreen program.

Tile-Based Backgrounds

You have seen what a simple scroller looks like, even though it relied on mouse input to scroll. A high-speed scrolling arcade game would automatically scroll horizontally or vertically, displaying a ground-, air-, or space-based terrain below the player (usually represented by an airplane or a spaceship). The point of these games is to keep the action moving so fast that the player doesn't have a chance to rest from one wave of enemies to the next.

Backgrounds and Scenery

A background is comprised of imagery or terrain in one form or another, upon which the sprites are drawn. The background might be nothing more than a pretty picture behind the action in a game, or it might take an active part, as in a scroller. When you are talking about scrollers, they need not be relegated only to the high-speed arcade games. Role-playing games are usually scrollers too, as are most sports games.

You should design the background around the goals of your game, not the other way around. You should not come up with some cool background and then try to build the game around it. (However, I admit that this is often how games are started.) You never want to rely on a single cool technology as the basis for an entire game, or the game will be forever remembered as a trendy game that tried to cash in on the latest fad. Instead of following and imitating, set your own precedents and make your own standards!

What am I talking about, you might ask? You might have the impression that anything and everything that could possibly have been done with a scrolling game has already been done ten times over. That's not true! Remember when *Doom* first came out? Everyone had been imitating *Wolfenstein 3D* when Carmack and Romero bumped up the notch a few hundred points and raised everyone's expectations so high that shockwaves reverberated throughout the entire game industry—console and PC alike.

Do you really think it has all been done before and there is no more room for innovation, that the game industry is saturated and it's impossible to make a successful "indie" game? That didn't stop Bungie from going for broke on their first game project. *Halo* has made its mark in gaming history by upping everyone's expectations for superior physics and intelligent opponents. Now, a few years hence, what kinds of games are coming out? What is the biggest industry buzzword? *Physics.* Design a game today without it, and suddenly your game is *so 1990s* in the gaming press. It's all about physics and AI now, and that started with *Halo.* There is no reason why you can't invent the next revolution in gaming.

Creating Backgrounds from Tiles

The real power of a scrolling game comes from a technique called tiling. *Tiling* is a process in which there really is no background, just an array of tiles that make up the background as it is displayed. In other words, it is a virtual background and it takes up very little memory compared to a full bitmapped background (such as the one in ScrollScreen). Take a look at Figure 15.4 for an example.

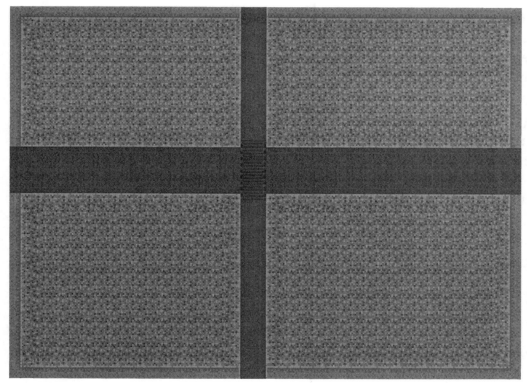

Figure 15.4
A bitmap image constructed of tiles.

Can you count the number of tiles used to construct the background in Figure 15.4? Eighteen tiles make up this image, actually. Imagine that—an entire game screen built using a handful of tiles, and the result is pretty good! Obviously a real game would have more than just grass, roads, rivers, and bridges; a real game would have sprites moving on top of the background. How about an example? I thought you'd like that idea.

Creating a Tile Map

I have generated a realistic-looking game map with source code, using an algorithm that matched terrain curves and straights (such as the road, bridge, and river) so that the map was created from scratch. Building a random landscape is one thing, but constructing it at runtime is not a great solution—even if your map-generating routine is very good. For instance, many games, such as *Civilization IV,* can generate the game world on the fly. Obviously, the programmers spent a lot of time perfecting the world-generating routines. If your game would benefit by featuring a randomly generated game world, then your work is cut out for you, but the results will be worth it. This is simply one of those design considerations that you must make, given that you have time to develop it.

Assuming you don't have the means to generate a random map at this time, you can simply create one within an array. Then you can modify the program so it uses the array instead of a single large bitmap, which is how the ScrollScreen program worked. Where do you start? First of all, you should realize that the tiles are numbered and should be referenced this way in the map array.

Here is what a tile map looks like in DB as a data sequence:

```
global MAP_ACROSS as integer = 10
global MAP_DOWN as integer = 6
data 1,1,1,1,1,1,1,1,1,1
data 1,2,2,2,2,2,2,2,2,1
data 1,2,2,2,2,2,2,2,2,1
data 1,2,2,2,2,2,2,2,2,1
data 1,2,2,2,2,2,2,2,2,1
data 1,1,1,1,1,1,1,1,1,1
```

It's not complicated—simply a bunch of twos (grass) bordered by ones (dirt). The trick here is that this is really only a single-dimensional array, but the listing makes it obvious how the map will look because there are 10 numbers in each row—the same number of tiles in each row. I did this intentionally so you can use this as a template for creating your own maps. And you can create more than one map if you want. Simply change the name of each map and reference the map you want when it's time to draw it. You might do this with a label (such as LEVEL1), which is how levels were done in Darkanoid in the previous chapter. Now are you starting to see the potential? You could use this simple scrolling code as the basis for any of a hundred different games if you have the creative gumption to do so.

I have prepared a legend of the tiles and the value for each in Figure 15.5. You can use the legend while building your own maps. That is, when using this particular tile sheet. You can use different sets of tile images for each game or each level if you want. This is just one simple example.

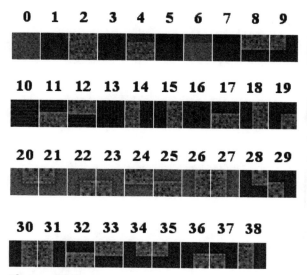

Figure 15.5
A legend of the tiles and their reference numbers used to create a map in the ScrollTiles program.

Note

All of the tiles used in this chapter were created by Ari Feldman, and are available in his free SpriteLib graphics library at http://www.flyingyogi.com.

Tile-Based Scrolling

Let's see how to create a real tile-based scroller. To make the program a bit easier to understand, the virtual background will be 800 pixels across. I know, I know—that's not much bigger than the 640 × 480 screen. The point is to demonstrate how it will work, not to build a game engine, so don't worry about it. If you want to type in the values to create a bigger map, by all means, go for it! That would be a great learning experience, as a matter of fact.

For our purposes here (and with my primary goal of being able to print an entire row of numbers in a single source code line in the book), I'll stick to maps that have fewer than 30 tiles across and down. You can work with a map that is deeper than it is wide, so that will allow you to test scrolling up and down fairly well. Figure 15.6 shows the output from the ScrollTiles program.

Figure 15.6
The ScrollTiles program scrolls a real tile map.

How about that source code? First, up near the top with the other defines, add these lines:

```
'define some convenient constants
global TILEW as integer = 32
global TILEH as integer = 32
global COLS as integer = 10
```

Then, of course, add the data statements that define the tile map below the variables.

```
'map definition
global MAP_ACROSS as integer = 29
global MAP_DOWN as integer = 25
data 0,0,0,0,0,0,0,0,0,0,0,0,0,0,0,0,0,0,0,0,0,0,0,0,0,0,0,0,0
data 0,1,1,2,2,2,2,2,2,2,2,2,2,2,2,2,2,2,2,2,2,2,2,2,2,2,1,1,0
data 0,1,1,2,2,2,2,2,2,2,2,2,2,2,2,2,2,2,2,2,2,2,2,2,2,2,1,1,0
```

```
data 0,1,1,2,2,2,2,2,2,2,2,2,2,2,2,2,2,2,2,2,2,2,2,2,2,2,2,1,1,0
data 0,1,1,2,2,2,2,2,2,2,2,2,2,2,2,2,2,2,2,2,2,2,2,2,2,2,2,1,1,0
data 0,1,1,2,2,2,2,2,2,2,2,2,2,2,2,2,2,2,2,2,2,2,2,2,2,2,2,1,1,0
data 0,1,1,2,2,2,2,2,2,2,2,2,2,2,2,2,2,2,2,2,2,2,2,2,2,2,2,1,1,0
data 0,1,1,2,2,2,2,2,2,2,2,2,2,2,2,2,2,2,2,2,2,2,2,2,2,2,2,1,1,0
data 0,1,1,2,2,2,2,2,2,2,2,2,2,2,2,2,2,2,2,2,2,2,2,2,2,2,2,1,1,0
data 0,1,1,2,2,2,2,2,2,2,2,2,2,2,2,2,2,2,2,2,2,2,2,2,2,2,2,1,1,0
data 0,1,1,2,2,2,2,2,2,2,2,2,2,2,2,2,2,2,2,2,2,2,2,2,2,2,2,1,1,0
data 0,1,1,2,2,2,2,2,2,2,2,2,2,2,2,2,2,2,2,2,2,2,2,2,2,2,2,1,1,0
data 0,1,1,2,2,2,2,2,2,2,2,2,2,2,2,2,2,2,2,2,2,2,2,2,2,2,2,1,1,0
data 0,1,1,2,2,2,2,2,2,2,2,2,2,2,2,2,2,2,2,2,2,2,2,2,2,2,2,1,1,0
data 0,1,1,2,2,2,2,2,2,2,2,2,2,2,2,2,2,2,2,2,2,2,2,2,2,2,2,1,1,0
data 0,1,1,2,2,2,2,2,2,2,2,2,2,2,2,2,2,2,2,2,2,2,2,2,2,2,2,1,1,0
data 0,1,1,2,2,2,2,2,2,2,2,2,2,2,2,2,2,2,2,2,2,2,2,2,2,2,2,1,1,0
data 0,1,1,2,2,2,2,2,2,2,2,2,2,2,2,2,2,2,2,2,2,2,2,2,2,2,2,1,1,0
data 0,1,1,2,2,2,2,2,2,2,2,2,2,2,2,2,2,2,2,2,2,2,2,2,2,2,2,1,1,0
data 0,1,1,2,2,2,2,2,2,2,2,2,2,2,2,2,2,2,2,2,2,2,2,2,2,2,2,1,1,0
data 0,1,1,2,2,2,2,2,2,2,2,2,2,2,2,2,2,2,2,2,2,2,2,2,2,2,2,1,1,0
data 0,1,1,2,2,2,2,2,2,2,2,2,2,2,2,2,2,2,2,2,2,2,2,2,2,2,2,1,1,0
data 0,1,1,2,2,2,2,2,2,2,2,2,2,2,2,2,2,2,2,2,2,2,2,2,2,2,2,1,1,0
data 0,1,1,2,2,2,2,2,2,2,2,2,2,2,2,2,2,2,2,2,2,2,2,2,2,2,2,1,1,0
data 0,0,0,0,0,0,0,0,0,0,0,0,0,0,0,0,0,0,0,0,0,0,0,0,0,0,0,0,0,0
```

Next comes some global constants and variables and the code that loads the bitmap containing the tiles. Also, this code creates the virtual scroll buffer using the create bitmap command.

```
'temp bitmap
global TILE_BITMAP as integer = 5

'virtual background buffer
global SCROLL_BITMAP as integer = 6

'scrolling variables
global scrollx as integer = 0
global scrolly as integer = 0
global tilex as integer
global tiley as integer

'create the virtual background
create bitmap SCROLL_BITMAP, MAP_ACROSS * TILEW, MAP_DOWN * TILEH
```

```
'load the tile bitmap
load bitmap "tiles.bmp", TILE_BITMAP
```

Next, we need to copy the individual tiles onto the virtual scroll buffer using the copy bitmap command. Be sure to type the copy bitmap command below onto a single line of code (as it will not fit on a single line on the printed page).

```
'draw tiles onto virtual scroller bitmap
for tiley = 0 to MAP_DOWN-1
   for tilex = 0 to MAP_ACROSS-1
      read tilenumber
      x = (tilenumber MOD COLS) * (TILEW+1)
      y = (tilenumber / COLS) * (TILEH+1)
      copy bitmap TILE_BITMAP, x, y, x+TILEW, y+TILEH, SCROLL_BITMAP, tilex*
TILEW, tiley*TILEW, tilex*TILEW+TILEW, tiley*TILEH+TILEH
   next tilex
next tiley
```

Okay, now that the tile information is in the program, we can focus on the normal stuff like the game loop and the functionality that scrolls the game world based on user input.

```
sync on
sync rate 40
hide mouse
set current bitmap 0
width = screen width()-1
height = screen height()-1

'main loop
repeat
   'check mouse motion
   movex = mousemovex()
   movey = mousemovey()

   'left/right movement
   if movex <> 0
      scrollx = scrollx + movex
      if scrollx < 0 then scrollx = 0
      scrollw = bitmap width(SCROLL_BITMAP)
      if scrollx > scrollw - width then scrollx = scrollw - width
   endif
```

```
'up/down movement
if movey <> 0
   scrolly = scrolly + movey
   if scrolly < 0 then scrolly = 0
   scrollh = bitmap height(SCROLL_BITMAP)
   if scrolly > scrollh - height then scrolly = scrollh - height
endif

cls

'draw the scroll window portion of the virtual buffer
copy bitmap SCROLL_BITMAP, scrollx, scrolly, scrollx + width, scrolly +
height, 0, 0, 0, width, height

'display status info
text 10, 10, "Position = " + str$(scrollx) + "," + str$(scrolly)

sync
until escapekey() = 1

delete bitmap SCROLL_BITMAP
delete bitmap TILE_BITMAP
```

Be sure to type the copy bitmap command above onto a single line of code, or DB will complain. We can't fit the entire line of code onto the printed page.

I encourage you to modify and experiment with the ScrollTiles program to see what it can do. Enlarge the map to see how big you can make it. Try having the program scroll the map (with wrapping) without requiring user input. This is actually a fairly advanced topic. You should definitely play around with the map array to come up with your own map, and you can even try a different set of tiles. If you have found any free game tiles on the web (or if you have an artist friend draw some custom tiles for your game), note the layout and size of each tile, and then you can modify the constants in the program to accommodate the new tile set. See what you can come up with; experimentation is what puts the "science" in computer science.

Dynamic Tile-Based Scrolling

The previous two programs show two possible ways to create a scrolling game world. The real flaw in these programs is that they can't handle a truly huge game world. The reason for this limitation is that the ScrollTiles program preallocates memory for the entire level before the tiles are drawn onto the screen. At this

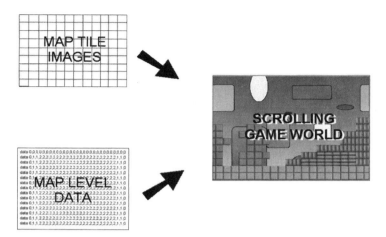

Figure 15.7
A dynamically rendered scroller needs a set of tile images and an array of data filled with tile numbers that describe the game world.

point, it behaves just like the ScrollScreen program; the only difference is that the image was constructed rather than loaded from a bitmap file. A truly robust scroller must be able to render tiles on the screen dynamically when they are needed, without using an offscreen game world bitmap.

There are several ways to describe the next stage of scrolling. I would like to call it a *dynamic scroller*, or perhaps a *just in time scroller*, because of how it works. The dynamic tile-based scroller does not have to allocate a huge bitmap in memory to hold the game world because a *dynamic* scroller draws the tiles onto the screen directly, as they are needed according to the current scroll position (X and Y). It is the job of the dynamic scroller engine to figure out where tiles should be drawn, so this type of scroller is far more complicated than either of the previous two examples you have seen in this chapter. Figure 15.7 shows an illustration of the process involved in rendering tiles using a dynamic scroller. To make this work, you need a source image containing the images for the tiles. You also need a data source (the map level data) that describes the tile map using numbers representing the number for each tile.

The dynamic scroller works on the same principle as the previous two examples, where a portion of a large scroll buffer is copied to the screen. However, it is the way this scroll buffer is constructed that makes the dynamic scroller vastly more efficient than the previous two examples. In this new algorithm, the tiles are being drawn onto the scroll buffer during each frame of the game loop, *and* the scroll buffer is very small in comparison. You can easily fill the screen with tiles by using two for loops to copy *N* tiles onto the screen, where *N = Screen Width / Tile Width*. If your screen is 640×480, and your tiles are 32×32 in size, then you can draw 640/32 = 20 tiles across, and 480/32 = 15 tiles down. Some screen resolutions do not divide evenly by the tile width or height, and will end up having a small empty portion at the right or bottom edge of the screen. You can stretch the image to fill the entire screen if you want (using the copy bitmap command, which allows you to specify the source and destination dimensions in order to stretch [or scale] the image). This tends to slow the program down a bit, which is why I recommend just adjusting the position of the tiles to center them on the screen rather than stretching the image.

By using the simple formulas just explained, you can correctly position the tile map onto the screen at the desired scroll position. But when you draw the tiles in this manner, they will jump from one tile to the next while the scroller is moving. This is because only an entire row or column of tiles may be drawn at a time. To smooth out the rendering of the tiles, one technique I have used successfully is to create a scroll buffer that is slightly larger than the screen. As Figure 15.8 shows, the scroll buffer has enough room to accommodate the screen and one tile's width and height around the outside of the screen.

As long as the scrolling does not move farther than the width or height of one tile, then the current scroll buffer is used to fill the screen with the tile map. When the scrolling goes beyond one tile's worth of pixels in the horizontal or vertical direction, then the scroll buffer must be reloaded with tiles. It is loaded with tiles using the simple division described in the previous two paragraphs. Since that is understood, how about moving the current scroll position around within the

Figure 15.8
The scroll buffer is slightly larger than the screen (one tile's worth).

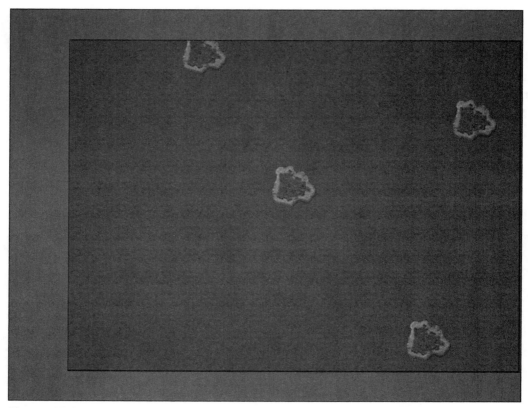

Figure 15.9
The scroll position is moving to the right edge of the scroll buffer.

boundary of the scroll buffer? As Figure 15.8 shows, the scroll buffer has room for the entire screen and room for one more tile completely around the screen. The trick is to move the screen (or rather, the scroll position) inside the scroll buffer until it reaches the edge. As soon as that happens, then you have to fill the scroll buffer with a new set of tiles that are adjusted in the direction of the scrolling.

Let me give you some illustrations to help you visualize what's going on. Figure 15.9 shows the situation where the scroll position has moved to the right inside the scroll buffer and is about to hit the right edge of the scroll buffer. Keep in mind that there is room for one whole tile completely around the edge of the screen (in this case, the tiles are 32×32, so we have 32 pixels of movement in every direction).

When the scroll position reaches the right edge of the scroll buffer, then the buffer has been exceeded and it must be reloaded with a new set of tiles that have been shifted to the left by one whole tile. This allows the scroller to keep moving in that direction, and to the viewer it will appear as if the tiles are just moving along from one large bitmap buffer. The situation is very much like a treadmill, where the "floor" you walk upon while using a treadmill just presents you with enough room to walk or jog in place, but it does not give you an entire hiking trail or track to jog on. As a result, the "virtual track" only takes up a few square feet of the floor. In contrast, an entire track would be very inefficient and wasteful for a single individual (are you still following the analogy?). The dynamic scroller works in a similar way. The tiles are created literally under the foot of the screen, which is represented by the scroll position.

When the scroll position has exceeded the scroll buffer, as shown in Figure 15.10, then the buffer must be reloaded. Note that the scroll position will never actually move beyond the buffer as shown in this figure, but it illustrates the situation where the buffer must be reloaded and shifted to the left. Note also in this figure that the dark gray portion that represents the scroll buffer will actually contain tile images as well; I left out the tiles so you can see exactly what portion of the buffer is seen on the screen.

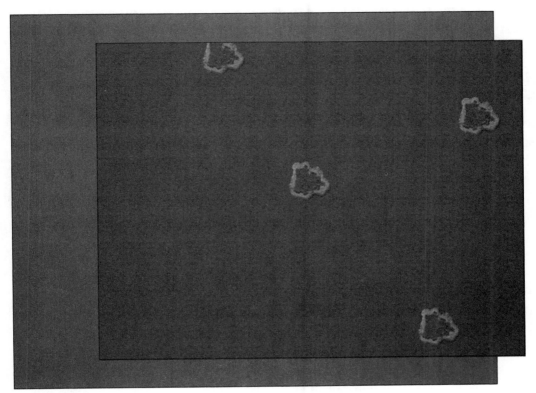

Figure 15.10
The scroll position has moved beyond the right edge of the scroll buffer.

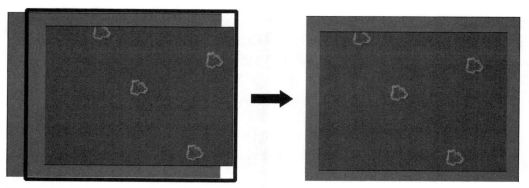

Figure 15.11
The scroll buffer has been loaded with tiles shifted to the left to accommodate the new scroll position.

When this happens, the scroll buffer must be reloaded with tiles. Figure 15.11 shows how the problem is handled. When the scroll position reaches the edge of the scroll buffer, then the tiles are shifted to the left by one entire tile width and the next column of tiles is added to the right side of the scroll buffer. If you look carefully at the figure you'll notice that the tiles are indeed shifted to the left by one tile's width.

The DynamicScroller Program

The DynamicScroller program is an example of dynamic or just-in-time scrolling, and is shown in Figure 15.12. This program only requires enough memory for the source bitmap image containing tiles, and a scroll buffer that is just slightly larger than the screen. If you understand the concept of a dynamic scroller at this point, then you will be able to visualize how the following code works intuitively. If you find that any part of the theory behind this algorithm confuses you, then just jump back a few pages and read the explanation of dynamic scrolling again while reading through the code, and I'm sure you will get the hang of it.

The DynamicScroller Source Code

The DynamicScroller program only has a few key functions that you will need to understand in order to adapt the code to your own tile-based game. I will explain every part of the program in the following pages. First, let's start with the global variables and constants used by the program. This section of code is very important because it defines all of the settings of the scroller. This code might need to be made more reusable by moving some of these globals into parameters

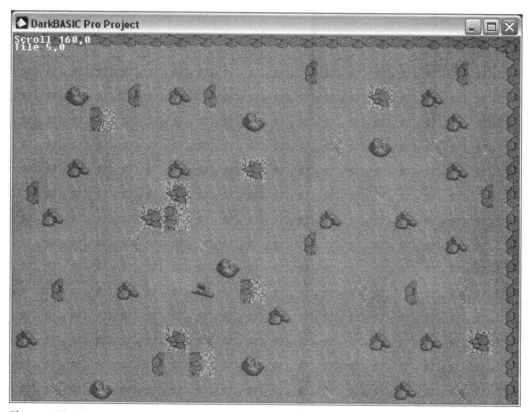

Figure 15.12
The DynamicScroller program is a demonstration of dynamic tile-based scrolling.

for the various scroller support functions. At this point, clarity is more important than efficiency and code reuse. You will want to modify the TILEWIDTH and TILEHEIGHT constants if you change the size of your tiles (they are currently 32×32). Most of the remaining constants rely on these two.

```
global ScrollX as integer = 0
global ScrollY as integer = 0
global TileX as integer = 0
global TileY as integer = 0

global IMG_SCROLLBUFFER as integer = 10
global IMG_TILES as integer = 20

global MAPWIDTH as integer = 25
global MAPHEIGHT as integer = 50
```

```
global TILEWIDTH as integer = 32
global TILEHEIGHT as integer = 32

global GAMEWORLDWIDTH as integer
GAMEWORLDWIDTH = TILEWIDTH * MAPWIDTH
global GAMEWORLDHEIGHT as integer
GAMEWORLDHEIGHT = TILEHEIGHT * MAPHEIGHT

'scrolling window size
global WINDOWWIDTH as integer
WINDOWWIDTH = (screen width() / TILEWIDTH) * TILEWIDTH
global WINDOWHEIGHT as integer
WINDOWHEIGHT = (screen height() / TILEHEIGHT) * TILEHEIGHT

'scroll buffer size
global SCROLLBUFFERWIDTH as integer
SCROLLBUFFERWIDTH = screen width() + TILEWIDTH * 2
global SCROLLBUFFERHEIGHT as integer
SCROLLBUFFERHEIGHT = screen height() + TILEHEIGHT * 2
dim MAPDATA(MAPWIDTH,MAPHEIGHT) as integer
```

The Map Data

I wanted to create a large map for this example so you can actually scroll the game world around quite a bit before hitting the edges. This map definition doesn't quite fit on one printed line in the book, so just be sure to put all of the values on a single line as they appear after each data statement. When you are working with very large game levels, it's a good idea to define the level using the actual width of the level, rather than making the values all line up in your code. You should be able to see basically what the game level looks like just by examining the level's data values.

```
data 80, 81, 81, 81, 81, 81, 81, 81, 81, 81, 81, 81, 81, 81, 81, 81, 81, 81, 81, 81,
81, 81, 81, 81, 82
data 90, 3, 3, 3, 3, 3, 3, 3, 3, 3, 3, 3, 3, 3, 3, 92, 3, 3, 3, 3, 3, 92, 3, 92
data 90, 3, 13, 83, 96, 3, 3, 23, 3, 92, 3, 13, 92, 3, 3, 3, 3, 3, 3, 11, 3, 13, 3, 3,
92
data 90, 3, 3, 3, 3, 3, 3, 3, 10, 3, 3, 3, 3, 3, 23, 3, 3, 3, 3, 3, 3, 3, 13, 3, 92
data 90, 3, 96, 3, 13, 3, 3, 3, 3, 3, 3, 3, 3, 3, 3, 3, 96, 3, 23, 3, 96, 3, 3, 92
data 90, 3, 3, 3, 3, 3, 3, 13, 3, 3, 3, 13, 3, 3, 11, 3, 3, 3, 3, 3, 3, 3, 13, 3, 92
data 90, 3, 83, 11, 3, 92, 3, 3, 3, 3, 3, 11, 3, 3, 3, 3, 3, 3, 3, 83, 3, 3, 3, 92, 92
```

```
data 90, 3, 3, 3, 96, 3, 13, 3, 3, 3, 11, 10, 3, 3, 3, 3, 3, 13, 3, 3, 13, 3, 3, 3, 92
data 90, 3, 23, 3, 3, 3, 3, 3, 3, 96, 3, 3, 83, 3, 3, 3, 92, 3, 3, 3, 3, 3, 13, 3, 92
data 90, 3, 3, 3, 3, 3, 3, 3, 3, 3, 3, 3, 3, 23, 3, 3, 3, 3, 3, 3, 3, 3, 3, 3, 92
data 90, 3, 3, 3, 11, 3, 92, 3, 3, 13, 3, 3,131, 3, 10, 3, 3, 3, 96, 3, 92, 3, 96, 3, 92
data 90, 3, 13, 83, 3, 3, 3, 3, 3, 3, 3, 3, 3, 3, 13, 3, 3, 3, 3, 3, 3, 3, 3, 92
data 90, 3, 3, 3, 3, 13, 3, 3, 3, 3, 3, 11, 96, 3, 3, 3, 3, 3, 3, 13, 3, 13, 3, 11, 92
data 90, 92, 3, 13, 3, 3, 3, 3, 3, 3, 92, 3, 10, 3, 23, 3, 3, 3, 3, 3, 3, 3, 3, 3, 92
data 90, 3, 3, 3, 3, 3, 96, 3, 23, 3, 3, 3, 3, 3, 3, 3, 3, 83, 3, 3, 13, 3, 96, 3, 92
data 90, 3, 3, 3, 3, 92, 3, 3, 3, 3, 3, 13, 3, 3, 3, 13, 3, 3, 3, 11, 3, 3, 3, 3, 92
data 90, 3, 13, 3, 3, 3, 3, 3, 3, 3, 96, 3, 3, 3, 3, 3, 3, 3, 3, 3, 3, 92, 3, 3, 92
data 90, 3, 3, 3, 96, 3, 13, 3, 3, 3, 11, 10, 3, 3, 3, 3, 3, 13, 3, 3, 13, 3, 3, 3, 92
data 90, 3, 23, 3, 3, 3, 3, 3, 3, 96, 3, 3, 83, 3, 3, 3, 92, 3, 3, 3, 3, 3, 13, 3, 92
data 90, 3, 3, 3, 3, 3, 3, 3, 3, 3, 3, 3, 3, 23, 3, 3, 3, 3, 3, 3, 3, 3, 3, 3, 92
data 90, 3, 3, 3, 11, 3, 92, 3, 3, 13, 3, 3,131, 3, 10, 3, 3, 3, 96, 3, 92, 3, 96, 3, 92
data 90, 3, 13, 83, 3, 3, 3, 3, 3, 3, 3, 3, 3, 3, 13, 3, 3, 3, 3, 3, 3, 3, 3, 92
data 90, 3, 3, 3, 13, 3, 3, 3, 3, 3, 11, 96, 3, 3, 3, 3, 3, 3, 13, 3, 13, 3, 11, 92
data 90, 92, 3, 13, 3, 3, 3, 3, 3, 3, 92, 3, 10, 3, 23, 3, 3, 3, 3, 3, 3, 3, 3, 3, 92
data 90, 3, 3, 3, 3, 3, 96, 3, 23, 3, 3, 3, 3, 3, 3, 3, 3, 83, 3, 3, 13, 3, 96, 3, 92
data 90, 3, 3, 3, 3, 92, 3, 3, 3, 3, 3, 13, 3, 3, 3, 13, 3, 3, 3, 11, 3, 3, 3, 3, 92
data 90, 3, 13, 3, 3, 3, 3, 3, 3, 3, 96, 3, 3, 3, 3, 3, 3, 3, 3, 3, 3, 92, 3, 3, 92
data 90, 3, 96, 3, 13, 3, 3, 3, 3, 3, 3, 3, 3, 3, 3, 3, 3, 96, 3, 23, 3, 96, 3, 3, 92
data 90, 3, 3, 3, 3, 3, 3, 13, 3, 3, 3, 13, 3, 3, 11, 3, 3, 3, 3, 3, 3, 3, 13, 3, 92
data 90, 3, 83, 11, 3, 92, 3, 3, 3, 3, 3, 11, 3, 3, 3, 3, 3, 3, 3, 83, 3, 3, 3, 92, 92
data 90, 3, 3, 3, 96, 3, 13, 3, 3, 3, 11, 10, 3, 3, 3, 3, 3, 13, 3, 3, 13, 3, 3, 3, 92
data 90, 3, 23, 3, 3, 3, 3, 3, 3, 96, 3, 3, 83, 3, 3, 3, 92, 3, 3, 3, 3, 3, 13, 3, 92
data 90, 3, 3, 3, 3, 3, 3, 3, 3, 3, 3, 3, 3, 23, 3, 3, 3, 3, 3, 3, 3, 3, 3, 3, 92
data 90, 3, 3, 3, 11, 3, 92, 3, 3, 13, 3, 3,131, 3, 10, 3, 3, 3, 96, 3, 92, 3, 96, 3, 92
data 90, 3, 13, 83, 3, 3, 3, 3, 3, 3, 3, 3, 3, 3, 13, 3, 3, 3, 3, 3, 3, 3, 3, 92
data 90, 3, 3, 3, 3, 13, 3, 3, 3, 3, 3, 11, 96, 3, 3, 3, 3, 3, 3, 13, 3, 13, 3, 11, 92
data 90, 92, 3, 13, 3, 3, 3, 3, 3, 3, 92, 3, 10, 3, 23, 3, 3, 3, 3, 3, 3, 3, 3, 3, 92
data 90, 3, 3, 3, 11, 3, 92, 3, 3, 13, 3, 3,131, 3, 10, 3, 3, 3, 96, 3, 92, 3, 96, 3, 92
data 90, 3, 13, 83, 3, 3, 3, 3, 3, 3, 3, 3, 3, 3, 13, 3, 3, 3, 3, 3, 3, 3, 3, 92
data 90, 3, 3, 3, 3, 13, 3, 3, 3, 3, 3, 11, 96, 3, 3, 3, 3, 3, 3, 13, 3, 13, 3, 11, 92
```

```
data 90, 92, 3, 13, 3, 3, 3, 3, 3, 3, 92, 3, 10, 3, 23, 3, 3, 3, 3, 3, 3, 3, 3, 3, 92
data 90, 3, 3, 3, 3, 3, 96, 3, 23, 3, 3, 3, 3, 3, 3, 3, 3, 83, 3, 3, 13, 3, 96, 3, 92
data 90, 3, 3, 3, 3, 92, 3, 3, 3, 3, 3, 13, 3, 3, 3, 13, 3, 3, 3, 11, 3, 3, 3, 3, 92
data 90, 3, 13, 3, 3, 3, 3, 3, 3, 96, 3, 3, 3, 3, 3, 3, 3, 3, 3, 3, 92, 3, 3, 92
data 90, 3, 96, 3, 13, 3, 3, 3, 3, 3, 3, 3, 3, 3, 3, 3, 3, 96, 3, 23, 3, 96, 3, 3, 92
data 90, 3, 3, 3, 3, 3, 3, 13, 3, 3, 3, 13, 3, 3, 11, 3, 3, 3, 3, 3, 3, 3, 13, 3, 92
data 90, 3, 83, 11, 3, 92, 3, 3, 3, 3, 3, 11, 3, 3, 3, 3, 3, 3, 3, 83, 3, 3, 3, 92, 92
data 90, 3, 3, 3, 96, 3, 13, 3, 3, 3, 11, 10, 3, 3, 3, 3, 3, 13, 3, 3, 13, 3, 3, 3, 92
data 90, 3, 23, 3, 3, 3, 3, 3, 3, 96, 3, 3, 83, 3, 3, 3, 92, 3, 3, 3, 3, 3, 13, 3, 92
data 100, 101, 101, 101, 101, 101, 101, 101, 101, 101, 101, 101, 101, 101, 101,
101, 101, 101, 101, 101, 101, 101, 101, 101, 102
```

Main Code

The following three lines of code are the core of the program. Game_Init() is called to initialize the variables, load the tile images, and allocate memory for the scroll buffer, among other things. Game_Run() contains the game loop.

```
Game_Init()
Game_Run()
end
```

Initializing the Program

The Game_Init() function has the task of loading the tile images and filling the MAPDATA array from the data statements. Although you could use the RESTORE and READ commands to read the data statements directly, this process is slow and would cause the scroller to update slowly. That is why we copy the data values into an array first, because an array is instantly available. This function also must create the scroll buffer and set some basic starting values for the program, such as the sync rate.

```
function Game_Init()
  'load the tile images
  load bitmap "groundtiles.bmp", IMG_TILES

  'create the scroll buffer surface in memory, slightly bigger than the screen
  create bitmap IMG_SCROLLBUFFER, SCROLLBUFFERWIDTH, SCROLLBUFFERHEIGHT
```

```
   'load the map data into the array
   for y = 0 to MAPHEIGHT-1
      for x = 0 to MAPWIDTH-1
         read MAPDATA(x,y)
      next x
   next y

   sync on
   sync rate 0
   hide mouse
   set current bitmap 0
endfunction
```

The Game Loop

The Game_Run() function contains the game loop for this program, which operates inside a loop to continuously draw the tiles on the screen based on the scroll position (which is moved using the arrow keys). This function calls several support functions to update the scroll position, draw the tile map, and display some information on the screen showing the scroll position.

```
function Game_Run()
   repeat
      'update the scrolling view
      UpdateScrollPosition()

      'draw tiles onto the scroll buffer
      DrawTileMap()

      text 0,0,"Scroll " + str$(scrollx) + "," + str$(scrolly)
      text 0,10,"Tile " + str$(tilex) + "," + str$(tiley)

      'display the back buffer on the screen
      sync
   until escapekey() = 1
endfunction
```

Drawing a Tile

The DrawTile() function has the sole job of drawing a single tile. The tile to draw is specified by passing the image number, tile number, width, and height to the function. In addition, this function needs to know how many columns are found in the tile image. It then expects to receive the destination bitmap where the tile should be drawn, and the position for the tile. Be sure to type in the code for copy bitmap entirely on a single line, as some of the line wrapped onto the next line due to the size of the printed page.

```
'This function does the real work of drawing a single tile from the source image
'onto the tile scroll buffer. Parameters provide much flexibility.
function DrawTile(source as integer,tile as integer,width as integer,height as
integer,columns as integer,dest as integer,destx as integer,desty as integer)

    'describe the source image
    left = (tile MOD columns) * width
    top = (tile / columns) * height
    right = left + width
    bottom = top + height

    'draw the tile
  copy bitmap source, left, top, right, bottom, dest, destx, desty, destx+width,
desty+height
endfunction
```

Drawing the Tile Map

The DrawTileMap() function has the job of drawing the tile map on the screen based on the current scroll position (ScrollX and ScrollY). This is the most complicated function in the program because of all the work it must do to keep the tiles scrolling smoothly. This function implements the partial-tile scrolling method discussed earlier, where a scroll buffer is used to contain a small border of tiles around the central part of the buffer that represents the screen. Study this function well because it is the core of a tile-based game. There are two lines of code in this function that are highlighted in bold. Be sure to keep the code for these two calls to copy bitmap each on a single line of code. Because of the large number of parameters passed to this command, they would not fit entirely on one line in the code listing, but they must be on a single line or the DB compiler will complain.

```
'This function fills the tilebuffer with tiles representing
'the current scroll display based on scrollx/scrolly.
function DrawTileMap()
```

```
'calculate starting tile position
tilex = int(ScrollX / TILEWIDTH)
tiley = int(ScrollY / TILEHEIGHT)

columns = int(WINDOWWIDTH / TILEWIDTH)
rows = int(WINDOWHEIGHT / TILEHEIGHT)

'draw tiles onto the scroll buffer surface
for y = 0 to rows
   for x = 0 to columns
      'retrieve the tile number from this position
      tilenum = MAPDATA(tilex+x, tiley+y)

      'draw the tile onto the scroll buffer
   DrawTile(IMG_TILES, tilenum, TILEWIDTH, TILEHEIGHT, 16, IMG_SCROLLBUFFER,
x*TILEWIDTH, y*TILEHEIGHT)
   next x
next y

'draws the portion of the scroll buffer onto the back buffer
'according to the current "partial tile" scroll position.
left = ScrollX MOD TILEWIDTH
top = ScrollY MOD TILEHEIGHT

'set dimensions of the source image as a rectangle
right = left + WINDOWWIDTH
bottom = top + WINDOWHEIGHT

'draw the partial tile scroll window onto the back buffer
 copy bitmap IMG_SCROLLBUFFER, left, top, right, bottom, 0, 0, 0, WINDOWWIDTH,
WINDOWHEIGHT
endfunction
```

Updating the Scroll Position

The UpdateScrollPosition() function has the job of moving the scroll position around based on user input. Pressing any of the up, down, left, or right arrow keys will adjust the ScrollX and ScrollY variables, which determines where in the game world the current view is positioned.

```
'This function updates the scrolling position and speed
function UpdateScrollPosition()
```

```
'scroll based on keyboard input
if leftkey() then dec ScrollX, 1
if rightkey() then inc ScrollX, 1
if upkey() then dec ScrollY, 1
if downkey() then inc ScrollY, 1

'update horizontal scrolling position and speed
if ScrollX < 0
   ScrollX = 0
else
   if ScrollX > GAMEWORLDWIDTH - WINDOWWIDTH
      ScrollX = GAMEWORLDWIDTH - WINDOWWIDTH
   endif
endif

'update vertical scrolling position and speed
if ScrollY < 0
   ScrollY = 0
else
   if (ScrollY > GAMEWORLDHEIGHT - WINDOWHEIGHT-1)
      ScrollY = GAMEWORLDHEIGHT - WINDOWHEIGHT-1
   endif
endif
endfunction
```

Summary

This marks the end of yet another graphically intense chapter. We talked about tile-based scrolling and spent most of the time exploring dynamic scrolling backgrounds—how they are created and how to use them in a game. Working with tiles to create a scrolling game world is by no means an easy subject! If you skimmed over any part of this chapter, be sure to read through it again before you move on because the next three chapters dig even deeper into scrolling.

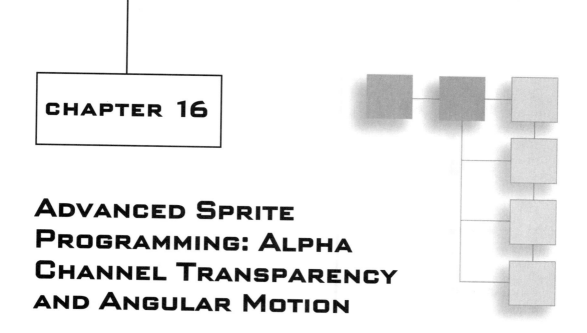

CHAPTER 16

ADVANCED SPRITE PROGRAMMING: ALPHA CHANNEL TRANSPARENCY AND ANGULAR MOTION

This chapter covers two advanced topics in sprite programming that will give your games a serious edge over the competition. First, you'll learn how to create sprite images that use an alpha channel instead of a color key for transparency. This advanced technique produces much higher quality sprites than a color keyed sprite (which uses a specific color for pixel-level transparency). Next, you'll learn an advanced technique to move a sprite using angular motion. This type of sprite control produces a realistic simulation of momentum which looks great in a space-based game. To demonstrate how these two advanced topics work, this chapter provides a hands-on tutorial and an example game. Specifically, in this chapter you'll learn about

- Alpha channel transparency

- Angular motion

Alpha Channel Transparency

In the previous chapters on sprite programming, you learned a technique for drawing transparent sprites using a color key. The color key of an image is a specific color that is defined as the *transparent color*, so that when the image is drawn, you can see through the transparent pixels in the image and the background will show. This is a reasonable way to draw transparent sprites, but it has some disadvantages. For one thing, you have to know the color key of a sprite, and unless you use the set image colorkey command for any images that have a different transparent color, some of your sprites won't render transparently. (This problem is lessened if you choose a standard color key.)

Comparing Color Key and Alpha Channel Transparency

Figure 16.1 shows a sprite loaded up in Paint Shop Pro with a white color key.

Note

The spaceship sprite featured in this chapter was drawn by artist Levi Bath (http://www.levibath.com). The alien UFO ship featured later on, as well as the background and bullet images, were drawn by Reiner Prokein (http://www.reinerstileset.de).

You can use any color for the color key of an image, such as the white color key in the previous figure, although this is an unusual color. Most color keys are either black (0,0,0) or magenta (255,0,255), which looks more like pink to me. For the

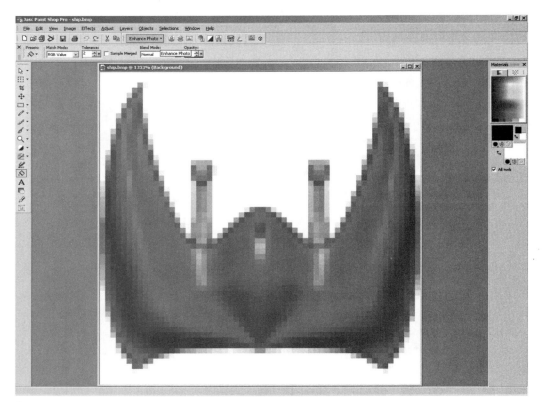

Figure 16.1
This sprite image has no alpha channel, but rather uses a color key.

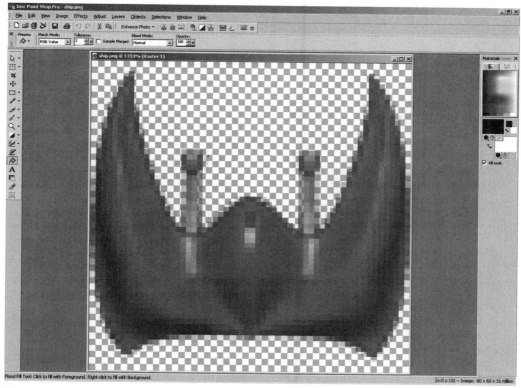

Figure 16.2
This sprite does have an alpha channel.

white color in the previous figure, you could use set image colorkey 255,255,255 to set white as the transparent color.

Now let's take a look at an image that uses an alpha channel instead of a color key. Figure 16.2 shows the same spaceship image in Paint Shop Pro that now has an alpha channel. You can tell that an alpha channel is in use in graphic editors (such as Paint Shop Pro and Photoshop) because the background will show a checkerboard pattern. This pattern shows you exactly what the image will look like when drawn over a background in a game.

Alpha channel transparency is a more advanced way to draw an image with transparency. The alpha channel refers to a color channel in a 32-bit image that represents a mask that filters out a portion of the image. An alpha channel can cause an image to blend with the background (making it partially see-through), or it can render certain pixels of the image with 100 percent transparency.

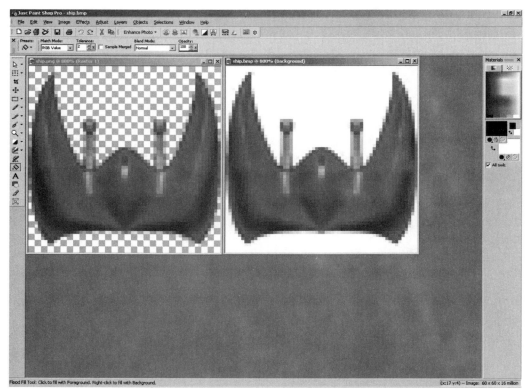

Figure 16.3
Two versions of the spaceship sprite, one with color key and the other with alpha channel transparency.

Figure 16.3 shows the two versions of the sprite side by side so you can see the difference at a glance.

Artists tend to prefer alpha channel transparency over color key because it is very obvious how the image will look in the game. DarkBASIC supports 32-bit images with an alpha channel in the PNG (Portable Network Graphics) file format. All popular graphic editors support the PNG format, so it is easy to convert from BMP to PNG.

Creating an Alpha Channel in an Image

Let's look at the steps involved in creating an alpha channel. You can take an existing image with a color keyed background color and add an alpha channel to the image using most graphic editors. For the purpose of this tutorial, I will be using Paint Shop Pro 8, though later versions have similar functionality.

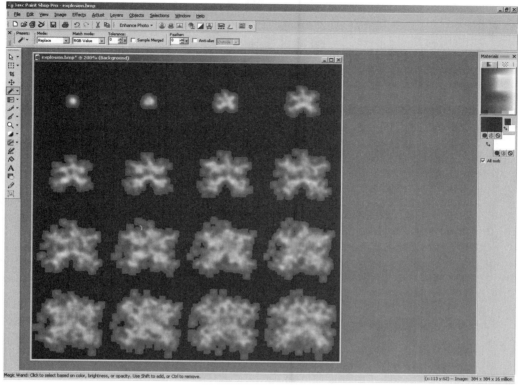

Figure 16.4
An alpha channel will be added to this animated explosion image.

Let's start with an animated sprite. Figure 16.4 shows an explosion sprite with 16 frames of animation that will work well for this tutorial. All modern graphic editors come with a tool called Magic Wand. You can look for this tool on the toolbar of your graphic editor, which is usually found with the other standard tools like Pen and Flood Fill. Now, using the Magic Wand, click somewhere on the background of the image, which in this example is any of the black portion of the image. The Magic Wand tool will locate the edges of the animation frames as shown in Figure 16.5.

Next, you want to zoom in to the image and add any additional transparent regions that are located inside the image, where the Magic Wand did not penetrate. By using the Shift key and clicking these additional pixels, you can add those regions to the existing selection, as you can see in Figure 16.6.

When you finally have the transparent regions all highlighted, the next step is to *invert* the selection. This will cause the selection to shift from the transparent

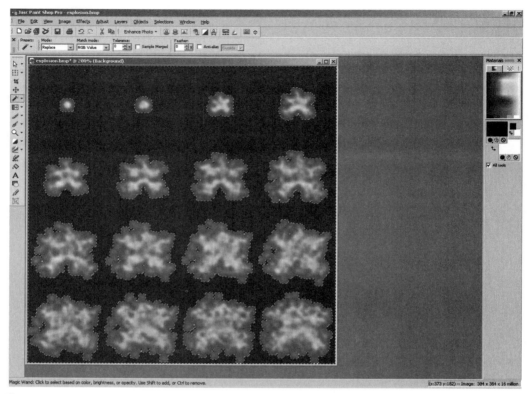

Figure 16.5
Using the Magic Wand tool to highlight the color keyed background color.

region to the actual image that you want to show up. By doing this, you will be able to erase the transparent portion from the image by creating a mask (or alpha channel) layer. The Invert option in Paint Shop Pro 8 can be found in the Selections menu as shown in Figure 16.7.

After the invert process is done, the resulting selection will look like that shown in Figure 16.8. Note that now only the true portions of the sprite frames are selected, and the background (or transparent) portion of the image is not selected. We will create the alpha channel using this selection so that the background color key will be removed from the image.

To create a mask layer, which will be the alpha channel, open the Layers menu and choose New Mask Layer, and then Show Selection, as shown in Figure 16.9. The new alpha channel will be added and the image will look like the one in Figure 16.10. You can now see the checkerboard pattern behind the image, which tells you that the alpha channel is working.

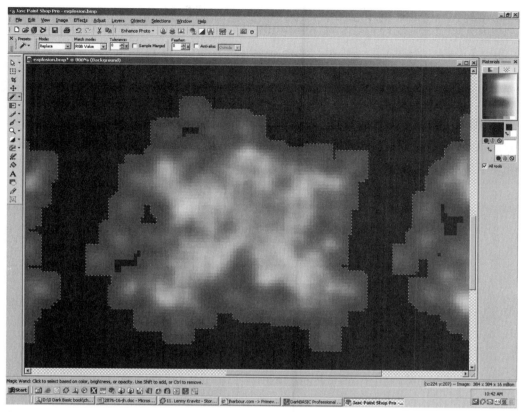

Figure 16.6
Adding additional selections with the Magic Wand tool by using the Shift key.

Now for saving the new image. You can't just save a 32-bit image with an alpha channel back to a BMP file, because that format doesn't support an alpha channel. Instead, we need to save the file as a PNG. Open the file menu and choose Save As, as shown in Figure 16.11. This will bring up the Save As dialog box. Using the Save As Type drop-down list, look for the file type called Portable Network Graphics (*.png), as shown in Figure 16.12. Type a name for the file and then click Save.

Angular Motion

Angular motion is an interesting technique for moving sprites in a realistic manner on the screen. Traditional methods of sprite movement, where the

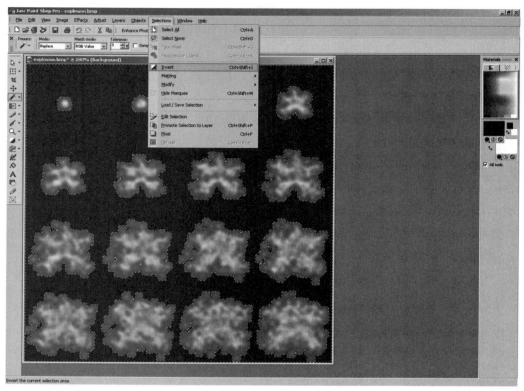

Figure 16.7
Inverting the selections.

position of the sprite is updated based on a fixed velocity, tend to produce games with a very limited and unrealistic level of gameplay. Typically, sprites that do not use angular motion are limited to only eight directions of travel. Figure 16.13 shows an example of an airplane with this limitation.

Another example is the tank sprite shown in Figure 16.14, which also has eight directions of travel, but it is oriented and numbered to give you a better idea of how it will move in a game.

Fixed Angles of Travel

Not only are these sprites limited in their range of movements, but they require a lot of hard-coded values to be inserted into the game, and each direction has an associated X and Y velocity that is fixed. The result is a very jerky-looking game with a very unrealistic sense of movement. In addition, firing a bullet or other

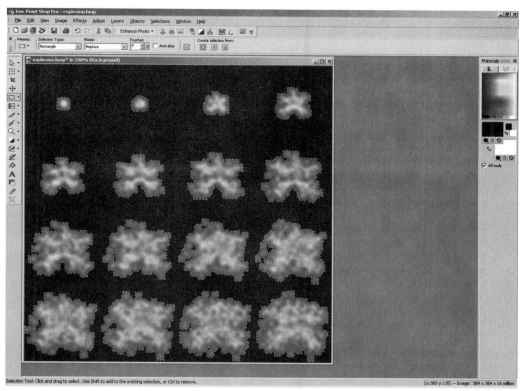

Figure 16.8
The selected portion of the image has been inverted.

weapon, as is usually required in most games, requires that the bullets also conform to this limited range of movement.

For instance, somewhere in your game loop is the code to update the sprite's position on the screen based on its velocity:

```
inc X, SpeedX
inc Y, SpeedY
```

The SpeedX and SpeedY variables are set to specific values such as 1, 2, or more. These represent the number of pixels that the sprite will move by in a single iteration of the game loop. One solution to improve realism is to add a delay value for both X and Y, so that a game sprite will move more realistically:

```
inc CounterX, 1
if (CounterX > DelayX)
```

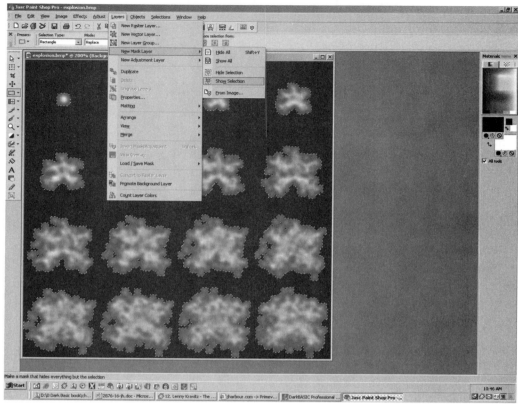

Figure 16.9
Adding a new mask layer to the image based on the image selection.

```
    CounterX = 0
    inc X, SpeedX
endif
```

The trick, then, is to fine-tune DelayX and SpeedX to values appropriate for the object you are trying to animate in the game. Take the direction that is due east, for example. As you can see in Figure 16.15, due east is 90 degrees from due north. Thus, the velocity for X should be positive, while the velocity for Y should be zero.

In a game that uses eight directions, each of the directions has an associated and fixed velocity that causes the sprite to move in that general direction. You must also have the eight different rotated images of the sprite, unless you plan to rotate them using the rotate sprite command, in which case you only need the north-facing sprite.

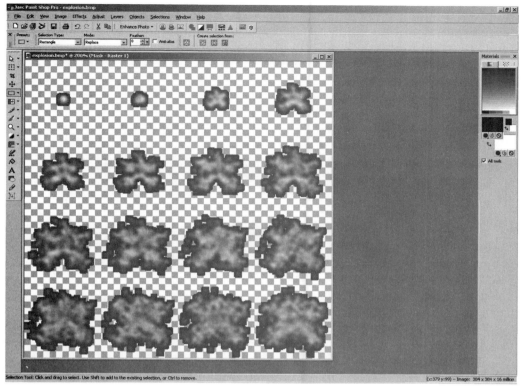

Figure 16.10
The new alpha channel has been added to the image.

Free Angles of Travel

Instead of limiting your game to just a handful of directions of travel, why not give your game objects the ability to move in *any direction* around the full 360 degrees? Yes, this is possible, and can be applied to any sprite with just a little bit of setup. I call this technique *angular motion* because the movement of a sprite is based on the angle it must travel.

A far better solution is to calculate the SpeedX and SpeedY values instead of setting them manually. What if SpeedX and SpeedY are floating-point instead of integer based? By switching to a float or double, you can use values such as:

```
SpeedX = 2.3455
SpeedY = 0.0023
```

These values might be small, even fractional, but keep in mind a game runs upwards of 60 frames per second. When iterated through a loop many times in a

Figure 16.11
Opening the File menu to save the file as a PNG.

second, a sprite with these types of values will move! The problem is figuring out which fractional values to assign to SpeedX and SpeedY to account for many directions of travel.

Programming Angular Motion

You could do that manually by playtesting to figure out which SpeedX and SpeedY values result in proper motion at a given angle, but this is tedious and imprecise. A better method is to calculate these values! Let me introduce you to two lovely functions that can help.

```
function calcVelocityX(angle as float)
   'calculate X velocity based on direction angle
   value# = sin(angle)
endfunction (value#)
```

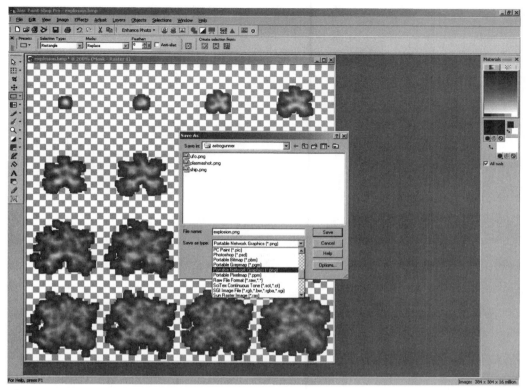

Figure 16.12
Saving the image as a PNG.

Figure 16.13
A sprite with only eight directions of movement is very limited.

```
function calcVelocityY(angle#)
   'calculate Y velocity based on direction angle
   value# = -cos(angle#)
endfunction value#
```

These two functions, calcVelocityX and calcVelocityY, make it possible to assign a floating-point value to the velocity of a sprite. To calculate a partial-pixel velocity for X, you calculate the sine of the angle. For the velocity of Y, you calculate the cosine of an angle. We multiply the cosine value by −1 because sine and cosine produce results that are based on the Cartesian coordinate system

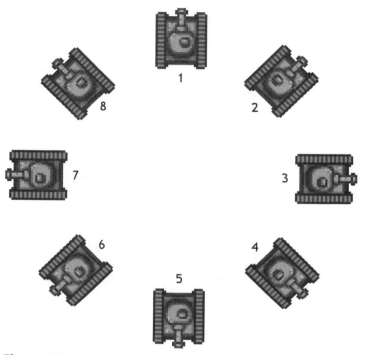

Figure 16.14
This tank sprite is also limited to eight directions of movement.

(remember basic geometry?), and the vertical orientation is inverted from the computer monitor. Then, instead of moving a sprite by a fixed 1 or 2 pixel per frame rate of speed, the sprite is moving at partial-pixel rates. What you want to do is choose a direction angle (as a double or float) and then call `calcAngleMoveX` and `calcAngleMoveY`, pass the angle to these functions, and then you are given a velocity value for X and Y.

This is quite different from the previous technique of forcing a sprite to move at a specific angle, with only 45 degrees of precision. Using angular motion, your sprite can move at 1 degree or 258 degrees or any other value from 0 to 359. Figure 16.16 shows a screenshot of the game that you will learn to create to demonstrate angular motion. Notice how the sprites are not only moving at arbitrary angles, but they're firing weapons along those trajectories as well!

Pay close attention to the values being printed at the top of the screen in this figure. See the first value at the upper left labeled "Vel"? These are the velocity X and Y values, which are, respectively, 1.030 and 0.543 in this example. The "Face" and "Move" values represent the angles that the ship is facing, which is not the

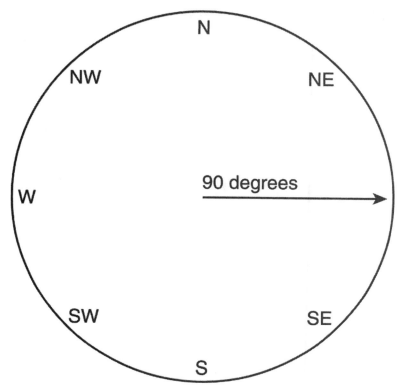

Figure 16.15
Each of the eight directions of travel require a specific velocity for X and Y.

same as the move angle. The ship can move in one direction, and then rotate and fire in a different direction without affecting the movement direction. This works great for a space-based game that must follow Newtonian physics. Remember Newton's first law of motion? It states "Every object in a state of uniform motion tends to remain in that state of motion unless an external force is applied to it."

Testing Angular Motion

I've written a simple demonstration program that will give you a good opportunity to play around with angular motion. This game is called Astro Gunner, and it is little more than a game of target practice, since the alien ship does not fire back. This program might be a good basis for an entire game if you add more functionality to it, such as enemies that shoot back, some other objects like asteroids, and possibly weapon upgrades, shields, and other features. At this stage, the game was intended solely to demonstrate angular motion, and as such

Vel: 1.030, 0.543   Pos: 618, 286   Face: 248   Move: 248   FPS 57

Figure 16.16
This game features sprites that are moved using angular motion calculations.

the code has been kept as lightweight and simple as possible. The alien UFO sprite is shown in Figure 16.17.

Defining Constants Used by the Game

Let's get started on the source code for the game, which I will explain in detail so you will have a solid grasp of how the game works. First up we have the usual constants used by the program. I like to use variables as constants so that the game doesn't have any image or sprite numbers used directly in the game's source code—which is very difficult to modify because you have to keep track of all the sprite and image numbers. It's far easier to use variables like SPR_SHIP instead.

```
'set screen to manual update
sync on
```

Figure 16.17
The alien UFO spaceship is a 32-bit image with an alpha channel.

```
sync rate 60
hide mouse

'define all sprite #'s
global IMG_BG as integer = 1
global SPR_SHIP as integer = 2
global SPR_UFO as integer = 3
global SPR_EXPLOSION as integer = 4
global IMG_BULLET as integer = 20
global SPR_BULLET as integer = 200

'ship constants
global ROTATIONRATE as float = 2.0
global ACCELERATION as float = 0.04
global TOPSPEED as float = 2.0
```

```
'bullet constants
global FIRINGRATE as integer = 4 'per second
global BULLETSPEED as float = 5.0
```

Defining the Sprite Structure

You have seen a rudimentary version of this sprite structure (a custom data type) in prior chapters, but now it has grown quite a bit and includes a lot of new features. Most notably, there are two new properties called imagenum and spritenum. These make it possible to assign a number to the sprite's structure variable for the image and sprite number, and then just use these properties any time you need to draw the sprite. This significantly cleans up the code and makes it possible to build a more complex game with many sprites.

```
'define a custom sprite datatype
type mySPRITE
    alive as byte
    x as float
    y as float
    velx as float
    vely as float
    faceangle as integer
    moveangle as integer
    velocity as float
    animframe as integer
    animcount as integer
    animdelay as integer
    imagenum as integer
    spritenum as integer
endtype
```

The Sprite Variables

After defining the sprite structure, which is called mySPRITE, next comes the sprite variables used in the game. The only sprites this simple game needs are the player, alien, and explosion, in addition to the bullets.

```
'define the sprites
global player as mySPRITE
global NUMBULLETS as integer = 10
dim bullets(10) as mySPRITE
global ufo as mySPRITE
global expl as mySPRITE
```

Getting the Game Rolling

Next up is some code that initializes the game and prepares it to run. Think of this code as the pre-launch checklist before the Space Shuttle is fired off into space.

```
'framerate variables
global fps as integer
global ticks as integer
global start as integer = timer()

'use manual timing for bullets
global firestart as integer = timer()

'load the game graphics
loadGraphics()

'make sure all drawing now goes to the screen
set current bitmap 0
```

The Game Loop

Now we have come to the most important part of the program, the game loop. This game loop uses the do . . . loop instead of repeat or while because in this particular example, we don't need any condition to exit out of the loop. The game loop calls on numerous support functions to get things happening on the screen, such as checkInput() and updateSprites().

```
do
  'draw the background
  paste image IMG_BG, 0, 0
  'move the player's ship
  checkInput()
  'update all sprites
  updateSprites()
  'test for collisions
  testCollisions()
  'display status info
  printInfo()
  'calculate frame rate
  ticks = ticks + 1
```

```
   if timer() > start + 999
      fps = ticks
      ticks = 0
      start = timer()
   endif
   sync
   if escapekey() = 1 then exit
loop
```

Loading and Initializing the Sprites

The `loadGraphics()` function loads the bitmap images and creates sprites out of them, in addition to loading up the background image. This game uses three sprite images: the player's ship, the alien UFO, and bullets. These sprites are all initialized using the `mySPRITE` struct properties. The nice thing about this structure is that you can add a lot of functionality to a sprite by setting its properties at startup, and then the code to manipulate a sprite is much less work later on.

```
function loadGraphics()
   'set transparent color to pink
   set image colorkey 255, 0, 255

   'load sprite graphics
   load image "space1.bmp", IMG_BG
   load image "ship.png", SPR_SHIP
   load image "ufo.png", SPR_UFO
   load image "bullet.png", IMG_BULLET

   'init the player
   player.x = 400.0
   player.y = 300.0
   player.imagenum = SPR_SHIP
   player.spritenum = SPR_SHIP
   sprite player.spritenum, player.x, player.y, player.imagenum
   xo = sprite width(player.spritenum)/2
   yo = sprite height(player.spritenum)/2
   offset sprite player.spritenum, xo, yo

   'init the bullets
   for n = 0 to NUMBULLETS-1
      bullets(n).imagenum = IMG_BULLET
      bullets(n).spritenum = SPR_BULLET + n
```

```
        bullets(n).alive = 0
        sprite bullets(n).spritenum, 999, 999, bullets(n).imagenum
        xo = sprite width(bullets(n).spritenum)/2
        yo = sprite height(bullets(n).spritenum)/2
        offset sprite bullets(n).spritenum, xo, yo
    next n


    'init the ufo
    ufo.x = rnd(screen width())
    ufo.y = rnd(screen height())
    ufo.moveangle = rnd(359)
    ufo.faceangle = ufo.moveangle
    ufo.velx = calcVelocityX(ufo.moveangle)
    ufo.vely = calcVelocityY(ufo.moveangle)
    ufo.imagenum = SPR_UFO
    ufo.spritenum = SPR_UFO
    sprite ufo.spritenum, ufo.x, ufo.y, ufo.imagenum
    xo = sprite width(ufo.spritenum)/2
    yo = sprite height(ufo.spritenum)/2
    offset sprite ufo.spritenum, xo, yo
    rotate sprite ufo.imagenum, ufo.faceangle


    'init the explosion
    spr = SPR_EXPLOSION
    create animated sprite spr, "explosion.png", 4, 4, spr
    expl.alive = 0
    expl.x = 999
    expl.y = 999
    expl.imagenum = SPR_EXPLOSION
    expl.spritenum = SPR_EXPLOSION
    sprite expl.spritenum, expl.x, expl.y, expl.imagenum
    xo = sprite width(expl.spritenum)/2
    yo = sprite height(expl.spritenum)/2
    offset sprite expl.spritenum, xo, yo
endfunction
```

Updating the Sprites

The updateSprites() function updates the position and animation of the sprites used in the game. This includes the player's ship, the alien UFO, the explosions, and the bullets. This is a pretty big function, but just take a look at the code for a minute and you'll see that it's all very repetitive. A sprite's position (X and Y) is updated using the sprite's velocity (velX and velY), and so on.

```
function updateSprites()
   'update player's x pos
   player.X = player.X + player.velX
   if player.X < 0 then player.X = screen width()
   if player.X > screen width() then player.X = 0

   'update player's y pos
   player.Y = player.Y + player.velY
   if player.Y < 0 then player.Y = screen height()
   if player.Y > screen height() then player.Y = 0

   'move the ufo
   ufo.X = ufo.X + ufo.velX
   if ufo.X < 0 then ufo.X = screen width()
   if ufo.X > screen width() then ufo.X = 0

   'update ufo
   ufo.X = ufo.X + ufo.velX
   if ufo.X < 0 then ufo.X = screen width()
   if ufo.X > screen width() then ufo.X = 0
   ufo.Y = ufo.Y + ufo.velY
   if ufo.Y < 0 then ufo.Y = screen height()
   if ufo.Y > screen height() then ufo.Y = 0
   sprite ufo.spritenum, ufo.x, ufo.y, ufo.imagenum

   'update explosion
   if expl.alive = 1
      if sprite frame(expl.spritenum) = 16
         expl.alive = 0
      else
         paste sprite expl.spritenum, expl.x, expl.y
         play sprite expl.spritenum, 1, 16, 30
      endif
   endif

   'draw the player's ship
   spr = player.imagenum
   sprite spr, int(player.X), int(player.Y), spr
```

```
    for n = 0 to NUMBULLETS-1
      if bullets(n).alive = 1
        'update sprite's x pos
        bullets(n).x = bullets(n).x + bullets(n).velx * BULLETSPEED
        if bullets(n).x < 0 or bullets(n).x > screen width()
          bullets(n).alive = 0
          hide sprite bullets(n).spritenum
        endif

        'update sprite's y pos
        bullets(n).y = bullets(n).y + bullets(n).vely * BULLETSPEED
        if bullets(n).y < 0 or bullets(n).y > screen height()
          bullets(n).alive = 0
          hide sprite bullets(n).spritenum
        endif

        'draw the sprite
        spr = bullets(n).spritenum
        img = bullets(n).imagenum
        sprite spr, int(bullets(n).x), int(bullets(n).y), img
      endif
    next n
endfunction
```

Getting Player Input

The checkInput() function checks for user input and manipulates the player's ship in the process. The left and right arrow keys are used to rotate the ship, while the up arrow is used to apply thrust to the ship. The spacebar fires a bullet. This is the second most important part of the game next to the game loop because it is here that the angular motion calculations are made by calling the calcVelocityX and calcVelocityY functions. These calculations must be made every time the ship rotates to a new angle.

```
function checkInput()
  vel as float

  if upkey()
    'apply some thrust using calculated velocity
    player.moveangle = wrapvalue(player.faceangle)
```

```
            'calculate X velocity
            vel = calcVelocityX(player.moveangle) * ACCELERATION
            player.velx = player.velx + vel

            'limit the throttle
            if player.velx < -TOPSPEED then player.velx = -TOPSPEED
            if player.velx > TOPSPEED then player.velx = TOPSPEED

            'calculate Y velocity
            vel = calcVelocityY(player.moveangle) * ACCELERATION
            player.vely = player.vely + vel

            'limit the throttle
            if player.vely < -TOPSPEED then player.vely = -TOPSPEED
            if player.vely > TOPSPEED then player.vely = TOPSPEED
        endif

    if leftkey()
        'turn ship left
        player.faceangle = wrapvalue(player.faceangle - ROTATIONRATE)
        rotate sprite player.imagenum, player.faceangle
    endif

    if rightkey()
        'turn ship right
        player.faceangle = wrapvalue(player.faceangle + ROTATIONRATE)
        rotate sprite player.imagenum, player.faceangle
    endif

    'fire a bullet
    if spacekey()
        fireBullet()
    endif
endfunction
```

Calculating Angular Motion

The calcVelocityX() and calcVelocityY() functions calculate the angular motion velocity values for X and Y, which must be floats (not integers). These functions use sine for X, and cosine for Y.

```
function calcVelocityX(angle as float)
    'calculate X velocity based on direction angle
```

```
   value# = sin(angle)
endfunction (value#)

function calcVelocityY(angle#)

   'calculate Y velocity based on direction angle
   value# = -cos(angle#)
endfunction value#
```

Firing Bullets

The fireBullet() function iterates through the bullets array to locate an unused bullet. Any time a bullet hits the edge of the screen, or hits the alien UFO, it is destroyed. Actually, the sprite is just hidden and its *alive* property is set to 0 (which equates to false). So, the for loop in this function looks for an unused bullet, in which case its alive property will be zero. When found, the function sets the bullet equal to the ship's position and direction of travel, and then the bullet is picked up by the updateSprites() function (where it is then moved). After preparing a bullet, this function is only needed again when another bullet is fired, and is not needed during the game loop to move anything.

```
function fireBullet()
   done as integer = 0

   'slow down the firing rate
   if timer() > firestart + 1000 / FIRINGRATE

      for n = 0 to NUMBULLETS-1

         'break out of loop when we find an unused bullet
         if done = 0 and bullets(n).alive = 0
            bullets(n).alive = 1
            bullets(n).x = player.x
            bullets(n).y = player.y
            bullets(n).faceangle = player.faceangle
            bullets(n).moveangle = player.faceangle
            bullets(n).velx = calcVelocityX(bullets(n).moveangle)
            bullets(n).vely = calcVelocityY(bullets(n).moveangle)

            'draw the bullet sprite at the correct angle
            rotate sprite bullets(n).spritenum, bullets(n).faceangle

            'move the bullet sprite
            spr = bullets(n).spritenum
```

```
            img = bullets(n).imagenum
            sprite spr, bullets(n).x, bullets(n).y, img
            show sprite bullets(n).spritenum
            done = 1
        endif
    next n

    'pause before allowing another shot to be fired
    firestart = timer()
  endif
endfunction
```

Testing for Collisions

The testCollisions() function looks at all of the bullet sprites and checks to see if one has collided with the alien UFO. When this happens, the bullet is hidden, an explosion animation is started, and the UFO is respawned elsewhere on the screen. For a real game, this function would need to do more things like update the player's score, check for collisions with the player's ship, and so on.

```
function testCollisions()
  'look at all the bullets for a collision
  for n = 0 to NUMBULLETS-1
    if bullets(n).alive = 1

        'collision test: bullet and ufo
        if sprite collision(bullets(n).spritenum, ufo.spritenum)

          'erase the bullet
          bullets(n).alive = 0
          hide sprite bullets(n).spritenum

          'start the explosion
          expl.x = ufo.x
          expl.y = ufo.y
          expl.alive = 1
          set sprite frame expl.spritenum, 1

          'restart the ufo somewhere else
          ufo.x = rnd(screen width())
          ufo.y = rnd(screen height())
          ufo.moveangle = rnd(359)
```

```
        ufo.faceangle = ufo.moveangle
        ufo.velx = calcVelocityX(ufo.moveangle)
        ufo.vely = calcVelocityY(ufo.moveangle)
        rotate sprite ufo.imagenum, ufo.faceangle
        exit

    endif

  endif

 next n
endfunction
```

Printing Detailed Information

The printInfo() function is a debugging tool, for the most part. This function prints out detailed information about the game's current state so you can see what is happening to the player's ship as it is moved around on the screen. This is helpful for understanding how angular motion works. Just watch the velocity and position values adjust whenever you rotate or apply thrust to the ship.

```
function printInfo()
   'set up a nice font
   set text font "Arial"
   set text to bold
   set text size 18
   ink rgb(255,255,0),0

   'display ship's velocity
   vx$ = left$(str$(player.velX),5)
   vy$ = left$(str$(player.velY),5)
   text 0,0,"Vel: " + vx$ + ", " + vy$

   'display ship's position
   text 140,0,"Pos: "+str$(int(player.X))+", "+str$(int(player.Y))

   'display angles
   text 300,0,"Face: " + str$(player.faceangle)
   text 400,0,"Move: " + str$(player.moveangle)
   text screen width()-80,0,"FPS " + str$(fps)
endfunction
```

Summary

This chapter has been a romp through some seriously advanced topics! You first learned about alpha channel transparency and then you learned how to program angular motion to move a sprite realistically in a game. Although the game demonstrated in this chapter was based in space, you can apply the knowledge to any type of game genre, and the calculations here will save you a lot of time that would have been spent setting up sprites to move realistically. Don't you love a good algorithm?

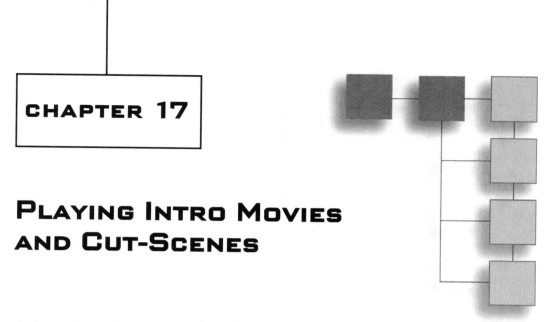

CHAPTER 17

PLAYING INTRO MOVIES AND CUT-SCENES

Animated movie sequences have become a standard feature of video games, so much so that introductory movies and cut-scenes for games are often used as demo reels and trailers before the game is finished. If a high-end game is released without an introductory movie or narrative of some kind, it is possible that the game will make a poor first impression on reviewers and consumers alike. A two-minute game "teaser" trailer or introductory movie can take up to a year and cost upwards of a million dollars to produce, due to the excruciating detail put into 3D animation sequences that are rendered for the movie. Game studios often hire 3D animators and concept artists to use programs such as Maya and LightWave for both game artwork and movies.

This chapter teaches you how to add intro movies and cut-scenes to your DB games. As you will learn, DB can be used for playing movie files, which can be embedded inside the executable. If you are an animator or 3D modeler learning DB to enhance your portfolio, then you might use this feature to make your demos into self-running programs! I won't be talking about creating videos, only how to play video files.

This chapter covers the following topics:

- Introduction to movies
- Loading and playing movie files
- Changing the position and size of a movie
- Movie trailers

Introduction to Movies

In the early days of video games, the "intro movie" was usually a paragraph of text on the screen with perhaps a single-channel soundtrack. As games became more complex and budgets were increased, intro movies and cut-scenes became more elaborate, moving from text to game engine cinematics. One of the first games to feature cut-scenes within the game was *Wing Commander II: Vengeance of the Kilrathi,* and later games in the Wing Commander series followed suit to much acclaim, with custom movie-quality sets and popular actors reprising the roles of lead characters in the game.

Game Cinema

Wing Commander II was a trend-setting game featuring extraordinary movies that told the story within the game. Keep in mind that when this game came out, the average PC was a 486/33 with 8 MB of memory and an Adlib or Sound Blaster card. Windows 3.0 was not even around yet. That the game had movie sequences and voice-overs was extraordinary. Granted, the speech kit was an add-on for the game, sold separately. The game wasn't even distributed on a CD-ROM. Actually, CD-ROM technology had not hit the mainstream yet so games were still being put on 5 1/4" or 3 1/2" floppy diskettes (1.2 MB and 1.4 MB, respectively). The movie sequences in *Wing Commander II* were recorded on video and then digitized using a video capture card. In other words, the movies were not rendered in 3D as they are today.

Video capture movies were used in the follow-up *Wing Commander* games, but they dropped in popularity as the game industry was flooded with video-capture games in the great multimedia revolution. In-game movies are almost always rendered in 3D today. If you are looking for ideas about how to create intro movies for your own games, consider recording a video of your game actually running (perhaps in demo mode), adding a catchy music soundtrack, and using the demo trailer for your game as the intro movie.

What Is a Movie File?

Movie files store the video frames and audio streams that make up a movie sequence. The AVI (*Audio-Video Interleaved*) format was a standard for Windows multimedia PCs at the start of the multimedia revolution in the early 1990s, and it is still the most popular movie file format for Windows. However, there are many competing video formats, such as Apple's QuickTime (.mov),

RealNetwork's RealMedia (.rm), the open-source Xvid, and the professional MPEG (.mpg) formats. Since that time, AVI has been expanded with multiple compressor-decompressor (*codec*) formats, making it extremely versatile at the expense of complexity. When encoding or decoding to or from an AVI, which codec you should use can be confusing. Despite the growing list, there are two formats that are compatible with most AVI players—Indeo and Cinepak. If you have ever played around with a video capture card or video mastering software, you have likely come across these codecs.

Loading and Playing Movie Files

Despite the confusing plethora of audio-video formats and codecs, DB makes loading and playing AVI files as simple as loading and displaying a bitmap image. Not only does DB let you load and play a movie file with only a couple of lines of source code, you can even play several movies on the screen at the same time!

Basic Movie Playback Commands

There are quite a few commands to help you get the most out of your movie-going experience, but only a couple of those commands are absolutely necessary. This section will show you the commands that simply load and play a movie, along with some helper commands. First, I want to introduce you to the command to load a movie file.

Loading a Video File

You can use the LOAD ANIMATION command to load an AVI movie file into DB. The syntax of the command is LOAD ANIMATION *Filename, Animation Number*. The first parameter is the name of an AVI file, which is relative to the current folder in which the program was run. The second parameter is a number from 1 to 32 for the position in which to store the movie in DB. You can load up to 32 movies at a time and play any or all of them at any time. However, keep in mind that movie files can be large, and you might extinguish available memory by trying to load them all at once.

Checking a Video's Status

After you have loaded a movie file into DB, there are several helper commands available to tell you about the movie. One such command is ANIMATION EXIST, which has the syntax Return Value = ANIMATION EXIST (*Animation Number*). If the animation has been loaded, then the ANIMATION EXIST command will return a 1; otherwise, it will return a 0. You can use this command after loading a movie file to determine whether it loaded correctly. Another way to make sure the movie was loaded correctly is by checking its dimensions, as the next two commands demonstrate. The term *animation* is synonymous with the term *movie* in DB.

Some movie files are short, and others can be very long. In fact, some games have high-resolution intro movies that weigh in at several hundred megabytes. You can use the ANIMATION PLAYING command to determine when a movie is done playing. The syntax is Return Value = ANIMATION PLAYING (*Animation Number*).

Getting a Video's Properties

The ANIMATION WIDTH command returns the horizontal resolution of a movie after it has been loaded by referencing the animation number parameter. The syntax for the command is Return Value = ANIMATION WIDTH (*Animation Number*). This command comes in handy when you want to resize or reposition the movie. As I'll show you later in this chapter, you can scale the movie or center it on the screen. Likewise, ANIMATION HEIGHT returns the vertical resolution of a movie after it has been loaded by referencing the animation number parameter. The syntax for the command is Return Value = ANIMATION HEIGHT (*Animation Number*).

Playing a Video

After you have loaded and verified a movie file, you can play it using the PLAY ANIMATION command. The syntax for this command is PLAY ANIMATION *Animation Number*, *Bitmap Number*, *Left*, *Top*, *Right*, *Bottom*. The first parameter is required, but the other parameters are optional. By specifying the bitmap number, you can send playback to a specific bitmap. The last four parameters (Left, Top, Right, and Bottom) resize and reposition the movie on the screen.

Removing a Video from Memory

After you have finished playing a particular movie that you might not need again, always consider deleting the movie to free up memory and make room for other movies. You can delete a movie using the DELETE ANIMATION command. The syntax is DELETE ANIMATION *Animation Number*. It is usually better to load a movie, play it, and then delete it from memory using the DELETE ANIMATION command. You don't want to keep a large movie in memory if you will only play it once.

Testing Video File Playback

All right, how about a demonstration of loading and playing an AVI video file? Nothing beats a little source code to see how something works. I wrote the PlayAnim program just for that purpose. It is simple enough that you can see how easy it is to load and play a movie file. Take a look at Figure 17.1, which shows a movie file playing with the default resolution. Figure 17.2 shows a movie playing in full-screen mode, which is possible by simple changing the size parameters of the PLAY ANIMATION command.

Note that the PlayAnim program (and all the other programs in this chapter) runs at 640×480 in 32-bit color mode. Although all of the sample programs run at this screen resolution, the color depth is not quite as important. Aside from the fact that 32-bit color is of a higher quality than 16-bit color, and special effects such as transparency are possible with 32-bit color mode, you may feel free to use

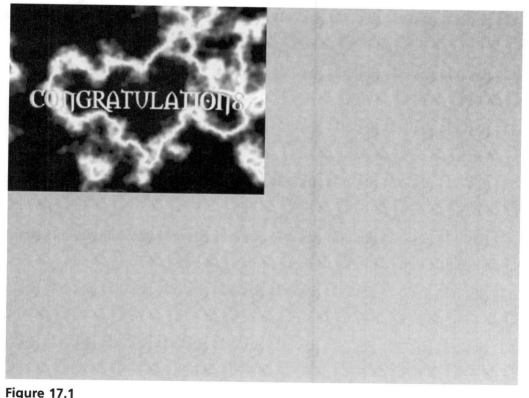

Figure 17.1
The PlayAnim program loads and plays an AVI movie file using the default width and height of the movie.

Figure 17.2
The PlayAnim program can be set to run full screen by changing the `Right` and `Bottom` parameters to the resolution of the screen.

either 32-bit or 16-bit color (using the third parameters of the SET DISPLAY MODE command). If your video card is unable to run in 32-bit color mode (or if it runs slowly), feel free to change the display mode command so it uses 16-bit color instead. DB supports this command, but it is preferred that you use the Project Manager to configure the video mode instead.

```
'initialize the program
SET DISPLAY MODE 640, 480, 32
HIDE MOUSE

'load background bitmap
LOAD BITMAP "background.bmp", 0

'load the animation file
LOAD ANIMATION "congrat2.avi", 1
```

```
'play the animation
PLAY ANIMATION 1, 0, 0, 320, 240

'wait for keypress
WAIT KEY

'remove the movie from memory
DELETE ANIMATION 1
END
```

Looping Movie Playback

One thing you probably noticed right away was how short the movie was in the PlayAnim program. It was only a few seconds long! That file, like many of the others in this chapter, is one of the movie files that comes with DB. You can use those animated movies to enhance your game by playing the Congratulations movie when the player wins or the Game Over movie when the game ends.

Starting and Stopping a Looped Video

The animation in the PlayAnim program doesn't last long because that particular movie file simply is supposed to display the Congratulations message on the screen. But what if you want to repeat the movie after it has stopped? For example, you can use the LOOP ANIMATION command to loop the movie to play until the player presses a key or clicks a mouse button. The syntax for this command is LOOP ANIMATION *Animation Number, Bitmap Number, Left, Top, Right, Bottom*. The last four parameters (Left, Top, Right, and Bottom) are optional, as is the Bitmap Number parameter. I will explain movie scaling shortly, but for now I'll focus on looping.

Since a movie that is looping will continue to loop indefinitely, you need a way to stop the playback at some point (such as at the end of the program). You can stop playback of a movie using the STOP ANIMATION command. The syntax is STOP ANIMATION *Animation Number*.

When a movie is playing in loop mode, the ANIMATION LOOPED command will return a 1 for that movie; otherwise, it returns a 0. The syntax for the command is Return Value = ANIMATION LOOPED (*Animation Number*).

Pausing and Resuming Playback

Now for some support commands, as promised. There are several commands you can use while a movie file is playing that might come in handy. For example, to pause playback at the current position, you can use the PAUSE ANIMATION command. The syntax is PAUSE ANIMATION *Animation Number*. Once a movie has been paused, you can check the status of the paused property using the ANIMATION PAUSED command. The syntax is Return Value = ANIMATION PAUSED (*Animation Number*).

Another useful command is the RESUME ANIMATION command, which resumes playback after it has been paused. The syntax for this command is RESUME ANIMATION *Animation Number*. Keep in mind that while these commands are all similar in syntax, you can use any animation number from 1 to 32 when calling them, which gives you the ability to manipulate multiple movies at the same time. I would think that playing just one movie on the screen would be enough to ask of DB, but it goes a step further by allowing you to play several at a time!

The MultiAnim Program

The MultiAnim program plays four movies on the screen at the same time. By pressing the number keys 1 to 4, you can pause and resume playback of each of the four movies. The Esc key ends the program. Figure 17.3 shows the output of the MultiAnim program. This program is very demanding of your PC, so if the program doesn't respond immediately to the number keys, just hold the key down for a second and you should see something happen.

```
'initialize the program
SET DISPLAY MODE 640, 480, 16
HIDE MOUSE
DISABLE ESCAPEKEY
CLS

'load and start each of the movies
LOAD ANIMATION "youwin1.avi", 1
LOOP ANIMATION 1
LOAD ANIMATION "congrat2.avi", 2
LOOP ANIMATION 2, 0, 320, 0, 640, 240
LOAD ANIMATION "gameover2.avi", 3
LOOP ANIMATION 3, 0, 0, 240, 320, 480
LOAD ANIMATION "loading3.avi", 4
LOOP ANIMATION 4, 0, 320, 240, 640, 480

'loop until ESC key pressed
REPEAT
```

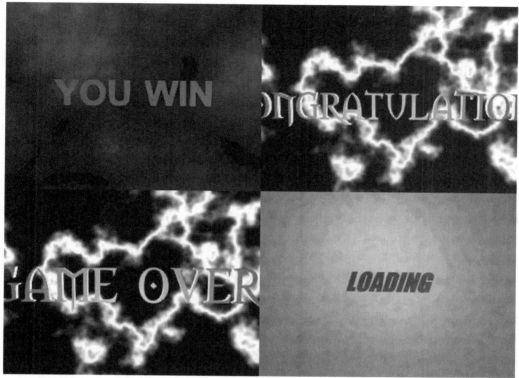

Figure 17.3
The MultiAnim program plays four movie files at the same time and allows the user to pause and resume playback of each video stream.

```
   FOR N = 1 TO 4
      IF VAL(INKEY$()) = N
         IF ANIMATION PAUSED(N)
            RESUME ANIMATION N
         ELSE
            PAUSE ANIMATION N
         ENDIF
      ENDIF
   NEXT N
   'update the screen
   SYNC
UNTIL ESCAPEKEY()

'delete the movies
DELETE ANIMATION 1
DELETE ANIMATION 2
```

```
DELETE ANIMATION 3
DELETE ANIMATION 4
END
```

Changing the Position and Size of a Movie

Now that you've had a little experience playing and looping movie files, I'd like to explain some advanced playback features. This section will explain how to change the scale and position of a movie during playback, with some interesting results.

Changing the Position of a Movie

Although you can simply play a movie using the full resolution of the screen, it is far more likely that you will want to use DB's fantastic movie-playing capabilities for many small animations in a game or program. For this, you will need a way to reposition the playback to any place on the screen, and then return the position of the movie. Following are some commands that will help you to do just that.

PLACE ANIMATION is one of the most versatile movie playback commands in DB. The syntax is PLACE ANIMATION *Animation Number, Left, Top, Right, Bottom*. Using this command, you can reposition and scale a movie *during playback*. That is the significant phrase—*during playback*. You can set the scale and position using the PLAY ANIMATION command. However, once the movie has started, you must use PLACE ANIMATION to make changes during playback. The MoveAnim and ScaleAnim programs, which are featured later in this chapter, demonstrate how to use this command.

When you are using the PLACE ANIMATION command, it is often convenient to be able to return the position of the movie on the screen. There are two commands for determining the position of the movie. The first command, ANIMATION POSITION X, returns the X position of a movie. The syntax is Return Value = ANIMATION POSITION X (*Animation Number*). The other command for determining the position of a movie is the ANIMATION POSITION Y command, which returns the Y position of a movie. The syntax is Return Value = ANIMATION POSITION Y (*Animation Number*).

Changing the Scale of a Movie

Moving the position of a movie is pretty impressive, but it is nothing compared to real-time scaling! *Scale* refers to not only the size of something, but also the ratio of width to height. Although you could scale the horizontal dimension of a 2D object to stretch it left to right, and you could likewise scale the vertical dimension to stretch it top to bottom, that is not true scaling (and it is not particularly useful in any case). Scaling involves resizing both dimensions (horizontal and vertical) by the same amount. That is really the only way to get clean results with a movie.

To change the scale of a movie, you use the same command that you used earlier to reposition a movie—the PLACE ANIMATION command. For reference, the syntax for this command is PLACE ANIMATION *Animation Number, Left, Top, Right, Bottom*. The key to scaling a movie lies with the last two parameters: Right and Bottom. To change the scale of a movie, you simply modify the Right and Bottom values by a set percent, and the output will either shrink or grow by that percent.

The ScaleAnim Program

To demonstrate movie scaling, I have written a program called ScaleAnim. Figure 17.4 shows a movie with a very small scale, and Figure 17.5 shows the same movie at 165% of its normal size, nearly filling the screen.

Figure 17.4
The ScaleAnim program changes the scale of a movie during playback. Here, the movie is reduced down to a very small size.

Figure 17.5
The ScaleAnim program loops the animation while changing the scale from 10% to 200%.

```
'create some variables
scale = 1.0
change = 0.05
SX = 0
SY = 0
X = 0
Y = 0

'initialize the program
SET DISPLAY MODE 640, 480, 32
HIDE MOUSE
SYNC ON

'load background bitmap
LOAD BITMAP "background.bmp", 1
COPY BITMAP 1, 0
SET CURRENT BITMAP 0
```

```
'load and play the animation file
LOAD ANIMATION "gameover2.avi", 1
LOOP ANIMATION 1

'loop until ESC key pressed
REPEAT
    'redraw background
    COPY BITMAP 1, 0

    'change the scale
    scale = scale + change
    IF scale < 0.1 OR scale > 2.0
        change = change * -1
    ENDIF

    'reposition the movie
    SX = INT(320 * scale)
    SY =  INT(240 * scale)
    X = 320 - SX / 2
    Y = 240 - SY / 2
    PLACE ANIMATION 1, X, Y, X + SX, Y + SY

    TEXT 0,0,"Scale: " + STR$(scale)

    'update the screen
    SYNC
UNTIL ESCAPEKEY()

DELETE ANIMATION 1
END
```

Movie Trailers

So you can really get a feel for what an introductory movie is like, I recommend that you download some movie or video game trailers from http://www .apple.com/trailers or http://www.ifilm.com. Some movie files are not in a format supported by DB. The three most popular movie formats are Windows Media, Apple QuickTime, and RealPlayer. In order to play a movie file, it must be an AVI file in a standard format like Indeo or Cinepak. As long as you use a standard format when converting a movie file to AVI for use in DB, the movie will be playable. There are many sample movies that come with DB, such as those used in the sample programs in this chapter.

As for converting video files, there are numerous programs on the Internet that you can download and try out or purchase. One such program that I recommend is EO Video by McGray Ltd. You can learn more about EO Video and download a trial version from http://www.eo-video.com. I like this program because it can convert from any movie format to another, and it can even combine multiple movie files into a single output file using any codec (compressor-decompressor) format.

Feel free to modify the PlayMovie program to scale the movies to fill the whole screen. However, at higher than 320×240 (the most common resolution), some movies look grainy, so I prefer to watch them at their native resolution. The amazing thing about DB is that you can compile the movies *into* the executable file by adding files to the Media list in the project window (on the bottom-right corner of the DB IDE). Then go to Settings, and set the "EXE with Attached Media" option.

The PlayMovie Program

The PlayMovie program is similar to the PlayAnim program, with the added feature that it centers the movie on the screen. This program also shows how to check the horizontal and vertical resolution of the movie file so it can be centered properly. Previous programs in this chapter hard-coded the playback resolution, but this one retrieves the dimensions of the video and centers it regardless of the size. For large, high-resolution videos, you might want to increase the resolution of the program (which is currently set to 640×480).

```
'create some variables
Width = 0
Height = 0
X = 0
Y = 0


'initialize the program
SET DISPLAY MODE 640, 480, 32
HIDE MOUSE
DISABLE ESCAPEKEY
CLS


'modify the following line with the appropriate filename
LOAD ANIMATION "moviefile.avi", 1
```

```
'get resolution of the movie
Width = ANIMATION WIDTH(1)
Height = ANIMATION HEIGHT(1)
X = 320 - Width / 2
Y = 240 - Height / 2

'play the animation
PLAY ANIMATION 1, X, Y, X + Width, Y + Height

'wait for keypress
WAIT KEY

'remove the movie from memory
DELETE ANIMATION 1
END
```

Summary

This chapter explored the subject of playing movies for the introduction to a game and for cut-scenes within a game. DB supports the AVI format most common on Windows PCs. It is capable of playing any Indeo, Cinepak, or similar codec in an AVI file. This chapter also showed you how to position a movie on the screen, how to move the movie during playback, and how to change the size of the movie by scaling the output rectangle.

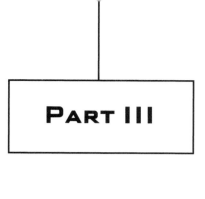

PART III

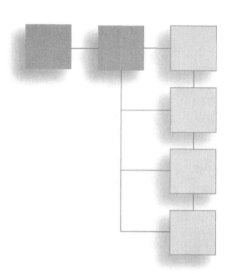

3D GAME PROGRAMMING

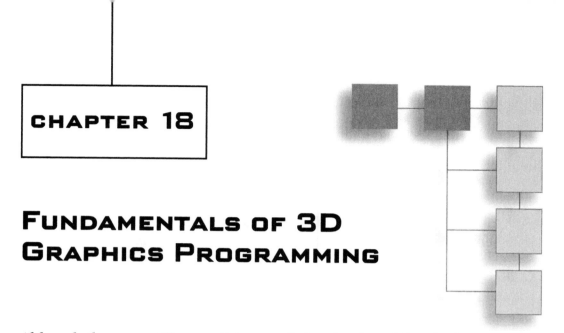

CHAPTER 18

FUNDAMENTALS OF 3D GRAPHICS PROGRAMMING

Although there are still many 2D games being developed for platforms such as Game Boy Advance and web-based casual games, such games are in the minority. This chapter is the first of several chapters that focuses on 3D graphics programming. Starting with this chapter, you will learn the basics of how to create and draw 3D objects, such as triangles, rectangles, cubes, cones, and cylinders, as well as how to apply textures to such objects. This chapter provides you with what might be called the low-level view of 3D graphics because you will have an opportunity to create 3D objects from scratch using source code, providing that extremely important foundation for more advanced techniques (such as meshes).

The one thing that this chapter does *not* do is bore you with 3D theory. Instead, I have designed this chapter to explain the specific DarkBASIC commands that you need to write 3D programs. There is value in understanding the underlying matrix mathematics involved in rendering a 3D scene, but the subject can become quickly overwhelming! If you struggle with any specific subject related to 3D graphics, you will surely be able to figure out what is going on by running the sample programs in this chapter. This chapter covers the following topics:

- Introduction to 3D graphics

- Basic 3D graphics commands

Introduction to 3D Graphics

The subject of 3D graphics consists of a monumental amount of information. Not only have entire books been written just about the basics of 3D graphics, but entire sets of volumes have been dedicated to the subject of advanced 3D rendering techniques. The 3D graphics business is a multi-billion dollar industry that encompasses video games and the motion picture industry, as well as commercial aviation and military applications. The astonishing thing about 3D graphics is how much it has improved over the years, both in theory and in application. There are techniques in use today, such as mip-mapping and multi-texturing, that are staggering in their realism. It is quite possible to mistake a real-time 3D demonstration for a prerendered video because the quality of rendered graphics today is so astonishing.

Although visual quality is really just a factor of your video card's features and capabilities, it does not take extraordinarily complex scenes to make a great game. Realism is definitely a good thing, but only if the majority of PCs in the world are able to run the game! The one thing you definitely do not want to do is limit the potential audience for your game by putting in so many high-quality scenes and models that it requires the very latest generation of video card to run the game. The latest generation of graphics processors (GPUs) are the nVidia GeForce 7900 and ATI Radeon X1900, which is capable of drawing billions of polygons per second.

The GPU in your video card does all the complicated work involved in rendering the 3D graphics in a game. In the old days before 3D accelerators came along (such as during the early '90s), the main CPU was tasked with doing all of the 3D calculations. Suffice it to say, CPUs in the early '90s were not particularly fast in the first place, let alone when required to render a 3D scene. Today, a single ATI Radeon X1900 or nVidia GeForce 7900 is capable of more than a trillion calculations per second—many thousands of times faster than an original Intel Pentium chip. Due to such advances in silicon technology, we have extraordinarily powerful graphics workstations available in the most common new PCs that you might peruse at a local computer store, and usually for less than $1,500. Such a thing was unheard of just a few years ago!

DB does a great job at simplifying the complexity of programming 3D graphics. The most recent update to DB requires the latest version of DirectX 9.0 (June 2006), with a large assortment of special effects and next-generation graphical features (such as shaders). One of the goals of this chapter is to demonstrate the difference that the video card can make in visual quality and performance, because these factors are so important when it comes to 3D graphics programming. If you have an older video card that does not provide shader technology or at least transform and lighting (T&L), then you will not be able to use the advanced features available with DirectX 9.0.

Introduction to Vertices

Now let's jump into the details and learn the basics of 3D graphics. Trust me, you will appreciate this information down the road when you start working with advanced 3D scenes and 3D objects. It's okay if you have never written a 3D program before, because this chapter will show you how to draw basic 3D objects on the screen. For now, let's start at the beginning.

What Is a Vertex?

The first question that you must ask before doing anything in 3D is: What is a vertex? It is the atom of the 3D realm, the lowest common denominator, the most basic entity of a 3D world. If you think of a 3D world as a pool of water, then a vertex is analogous to an H_2O molecule. A vertex is actually a point in geometric space. Do you have any experience with geometry? In high school the class that unifies geometry with algebra is called trigonometry. Whether you are interested in the subject or not, I can't stress enough how a little background refresher in trigonometry will make you a more competent 3D programmer. As the previous chapters in this book have testified, it takes a lot to explain the basics of something that is rather complicated—like programming a game.

Now, don't let me worry you. You won't need to know how to solve complex geometry or trigonometry to write a 3D game with DB because it was designed to make game programming as simple as possible, handling all the math in the background for you. In the 3D graphics world, trigonometry describes how 3D objects can be rotated, moved, and scaled on the screen. I will explain the different ways that DB uses trigonometry to create 3D objects throughout this chapter.

A vertex can be described as a 3D geometric point. The 3D world is mapped around the Cartesian coordinate system. A 3D point has three components: X, Y, and Z. Three vertices make up a polygon, the basis for 3D graphics. Take a look at Figure 18.1 for an illustration of vertices.

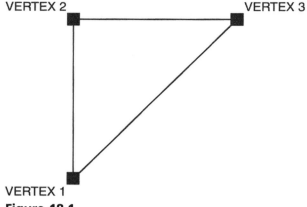

VERTEX 2

VERTEX 3

VERTEX 1

Figure 18.1
Three vertices make up a polygon.

Definition

A *vertex* is a point in 3D space represented by three coordinates: X, Y, and Z.

Because 3D graphics are based on trigonometry, 3D formulas also use the Cartesian coordinate system for drawing, moving, rotating, and scaling vertices. The Cartesian coordinate system (shown in Figure 18.2) is the basis for all 3D graphics rendering.

If you have a hard time visualizing the Z axis, just think of Z as moving away from you (see Figure 18.3). Hold your hand in the air in front of your face and move it away from you, and then back in toward you. That is the Z axis. The motion going away from you is the positive Z axis, while moving your hand back in toward you is the negative Z axis. As for Figure 18.3, imagine the X and Y axes moving back and forth along the Z axis. That is exactly what happens when you are dealing with three dimensions. The lesser two dimensions are represented "on" the third dimension in what seems like many copies of those two dimensions. On the computer screen, when you are rendering an object in 3D space, the Z axis determines how far away the object is from the camera. Although there might be an absolute origin (0,0,0) in the 3D scene, you might think of the camera as the local origin. Every object in 3D space in relation to the game's camera can be represented by distance as a Z axis value.

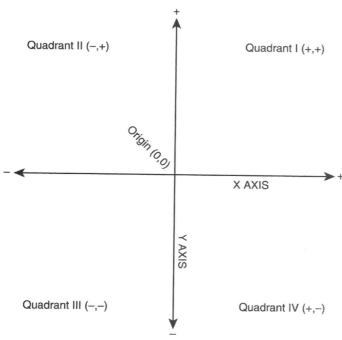

Figure 18.2
3D math is based on the Cartesian coordinate system.

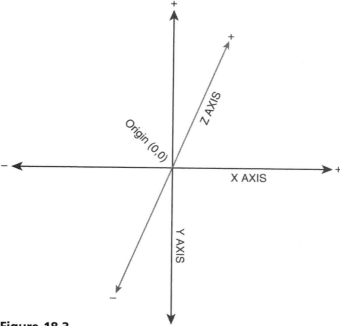

Figure 18.3
A 3D coordinate system with a Z axis.

Table 18.1 Four-Dimensional Space/Time

Dimension	Axis	Description
First	X	Left and right
Second	Y	Up and down
Third	Z	In and out
Fourth	T	Forward and backward

Does this illustration and analogy help you to visualize the Z axis and the third dimension? If you understand this, then you also should be able to visualize the fourth dimension (or 4D), which is time. I don't want to sound like a guest speaker at a science-fiction convention, but time is just as important in a 3D game as the other three dimensions. Unfortunately, there is no easy way to illustrate a 4D coordinate system on paper. Table 18.1 puts the four dimensions into words.

Let me take the illustration with your hand one step further to explain time. Hold up your hand again to represent an object in 3D space. If you move your hand left to right, it is moving in the X axis. Move your hand up and down, and that is the Y axis. As I explained before, move your hand away from you and then back, and that is the Z axis. Now what about the T axis, representing the fourth dimension of time? While still holding your hand out in front of you (and moving it any way you want), stand up and take a step forward. Now take a step back. You have just translated your imaginary hand coordinate system into the fourth dimension.

Interested in whacking your brain even further? It's really all just a matter of perspective. Imagine where you are located in relation to your surroundings. Your body is a coordinate system. You can move left to right, up and down, in and out, and forward and backward. But what if you are walking around doing this on a train or a commercial airplane? Your imaginary coordinate system stays with you, and yet that whole coordinate system is moving *in another coordinate system itself*! You have just imagined how a fifth dimension might work. Of course, that is not useful for anything other than a fascinating discussion.

Vertices Are the Point

A 3D scene is nothing more than a huge collection of points, which is all the computer really sees. The video card fills in the pixels between the points, and that's about all there is to 3D rendering. When you look at the stratospheric polygon counts announced with each new video card release, the figure is only relevant when you consider that a polygon can be made up of just three points. There is no rule that there *must* be something between the points, although common sense would dictate as much. Video card manufacturers publish the capabilities of their GPUs on the smallest of triangles, essentially three adjacent pixels, which is technically a polygon even if only three pixels are being filled. That is why published specifications are next to useless, and you should measure GPU performance on real-world tests (such as a frame rate test with a specific game). What is the reasoning behind this? Why would anyone want to announce a polygon fill rate that is half the fill rate of a competitor's card? Realistically, fill rates are only as useful as the game that uses them, and that is the point at which true benchmarks should be measured. There might be a video card with published polygon fill rates of ten billion triangles that can only run *Star Wars: Empire at War* at 20 FPS at the highest resolution. Given that performance statistic, who cares about fill rates?

What is far more important than raw fill rate is the quality of a rendered scene. The latest video cards support vertex shaders and pixel shaders, which allow a 3D programmer to write a mini program that draws every pixel in a polygon. The previous graphics card technology worked with a technology called transform and lighting, and one big issue during that period was full-screen anti-aliasing (or FSAA). This is a technique that smoothes the jagged edges of objects on the screen, making a game look more realistic and less pixelated. Transform and lighting (which is often referred to as T&L or TnL) is one of those unfortunate computing technologies, such as MMX, that everyone wants but that few consumers truly understand. The first T&L chip was invented by nVidia and called the GeForce GPU (*Graphics Processing Unit*). This new naming convention was nothing short of brilliant marketing on the part of nVidia, and it made the GeForce chip clearly stand out as the next greatest thing in computer graphics. But that technology is now ancient history.

The GeForce name comes from "geometry force," not the term "G-force," which is familiar to pilots and flight simulator fans. But to the core, this new chip *is* a geometry force, the first chip of its kind to offload the mathematics required to rotate, translate, and scale points in 3D, as well as apply lighting effects to a polygon. Thus, the term *transform and lighting* was born. In fact, modern GPUs perform so many astounding special effects that even the first shaders are now obsolete. Now that a base standard for graphics has arisen from the competitive conflict between ATI and nVidia—the two chief rivals of the PC graphics industry today—the technology has reached a plateau in which astounding quality in addition to dazzling performance is to be expected. New techniques such as normal mapping are giving normally flat polygons a real-life texture when viewed from any angle, and that raises the quality bar a number of levels and brings cinema-quality graphics to computer games.

Introduction to Polygons

The ironic thing about all this new technology is that it all comes back to the vertices, the points that make up a polygon, which makes up an object, which makes a scene. Vertices are useless unless they are connected to form lines. Three connected lines make the simplest polygon—a triangle. Although it might seem like three lines would have six points, that is only relevant if the lines are disconnected. By adding each line to the end of another line, the three lines are connected with only three points. A polygon with three vertices is called a triangle. There are many types of polygons, as described in Table 18.2.

Drawing a Wireframe Triangle

Ready for your first sample 3D program? Okay, this one is really short, but the educational value of this small program is significant when you read the paragraphs that follow the listing. For now, type this program into DB and then save it as Wireframe. Alternatively, you can load this project off the CD-ROM under the folder for this chapter.

Table 18.2 Polygons and Vertex Count

Polygon Name	Number of Vertices
Triangle	3
Quadrilateral	4
Pentagon	5
Hexagon	6
Heptagon	7
Octagon	8
Nonagon	9
Decagon	10

```
'set up the screen
SYNC ON
SYNC RATE 30
COLOR BACKDROP RGB(0,0,0)
INK RGB(255,255,255),0

'create a triangle
MAKE OBJECT TRIANGLE 1,0,0,0,0,10,0,10,10,0

'center triangle at the origin
MOVE OBJECT LEFT 1, 5
MOVE OBJECT DOWN 1, 5

'draw the triangle as a wireframe
SET OBJECT WIREFRAME 1, 1

'drag camera back away from object
MOVE CAMERA -12

'wait for a keypress
REPEAT
    SYNC
UNTIL ESCAPEKEY() = 1
END
```

Now go ahead and run the program, and you should see a triangle like the one shown in Figure 18.4. If you look closely at the figure, it might seem a bit fuzzy at the edges. In fact, the lines are not quite distinct, particularly when you look at the output of the program in contrast to the printed figure.

Here, let me zoom in on the figure and show you a closer view of the triangle in Figure 18.5. Do you see how smooth the edges of the lines that make up this triangle look?

Do you see how there is a somewhat brighter central line with several levels of darker shading around each pixel of the line? That dark-gray color was supposed to be white, because the Wireframe program was given a color of RGB (255,255,255), which is pure white. However, the video card automatically anti-aliased the scene, producing this altered representation of the white line. Although it is possible (and in some cases, desirable) to turn off anti-aliasing in the Windows Display Settings (via the Control Panel), a fully textured game world looks magnificent with this feature enabled. The only downside is that simple wireframe polygons like this triangle will emphasize the slight imperfections that anti-aliasing inflicts on the geometry of a scene.

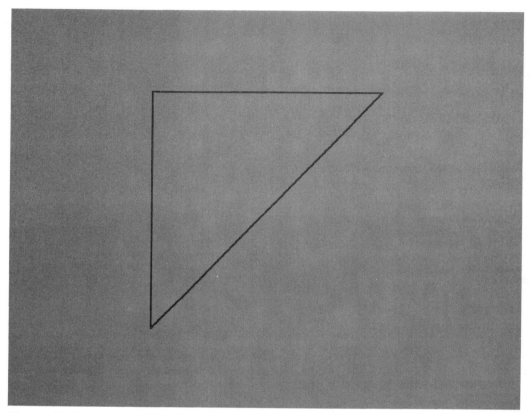

Figure 18.4
The Wireframe program draws a wireframe triangle on the screen.

Some games look terrific with full-screen anti-aliasing (FSAA) turned on, while others run poorly, so it is up to you to decide whether to use FSAA (if your video card supports it, that is). There are also several different FSAA modes from which to choose. Consult your video card manufacturer as well as reviews to determine which FSAA method works best on your card. One interesting thing you can do with the FSAA settings is select each mode in your display settings and then run a sample program in DB (such as the TexturedCube program later in this chapter) to see for yourself how each FSAA mode affects the quality and performance of the program. Better yet, run a complete game with each mode for a more effective demonstration!

Drawing a Wireframe Cube

Let's take the wireframe concept a step further and draw a wireframe cube. The only difference between a wired cube and a shaded cube is a command called SET OBJECT WIREFRAME, which must be set in order to view something in a

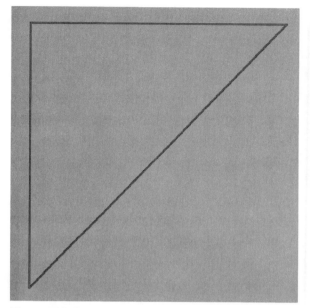

Figure 18.5
The zoomed-in triangle produced by the Wireframe program.

wireframe, but the results can be very interesting, not to mention educational. Figure 18.6 shows the WiredCube program with culling turned off. *Culling* is the process of removing non-visible polygons from an object where a polygon is behind another polygon in the Z axis. Compare this figure with the one in Figure 18.7, which shows the same cube with culling turned on (the default), hiding the invisible polygons.

```
'set up the screen
SYNC ON
SYNC RATE 30
COLOR BACKDROP RGB(0,0,0)
INK RGB(255,255,255),0

'create a triangle
MAKE OBJECT CUBE 1, 50

'draw the triangle as a wireframe
SET OBJECT WIREFRAME 1, 1

'uncomment to show away-facing polygons
'SET OBJECT CULL 1, 0
```

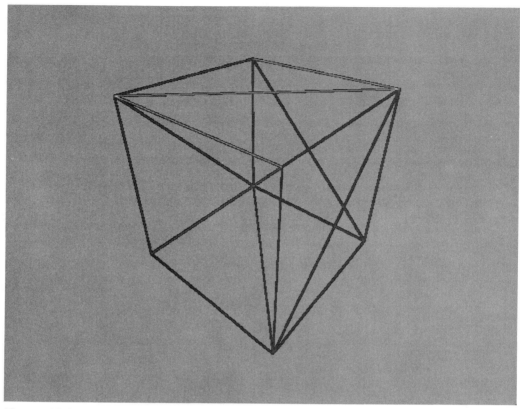

Figure 18.6
The WiredCube program with culling turned off shows all of the triangles that make up the cube.

```
'move the camera out for a better view
POSITION CAMERA 50, 50, -60
POINT CAMERA 0, 0, 0

'wait for a keypress
REPEAT
   SYNC
UNTIL ESCAPEKEY() = 1
END
```

Drawing a Shaded Polygon

Wireframe models make for an interesting discussion on 3D theory, but they are really not much to see. After all, who is writing wireframe vector graphics games today? That sort of thing ended a couple decades ago! If you have a

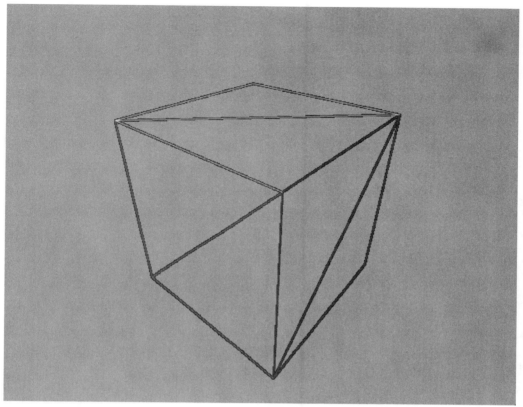

Figure 18.7
The WiredCube program with culling turned on shows only those triangles in view of the camera.

modern video card, it should be against the law to use your billion-operations-per-second GPU to draw wireframe models. So let's learn how to add some color and shading to a polygon. Later, I will show you how to fully texture a polygon with a bitmap image, which is the goal of this discussion, and the way games are designed today.

A simple triangle without the SET OBJECT WIREFRAME command will result in a shaded white surface, which is rather dull. Instead of white, it is usually prettier to apply some other color to the surface when dealing with shaded polygons. To do so you can employ the SET OBJECT COLOR command, as the following Triangle program demonstrates. Figure 18.8 shows the output of the Triangle program, which draws and rotates a triangle on the screen. Figure 18.9 shows another random triangle on the screen, but I have added some labels to the figure so you can see the vertices that make up the polygon.

Figure 18.8
A triangle is made up of three vertices (and therefore, three sides).

The Triangle program uses two new commands for working with polygons, XROTATE OBJECT and YROTATE OBJECT. These commands are passed the object number and a value by which the relevant axis should be rotated. To rotate an object in the same direction endlessly, you can use the OBJECT ANGLE X(), OBJECT ANGLE Y(), and OBJECT ANGLE Z() commands.

```
'enable manual screen refresh
SYNC ON
SYNC RATE 100

'set some initial settings
HIDE MOUSE
COLOR BACKDROP RGB(0,40,40)
RANDOMIZE TIMER()
```

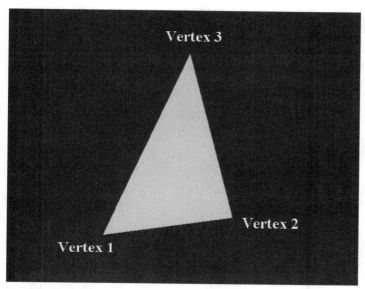

Figure 18.9
The Triangle program demonstrates the simplest 3D object that can be rendered in DB.

```
'create a colored triangle
MAKE OBJECT TRIANGLE 1,-10,-10,0,-10,10,0,10,10,0
COLOR OBJECT 1,RGB(RND(255),RND(255),RND(255))

'move camera back away from object
MOVE CAMERA -20

'main loop
REPEAT
    'rotate the X axis of the triangle
    XROTATE OBJECT 1, OBJECT ANGLE X(1) + 1
    'rotate the Y axis of the triangle
    YROTATE OBJECT 1, OBJECT ANGLE Y(1) + 1
    'update the screen
    SYNC
UNTIL ESCAPEKEY() = 1

'clean up
SHOW MOUSE
END
```

Figure 18.10
A quadrilateral is made up of two joined triangles.

Drawing a Shaded Quadrilateral

A quadrilateral is a polygon with four vertices and four sides, which might not be made up of right triangles. (In other words, it might not be a perfect rectangle.) Most flat surfaces in a 3D scene are made up of triangles of varying sizes and shapes, and that is what this sample program demonstrates. The Quadrilateral program creates a shape by combining two rectangles on the same plane. The result is a two-tone quadrilateral surface, as shown in Figure 18.10.

Figure 18.11 shows the vertices that make up a polygon comprised of two triangles, called a triangle list. Although this is the best way to visualize the process while learning, there is actually an optimized way to render triangles that reduces the number of vertices by having adjacent triangles simply share vertices. This is called a triangle strip.

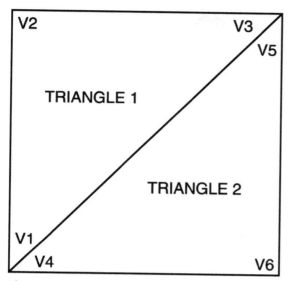

Figure 18.11
All polygons can be divided into interconnected triangles of varying levels of complexity.

Figure 18.12 shows another random quadrilateral, but I have inserted labels showing the position of each vertex and how the two triangles share two corners, similar to the diagram in Figure 18.12.

```
'enable manual screen refresh
SYNC ON
SYNC RATE 100

'set some initial settings
HIDE MOUSE
COLOR BACKDROP RGB(0,40,40)
RANDOMIZE TIMER()

'create a colored triangle
MAKE OBJECT TRIANGLE 1,-10,-10,0,-10,10,0,10,10,0
COLOR OBJECT 1,RGB(RND(255),RND(255),RND(255))
MAKE OBJECT TRIANGLE 2,-10,-10,0,10,10,0,10,-10,0
COLOR OBJECT 2,RGB(RND(255),RND(255),RND(255))

'move camera back away from object
MOVE CAMERA -20

'main loop
REPEAT
```

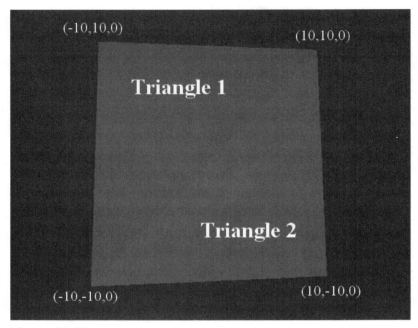

Figure 18.12
The output of the Quadrilateral program, with labels added to describe the vertices and triangles that make up the quadrilateral.

```
    'rotate the X axis of the triangle
    XROTATE OBJECT 1, OBJECT ANGLE X(1) + 1
    XROTATE OBJECT 2, OBJECT ANGLE X(2) + 1
    'rotate the Y axis of the triangle
    YROTATE OBJECT 1, OBJECT ANGLE Y(1) + 1
    YROTATE OBJECT 2, OBJECT ANGLE Y(2) + 1
    'update the screen
    SYNC
UNTIL ESCAPEKEY() = 1

'clean up
SHOW MOUSE
END
```

Drawing a Rectangle

DB Pro has a command called MAKE OBJECT PLAIN (yes, this is a spelling error in the DB language) that creates a rectangle (a quadrilateral with 90-degree angles) without the need to join two triangles, as you did previously. Figure 18.13 shows the output of the Rectangle program, in which the rectangle

Figure 18.13
A simple plane object is made up of two right triangles and can be a root limb for a more complex object.

is rotating in 3D space. I have also included a picture of the rectangle as a wireframe by using the command SET OBJECT WIREFRAME, as you saw earlier. The output shown in Figure 18.14 demonstrates how DB Pro builds a stock "surface" out of triangles.

Note

Note that in standard DB, you would use the SET OBJECT command to turn on wireframe.

```
'enable manual screen refresh
SYNC ON
SYNC RATE 100

'set some initial settings
HIDE MOUSE
COLOR BACKDROP RGB(0,40,40)
RANDOMIZE TIMER()

'create a colored triangle
MAKE OBJECT PLAIN 1, RND(10) + 1, RND(10) + 1
COLOR OBJECT 1,RGB(RND(255),RND(255),RND(255))
```

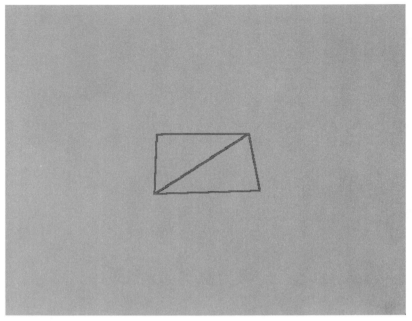

Figure 18.14
Setting the plane object to be drawn in wireframe reveals that the object is actually made up of two triangles.

```
'uncomment to draw in wireframe
'SET OBJECT WIREFRAME 1, 1

'main loop
REPEAT
    'rotate the X axis of the triangle
    XROTATE OBJECT 1, OBJECT ANGLE X(1) - 0.75

    'rotate the Y axis of the triangle
    YROTATE OBJECT 1, OBJECT ANGLE Y(1) + 1
    'update the screen
    SYNC
UNTIL ESCAPEKEY() = 1

'clean up
SHOW MOUSE
END
```

Basic 3D Graphics Commands

That was quite a fast-paced first half of the chapter, wouldn't you agree? It has been fun to learn all about wireframe and solid objects and how DB creates objects and draws them. Now I would like to up the ante, so to speak, and give you more 3D graphics programming power by talking about some of the more powerful commands in DB.

Creating Stock Objects

You have already seen some of the stock objects in DB, such as the triangle, plane, and cube. Now I would like to cover all of the stock objects and then provide you with a demonstration program to show you how to use these objects.

Making a Triangle

I'll start with the easiest object, just for reference. This command is used to create a simple triangle in whatever shape you prefer. The syntax for this command is `MAKE OBJECT TRIANGLE Object Number, X1, Y1, Z1, X2, Y2, Z2, X3, Y3, Z3`. There are so many parameters for this command because a triangle is the polygon by which all other 3D objects are constructed, and it requires the most flexibility. There are many different shapes and sizes possible with a triangle, not just the right-triangle variety with a 90-degree angle. With enough creativity, you can create any 3D object that you can imagine entirely out of triangles. This object is the building block of all others.

Making a Surface (Plane)

A plane is a quadrilateral (or rectangle) with two sets of equal sides and four right angles that equal 360 degrees in total. To create a rectangle, simply pass the width and height to the `MAKE OBJECT PLAIN` command. The syntax is `MAKE OBJECT PLAIN Object Number, Width, Height`. (Note the spelling difference; this is the way the command is spelled in DB).

Making a Cube

The `MAKE OBJECT CUBE` command constructs a cube that is comprised of six sides (and therefore 12 triangles). Due to the number of polygons involved, a cube has eight vertices—one for each corner. The important thing to remember is that this command constructs a cube of equal dimensions on all sides. (In contrast, the MAKE OBJECT BOX command builds an object with a different height, width, and depth.) The syntax for this command is MAKE OBJECT CUBE *Object Number, Size*.

Making a Box

The MAKE OBJECT BOX command creates a 3D object that is similar to a cube, but that might have different dimensions for the width, height, and depth. The result is akin to a 3D rectangle. (In contrast, the MAKE OBJECT CUBE command builds an object with the same height, width, and depth.) The format for this command is MAKE OBJECT BOX *Object Number, Width, Height, Depth*.

Making a Cylinder or a Cone

To create a cylinder object, such as a telephone pole or drinking cup, use the MAKE OBJECT CYLINDER command. The syntax is MAKE OBJECT CYLINDER *Object Number, Size*. The MAKE OBJECT CONE command creates a cone-shaped object that resembles an ice cream cone. The syntax is MAKE OBJECT CONE *Object Number, Size*.

Making a Sphere

A sphere is a complex 3D object consisting of many triangles in the proper orientation to give a spherical appearance (which might be used, for example, to render a planet in space). You can use the Rows and Columns parameters for this command to provide DB with more detail on the number of polygons in the sphere. You can create a sphere using the MAKE OBJECT SPHERE command. The syntax is MAKE OBJECT SPHERE *Object Number, Size, Rows, Columns*.

Transforming and Drawing 3D Objects

When you have created a stock 3D object using one of the commands covered earlier, you can then instruct DB to manipulate and draw the object on the screen. Transforming is a process by which something changes orientation, position, or scale. The precise terms for this are rotation, translation, and scaling, respectively. *Rotation* refers to the angle by which an object is displayed on each of the three axes (X, Y, and Z). *Translation* is the process of moving an object in 3D space using the three axes. *Scaling* involves changing the size of an object.

The most important thing to consider when you are working in 3D is the viewpoint, or the position of the so-called "camera." Although there is no physical (or logical) camera in the 3D scene, it is a practical analogy to describe the process of setting the viewpoint (and viewport) of the scene. The camera can be moved and rotated independently of any 3D objects in the scene, which can be quite useful. Often the functioning of the camera will make or break a game, despite the amount of work that has gone into it. If the camera is unwieldy, moves too often, and prevents the player from seeing what is going on in the game (such as the infamous problem with the player walking "toward" the camera and thus being unable to see anything), it will simply ruin a game. You must take great care and pay attention to the code that positions the camera in a scene. Often the best policy is just to leave the camera at a bird's-eye view and let the game run normally below the camera. (This might be useful in a strategy war game, for example.)

Although scaling is also a transformation, I don't use it very often. Scaling might be useful if you wanted to use a common stock size for all enemies in a game, and you want to enlarge some models for boss characters. You might also have a stock size and want to reduce models; for instance, to render a flock of birds where the model size is rather large by default.

The MakeObjects Program

The MakeObjects program demonstrates how to create several stock 3D objects and then rotates and moves those objects around in a circular formation. This program shows how to transform objects (remember: rotation, translation, and scaling) and position the camera. Figure 18.15 shows the output of the MakeObjects program running in normal mode, while Figure 18.16 shows the program running at the fastest possible speed (which is useful for benchmarking the game loop).

```
'create some arrays
DIM angle(5)
DIM posx(5)
DIM posz(5)

'initialize the program
SYNC ON
SYNC RATE 60  'set this to 0 for fastest speed
HIDE MOUSE
COLOR BACKDROP RGB(0,40,40)

'create a cube
MAKE OBJECT CUBE 1,50
COLOR OBJECT 1, rgb(255,0,0)
```

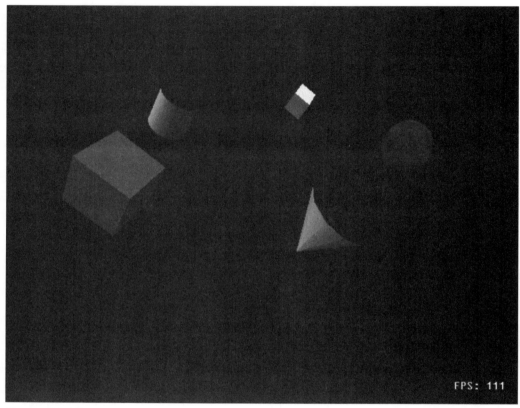

Figure 18.15
The MakeObjects program draws five stock 3D objects rotating in a circle on the screen.

```
'create a cone
MAKE OBJECT CONE 2,50
COLOR OBJECT 2, RGB(0,255,0)

'create a sphere
MAKE OBJECT SPHERE 3,50
COLOR OBJECT 3, RGB(0,0,255)

'create a box
MAKE OBJECT BOX 4, 50, 25, 25
COLOR OBJECT 4, RGB(255,255,0)

'create a cylinder
MAKE OBJECT CYLINDER 5, 50
COLOR OBJECT 5, RGB(0,255,255)
```

Figure 18.16
The MakeObjects program, running without a frame rate limit.

```
'reposition the camera to get the whole view
PITCH CAMERA DOWN 25
MOVE CAMERA -200

'set initial angles for each object
angle(1) = 0
angle(2) = 72
angle(3) = 144
angle(4) = 216
angle(5) = 288
radius = 150

'start the loop
REPEAT
```

```
      'move the objects in a circle
      FOR n = 1 TO 5
         'calculate X position using cosine
         posx(n) = COS(angle(n)) * radius
         'calculate Y position using sine
         posz(n) = SIN(angle(n)) * radius
         'increment the angle
         angle(n) = angle(n) + 1
         'move and rotate the object
         POSITION OBJECT n, posx(n), 0, posz(n)
         XROTATE OBJECT n, OBJECT ANGLE X(n) + 1
         YROTATE OBJECT n, OBJECT ANGLE Y(n) + 0.5
      next n

      'display frame rate and update the screen
      TEXT SCREEN WIDTH()-80, SCREEN HEIGHT()-30, "FPS: " + STR$(SCREEN FPS())
      SYNC
   UNTIL ESCAPEKEY() = 1

   'clean up
   SHOW MOUSE
   END
```

Adding Textures to 3D Objects

For many years, video games used shaded polygons to build their 3D worlds, and before that, wireframe graphics (remember *Battlezone?*). What truly makes a game realistic, though, is the use of textures. Texturing is a process by which a bitmap image is pasted onto a polygon. That is the gist of it in simple terms. However, the process of mapping pixels to a polygon and even wrapping a texture around an entire 3D object is quite complicated. Add to this the real-world need for extreme speed in a texture mapper, and there can be some serious problems in a software-only solution. That is why all modern video cards paste textures to polygons in the hardware—the silicon 3D chip itself does the texture mapping. As you have probably noticed while playing a recent game, hardware 3D is impressive. Before hardware texture mapping was brought to the PC, software texture mapping code relied on a fast processor to work.

Half-Life featured a software texture mapper within its 3D engine that was quite sophisticated (no surprise, given that it was based on *Quake II*). However, the most impressive software texturing algorithm in the world has no hope of competing with a hardware renderer. I remember the first time I saw a game running on a 3D-accelerated PC. It was the original *Quake*, running an OpenGL driver on a 3Dfx Voodoo card. The difference between software-rendered *Quake* and hardware-rendered *Quake* was astounding! Suffice it to say, it is a given today that all 3D games must be textured and hardware accelerated. Software-only solutions don't have a hope of competing (nor should anyone argue any longer against a game that is dependent on 3D hardware).

Loading a Texture

DB makes texturing very easy. In fact, just slap yourself right now for not skipping to this part of the chapter. No wait, just kidding! There is true educational value to be had from going through the process. So many programmers today take the rendering pipeline for granted without considering exactly how much work is involved in drawing a complex textured 3D scene. I suppose after writing some 3D code in DB, you will start to take it for granted too. Such is the nature of computers. Ah, well. Let me show you how to load a texture.

Basically, a texture is just a bitmap file. Why are they called textures, then, rather than bitmaps? That's a funny question. Actually, doesn't "texture" have something to do with how things feel? When I think of the word "texture," I am reminded of what the bark on a tree feels like, because that is a significant feeling. I also think of a brick wall as being very textured. Wait, that is bump-mapping. You know, computer science people are weird, okay? Please stop asking silly questions and just take my word for it that a texture is a bitmap.

Note

Actually, a texture could be a JPG, PNG, BMP, TGA, DDS, or DIB file! Just thought I'd throw that little tidbit in there to confuse you a little more.

You use the LOAD IMAGE command to load a texture. The format is LOAD IMAGE *Filename, Image Number*.

Applying a Texture to a Polygon

After loading a texture into an image, you can then apply that texture to a polygon using the TEXTURE OBJECT command. This command is quite easy to use, despite the complexity behind it. The format of the command is TEXTURE OBJECT *Object Number, Image Number*.

Simply pass the object number and image number to the command, and the bitmap image stored in that image number will be textured onto the passed object (which can be a single polygon, a stock 3D object, or an object that you have constructed).

The TexturedCube Program

Texturing a 3D object is really easy to do, and I would like to provide you with a sample program to prove it. The TexturedCube program creates several stock objects, including a rotating cube in the center of the other objects with a texture applied to it. The TexturedCube program is similar to the MakeObjects program. I have removed two of the objects and placed the new cube in the center, rotating opposite of the motion of the other objects. Figure 18.17 shows the program running at normal speed, and Figure 18.18 shows the program running at top speed.

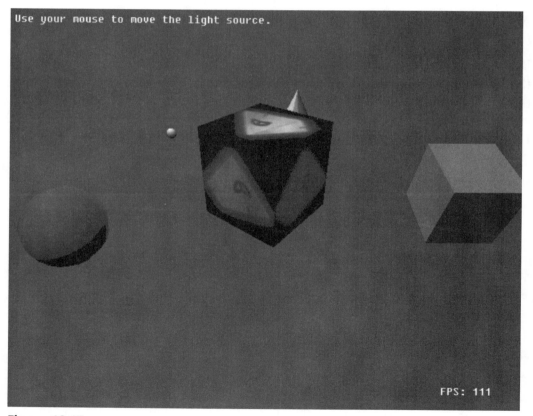

Figure 18.17
The TexturedCube program draws a textured cube with several colored objects rotating around it.

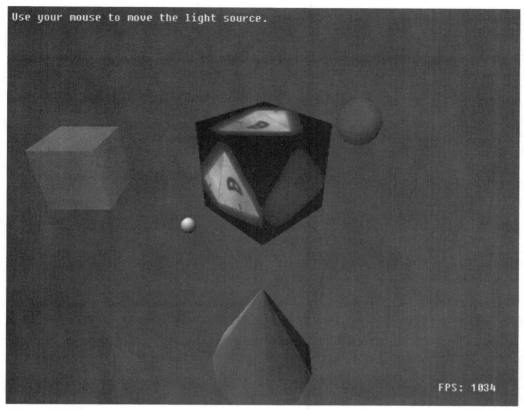

Figure 18.18
The TexturedCube program running without a frame rate limiter results in a very high frame rate.

You can type this program into DB or load the project from the CD-ROM.

```
'declare some arrays
DIM angle(4)
DIM posx(4)
DIM posz(4)

'initialize program
SYNC ON
SYNC RATE 60   'set to 0 for fastest speed
HIDE MOUSE
COLOR BACKDROP RGB(0,60,60)

'create a light source
SET AMBIENT LIGHT 0
```

```
MAKE LIGHT 1
MAKE OBJECT SPHERE 9, 10
COLOR OBJECT 9, RGB(255,255,255)

'create the central textured cube
MAKE OBJECT CUBE 1, 75
LOAD IMAGE "pyramid.bmp",1
TEXTURE OBJECT 1, 1

'create a cone
MAKE OBJECT CONE 2, 50
COLOR OBJECT 2, RGB(0,255,0)

'create a sphere
MAKE OBJECT SPHERE 3, 50
COLOR OBJECT 3, RGB(0,0,255)

'create a cube
MAKE OBJECT CUBE 4, 50
COLOR OBJECT 4, RGB(255,0,0)

'position the camera
PITCH CAMERA DOWN 25
MOVE CAMERA -200

'set the starting position of each object
angle(2) = 0
angle(3) = 135
angle(4) = 270


'set the radius of the rotation circle
radius = 150

'start the loop
REPEAT
  'move the objects in a circle
  FOR n = 2 TO 4

    'set the X position with cosine
    posx(n) = COS(angle(n)) * radius
    'set the Y position with sine
    posz(n) = SIN(angle(n)) * radius
    'increment the angle
```

```
      angle(n) = angle(n) + 1
      'move the object
      POSITION OBJECT n, posx(n), 0, posz(n)
   NEXT n

   'rotate the objects individually
   YROTATE OBJECT 1, OBJECT ANGLE Y(1) + 0.5
   YROTATE OBJECT 2, OBJECT ANGLE Y(2) + 1
   XROTATE OBJECT 3, OBJECT ANGLE X(3) + 1
   XROTATE OBJECT 4, OBJECT ANGLE X(4) + 1

   'move the light source according to mouse position
   POSITION LIGHT 1, MOUSEX() - 320, 0, 240 - MOUSEY()
   POSITION OBJECT 9, MOUSEX() - 320, 0, 240 - MOUSEY()

   'display some text messages and refresh the screen
   TEXT 5, 5, "Use your mouse to move the light source."
   TEXT SCREEN WIDTH()-100,SCREEN HEIGHT()-30,"FPS: "+STR$(SCREEN FPS())
   SYNC
UNTIL ESCAPEKEY() = 1

'clean up
SHOW MOUSE
END
```

Summary

Thus ends one of the biggest and most complicated, but surely the most exciting chapter of the book so far! I hope you enjoyed this chapter because 3D programming is where the action is, and this is what you should strive to master to write your own cutting-edge games. 2D games are fun and may always be around, but 3D is the place to be. To be honest, I personally find 3D programming just as easy as (if not easier than) 2D programming. It just seems that DB handles all the details and makes it so much fun! It's wonderful to be able to write a 3D demo or even a complete game without having to learn matrix math or trigonometry. You can move or rotate any object, light source, or camera with only a single command (which is the topic of the next chapter). Now that's real programming power!

CHAPTER 19

LIGHTS, CAMERA, ACTION: 3D LIGHTING AND CAMERA CONTROL

This chapter continues the coverage of basic 3D programming in DarkBASIC that was started in the previous chapter. Now you will learn the key concepts of lighting and camera control, which are crucial to a game. First, lighting improves the visual appearance of a 3D model, and we have several different types of hardware lights (which are handled by the video card) to use in a scene. Camera control describes where the camera is positioned within a scene, and which direction the camera is pointing, which affects what you see on the screen. Here are the key topics covered in this chapter:

- Lighting the scene

- Controlling the camera

Lighting the Scene

The difference between a simple 3D game and a complex one is often the amount of varied lighting in the game. As one of the most complicated themes in 3D graphics programming, lighting is such a difficult task that many games feature pre-lit scenes in order to simulate the effects of light. For example, a streetlight might seem to emit a directional light on the ground below when the texture of the ground below the light has simply been pre-rendered with the appearance of a light shining on it. This can result in a realistic scene that avoids the difficulties involved in programming real-time lighting effects. Even when using a library that might include support for hardware lights supported in the video card, such as OpenGL or Direct3D, you must still design a game engine in such a way that textures and objects in the game are set up to support hardware lights. DB has support for several types of lights that affect the characters and surroundings in a game. The built-in lighting effects in DB are so easy to set up and use that you will be surprised by the results.

Ambient Light

Ambient light is the uniform level of lighting present in a scene. If you are standing in a room that is lighted by fluorescent light bulbs, such as in an office building, the level of light might be viewed as ambient, and there would be a certain ambient level in the room. If you stand outside on a bright sunny day, though, ambient light will be significantly different from the light level in an office building. For one, the sun is a large bright point light source. There is so much light (and heat) emitted from the sun that it might seem to be ambient, but it is not. For one thing, sunlight creates shadows on the ground under trees, buildings, people, or anything else. Ambient light by nature does not create shadows. You might think of ambient light as a filler—somewhat like fog that is not emitted from a specific source. Some people, myself included, have a hard time visualizing ambient light. It is easy to understand a directional light, a point light, or a spot light, but ambient light is an abstract concept. When 3D objects are rendered in a scene with ambient light, all faces are lit equally without shadow.

Setting the Ambient Light Level and Color

You can set the level of ambient light using the SET AMBIENT LIGHT command. The format is SET AMBIENT LIGHT *Percentage Value*. This command expects a single parameter, 0 to 100, indicating the value of ambient light to apply to the scene as a percentage. Setting ambient light to 100 will result in no shadows (and is too bright to be used in a game) while a value of 0 is useful when you want to use directional lights in the scene (which I'll discuss further in the upcoming "Directional Lights" section). In addition to changing the level of ambient light, you also have the capability to change the color of the ambient light to any RGB color value using the COLOR AMBIENT LIGHT command. The syntax is COLOR AMBIENT LIGHT *Color Value*.

The AmbientLight Program

The best way to demonstrate how to use ambient light is by showing you a sample program. The AmbientLight program draws a textured cube in the center of the

Figure 19.1
The AmbientLight program demonstrates varying levels of ambient light in a scene.

screen, rotates the cube, and oscillates the light level and color of the ambient light. Figure 19.1 shows the AmbientLight program while near the peak of full ambient color, and Figure 19.2 shows the cube at a low ambient level. At the same time, varying degrees of RGB color are being changed while the program is running, producing some interesting texture colors.

```
'create some variables
Ambient = 0
Direction = 1
Red = 0
Green = 0
Blue = 0

'initialize program
SYNC ON
SYNC RATE 60
```

Figure 19.2
A low ambient light setting in the AmbientLight program results in dark, shadowed textures.

```
HIDE MOUSE
COLOR BACKDROP RGB(0,60,60)

'create a textured cube
MAKE OBJECT CUBE 1, 75
LOAD IMAGE "cube.bmp",1
TEXTURE OBJECT 1, 1
POSITION OBJECT 1, 0, -20, -120

'position the camera
MOVE CAMERA -150
PITCH CAMERA DOWN 20

'start the loop
REPEAT
```

```
'rotate the objects individually
YROTATE OBJECT 1, OBJECT ANGLE Y(1) + 1

'update ambient variable
Ambient = Ambient + Direction
IF Ambient > 100
   Ambient = 100
   Direction = -1
ENDIF
IF Ambient < 0
   Ambient = 0
   Direction = 1
ENDIF

'set the ambient light
SET AMBIENT LIGHT Ambient

'update the ambient color variables
IF Red > 254
   IF Green > 254
      IF Blue > 254
         Red = 0
         Green = 0
         Blue = 0
      ELSE
         Blue = Blue + 1
      ENDIF
   ELSE
      Green = Green + 1
   ENDIF
ELSE
   Red = Red + 1
ENDIF

'set the ambient color
COLOR AMBIENT LIGHT RGB(Red,Green,Blue)

'display the ambient variable
TEXT 10, 10, "Ambient level: " + STR$(Ambient)
TEXT 10, 20, "Color: "+STR$(Red)+ ","+STR$(Green)+ ","+STR$(Blue)

'update the screen
```

```
    SYNC
UNTIL ESCAPEKEY() = 1

'clean up
SHOW MOUSE
END
```

Ambient light will suffice for almost any game that you plan to write. Most of the time, you need nothing more than the default ambient light level. However, you might want to add some pizzazz to your games. In addition to ambient light, DB Pro provides three special-case lights that you can use in your programs.

■ Directional lights

■ Point lights

■ Spot lights

Directional Lights

Directional lights will illuminate a scene by shining a light from a point toward any point in space that you specify. The light shines in a conical shape that points to a specific location, which will be at the center of the cone. A directional light is similar to a spotlight, but it does not have a changeable angle of effect. Probably the most obvious use for a directional light would be a streetlamp or headlights on a car.

You can use the SET DIRECTIONAL LIGHT command to turn an existing light into a directional light. The syntax for this command is SET DIRECTIONAL LIGHT *Light Number*, *DirX*, *DirY*, *DirZ*. The DirX, DirY, and DirZ parameters define the direction that the light is pointing.

Testing Directional Light

I have written a program called DirectionalLight to demonstrate how to use directional lights. This program revolves a small sphere (representing the light source) in a circle around a larger sphere, constantly shining the directional light at the larger sphere. The result is a bright surface on the larger sphere that moves according to the position of the light source, as shown in Figure 19.3. This project, like all of the programs in this chapter, is available on the CD-ROM in the \sources\chapter19 folder.

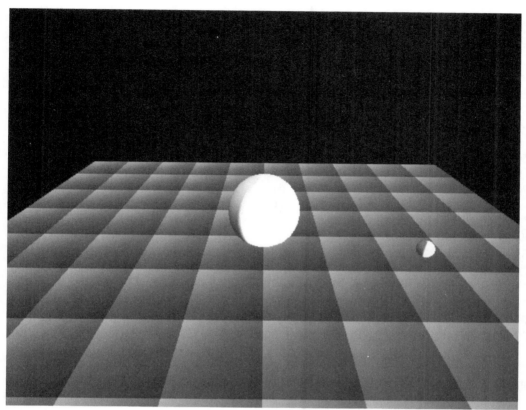

Figure 19.3
The DirectionalLight program demonstrates one of the many ways you can use directional lights.

```
'create variables
posx = 0
posz = 0
angle = 0
radius = 200

'initialize program
SYNC ON
SYNC RATE 60
HIDE MOUSE
COLOR BACKDROP RGB(0,40,40)

'create the floor
MAKE MATRIX 1, 1000, 1000, 10, 10
LOAD IMAGE "floor.bmp", 2
POSITION MATRIX 1, -500, -100, -500
```

```
PREPARE MATRIX TEXTURE 1, 2, 1, 1
UPDATE MATRIX 1

'create the large sphere
MAKE OBJECT SPHERE 1, 100
COLOR OBJECT 1, RGB(245,200,0)

'create the small sphere
MAKE OBJECT SPHERE 2, 20
COLOR OBJECT 2, RGB(255,0,255)
POSITION OBJECT 2, 200, 0, 200

'create the directional light
MAKE LIGHT 1
SET DIRECTIONAL LIGHT 1, 0, 0, 0
'COLOR LIGHT 1, RGB(255,0,0)

'set up the camera
POSITION CAMERA 0, 200, -400
POINT CAMERA 0, 0, 0

'start the loop
REPEAT
   'move the small sphere and light source
   posx = COS(angle) * radius
   posz = SIN(angle) * radius
   angle = angle + 1
   POSITION OBJECT 2, posx + 20, 0, posz + 20
   POSITION LIGHT 1, posx, 0, posz
   POINT LIGHT 1, 0, 0, 0

   'update the screen
   SYNC
UNTIL ESCAPEKEY() = 1

'clean up
SHOW MOUSE
END
```

Point Lights

Point lights are fascinating because they emit light in all directions and have limited range, which allows for local lighting effects. One possible use for a point light is a projectile fired from a weapon, such as a plasma bolt fired from a gun, for instance, in a futuristic tank battle or first-person shooter. Having a projectile that lights up objects that it passes is a particularly impressive special effect in a game. Keep in mind, however, that DB has only a limited supply of lights available, and some video cards might not support hardware lights (which will slow down the program, because lighting effects are a serious drag on the processor).

You can set an existing light to a point light by using the SET POINT LIGHT command. The format is SET POINT LIGHT *Light Number, PosX, PosY, PosZ*. The PosX, PosY, and PosZ parameters define the position of the light.

Testing Point Lights

The PointLight program demonstrates how to use point lights. I was really happy with the way this program turned out because it surprised me the first time I ran it! The scene was supposed to be lit already, but I inadvertently set the ambient light level to a very low value. The result is that the point light circling the object in the center of the screen actually lights the surface of the object, which is a yellow sphere. The result is very interesting, as you can see in Figure 19.4.

```
'create some variables
posx = 0
posz = 0
angle = 0
radius = 120

'initialize program
SYNC ON
SYNC RATE 60
HIDE MOUSE
COLOR BACKDROP RGB(0,0,0)

'set the ambient light
SET AMBIENT LIGHT 5

'create a point light
SET POINT LIGHT 0, 0, 0, 0
COLOR LIGHT 0, RGB(245,200,0)
SET LIGHT RANGE 0, 200

'create the central sphere
MAKE OBJECT SPHERE 1, 100
COLOR OBJECT 1, RGB(245,200,0)
```

Figure 19.4
The PointLight program revolves a small point light around a sphere with low ambient light.

```
'set up the camera
POSITION CAMERA 0, 50, -100
POINT CAMERA 0, 0, 0

'start the loop
REPEAT
    'orbit the point light around the sphere
    posx = COS(angle) * radius
    posz = SIN(angle) * radius
    angle = angle + 2
    POSITION LIGHT 0, posx, 0, posz

    'rotate the central sphere
    YROTATE OBJECT 1, OBJECT ANGLE Y(1) + 1
```

```
    'update the screen
    SYNC
UNTIL ESCAPEKEY() = 1

'clean up
SHOW MOUSE
END
```

Spot Lights

Spot lights are my favorite kind of light in DB because color can be applied to a spot light with attractive results. A spot light is similar to a directional light in that there is a conical-shaped light source, but spot lights have the added benefit of having internal and external light cone angles that you can set. The inner cone determines how large the spot light will be when it strikes a surface, and the outer cone determines how much residual light will pour out of the inner cone onto an object in a faded manner.

You can set an existing light to a spot light by using the SET SPOT LIGHT command. The format is SET SPOT LIGHT *Light Number, Inner Angle, Outer Angle*. The PosX, PosY, and PosZ parameters define the position of the light.

Testing Spot Lights

The SpotLight program is my favorite among the light source demos because it works so well and the result is fantastic (see Figure 19.5). By applying a different color to each of the two light sources in this program and shining them both at a textured cube, the result is very colorful and shows the great effects possible with spot lights. The only thing I might have done differently is to have the light sources move instead of the camera, but the result would have been attractive either way.

```
posx = 0
posz = 0
angle = 0
height = 150
radius = 400

'initialize program
SYNC ON
SYNC RATE 60
HIDE MOUSE
COLOR BACKDROP RGB(0,60,60)
```

Figure 19.5
The SpotLight program demonstrates how to use spot lights.

```
'create a textured cube
MAKE OBJECT CUBE 1, 100
LOAD IMAGE "cube.bmp",1
TEXTURE OBJECT 1, 1

'create the "floor"
MAKE MATRIX 1, 1000, 1000, 10, 10
LOAD IMAGE "floor.bmp", 2
POSITION MATRIX 1, -500, -100, -500
PREPARE MATRIX TEXTURE 1, 2, 1, 1
UPDATE MATRIX 1

'marker object for green light
MAKE OBJECT SPHERE 10, 10
```

```
COLOR OBJECT 10, RGB(0,0,255)
POSITION OBJECT 10, 200, 0, 200

'create a green spot light
MAKE LIGHT 1
SET SPOT LIGHT 1, 30, 10
COLOR LIGHT 1, RGB(0,0,255)
POSITION LIGHT 1, 200, 0, 200
POINT LIGHT 1, 0, 0, 0

'marker object for red light
MAKE OBJECT SPHERE 11, 10
COLOR OBJECT 11, RGB(255,255,0)
POSITION OBJECT 11, -200, 0, -200

'create a red spot light
MAKE LIGHT 2
SET SPOT LIGHT 2, 30, 10
COLOR LIGHT 2, RGB(255,255,0)
POSITION LIGHT 2, -200, 0, -200
POINT LIGHT 2, 0, 0, 0

'start the loop
REPEAT
    'rotate the camera around the scene
    posx = COS(angle) * radius
    posz = SIN(angle) * radius
    angle = angle + 1
    POSITION CAMERA n, posx, height, posz
    POINT CAMERA 0, 0, 0

    'update the screen
    SYNC
UNTIL ESCAPEKEY() = 1

'clean up
SHOW MOUSE
END
```

Controlling the Camera

You have already seen some of the possible uses for the camera earlier in this chapter, such as moving it around the perimeter of a scene instead of moving individual objects in the scene—a very useful technique, particularly when you just want to show off a 3D model that you have loaded. The camera is the most important aspect of the 3D engine, and DB is no exception, although support for multiple cameras is a fascinating idea. The concept of a "camera" in 3D graphics is abstract. As far as DB knows, there is a 3D world and there really is no computer screen or monitor. The 3D objects, lights, and cameras will move around and do their thing regardless of whether someone is watching. (In this sense, the word "watching" refers to not only the player—you, the programmer—but also to a camera.) By default, DB sets up camera 0 as the standard camera and displays the camera's view on the screen. But you can just as easily create another camera elsewhere in the scene and set the screen to display what that camera is viewing! That is what I meant when I stated that cameras are abstract views in 3D space. Often the impression is that a 3D scene is rendered on the screen using some sort of ray-tracing algorithm, and that impression somehow links the 3D objects to the screen as if they are glued in place. In fact, those objects are totally independent of the screen.

The 3D chip in your video card optimizes the mathematics involved in rendering these objects. The resulting impression of modern 3D graphics is that the scene can be rendered regardless of who is watching. This sort of reminds me of the philosophical argument that poses this question: If a tree falls in a forest where no one is around to witness it, did the tree really fall? I have questioned the sanity of this argument more often than I have given the argument mental processing time. However, in the 3D graphics realm, that argument is precisely relevant. If there is no camera in place to display a scene on the screen, then the CPU will spend no time processing the scene. Although the CPU might continue to update the position of objects in the scene, rendering is by far the most intensive operation. This simply does not occur if there are no virtual cameras in place.

Creating New Cameras

DB provides a default camera (0) that is set slightly back (in the Z axis) and focused on 0,0,0. You will almost always need to move the default camera out a certain distance, depending on the size of the objects in your scene in order to see those objects. If you are writing a game like a third-person shooter, you will probably want to set the camera just above and behind the main object in the game. You can use the default camera or create additional cameras using the MAKE CAMERA command. The syntax is MAKE CAMERA *Camera Number*.

After having created a new camera, you can position and point it to a new location in the scene, and then easily switch from one camera to another by simply calling the SET CURRENT CAMERA command, which immediately sets the view to that seen by the specified camera. The syntax of this command is SET CURRENT CAMERA *Camera Number*.

If you would rather display the feed of a particular camera right on the screen, you can do just that with the SET CAMERA VIEW command, which sets up a portion of the screen as an overlay video. The syntax is SET CAMERA VIEW *Camera Number, Left, Top, Right, Bottom.*

Adjusting the Camera's Position

It is your job to manage the camera's position. Although there is a command called AUTOCAM ON, it simply focuses on the last 3D object that was created or loaded and does not follow the correct field of view. To set a camera's position in 3D space, you can use POSITION CAMERA in the syntax POSITION CAMERA *Camera Number, X, Y, Z.*

Anytime you need to know the exact position of a camera or you need to move the camera based on its current position (for instance, to move the camera using absolute coordinates), you can use one of the following commands:

- CAMERA POSITION X(*Camera Number*)

- CAMERA POSITION Y(*Camera Number*)

- CAMERA POSITION Z(*Camera Number*)

Pointing the Camera

After positioning, the next most important factor to consider in camera management is the direction the camera is pointing. This determines what the camera is looking at and what is displayed on the screen (or in a window, as you will see later). To set a camera's direction, you can use the POINT CAMERA command, which is almost always necessary after moving the camera to a new location. The syntax is POINT CAMERA *Camera Number, X, Y, Z.* Surprisingly, those are all the commands you need to effectively manage one or more cameras in a game.

Testing the Camera Commands

There are many more commands in DB for manipulating and reading the status of the cameras in your programs, but I have covered only those commands that

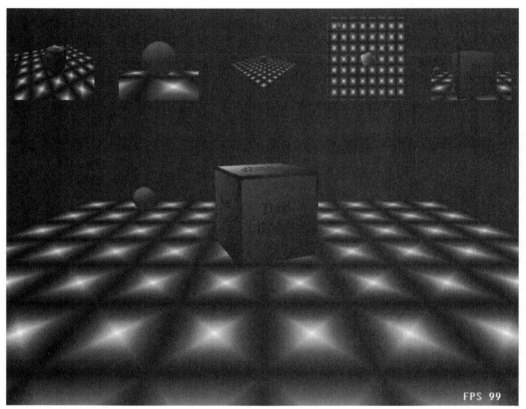

Figure 19.6
The CameraView program demonstrates how to position and orient cameras in a scene and then display the output from each camera on the screen.

are immediately useful. To demonstrate how these commands work, I have written a program called CameraView. This program creates five cameras and positions them at various points in the scene, even moving the cameras in relation to objects. The top portion of the screen features five mini-overlays that show the view of each camera, in addition to the default camera (which fills the screen by default). See Figure 19.6 to get an idea what the output of the program looks like.

As has been the case throughout the book, I am taking liberty with the texture files being referenced in this program, assuming that the files exist. You can copy the texture files (floor.bmp and cube.bmp) to the program folder where you have saved the listing for CameraView or you can create your own textures. The standard size for a texture is 512×512 pixels.

```
'create some variables
posx = 0
posz = 0
angle = 0
height = 150
radius = 300
screenw = SCREEN WIDTH()
screenh = SCREEN HEIGHT()

'initialize program
SYNC ON
SYNC RATE 100
HIDE MOUSE
COLOR BACKDROP RGB(0,60,60)

'create the "floor"
MAKE MATRIX 1, 1000, 1000, 10, 9
LOAD IMAGE "floor.bmp", 2
POSITION MATRIX 1, -500, -100, -500
PREPARE MATRIX TEXTURE 1, 2, 1, 1
UPDATE MATRIX 1

'create a textured cube
MAKE OBJECT CUBE 1, 100
LOAD IMAGE "cube.bmp",1
TEXTURE OBJECT 1, 1

'create the moving sphere
MAKE OBJECT SPHERE 2, 50
COLOR OBJECT 2, RGB(245, 0, 200)

'create and set up the cameras
MAKE CAMERA 1
SET CAMERA VIEW 1, 10, 10, 110, 110
MAKE CAMERA 2
SET CAMERA VIEW 2, screenw-110, 10, screenw-10, 110
MAKE CAMERA 3
SET CAMERA VIEW 3, 140, 10, 240, 110
MAKE CAMERA 4
POSITION CAMERA 4, 0, 600, 0
POINT CAMERA 4, 0, 0, 0
SET CAMERA VIEW 4, screenw-240, 10, screenw-140, 110
```

```
MAKE CAMERA 5
POSITION CAMERA 5, 900, 400, -900
POINT CAMERA 5, 0, 0, 0
SET CAMERA VIEW 5, screenw/2-50, 10, screenw/2+50, 110
POSITION CAMERA 0, 0, 100, -400
POINT CAMERA 0, 0, 0, 0


'start the loop
REPEAT

    'rotate the cube and point camera 2 at it
    YROTATE OBJECT 1, OBJECT ANGLE Y(1) + 1
    SET CAMERA TO FOLLOW 2, 0, 0, 0, 0, 200, 30, 1.0, 0


    'rotate a point around the scene
    posx = COS(angle) * radius
    posz = SIN(angle) * radius
    angle = angle + 1


    'move camera 1
    POSITION CAMERA 1, posx, height, posz
    POINT CAMERA 1, 0, 0, 0


    'move the sphere
    POSITION OBJECT 2, -1*posx, COS(angle)*posz/2, -1*posz+200


    'move camera 3
    X = OBJECT POSITION X(2)
    Y = OBJECT POSITION Y(2)
    Z = OBJECT POSITION Z(2)
    SET CAMERA TO FOLLOW 3, X, Y, Z, 0, 100, Y, 1.0, 0


    'display frame rate and update the screen
    TEXT screenw-70, screenh-20, "FPS " + STR$(SCREEN FPS())
    SYNC
UNTIL ESCAPEKEY() = 1


'clean up
SHOW MOUSE
END
```

Summary

This chapter continued to educate you in the ways of the 3D zen programmer. This is such a monumental subject that we have only just scratched the surface in this chapter. However, what you have learned here is more than just the basics—you have experienced the fundamentals of 3D graphics programming from a very functional and applied point of view. You could take the concepts you've learned in this chapter (and those that came before it) to create a complete 3D game using the stock 3D objects that DarkBASIC can create for you. Of course, there is an even more advanced way to make a game—by loading and animating a 3D model from a mesh file. And that is the subject of the next chapter.

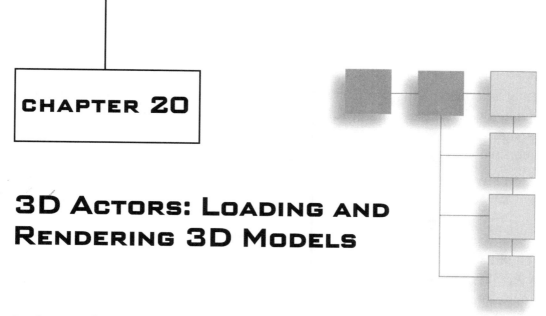

CHAPTER 20

3D Actors: Loading and Rendering 3D Models

DarkBASIC has an extensive command library for manipulating and drawing 3D animated models that have been loaded from a model file or created at runtime. This chapter covers the basic 3D commands for loading and animating models. Here are the key topics:

- Learning about 3D models

- Loading and drawing 3D models

Learning about 3D Models

DB supports two common 3D mesh file formats and three file formats used in popular games like *Quake III: Arena:*

DirectX	.X
3D Studio	.3DS
Quake	.MDL
Quake II	.MD2
Quake III	.MD3

These file formats are very common in the 3D industry, although most professional games are developed using 3D Studio *MAX* and Maya, which are high-performance modeling packages with complex file formats. Most of the professional tools provide an exporter for the DirectX format, though.

Loading a Mesh File

In 3D modeling terms, a model is called a *mesh*. A mesh describes the object more explicitly than the word "model," because a mesh is comprised of many vertices. A vertex, as you'll recall from Chapter 18, is a single point, and three vertices are required to create the simplest polygon—a triangle.

Let's learn about DB's mesh file commands. The command to load a mesh file is LOAD OBJECT:

```
LOAD OBJECT Filename, Object #
```

This is a simple command that just needs to know the filename of the mesh file (.X, .3DS, .MDL, .MD2, or .MD3). This command will load the mesh file into memory in the specified object number. From that point on, you can use that object number any time you want to do something with the mesh you have loaded. In this regard, DB makes 3D drawing and animation extremely easy, as you'll learn in a moment.

There are a ton of 3D commands that we won't have time to explore, because this is not an advanced 3D book (and I could fill 50 pages just listing all of the commands, let alone explaining all of them). However, you can browse the commands using the help system in DB. Many of the commands involve pixel and vertex shaders, which you can load from a shader script file and compile, or you can use predefined shaders. There are many other advanced topics that DB supports as well, and I encourage you to look them up in the built-in help system or browse examples and more detailed information at http://www.thegamecreators.com.

Drawing a 3D Object

Let's look at how to move and draw a 3D object. The position object command will set the position of a 3D object to a specified vector in 3D space (X, Y, Z). In order to see your 3D object, you must ensure the camera is pointing in the right direction and that both camera and 3D object are within 5000 units from each other. The object number should be specified using an integer value. The 3D coordinates should be decimal numbers.

```
POSITION OBJECT Object #, X, Y, Z
```

You can draw a 3D model using the SHOW OBJECT command, which simply requires the object number passed to it. This renders the first frame if the model contains animation. To play an animation, there are two options available. You can play an animation using the PLAY OBJECT command, or you can loop the animation using the LOOP OBJECT command. If you provide no start and end parameter, all of the animation is played.

```
PLAY OBJECT Object #[, start, end]
LOOP OBJECT Object #[, start, end]
```

Before an animation will render properly, you must specify the speed of the animation. This is closely related to the frame rate of the game, which is specified using the sync rate command. Most of the time, you will want to use sync rate 60 to arrive at a consistent frame rate, but you can use lower values. (DB does not typically render a scene at much faster than 60 fps unless you disable timing.) The object will only animate if you have set the animation speed using this command:

```
SET OBJECT SPEED Object #, Speed
```

Now let's take a look at a short but complete program that loads and draws a mesh file and points the camera at the model.

```
'load the object
load object "soldier.x", 1
position object 1, 0, 0, 0
're-orient the object so it is standing
xrotate object 1, -90
yrotate object 1, 90
'animate the object
set object speed 1,6000
loop object 1
'point the camera at the object
cy = object size y(1)/2
position camera 100, cy, -200
point camera 0, cy, 0
```

Testing 3D Animation

Let's test the theory you've learned about so far with a larger program. The AnimateModel program loads up a 3D model that was borrowed from a 3D file collection called *DarkMATTER 2*. This collection is available for a very reasonable price from The Game Creators at http://www.thegamecreators.com, and contains about a hundred fully animated models, for about the price of a retail game.

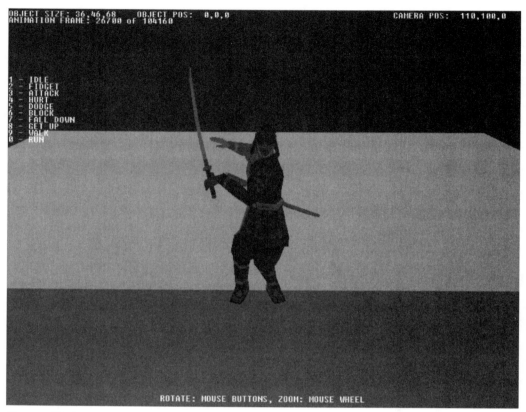

Figure 20.1
The AnimateModel program animates a 3D model.

The AnimateModel Program

The AnimateModel program loads up the Samurai.x model file and renders it at the center of the origin, which is intersected by the three axes (X, Y, and Z). Figure 20.1 shows the model, with the camera zoomed in. You can use the left and right mouse buttons to rotate the camera around the origin, and the mouse wheel zooms in and out. The main animation sequences in the model are listed on the left side of the screen. By pressing the number keys 0 to 9, you can change the animation of the model.

Tip

This Samurai model is featured later in Chapter 23 in the Battle Checkers game.

Figure 20.2 shows the program after the camera has zoomed out to show the entire scene. There are three axes (X, Y, and Z) that intersect at the origin. This is

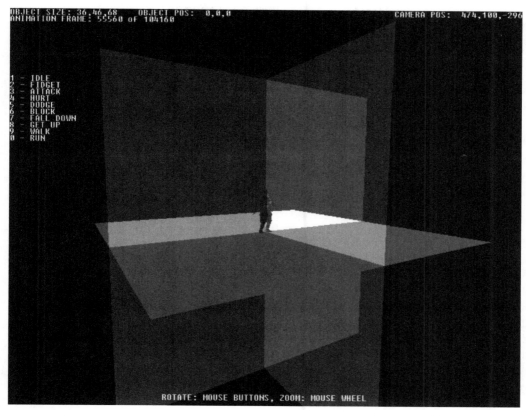

Figure 20.2
Zooming out to see the three axes intersecting at the origin.

a helpful way to see how a 3D model looks for testing purposes before it is loaded into a game.

The AnimateModel Source Code

Now for the source code to the AnimateModel program. Let's start with a bunch of constants that define the animation sequences found within the model file that I've used for this program (Samurai.x), as well as the data values for the sequence numbers. How do I know what these animations are and how many frames each one contains? That information was provided with DarkMATTER 2 in an information file describing the contents of the models.

```
'animation constants
ANI_IDLE = 1
ANI_FIDGET = 2
```

```
ANI_ATTACK = 3
ANI_HURT = 4
ANI_DODGE = 5
ANI_BLOCK = 6
ANI_FALLDOWN = 7
ANI_GETUP = 8
ANI_WALKSTART = 9
ANI_WALKING = 10
ANI_WALKSTOP = 11
ANI_RUNSTART = 12
ANI_RUNNING = 13
ANI_RUNSTOP = 14
ANIMATIONS:
data 0,12800           'idle
data 12800,24000       'fidget
data 24000,32000       'attack
data 32000,40000       'hurt
data 40000,48000       'dodge
data 48000,56000       'block
data 56000,64000       'fall down
data 64000,72000       'get up
data 72000,75200       'walk-position to loop
data 75200,84800       'walk-looping
data 84800,88000       'walk-return to stance
data 88000,91200       'run-position to loop
data 91200,100800      'run-looping
data 100800,104000     'run-return to stance
```

In order to make animation a little easier, here is a custom data type called ANIMTYPE that contains a start and stop variable which you can use to define the beginning and ending of an animation without hard-coding those values into your code. Once you've set up the range at the start of the program, you can use this to animate the model at any point.

```
'custom animation data type
type ANIMTYPE
   start as integer
   stop as integer
endtype

'create and fill the animation array
dim anim(14) as ANIMTYPE
for n = 1 to 14
```

```
    read anim(n).start
    read anim(n).stop
next n
```

Now for some global variables that are used in the program. The radius and angle integers are used to position the camera around the scene, while frame represents the current animation frame.

```
'global variables
global AXIS_SIZE as integer = 500
global radius as integer = 300
global angle as integer = 0
global frame as integer = 0
```

Now for the code that creates the three axes. After creating a plane to represent each axis, it is oriented in the X, Y, and Z orientations. (Note the difference in spelling in DB for the word "plain", which is not a typo.)

```
'show the X axis
make object plain 8, AXIS_SIZE, AXIS_SIZE
xrotate object 8, 90
color object 8, rgb(255, 0, 0)

'show the Y axis
make object plain 9, AXIS_SIZE, AXIS_SIZE
yrotate object 9, 90
color object 9, rgb(0,255,0)
ghost object on 9

'show the Z axis
make object plain 10, AXIS_SIZE, AXIS_SIZE
color object 10, rgb(0, 0, 255)
ghost object on 10
```

Next, let's load up the 3D mesh file. Since the models in DarkMATTER 2 are oriented on the X axis, and our program is oriented on the Z axis, the object has to be rotated up to a standing position, and rotated around to face the camera. This is very normal, since 3D meshes will never show up in the 3D scene exactly where you want them when loaded.

```
'load and position the Samurai model
load object "samurai.x", 1
position object 1, 0, 0, 0
```

```
xrotate object 1, -90
yrotate object 1, 90
set object speed 1, 9000
animate(ANI_WALKING)
```

Next comes the program's initialization code, which sets the frame rate, lighting, and camera position.

```
sync on
sync rate 60
color backdrop rgb(0,0,0)
set ambient light 50
set spot light 0, 10, 20
position light 0, 500, -1000, 500
point light 0, 0, 0, 0
set normalization on
```

Now for a helper function. The animate() function simply makes it easier to set a specific animation sequence without the sizeable call to loop object.

```
function animate(frame as integer)
   loop object 1, anim(frame).start, anim(frame).stop
endfunction
```

Okay, we've finally gotten to the game loop. For starters, the program looks at the keys 1 through 0 (for 10 keys total) that are used to change the animation sequence while the program is running.

```
'game loop
repeat
  key as string
  key = inkey$()
  select key
    case "1" : animate(ANI_IDLE) : endcase
    case "2" : animate(ANI_FIDGET) : endcase
    case "3" : animate(ANI_ATTACK) : endcase
    case "4" : animate(ANI_HURT) : endcase
    case "5" : animate(ANI_DODGE) : endcase
    case "6" : animate(ANI_BLOCK) : endcase
    case "7" : animate(ANI_FALLDOWN) : endcase
    case "8" : animate(ANI_GETUP) : endcase
    case "9" : animate(ANI_WALKING) : endcase
    case "0" : animate(ANI_RUNNING) : endcase
  endselect
```

Next we have some code to print out status information on the screen about the mesh, camera position, and animation frame.

```
'print the object size
sx$ = str$(int(object size x(1)))
sy$ = str$(int(object size y(1)))
sz$ = str$(int(object size z(1)))
text 0,0,"OBJECT SIZE: " + sx$ + "," + sy$ + "," + sz$

'print the object position
px$ = str$(int(object position x(1)))
py$ = str$(int(object position y(1)))
pz$ = str$(int(object position z(1)))
text 200,0,"OBJECT POS:  " + px$ + "," + py$ + "," + pz$

'print current animation frame
text 0,10,"ANIMATION FRAME: " + str$(object frame(1)) + " of " + str$(total
object frames(1))

'print camera position
px$ = str$(int(camera position x()))
py$ = str$(int(camera position y()))
pz$ = str$(int(camera position z()))
text 600,0,"CAMERA POS:  " + px$ + "," + py$ + "," + pz$

'animation key instructions
text 0, 100, "1 - IDLE"
text 0, 110, "2 - FIDGET"
text 0, 120, "3 - ATTACK"
text 0, 130, "4 - HURT"
text 0, 140, "5 - DODGE"
text 0, 150, "6 - BLOCK"
text 0, 160, "7 - FALL DOWN"
text 0, 170, "8 - GET UP"
text 0, 180, "9 - WALK"
text 0, 190, "0 - RUN"

'print instructions
center text screen width()/2, screen height()-20, "ROTATE: MOUSE BUTTONS,
ZOOM: MOUSE WHEEL"
```

Finally, the last portion of code in this program involves the movement of the camera view based on mouse input. The left mouse button rotates the camera to the left, while the right button rotates the camera to the right, while still focusing on the origin of the scene (at 0,0,0). The mouse wheel is used to zoom in and out.

```
    'rotate camera based on mouse buttons
    button = mouseclick()
    if button = 1 then angle = angle - 1
    if button = 2 then angle = angle + 1

    'mouse wheel zooms in and out
    zoom = mousemovez()
    if zoom > 0 then radius = radius - 10
    if zoom < 0 then radius = radius + 10

    'rotate the camera around the scene
    posx = COS(angle) * radius
    posz = SIN(angle) * radius
    position camera posx, 100, posz
    point camera 0, 40, 0

    sync
until escapekey()
```

Summary

This chapter provided the essential information for loading and rendering 3D meshes stored in files. You learned how to position and manipulate a mesh, and how to animate it (if the mesh contains animation frames, that is).

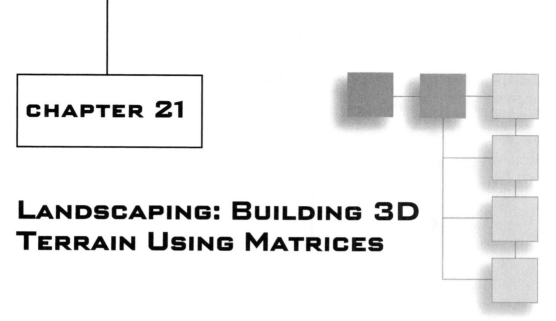

CHAPTER 21

LANDSCAPING: BUILDING 3D TERRAIN USING MATRICES

DarkBASIC provides some very easy-to-use commands for creating and manipulating bumpy terrain (that is, terrain with multiple levels that is not just flat). In this chapter we will take a look at some of the matrix commands for working with bumpy terrain and learn about

- Using bumpy terrain

- Following the contour

Using Bumpy Terrain

As with many features of the language, DB provides some very easy-to-use commands for working with terrain, and provides more complex commands for fine-tuning things. The easiest way to create bumpy terrain is to create a matrix, and then randomize it. A matrix is a complex surface constructed of quads. Each quad is called a *tile* by DB, and you can paint a texture onto each tile individually.

First, you can create a matrix using the make matrix command. This command will construct a simple flat matrix with the specified dimensions, and divide the matrix into the tiles specified using the x tiles and z tiles parameters.

```
make matrix matrix #, width, height, x tiles, z tiles
```

Next, you will want to load an image using the `load image` command, and then apply the image as a texture to the matrix. The image should contain a series of images like the tiles you used back in Chapter 15. The tiled image looks somewhat like a sprite sheet, also known as an animation strip. DB will use the tiles in the image to fill a matrix with those tiles. Depending on the quality of your tiles, this can be used to build a very realistic bumpy ground terrain with just a few commands. You use the PREPARE MATRIX TEXTURE command to apply a tiled image to the matrix.

`PREPARE MATRIX TEXTURE matrix #, image #, tiles across, tiles down`

The last two parameters (`tiles across` and `tiles down`) should describe the tiles contained in the image number you have passed in the second parameter, and this is where the matrix command somewhat resembles a sprite animation.

Next, we can use the RANDOMIZE MATRIX command to generate random heights for the tile end-points (vertices) in the terrain. The key to getting this command to create a decent landscape is to specify the correct number of tiles when you create the matrix, and then use a realistic value for the height when you randomize the matrix. If you want a very high-quality terrain, you have to use more tiles in the terrain (when you call the MAKE MATRIX command to create it). The quality of your texture is very important too.

`RANDOMIZE MATRIX matrix #, maximum height`

To set a specific tile inside the landscape to a tile number in the image, you can use the SET MATRIX TILE command.

`SET MATRIX TILE matrix #, tile x, tile z, tile #`

This command is really useful if you want to iterate through all the tiles in your terrain to set the tile image. For instance, if the matrix is 100 tiles across by 100 tiles down, then you can go through the entire matrix and set the tile image using code like this:

```
for z = 0 to 99
  for x = 0 to 99
    tile = rnd(3)+1
    SET MATRIX TILE 1, x, z, tile
  next x
next z
```

The most important thing to remember when working with a matrix is to update the changes you've made to the matrix. Since matrix manipulation is a time-consuming process, DB doesn't automatically update the matrix for you when you make a change to it. Therefore, to apply all of your changes, you must use the UPDATE MATRIX command.

```
UPDATE MATRIX 1
```

Following the Contour

Possibly the most common thing you will want to do with a matrix is to have a 3D model move over the terrain and follow the contour of the landscape. You might have an animated character walking over the terrain, or a vehicle driving over it. DB provides a convenient command to calculate the height of the matrix at any given coordinate. You can then use that height value to render your mesh at that location.

The command of interest here is called GET GROUND HEIGHT. There are three simple parameters: the matrix number, the x position, and the z position (which will usually be the location of your mesh object).

```
height = GET GROUND HEIGHT(matrix #, x position, z position)
```

Let's put this command to work by demonstrating how to animate a mesh object over the top of a landscape created as a matrix. The program I'm describing is called FollowTerrain, and is shown in Figure 21.1. I think you will find this example very useful for your own games.

Let's take a look at the short code listing for the FollowTerrain program. First up is the initialization code and declaration of some constants used by the mesh object's animation.

```
sync on
sync rate 60
color backdrop rgb(0,0,0)
randomize timer()

'animation constants
global WALK_START = 75200
global WALK_STOP = 84800
```

Figure 21.1
The FollowTerrain program.

Next is the code for creating the matrix and setting it up to a random height and
with random tile images.

```
'create a random matrix
load image "tiles.bmp", 30
MAKE MATRIX 1, 2000, 2000, 40, 40
PREPARE MATRIX TEXTURE 1, 30, 4, 1
RANDOMIZE MATRIX 1, 40
for z = 0 to 39
   for x = 0 to 39
      tile = rnd(3)+1
      SET MATRIX TILE 1, x, z, tile
   next x
next z
UPDATE MATRIX 1
```

Now we need to set the lighting. Simple ambient light is effective enough for this example program.

```
'set up the lighting
set ambient light 50
set normalization on
```

Now let's load up a mesh object to use in the example of terrain following. I'm loading up a model called Geisha.x, which was borrowed from the Dark-MATTER 2 collection. You can order this awesome 3D model collection at http://www.thegamecreators.com for a song and use them royalty-free in your own games.

```
'load and position the Samurai model
load object "geisha.x", 1
xrotate object 1, -90
yrotate object 1, 180
position object 1, 200, 0, 200
loop object 1, WALK_START, WALK_STOP
set object speed 1, 9000
```

Now for the main loop. This code gets the current height of the terrain at the specified coordinates of the mesh object. Then the mesh object is adjusted to the height of the terrain so that it will look like the Geisha character is walking over the landscape. This example is very low-resolution, but it demonstrates the functionality of this feature of DB very well. You can greatly improve the landscape by using more tiles in the grid and by using a good ground texture.

```
repeat
    'keep character on top of terrain
    x = object position x(1)
    z = object position z(1)
    y = GET GROUND HEIGHT(1, x, z)
    position object 1, x, y, z

    'move object using arrow keys
    if leftkey() then position object 1, x-5, y, z
    if rightkey() then position object 1, x+5, y, z
    if upkey() then position object 1, x, y, z+5
    if downkey() then position object 1, x, y, z-5
```

```
    'set the camera
    position camera -100, 200, -100
    point camera 2000, 0, 2000

    sync
until escapekey()
```

Summary

This chapter covered the very interesting subject of bumpy terrain and landscape following, which makes it possible to have a mesh object move over the top of the landscape and follow its contours realistically. You saw how to make use of this DarkBASIC feature by writing a short program called FollowTerrain.

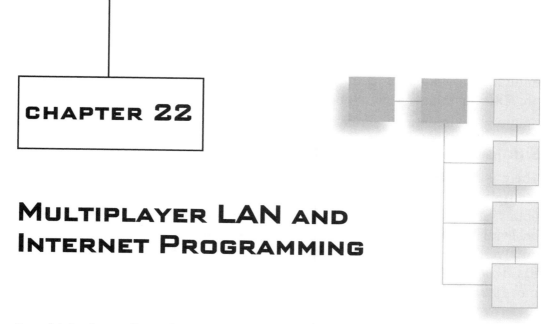

CHAPTER 22

MULTIPLAYER LAN AND INTERNET PROGRAMMING

Just think about all you have learned with DarkBASIC, from the basics of writing a program to 3D graphics. It has not always been easy! In this chapter, I am going to show you how to write code to communicate with other players over a network or the Internet. Regardless of the way you connect, you will be able to use the knowledge and code in this chapter to write your own multiplayer game, to challenge a friend in the other room or across the country!

Here are the key topics you'll learn about in this chapter:

- Introduction to multiplayer games
- Networking models
- TCP/IP protocol
- Writing a chat program

Introduction to Multiplayer Games

Multiplayer games are exceedingly popular today, and most game companies today are investing a lot of resources into researching new ways to build massively multiplayer online games (MMOGs). Everyone from Microsoft to EA is making them now. Some of the most notable multiplayer games are *Star Wars Galaxies, World of Warcraft,* and *Everquest II*. Each of these games uses multiplayer capabilities in different ways to achieve a fun factor that was not possible in previous generations of games.

Single-Player Versus Multiplayer

There is a question hanging around in the gaming world. Do consumers want multiplayer or single-player games? Multiplayer puts the world of human AI at your fingertips. There is no need to program the computer to simulate human behavior when you can just have humans do it for you. Single-player games, however, do have their place. Sometimes you just feel like playing a game without having to find someone else to play it with you. Single-player games are usually more story-driven, but that is changing as well.

Multiplayer Support in DarkBASIC

DB uses the DirectPlay component of DirectX to provide support for multiplayer games. DirectPlay is the networking component of DirectX that makes it possible to communicate with other players. It supports all of the functions required to play a network game.

DB has many commands to provide multiplayer support. For example, with just a few commands, you can create a multiplayer connection. DB supports two models of multiplayer connectivity—the client/server model and the peer-to-peer model. Each model starts with a host (server) and a client; the difference is how they pass the packets around. The default game settings use peer-to-peer.

Definition

A *packet* is a collection of data to be processed that is sent from one computer to another.

The Client/Server Model

The client/server model designates one computer as the master controller and the rest of the computers as slaves. Each slave sends its packets to the master controller, which then dictates where the packets are sent. Imagine there are three computers in a game—A, B, and C. If computer B is designated the master, computers A and C send their packets to B, which then sends the packets to the appropriate computer (A or C).

Anyone who has been in networking is very familiar with this model. This type of network connectivity is seen in systems such as Novell, UNIX, and Citrix, which generally include a server that hosts all the files and clients that connect to the server to retrieve files.

The Peer-to-Peer Model

The peer-to-peer model differs drastically from the client/server model. Although in DB you start with the client/server for connection, that is where the similarities end. When all of the computers are connected to the game, there is no designated master controller. Every computer can send packets to whichever computer they wish. Imagine computers A, B, and C in this scenario. Computer A could send all of its packets to both computers B and C. However, Computer A may have information only for computer B, in which case it would send that data only to computer B. The same applies to computers B and C.

You will find the peer-to-peer model mainly in Microsoft networking. In this model, one computer can talk to another computer without transferring any information through a central server. This is why, in a Microsoft network, you can connect from any computer to any computer on the network without logging into a master server. Higher functionalities of Microsoft networking merge both the client/server model and the peer-to-peer model.

Packet Transport

Once you are familiar with the network layout, the next thing you need to understand is how the packets are transported around the network. There are many different types of transportation for packets. DB supports four different types of network connections: serial (NULL Modem), modem, IPX/SPX, and TCP/IP. In this book I will only cover one—TCP/IP. TCP/IP is the most widely used protocol on networks today.

Definition

Network connection is just a fancy term for the mode of transportation for network packets.

Note

IPX/SPX stands for Internet Packet eXchange/Sequenced Packet eXchange.

TCP/IP stands for Transmission Control Protocol/Internet Protocol.

The TCP/IP Protocol

TCP/IP can be considered the taxicab of the Internet. Every time you view a webpage, TCP/IP transports the HTML packets to your web browser. Every time you check your e-mail, TCP/IP transports the e-mail packets to your e-mail client. If you think about it, TCP/IP is really quite amazing.

TCP/IP transports your packets through the use of the IP address. Every computer that is connected to a network using TCP/IP has an IP address. Currently, this address consists of four numbers ranging from 1 to 255, each separated by a period (.). A typical IP address is 209.232.223.40.

You're probably thinking, "If TCP/IP connects via numbered addresses, why do I type www.microsoft.com to get to Microsoft's website?" Well, there is a feature of the Internet known as DNS (*Domain Name System*) that converts IP addresses into numbers. Your computer keeps a repository that matches IP addresses to domain names so you do not have to memorize all those numbers. If your computer doesn't know an IP address, it checks with another computer to receive the answer. Domain names are like nicknames. You only have one real name (such as Robert), but you can have many different nicknames (Bob, Rob, etc.). You have one real IP address (such as 192.168.0.50), but you can have many different domain names (www.myaddress.com, www.bobshouse.com).

Selecting the Correct Transport

Now that you know about the TCP/IP, it's time to learn how to select it. Selecting the TCP/IP protocol is pretty easy; you just need to know what number it is by using PERFORM CHECKLIST FOR NET CONNECTIONS. This command will fill the checklist with all the transports available. CHECKLIST STRING$ will contain the name of the protocol associated with that number. You will have to search for or specifically select TCP/IP.

Establishing a Network Connection

After you select the connection, you must set up the game. A network game requires a minimum of two people. To that end, you need to call two different paths to create a network game—the client and server paths. There is only a difference of a single command between the two paths, but it's important to understand both of them.

Creating the Server Path

In the server/client model, the server is the computer that is hosting the game. In the peer-to-peer model, the server is the starting point for the game, but everyone acts as a server after the game is begun.

Before the game is established, you need to set the connection type that you got from PERFORM CHECKLIST FOR CONNECTIONS. Use the SET NET CONNECTION *Connection Number* command followed by a blank space in quotes: " ". You need the " " to establish that this computer is a host. The full command might look like this:

```
SET NET CONNECTION ConnectNumber, " "
```

The connection number variable, ConnectNumber, is the number you got from the PERFORM CHECKLIST FOR CONNECTIONS command.

After you set the game connection, you need to create a net game. To do so, you must use the CREATE NET GAME command, which looks like this:

```
CREATE NET GAME GameName, PlayerName, NumberOfPlayers, Flag
```

This command sets up DB to accept other players into the game. GameName is the name of the game being hosted. PlayerName is your name in the game. NumberofPlayers is the maximum number of players that you want to allow the game to include. You can have a maximum of 256 players including yourself in a game. Flag determines whether the game is connected in a peer-to-peer or client/server model. If Flag is a 1, the game is set to peer-to-peer. If the Flag is a 2, the game is set to client/server. After the game is established, the server will just wait for players.

Establishing the Client Path

Anyone that is not hosting a game is a client, and must connect to the host to play. Client computers first need to establish the connection by using the SET NET CONNECTION command, like this:

```
SET NET CONNECTION ConnectionNumber, AddressData
```

This is the same command used to establish the connection for the server, but you take a different approach in this instance. Address Data can either be blank

("") or it can have an address, such as 192.168.0.1 or www.mycomputer.com. AddressData is always a string and therefore its value must always be enclosed in quotes. If you leave AddressData blank, a dialog box will ask for any needed address data when the command is run.

Finding the games on the host is almost as easy as finding the connections. After you have established the connection, use the PERFORM CHECKLIST FOR NET SESSIONS command.

```
PERFORM CHECKLIST FOR NET SESSIONS
```

This will return a list of all the games running on the host computer. When you know what session to play, use the following command to establish a connection to the game.

```
JOIN NET GAME SessionNumber, Playername
```

SessionNumber is the number of the game you found using the PERFORM CHECKLIST FOR NET SESSIONS command. Playername is a string that contains your name.

Making the Connection

The following section of code for a program called ChatClient will connect two computers together via DB. When running the program, you will have to specify if the computer is the hosting machine or the client machine. If the computer is the client machine, the program will ask for the host's IP address. You can run two instances of this program on your PC at the same time (by running the ChatClient.exe file twice). Set up one as the host, and the other as the client, and connect to localhost or 127.0.0.1 or the IP address of your PC if you know it.

```
SYNC ON
SYNC RATE 30

' Keep track of what was said and who said it.
DIM ChatText$(32)
DIM PlayersName$(1)
DIM NumberOfPlayers(1)
DIM LastNumberOfPlayers(1)
```

```
' Find the TCP/IP connection number
TcpIpNumber = FindTCPIPConnectionNumber()
PRINT "Simple network chat client!"
PRINT
SYNC
' Get their Name
INPUT "Please Enter Your Name: ", MyName$
PlayersName$(1) = MyName$
SYNC
IF MyName$ = ""
   PRINT "You need to enter a name!"
   WAIT KEY
   END
ENDIF
' Find out who the host and clients are..
PRINT "(1) I'm the Host"
PRINT "(2) I'm the Client"
SYNC
A$ = ""
Answer = 0
' Get Host or Client
WHILE Answer = 0
   A$ = INKEY$()
   IF A$ = "1" THEN Answer = 1
   IF A$ = "2" THEN Answer = 2
ENDWHILE
' Do this if I'm the host..
IF Answer = 1
   PRINT "Creating net session. Please wait"
   SYNC
   Sleep 200
   SET NET CONNECTION TcpIpNumber, " "
   CREATE NET GAME "Sample Net session", MyName$, 16, 1
ENDIF
' Do this if I'm the client.
IF Answer = 2
   Input "Please enter the Hosts IP Address: ",AddressData$
   PRINT "Connecting to net session. Please wait"
   SYNC
   SET NET CONNECTION TcpIpNumber, AddressData$
   PERFORM CHECKLIST FOR NET SESSIONS
   NumberOfGames =CHECKLIST QUANTITY()
```

```
      IF NumberOfGames = 0
         PRINT "No session found at that address"
         SYNC
         WAIT KEY
         END
      ENDIF
      JOIN NET GAME 1, MyName$
      PRINT "Connected to session!"
      SYNC
   ENDIF
   ' Do the chat client
   ChatClient()
   END


   ' This function will determine which NET CONNECTION number
   ' is TCP/IP.
   FUNCTION FindTCPIPConnectionNumber()
      FLAG = 0
      CLS
      PERFORM CHECKLIST FOR NET CONNECTIONS
      FOR X = 1 TO CHECKLIST QUANTITY()
         Service$ = CHECKLIST STRING$(X)
         IF LEFT$(Service$,15)="Internet TCP/IP"
            FLAG = X
         ENDIF
      NEXT X
   ENDFUNCTION FLAG


   ' This function does all the chat client functionality.
   FUNCTION ChatClient()
      ' Clears the chat text from the array..
      ClearChatText()
      ' Displays the initial players in the room.
      PERFORM CHECKLIST FOR NET PLAYERS
      NumberOfPlayers(1) = CHECKLIST QUANTITY()
      FOR X = 1 to NumberOfPlayers(1)
         AddUserMessage(CHECKLIST STRING$(X))
      NEXT X

   '   Send a coming in message
      C$ = PlayersName$(1)+" has joined."
      SEND NET MESSAGE STRING 0,C$
```

```
        ' Displays the chat text..
        DisplayChatText()
        ' Set the entry buffers.
        A$ = ""
        B$ = ""
        C$ = ""
        CLEAR ENTRY BUFFER
    ' Capture Text Input and process it accordingly
        WHILE ESCAPEKEY()=0
            CheckIncomingMessages()
            A$ = INKEY$()
            IF ASC(A$) = 8
                C$ = C$ + ENTRY$()
                C$ = LEFT$(C$,LEN(C$)-1)
                CLEAR ENTRY BUFFER
                CLS
                DisplayChatText()
            ENDIF
            B$ = C$ + ENTRY$()
            TEXT 10,460,B$
            IF RETURNKEY()=1 and B$ <> ""
                SLEEP 250
    ' Send Remote Message
                D$ = PlayersName$(1)+": "+B$
                SEND NET MESSAGE STRING 0,D$
    ' Display Local Message
                AddStringToChat(D$)
                D$ = ""
                B$ = ""
                C$ = ""
                CLEAR ENTRY BUFFER
    ' Display New Chat Window
                DisplayChatText()
            ENDIF
            SYNC
        ENDWHILE
ENDFUNCTION


    ' Scans the incoming messages for strings
    ' and displays them.
FUNCTION CheckIncomingMessages()
    GET NET MESSAGE
    IF NET MESSAGE EXISTS()=0 THEN EXITFUNCTION
```

```
   WHILE NET MESSAGE EXISTS()<>0
      MsgType = NET MESSAGE TYPE()
      IF MsgType = 3
         Msg$ = NET MESSAGE STRING$()
         AddStringToChat(Msg$)
         DisplayChatText()
      ENDIF
      GET NET MESSAGE
   ENDWHILE
ENDFUNCTION

' Message to display if a User has joined
FUNCTION AddUserMessage(Name$)
   NewString$ = Name$+" is here."
   AddStringToChat(NewString$)
ENDFUNCTION

' Adds a string to the ChatText$ array
FUNCTION AddStringToChat(a$)
   FOR X = 1 to 32
      IF ChatText$(X) = ""
         ChatText$(X) = a$
         EXITFUNCTION
      ENDIF
   NEXT X
   FOR X = 32 TO 2
      Y = X - 1
      ChatText$(Y) = ChatText$(X)
   NEXT X
   ChatText$(32) = a$
ENDFUNCTION

' Clears the ChatText$ Variables
FUNCTION ClearChatText()
   FOR X = 1 to 32
      ChatText$(X) = ""
   NEXT X
ENDFUNCTION

' Displays the chat text on the screen
FUNCTION DisplayChatText()
   CLS
```

```
    SET CURRENT BITMAP 0
    CENTER TEXT 320,10,"Chat Client"
    FOR X = 1 To 32
      TEXT 10,10+(X*15),ChatText$(X)
    NEXT X
ENDFUNCTION
```

Passing the Data

After you have established the game, DarkBASIC provides you with many ways to pass data back and forth between the computers in the game. Passing data is a lot like passing notes in class. The data is written at your end, passed through the network, and read at the other end. If the other end has something to say to you, it performs the same series of events. The only difference between passing data and passing notes is that the teacher won't take your data and read it in front of the class.

Getting the Number and Names of Players

The very first piece of data you will probably want to obtain is the number of players and their names. You pass this data differently from the other data you send because it already resides on your computer. The PERFORM CHECKLIST FOR NET PLAYERS command will fill the checklist with the names and number of players in the game at the time the command is called. You can use this command to check to see whether someone else is in the game before you start it.

The checklist for PERFORM CHECKLIST FOR NET PLAYERS contains valuable information about the players. CHECKLIST STRING$(PlayerNumber) contains a string with that player's name. CHECKLIST VALUE A(PlayerNumber) contains a unique ID (or number) that was assigned to the player by the computer when he joined the game. This number will not change for the duration of the game; however, it is not the same on all computers in the game. CHECKLIST VALUE B(PlayerNumber) contains a special universal ID that is assigned to the player when he joins the game. This ID is the same for all of the computers on the network. CHECKLIST VALUE C(PlayerNumber) returns a number 1 if that player is you. CHECKLIST VALUE D(PlayerNumber) returns a 1 if this player is the host of the game.

Sending Information

There are quite a few commands for sending different types of information over the network. Each command follows a basic form, as shown in the following line of code.

```
SEND NET MESSAGE TYPE PlayerNumber, Value
```

Definition

Net message is DarkBASIC's terminology for a network packet. Any information sent over the network is considered a net message. You will see all packets from now on referred to as net messages.

PlayerNumber is the number of the player to whom you want to send the data. If you want to send the information to everyone except yourself, Player-Number would be 0. Table 22.1 lists all the commands and what type of data they send.

Each of the commands sends a specific type of data. Some of the commands take longer to get to the other computer than others. The SEND NET MESSAGE INTEGER command sends a small packet, whereas the SEND NET MESSAGE IMAGE can send a very large packet containing all the data in the image. You'll notice that the last five commands have a flag parameter after them. This flag is there in case of network slowdown. If it is set to 1, it guarantees that the data will get to the other computer. DB will drop any packets that don't have this flag if there is not enough time to send them.

Table 22.1 Network Message Send Commands

Command	Data Type Sent
SEND NET MESSAGE INTEGER	Integer
SEND NET MESSAGE FLOAT	Float
SEND NET MESSAGE STRING	String
SEND NET MESSAGE MEMBLOCK	Memblock
SEND NET MESSAGE BITMAP	Bitmap
SEND NET MESSAGE IMAGE	Image
SEND NET MESSAGE SOUND	Sound
SEND NET MESSAGE MESH	3D mesh

Reading Information

There are many commands for reading the data that is available to the computer. Because you don't want to be looking for packets every turn, the first command I will cover is NET MESSAGE EXISTS. This command returns a 1 if any messages are waiting to be processed. If no messages are waiting, there is no need to go through the process of reading them.

When you know that at least one message exists, you need to get that message. The GET NET MESSAGE command opens the packet so you can read it. For every message that comes to the computer, you must call a GET NET MESSAGE command. That is why when I am reading net messages, I simply do a loop while NET MESSAGES EXISTS is equal to 1.

After you have the message, and before you process it, you might want to know whom it is to and from. The NET MESSAGE PLAYER TO and NET MESSAGE PLAYER FROM commands return the player number to whom and from whom the message is sent, respectively. The commands should only be used if you need to know who the message is from or who it is directed to. In a server-client model, you will only get messages that are meant for you, so you can effectively ignore the NET MESSAGE PLAYER TO command. If your game requires you to keep track of who the message is from (in the case of games with more than two players), the NET MESSAGE PLAYER FROM command will return the ID of the player that sent the message.

If the computer knows the message is for you and has dealt with whom it is from, you might want to know what type of message it is. If the wrong read message is called, the data will not be valid for what you read. NET MESSAGE TYPE returns an integer that dictates the type of net message that is waiting. Table 22.2 lists the return values and the types of data they represent.

Table 22.2 Network Message Return Values

Return Value	Data Type
1	Integer
2	Float
3	String
4	Memblock
5	Bitmap
6	Image
7	Sound
8	Mesh

Table 22.3 Network Message Types

Command	Data Type
NET MESSAGE INTEGER	Integer
NET MESSAGE FLOAT	Float
NET MESSAGE STRING$	String
NET MESSAGE MEMBLOCK	Memblock
NET MESSAGE BITMAP	Bitmap
NET MESSAGE IMAGE	Image
NET MESSAGE SOUND	Sound
NET MESSAGE MESH	Mesh

Knowing the data type of the message waiting dictates what command you must call to retrieve the message. The commands will return the appropriate values for your game to process. NET MESSAGE INTEGER(), NET MESSAGE FLOAT(), and NET MESSAGE STRING() all return values appropriate to the type sent. The remaining five commands NET MESSAGE MEMBLOCK, NET MESSAGE BITMAP, NET MESSAGE IMAGE, NET MESSAGE SOUND, and NET MESSAGE MESH, have a parameter to indicate where to place the data (as referenced in Table 22.3).

Additional Multiplayer Commands

There are a few more multiplayer commands to cover. These commands give you a little extra data and control over what is occurring. You don't need to use all of the commands to play a multiplayer game, but they do provide you with extra information.

Buffer Size

The NET BUFFER SIZE() command returns how many messages are waiting to be received. This is the virtual pile of notes on your desk. If you don't want to process messages every time, you can use this command to determine how many are waiting before you do process them. However, there is a limit to the number of packets that can be waiting. If you go over that limit, you will start losing them.

Net Game Commands

The FREE NET GAME command frees the current game so you can create a new one. Even though you can have multiple games from PERFORM CHECKLIST FOR NET

SESSIONS, you can only have one game per application. Therefore, you will need to free the game before starting a new one.

The NET GAME LOST() command lets you know whether you have lost the current game. You should run this command to see whether the current net game has been freed. Once you know that the current net game has been freed, your program can quit the current game it's playing. There is no need to process or send any more net messages if no one is listening to them.

Adding and Removing Players

The CREATE NET PLAYER command allows you to add your own players into the game. The CREATE NET PLAYER command syntax is CREATE NET PLAYER Playername$ where PlayerName$ is a string containing the name of the player you want to create. When you create or join a net game, a player is automatically created for you. This command allows you to add secondary or AI players or other local players to the same net game.

The FREE NET PLAYER command allows you to free a player from a net game. The FREE NET PLAYER command syntax is FREE NET PLAYER PlayerNumber where PlayerNumber is the number of the player found in the PERFORM CHECKLIST FOR NET PLAYERS command. This is useful if you are dropping a local or AI player from the game because they have been destroyed or they are no longer needed.

The NET PLAYER CREATED command lets you know whether a net player was created by a CREATE NET PLAYER command. This command returns the number of the new net player that was created. The NET PLAYER DESTROYED command lets you know whether a net player was destroyed by a FREE NET PLAYER command. This command returns the number of the player that was destroyed.

Memory Blocks

One of the most powerful aspects of DB is the ability to create and manipulate memory blocks (memblocks). A memblock can be any size and can contain any data. Memblocks are powerful tools for passing multiple bits of information over a single network packet. They are a defined size that can be broken up into multiple bits of information.

D e f i n i t i o n

Memory blocks (memblocks) are chunks of memory allocated to store multiple types of information in one location. They have a specific size but do not conform to any specific data type. Memblocks can contain many different types of information in the same memory block.

Creating Memory Blocks

Creating a memblock is similar to creating an image, bitmap, or sound. You simply call the MAKE MEMBLOCK *Memblock Number, Size in Bytes* command. Make sure that you set the size of the memblock large enough to fit all the data you will be storing in it. The size is measured in bytes, so if you are placing four floats in the memory block, you should allocate the size as 12 bytes (4×3).

Destroying Memory Blocks

Destroying a memblock is *very* important. If you do not destroy a memblock when you are finished using it, you can create a memory leak in your program. To destroy a memblock, just use the DELETE MEMBLOCK *Memblock Number* command. This command will destroy the memblock and free any memory associated with it.

Writing Data to Memory Blocks

Writing data into a memblock is pretty easy. DB provides four different commands to write data into memblocks: WRITE MEMBLOCK BYTE, WRITE MEMBLOCK WORD, WRITE MEMBLOCK DWORD, and WRITE MEMBLOCK FLOAT. The syntax for each command looks like this:

```
WRITE MEMBLOCK BYTE MemblockNumber, Location, Value
WRITE MEMBLOCK WORD MemblockNumber, Location, Value
WRITE MEMBLOCK DWORD MemblockNumber, Location, Value
WRITE MEMBLOCK FLOAT MemblockNumber, Location, Value
```

Each of these commands has three parameters. The first parameter is the memblock number. This is the number you designated during the CREATE MEMBLOCK command.

The second parameter is the location in the memblock to write the data. When you created the memory block, you had to assign it a size. This is the maximum amount of data (in bytes) that can be placed into the memory block. Each value

Table 22.4 Memory Block WRITE Commands

Command	Data Size
WRITE MEMBLOCK BYTE	1
WRITE MEMBLOCK WORD	2
WRITE MEMBLOCK DWORD	4
WRITE MEMBLOCK FLOAT	4

Table 22.5 Memblock Read Commands

Command	Data Size
MEMBLOCK BYTE	1
MEMBLOCK WORD	2
MEMBLOCK DWORD	4
MEMBLOCK FLOAT	4

placed in a memblock takes up a specific number of bytes. You don't want to overwrite the data already added to a memblock. Table 22.4 contains the list of commands and how many bytes of memory they use.

The third parameter of the WRITE MEMBLOCK commands is the value of the data itself.

Reading Data from a Memory Block

Reading from a memory block is as easy as writing to one. There are four commands for reading from each memblock, and each command takes two parameters. The first parameter is the memblock number, and the second is the position in the memblock to start reading. Table 22.5 lists the commands for reading from a memblock. These commands return the value that you request from the memblock.

Miscellaneous Memory Block Commands

There are a few other memory block commands that don't fall into the create/destroy or the read/write categories. However, these commands are still useful for manipulating memory blocks.

Copying Part of a Memory Block

The COPY MEMBLOCK *From, To, PosFrom, PosTo, Bytes* command copies the contents of one memory block to another. You can specify the locations in the memory block you are copying the data from and to, along with the size of the memory to copy.

Determining the Existence of a Memory Block

The MEMBLOCK EXISTS(*Memblock Number*) command indicates whether or not a memblock has been allocated. If the memblock has been allocated, this command returns a 0.

Retrieving the Size of a Memory Block

The GET MEMORYBLOCK SIZE(*Memblock Number*) command returns the size of the specified memblock.

Using Memblocks

Using memblocks is a tough concept to handle. The following source code shows you how to use memblocks. This program asks for a few inputs, places the data into memblocks, and then returns the data back stored in the memblock. This program can be done using all variables, but the memblock is the most efficient way of collecting data and sending it as one net message.

```
' Create Memblock
MAKE MEMBLOCK 1,25
' Get the numbers
INPUT "Enter a byte (0-255)",MyByte
INPUT "Enter a word (0-65535)",MyWord
INPUT "Enter a dword (0-4294967295)",MyDWord
INPUT "Enter a float (A number with a . in it)",MyFloat#
' Make the Byte entered less than or equal to 255
WHILE MyByte > 255
   MyByte = MyByte - 255
ENDWHILE
' Make the Byte entered less than or equal to 65535
WHILE MyWord > 65535
   MyByte = MyByte - 65535
ENDWHILE
```

```
' Make the Byte entered less than or equal to 4294967295
WHILE MyDWord > 4294967295
   MyByte = MyByte - 4294967295
ENDWHILE
' Write the memory blocks
WRITE MEMBLOCK BYTE 1,0,MyByte
WRITE MEMBLOCK WORD 1,1,MyWord
WRITE MEMBLOCK DWORD 1,3,MyDWord
WRITE MEMBLOCK FLOAT 1,7,MyFloat#
' Clear the vars (to show memblocks are working)
MyByte = 0
MyWord = 0
MyDWord = 0
MyFloat# = 0.0
' Read the vars from the memblock
MyByte = MEMBLOCK BYTE(1,0)
MyWord = MEMBLOCK WORD(1,1)
MyDWord = MEMBLOCK DWORD(1,3)
MyFloat# = MEMBLOCK FLOAT(1,7)
' Display the vars gathered.
PRINT "Byte = "+STR$(MyByte)
PRINT "Word = "+STR$(MyWord)
PRINT "DWord = "+STR$(MyDWord)
PRINT "Float = "+STR$(MyFloat#)
'Delete Memory Block
DELETE MEMBLOCK 1
WAIT KEY
END
```

Summary

What an extensive chapter. Multiplayer and memory blocks are very advanced topics, but they give you powerful tools that can make your games stand out above the rest. By using the multiplayer commands, you can easily create a two-player LAN or Internet game, or you could go for broke and build your own multiplayer game server to host multiplayer games you've written in DarkBASIC.

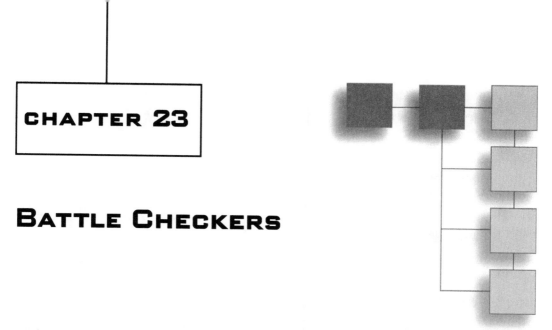

CHAPTER 23

BATTLE CHECKERS

Welcome to the final chapter of the book. It has been a long journey; wouldn't you agree? We are going to explore a lot of gameplay and logic while working on a complete game in this chapter. I'm going to show you how to build a game called Battle Checkers, which features 3D animated characters that fight for the squares, swing their swords, and fall down when they are killed! This makes an otherwise normal checkers game significantly more interesting. Here are the key topics in this chapter:

- Getting to know Battle Checkers

- Building the source code

Getting to Know Battle Checkers

Battle Checkers is a twist on the classic game of checkers, in which the checker pieces have been replaced by 3D animated characters. I've chosen a Samurai and a Geisha character for use in the game because they look nice when facing off on the board. These two characters were borrowed from the excellent 3D model collection called *DarkMATTER 2*. You can purchase this collection from The Game Creators (the company that created DB, in case you've forgotten) by visiting http://www.thegamecreators.com. There are several collections in the *DarkMATTER* series, and the price is very affordable, especially when you

Figure 23.1
Battle Checkers.

consider the high quality of these animated models. Out of fourteen total animation sequences stored in the model files, I am using about eight in the game!

Figure 23.1 shows Battle Checkers at startup. Note how the selector glows with a point light source, illuminating the board as it is moved around with the mouse. In this particular figure, the selector is hovering over tile (0,0). Many support functions are being called just to get the game started and up to this point. Most notably, a pair of functions called update_pointer() and update_selection() make it possible to move the spherical selector (a sort of cursor) with an attached light source. When you move the mouse, the game figures out what checker board square it is over and displays that information at the top of the screen. The tile at (0,0) is impassable because it is a white square, and in checkers you can only move on the black squares.

Figure 23.2 shows a clearer view of the mouse pointer in the center of the checker board. You can see that it is transparent and the light source is coming from the

Figure 23.2
The mouse cursor in Battle Checkers is a small transparent sphere with a point light source.

small sphere. The light shines on the board (which is a 3D matrix/plane made up of a grid of tiles) as well as on the pieces. The tile where the cursor is located is (3,4) and is reported as "unoccupied #99". What this means is that the tile is a valid square for play, but that it is currently empty.

You are allowed to move a piece in checkers in any forward diagonal direction. Since all the pieces start on black squares, the white squares are entirely unused in the game. The board in this game was constructed from black and white marble textures applied onto a matrix. A matrix in DB is a surface made up of a grid of tiles, each of which can be assigned a texture from a tiled texture image (which is similar in functionality to a sprite sheet filled with sprite frames in rows and columns).

Clicking a square with one of your checker pieces in it (which are represented by the Samurai characters) causes that square to be highlighted with a transparent

Pointer -300,6
Cursor over tile 3,7 - <impassable> #2
Selected object 2 at 2,5
Distance -1,-2

FPS 40

Figure 23.3
When you select a piece by clicking a square, a transparent cube-shaped selector appears over the square.

cube, as shown in Figure 23.3. If you notice where the mouse cursor is located (slightly down to the right of the selected piece), you'll see that the text at the top of the screen reports that a selection has been made. The current cursor position is at tile (3,7), which is impassable. Note also the distance values, which are showing (−1,−2). The distance values are key to programming a checkers game.

Since you can only move one square in a diagonal direction, your total possible moves in checkers are limited to two in most cases. The game displays the currently selected object (which is literally a number representing the 3D object in DB) along with the selected tile location. The game then keeps track of where you are moving the cursor in relation to the selected square and displays the distance to that tile.

Figure 23.4 shows the cursor over a valid destination square. How do you know if it is a valid square? Take a look at the distance values, which are (−1,1). These

Figure 23.4
To make a valid move, you can only choose a destination that is one diagonal square away.

two distance values represent the difference between the selected square and the target square. So, for instance, if you choose square (2,5) and then move to square (3,4), the distance will be reported as $(2 - 3 = -1)$ and the Y distance is $(5 - 4 = 1)$. These calculations are made when determining if a move is valid.

Depending on which side is currently making a move, you can figure out which squares are valid by considering these distance values. For the human player making a move forward, the Y distance can only be positive 1. Why? Because the forward direction for player 1 is always from a numerically higher square to a numerically lower square. Take a look at Figure 23.5 for an illustration of the checker board.

The first thing you should note is that a black square should always be located at the lower left corner when you set up the board. Next, consider the move shown in the illustration, from (2,5) to (3,4). You can figure out in your head that the

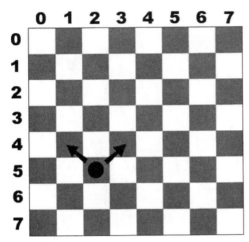

Figure 23.5
The numbered rows and columns in the checker board (zero based).

Y direction will always result in a value of 1, while the X direction will result in either 1 or −1, depending on whether you move diagonally left or right. This information is important when it comes to writing the code to validate a move.

Building the Game's Source Code

Now it's time to dig into the source code for the game. I'm going to go slowly and explain every variable declaration and function in the entire game, which is about 25 pages of code. This is actually quite small for a complete game. But Battle Checkers is not 100% polished, so there are some gameplay items that were left out of the game in order to keep the code shorter and more understandable. The two main features of checkers that were left out of the game are shown in the following list:

1. "Kinging" a pawn piece. Adding this capability would have significantly lengthened the key functions of the game, which currently work only in a single direction for each player. Adding kings to the game would have required new game states and revised functions.

2. Computer attack moves. This feature is very possible using the existing code for player jumps. But doing so would have required a revision to the perform_jump_move() function in order to add support for both directions (it currently only supports moves for the human-controlled pieces). This

function is lengthy, so a revision to it is a better solution than duplicating the entire function for a computer attack. Again, it was simply left out in the interest of space and time.

3. Sound and music. There are no sound effects or music in this game so that all you see is the minimal code needed to get the game running. This is yet another aspect of the game that you can implement on your own.

In defense of these two missing parts of the game, which are important for a complete checkers game, consider that the game does function as a single-player game with rudimentary computer A.I. (artificial intelligence) controlling the opponent pieces. I could have easily made this a two-player game by allowing two players to "hot-seat" the game by sharing the mouse and taking turns. That would have been extremely easy to do in comparison to the difficulty of giving the computer a rudimentary understanding of checkers. I believe you will appreciate the experience gained from this game after going over the source code, and will hopefully add these two missing ingredients on your own. Consider it a challenge!

Declarations

The start of the program contains a lot of variable declarations. I've used a lot of constants in the program (which are really just global variables written in uppercase to make them easily identified in the code). I like using constants because it significantly improves the readability of the source code. First up we have the definition of the 3D model orientation angles. These angles are used to make the Samurai and Geisha characters face the right direction when moving.

```
remstart
    BATTLE CHECKERS
    June, 2006
    DarkBASIC Pro Game Programming, 2nd Ed
remend

'character move angle constants
global SAMURAI_FORWARD_ANGLE as float = 90.0
global SAMURAI_TURN_LEFT_ANGLE as float = 45.0
global SAMURAI_TURN_RIGHT_ANGLE as float = 135.0
global GEISHA_FORWARD_ANGLE as float = -90.0
global GEISHA_TURN_LEFT_ANGLE as float = -45.0
global GEISHA_TURN_RIGHT_ANGLE as float = -135.0
```

Global Variables

Next up are the global variables. This is a pretty big list of globals, but they make the source code for the game *much* easier to follow and cut down on potential bugs that creep up whenever you are using local variables of the same name inside functions. For instance, I found myself repeatedly using `tilex` and `tiley` in support functions when working with tile numbers. So I moved the declaration up to the top of the program and made them globals, which eliminated two really difficult bugs.

```
'global variables
global posx as integer = 0
global posz as integer = 0
global angle as float = 0.0
global height as integer = 150
global radius as integer = 300
global pointerx as integer = 0
global pointery as integer = 0
global tilex as integer
global tiley as integer
global tilename as string
global selectstate as integer = 0
global selectedpiece as integer
global computerpiece as integer
global computer_moving_counter as integer = 0
global selx as integer
global sely as integer
global move_zdir as integer
global moving_counter as integer = 0
global move_while_animating_flag as integer = 1
global targetpiece as integer
global targetx as integer
global targety as integer
```

Animation Variables

There are many animation sequences stored inside the 3D models used in this game, including animations for walking, running, attacking, and falling down. The next section of code defines constants for the fourteen animations found within the Samurai and Geisha characters.

```
'animation constants
global ANI_SPEED = 15000 'this is dependent on sync rate
global ANI_IDLE = 1
global ANI_FIDGET = 2
```

```
global ANI_ATTACK = 3
global ANI_HURT = 4
global ANI_DODGE = 5
global ANI_BLOCK = 6
global ANI_FALLDOWN = 7
global ANI_GETUP = 8
global ANI_WALKSTART = 9
global ANI_WALKING = 10
global ANI_WALKSTOP = 11
global ANI_RUNSTART = 12
global ANI_RUNNING = 13
global ANI_RUNSTOP = 14
```

Animation Data

Next up is the data that defines the position within each model for the animation sequences defined above. The numbers are quite large because of interpolation. Basically, the actual numbers are inflated by a factor of 160 to arrive at the "smooth interpolated" animations, while the actual models *don't* have over 100,000 frames of actual mesh data contained within them.

```
'animation segments inside model file
ANIMATIONS:
data 0,12800           'idle
data 12800,24000       'fidget
data 24000,32000       'attack
data 32000,40000       'hurt
data 40000,48000       'dodge
data 48000,56000       'block
data 56000,64000       'fall down
data 64000,72000       'get up
data 72000,75200       'walk--position to loop
data 75200,84800       'walk--looping
data 84800,88000       'walk--return to stance
data 88000,91200       'run--position to loop
data 91200,100800      'run--looping
data 100800,104000     'run--return to stance
```

Animation Variables

I've created a custom data type to make it easier to work with animation sequences. The ANIMTYPE structure defines a start and stop frame for each animation. This is used to create an array called anim which is then used in the game to play a specific animation sequence, and they are pulled from the data statements you saw earlier.

```
'animation data type
type ANIMTYPE
   start as integer
   stop as integer
endtype

'create and fill the animation array
dim anim(14) as ANIMTYPE
restore ANIMATIONS
for n = 1 to 14
   read anim(n).start
   read anim(n).stop
next n
```

Checker Board

The checker board is defined with 64 data values arrayed like the actual board. This definition provides only the data for whether a square is valid or invalid. The actual pieces are added to the board array later on when they are moved to their starting squares.

```
'checker board definition
CHECKERBOARD:
data 0,99,0,99,0,99,0,99
data 99,0,99,0,99,0,99,0
data 0,99,0,99,0,99,0,99
data 99,0,99,0,99,0,99,0
data 0,99,0,99,0,99,0,99
data 99,0,99,0,99,0,99,0
data 0,99,0,99,0,99,0,99
data 99,0,99,0,99,0,99,0

'define the checker board array
dim board(8,8) as integer
```

Game State

To make it possible to move and attack pieces in the game with custom animations, this game would just not work without a form of game state to keep track of things. The constants defined below help to keep track of state in the game, while the global `game_state` variable makes it possible to change state at any point in the program.

```
'game state constants
global STATE_SELECTING = 0
global STATE_PLAYER_MOVE = 1
global STATE_PLAYER_ATTACK = 2
global STATE_COMPUTER_TURN = 9
global STATE_COMPUTER_MOVE = 10
global STATE_GAMEOVER = 99
global game_state as integer = STATE_SELECTING
```

Main Functions

The game calls on several functions to get the game going after all the variables have been defined. These functions create the game board, the character models, the pointer, the selector, and initialize the screen. Then `run_game()` is called to get the game loop going.

```
'initialize the game
create_board()
create_models()
create_pointer()
create_selector()
init_game()
run_game()
end
```

Game Loop

The `run_game()` function is listed below. You'll notice right away that game state rules this function, because it doesn't do much of anything outside of the `select...case` conditions. However, there is an exception. After the `select...case` is a quick check to determine if all of the computer pieces have been eliminated. When this condition occurs, the game is over, and the game goes into `STATE_GAMEOVER` mode, as shown in Figure 23.6.

```
function run_game()
    'main loop for the game
    repeat
        'hide the selection pointer
        hide object 40
```

Figure 23.6
"Game over, man! Game over!" Remember the *Twister* guy said that in the movie *Aliens*? That was awesome.

```
'animate the piece moving on the board
select game_state
  case 0 'STATE_SELECTING
    'no moves yet
    update_pointer()
    update_selection()
    endcase
  case 1 'STATE_PLAYER_MOVE
    'move player piece
    perform_normal_move()
    endcase
  case 2 'STATE_PLAYER_ATTACK
    'attack player piece
    perform_jump_move()
    endcase
```

```
            case 9 'STATE_COMPUTER_TURN
               'perform computer player move
               computers_turn()
               endcase
            case 10 'STATE_COMPUTER_MOVE
               'move computer player
               perform_computer_move()
               endcase
            case 99 'STATE_GAMEOVER
               set text size 36
               set text to bold
               ink rgb(255,0,255), rgb(0,0,0)
               center text screen width()/2, screen height()/2, "GAME OVER"
               endcase
         endselect

         'check board for end of game condition
         enemies = 0
         for y = 0 to 7
            for x = 0 to 7
               if board(x,y) > 12 and board(x,y) < 25
                  enemies = enemies + 1
               endif
            next x
         next y
         if enemies = 0 then game_state = STATE_GAMEOVER

         'print status info
         set text size 15
         set text to normal
         ink rgb(255,255,255), rgb(0,0,0)
         text 0,0, "Pointer " + str$(pointerx) + "," + str$(pointery)
         text 0,10, "Cursor over tile " + str$(tilex) + "," + str$(tiley) + " - " +
tilename + " #" + str$(selectedpiece)
         if selectstate = 1
         text 0,20,"Selected object " + str$(selectedpiece) + " at " + str$(selx) +
"," + str$(sely)
            text 0,30,"Distance " + str$(selx-tilex) + "," + str$(sely-tiley)
         endif

         text screen width() - 60,0, "FPS " + str$(screen fps())
         fastsync
      until escapekey() = 1
endfunction
```

Player Moves

It's kind of interesting how you perform a move in the game. You can't just grab a piece and move it to the destination square, because there's *animation* involved. Animation takes time, and the timing is crucial. So, it's just not possible to do a forced march on a piece without doing it *indirectly*. By indirectly, I mean that the game sets up a specific state for when an animated move should take place, and then that movement occurs later on in the game loop. Figure 23.7 shows a Samurai character moving to a new square. Indirect processes using game state is a difficult circular process to get your mind around, but it works and is the only practical way to do this sort of thing in a real-time game.

```
function perform_normal_move()
    x = object position x(selectedpiece) + 1
    z = object position z(selectedpiece) + move_zdir
    position object selectedpiece, x, −100, z
```

Figure 23.7
A human piece is moving to a new square after the move was validated.

```
    moving_counter = moving_counter + 1
    if moving_counter > 100
        moving_counter = 0
        game_state = STATE_COMPUTER_TURN
        move_piece_to_tile(selectedpiece, tilex, tiley)
        yrotate object selectedpiece, SAMURAI_FORWARD_ANGLE
        animate(selectedpiece, ANI_IDLE)
    endif
endfunction
```

Player Jump Attacks

The most interesting part of the game is when a piece jumps an enemy piece and removes it from the board. In Battle Checkers, this is really the fun part because there are many animation steps involved that help to add drama to the game. First, the character turns toward the target and begins moving in that direction. Figure 23.8 shows an attack in progress (look on the right side where most of the

Figure 23.8
The Samurai piece is attacking the enemy Geisha piece.

Figure 23.9
The enemy piece has been eliminated.

lighting is in the figure if you can't see where the animation is going on). You can see the Samurai's sword drawn in this figure.

After a short run animation, the Samurai draws his sword and slashes at the enemy character. The enemy Geisha first performs a dodge move and then is struck backward by the blow of the Samurai's sword. After a short pause, the Samurai continues on his way and the Geisha falls down. Figure 23.9 shows the fallen Geisha with the Samurai walking toward his destination square.

There are a lot of cases in the select statement below. Try not to get intimidated by them all. Instead, think of this as a series of animations that follow each other in order from smallest to largest number (starting at the bottom). The last bit of code to run in this sequence is actually at the top of the select statement, under the "case 400" condition. When the game loop has called this function 400 times, then the animation sequence is over and some cleanup code is called to end the animation and prepare the game for the next move. When you think of this as a series of animations, then it is much more comprehensible.

```
function perform_jump_move()
   moving_counter = moving_counter + 1

   'reached destination yet?
   select moving_counter
      case 400
         'done with attack sequence
         moving_counter = 0
         game_state = STATE_COMPUTER_TURN
         move_piece_to_tile(selectedpiece, tilex, tiley)
         yrotate object selectedpiece, SAMURAI_FORWARD_ANGLE
         animate(selectedpiece, ANI_IDLE)
         'get rid of enemy piece
         hide object targetpiece
         board(targetx,targety) = 99
         endcase
      case 310
       play object selectedpiece, anim(ANI_FIDGET).start, anim(ANI_FIDGET).stop
         move_while_animating_flag = 0
         endcase
      case 280
         play object selectedpiece, anim(ANI_WALKSTOP).start,
anim(ANI_WALKSTOP).stop
         move_while_animating_flag = 0
         endcase
      case 150
         'player continues walking
         animate(selectedpiece, ANI_RUNNING)
         move_while_animating_flag = 1
         endcase
      case 130
         'enemy piece dies
         play object targetpiece, anim(ANI_FALLDOWN).start,
         anim(ANI_FALLDOWN).stop
         'start walking again
         play object selectedpiece, anim(ANI_RUNSTART).start,
anim(ANI_RUNSTART).stop
         move_while_animating_flag = 0
         endcase
```

```
      case 80
        'enemy gets hit
        play object targetpiece, anim(ANI_HURT).start, anim(ANI_HURT).stop
        move_while_animating_flag = 0
        endcase
      case 70
        'player piece attacks
        play object selectedpiece, anim(ANI_ATTACK).start, anim
        (ANI_ATTACK).stop
        move_while_animating_flag = 0
        endcase
      case 60
        'player piece stops running
        play object selectedpiece, anim(ANI_RUNSTOP).start,
        anim(ANI_RUNSTOP).stop
        move_while_animating_flag = 0
        endcase
      case 40
        play object targetpiece, anim(ANI_DODGE).start, anim(ANI_DODGE).stop
        move_while_animating_flag = 1
        endcase
      case 1
        move_while_animating_flag = 1
        endcase
    endselect

    'move the piece along
    if move_while_animating_flag = 1
      x = object position x(selectedpiece) + 1
      z = object position z(selectedpiece) + move_zdir
      position object selectedpiece, x, -100, z
    endif
endfunction
```

The Mouse Pointer

The mouse pointer in this game is not your usual mouse pointer. Instead of the usual arrow image, the pointer in Battle Checkers is a glowing transparent sphere that follows the mouse's movement over the top of the checker board in 3D space. Since the mouse can only give us a general form of input, which is not tied to the 3D game board, this function has to calculate the correct location for the pointer based on the mouse position. While doing so, the code has to account for the 4:3 ratio screen by which the mouse is bound. To adjust for this ratio, the horizontal coordinate is multiplied by 1.33, which is the width divided by the height.

This function also has the important job of figuring out which tile on the checker board it is hovering over. This key information is passed along to the rest of the game in order to figure out which piece is selected, and where it is moved to, and so on.

```
function update_pointer()
   'show the pointer
   show object 40

   'move the pointer based on mouse position (and account for 4:3 screen)
   pointerx = 400 - int(mousey() * 1.33)
   pointery = 400 - mousex()
   position object 40, pointerx, -80, pointery
   position light 0, pointerx, -80, pointery

   'figure out tile num under cursor and adjust to upper left of checker board
   tilex = (400 - pointery) / 100
   tiley = (400 - pointerx) / 100

   'look at current tile
   tile = board(tilex,tiley)
   if tile = 0 then tilename = "<impassable>"
   if tile > 0 and tile < 13 then tilename = "Samurai"
   if tile > 12 and tile < 25 then tilename = "Geisha"
   if tile = 99 then tilename = "unoccupied"

   'don't try to grab pieces if we already have one
   if selectstate = 0
      selectedpiece = board(tilex,tiley)
   endif
endfunction
```

Selection Box

Whenever a piece is selected using the mouse pointer, there needs to be some way to identify which piece has been selected. This is important because only valid moves are allowed in checkers along diagonal black squares. This function draws a large transparent cube over the top of a square that has been selected. Likewise, when a valid move has been made, the selector cube has to be removed. This function is really the core of the entire game, because it controls how pieces are selected and how they are moved to new squares, and it calls on many support functions.

```
function update_selection()
   'see if player is trying to move a piece
   if mouseclick() = 1
      'okay to select this piece?
      if tilename = "Samurai" and selectstate = 0 and selectedpiece > 0
         selectstate = 1
         selx = tilex
         sely = tiley
         'show highlight box
         position object 50, 350 - sely * 100, -50, 350 - selx * 100
         show object 50
         wait 200
      else
         'ready to move piece to new square?
         if tilename = "unoccupied" and selectstate = 1
            'turn off the selection
            selectstate = 0
            'move the selection box out of the way
            position object 50, 2000,0,0
            hide object 50
            'is this a legal move?
            validate_move(selectedpiece,selx,sely,tilex,tiley)
            validate_attack(selectedpiece,selx,sely,tilex,tiley)

            'prevent multiple selection
            wait 200
         else
            'click same square to remove selection
            if selx = tilex and sely = tiley
               selectstate = 0
               position object 50, 2000,0,0
               hide object 50
               wait 200
            endif
         endif
      endif
   endif
endfunction
```

Valid Moves

To provide assistance to the selection function above, this new function helps to determine if a chosen destination square is a valid move for the selected piece. The move can only be forward on a diagonal black square, which means the Y distance must be 1, and the X distance can only be −1 or 1 (representing a right or left diagonal move). When a valid move is approved, then a game state of STATE_PLAYER_MOVE is enabled to cause the move animation to begin later on in the game loop.

```
function validate_move(piece as integer,sx as integer, sy as integer, dx as
integer, dy as integer)
   'only allow forward moves
   if dy > sy then exitfunction

   'move diagonally forward one square
   if sx - dx = 1 or sx - dx = −1
     'move the selected piece to the new tile
     board(sx,sy) = 99
     board(dx,dy) = piece
     animate(piece, ANI_RUNNING)

     'turn on the moving state in the game loop
     game_state = STATE_PLAYER_MOVE
     moving_counter = 0

     if sx - dx = 1
       yrotate object piece, SAMURAI_TURN_LEFT_ANGLE
       move_zdir = 1
     else
       yrotate object piece, SAMURAI_TURN_RIGHT_ANGLE
       move_zdir = −1
     endif
   endif
endfunction
```

Valid Attacks

In addition to validating moves, the game has to validate requested attack moves. The following function makes it possible for the human player to attack the computer pieces. To perform an attack, you must jump over an enemy piece to an empty square beyond it in the diagonal direction. To validate such a move, the function first checks to see if the Y and X distances are forward and two squares hence. If that condition is true, then a test is performed to see if the square in between contains an enemy piece. After all that is done, then STATE_PLAYER_ATTACK game state is enabled to get the attack animation sequences going.

```
function validate_attack(piece as integer,sx as integer, sy as integer, dx as
integer, dy as integer)
   'look for a jump attack move
   if (sy - dy = 2) and (sx - dx = 2 or sx - dx = -2)

      'jumping to the left?
      if sx - dx = 2
         'look at piece to attack
         targetpiece = board(sx-1, sy-1)
         'is this an enemy piece?
         if targetpiece > 12 and targetpiece < 25
            'lock on enemy target
            targetx = sx-1
            targety = sy-1
            'perform recordkeeping on the move
            board(sx,sy) = 99
            board(dx,dy) = piece
            animate(piece, ANI_RUNNING)
            game_state = STATE_PLAYER_ATTACK
            moving_counter = 0
            'orient the piece to the move direction
            yrotate object piece, SAMURAI_TURN_LEFT_ANGLE
            move_zdir = 1

         endif

      'jumping to the right?
      else
         'same process for left attack
         targetpiece = board(sx+1,sy-1)
         if targetpiece > 12 and targetpiece < 25
            targetx = sx+1
            targety = sy-1
            board(sx,sy) = 99
            board(dx,dy) = piece
            animate(piece, ANI_RUNNING)
            game_state = STATE_PLAYER_ATTACK
            moving_counter = 0
```

```
            yrotate object piece, SAMURAI_TURN_RIGHT_ANGLE
            move_zdir = -1
         endif
      endif
   endif
endfunction
```

Artificial Intelligence

The computer player is allowed a turn when the human player has successfully completed a normal move or an attack move. The computer's A.I. is not very intelligent, as it turns out. But the goal here is to make the game basically playable by automatically moving computer pieces and making valid moves in the process. The computer does not perform any attacking in this game. Are you up to the challenge of adding this functionality to the game? If you are, then see the validate_attack() and perform_attack_move() functions for clues on how to adapt them to computer attack moves. For starters, you could forego the animation and just claim a human piece in an attack move. You could then add the animations after basic attack moves are working.

```
function computers_turn()
   'examine board and take first legal move
   for cy = 7 to 0 step -1
      for cx = 7 to 0 step -1
         'is this a geisha piece that can move?
         computerpiece = board(cx,cy)
         if cy < 7 and computerpiece > 12 and computerpiece < 25
            'stay inside the board
            if cx < 7
               'look for an unoccupied square to the right
               if board(cx+1,cy+1) = 99
                  if computer_validate_move(computerpiece,cx,cy,cx+1,cy+1) = 1
                     game_state = STATE_COMPUTER_MOVE
                     exitfunction
                  endif
               endif
            endif
         endif
         'stay inside the board
         if cx > 0
            'look for unoccupied square to the left
            if board(cx-1,cy+1) = 99
```

```
            if computer_validate_move(computerpiece,cx,cy,cx-1,cy+1) = 1
               game_state = STATE_COMPUTER_MOVE
               exitfunction
            endif
          endif
        endif
      endif
    next cx
  next cy
  'no moves found, give up...
  game_state = STATE_SELECTING
endfunction
```

Valid Computer Moves

When the computers_turn() function finds a Geisha piece to use, it has to see if any valid moves are available for that piece. It does this by simply iterating through all of the pieces on the game board. This is a simple but effective way to move the computer's pieces without getting into too much complex A.I. code. Granted, a challenging computer opponent will significantly improve this game, but we have a solid foundation here for doing just that. The following function was adapted from the validate_move() function, which is for checking the validity of a human player move.

```
function computer_validate_move(piece as integer,sx as integer, sy as integer,
dx as integer, dy as integer)
   'only allow forward moves
   if sy > dy then exitfunction 0

   'move diagonally forward one square
   if sx - dx = 1 or sx - dx = -1
     'move the selected piece to the new tile
     tilex = dx
     tiley = dy
     board(sx,sy) = 99
     board(dx,dy) = computerpiece
     animate(computerpiece, ANI_RUNNING)

     if sx - dx = 1
       yrotate object computerpiece, GEISHA_TURN_LEFT_ANGLE
       move_zdir = 1
     else
```

```
        yrotate object computerpiece, GEISHA_TURN_RIGHT_ANGLE
        move_zdir = -1
      endif
      result = 1
      computer_moving_counter = 0
    else
      result = 0
    endif
endfunction result
```

Performing Computer Moves

Once the computer player has figured out that a certain piece can move to an adjacent diagonal square legally, it then triggers the animation sequence for moving that piece by setting the game state to STATE_COMPUTER_MOVE. That game state causes the following function to be called within the game loop. As long as this state is set, this function will continue to be called from the game loop in run_game(). You have to get your mind around this concept because it is crucial to understanding how a real-time game works.

This function has to animate the piece over a period of a few seconds, not immediately, so we have to take an indirect route. The solution is to use a variable called computer_moving_counter. This global variable is incremented each time this function is called, and when the counter reaches 100, then (and only then!) will the move be completed. When this happens, the function automatically changes the game state back to the default state called STATE_SELECTING. Just remember, in a real-time game, you have to go about things indirectly, and you have to use game state to get things done.

Each time this function is called, it moves the computer piece a little further toward its destination square. Conveniently, each square is exactly 100 points away from the others, so it is not necessary to calculate where the target square is located. Instead, the piece just moves 100 times toward the destination, and we rely on a specific *frame rate* to make the movement look realistic. Figure 23.10 shows a computer piece moving toward a new square.

```
function perform_computer_move()
  x = object position x(computerpiece) - 1
  z = object position z(computerpiece) + move_zdir
  position object computerpiece, x, -100, z
```

Figure 23.10
This computer-controlled piece is moving toward a new square.

```
   computer_moving_counter = computer_moving_counter + 1
   if computer_moving_counter > 100
      computer_moving_counter = 0
      game_state = STATE_SELECTING
      move_piece_to_tile(computerpiece, tilex, tiley)
      yrotate object computerpiece, GEISHA_FORWARD_ANGLE
      animate(computerpiece, ANI_IDLE)
   endif
endfunction
```

Creating the Board

Now we've come to some of the setup and initialization functions, including create_board(). This function creates the matrix and applies a texture to each tile to fabricate the checker board (using two for loops). The most important thing to remember when working with a matrix in DB is to call the update matrix command, because otherwise no changes are made. At the end of this function, the game board array is filled with the information in the data statements, which sets the board to initial valid/invalid squares.

```
function create_board()
   'create the checker board
   load image "marble.bmp", 30
   make matrix 1, 800, 800, 8, 8
   position matrix 1, -400, -100, -400
   prepare matrix texture 1, 30, 2,1

   'draw the black and white marble textures
   tile = 2
   for y = 0 to 7
     for x = 0 to 7
        set matrix tile 1, x, y, tile
        set matrix normal 1, x, y, 1.0, 1.0, 1.0
        tile = tile + 1
        if tile > 2 then tile = 1
     next x
     tile = tile + 1
     if tile > 2 then tile = 1
   next y

   'apply matrix changes
   update matrix 1

   'initialize the checkerboard array
   'starts out with just invalid and empty squares
   restore CHECKERBOARD
   for y = 0 to 7
     for x = 0 to 7
        read board(x,y)
     next x
   next y
endfunction
```

Creating the Models

The next function loads the Samurai.x and Geisha.x models and duplicates them with the clone object to create the 12 total pieces for each player in the game. Since the models are oriented in a face-down position with respect to our game world, some adjustment to the X and Y orientation is required when setting the models to their initial positions. The models are then moved onto their appropriate board squares.

```
function create_models()
   'load the Samurai model
   load object "samurai.x", 1
   position object 1, 0, -100, 0
   xrotate object 1, -90
   yrotate object 1, SAMURAI_FORWARD_ANGLE
   set object speed 1, ANI_SPEED
   set object specular power 1,5
   animate(1, ANI_IDLE)
   hide object 1

   'clone the samurai model
   for n = 2 to 12
      clone object n, 1
      set object speed n, ANI_SPEED
      animate(n, ANI_IDLE)
      hide object n
   next n

   'samurai models for player 1
   move_piece_to_tile(1, 0, 5)
   move_piece_to_tile(2, 2, 5)
   move_piece_to_tile(3, 4, 5)
   move_piece_to_tile(4, 6, 5)
   move_piece_to_tile(5, 1, 6)
   move_piece_to_tile(6, 3, 6)
   move_piece_to_tile(7, 5, 6)
   move_piece_to_tile(8, 7, 6)
   move_piece_to_tile(9, 0, 7)
   move_piece_to_tile(10, 2, 7)
   move_piece_to_tile(11, 4, 7)
   move_piece_to_tile(12, 6, 7)

   'load the Geisha model
   load object "geisha.x", 13
   position object 13, 0, -100, 0
   xrotate object 13, -90
   yrotate object 13, GEISHA_FORWARD_ANGLE
   set object speed 13, ANI_SPEED
```

```
set object specular power 13,5
animate(13, ANI_IDLE)
hide object 13

'clone the Geisha model
for n = 14 to 24
    clone object n, 13
    set object speed n, ANI_SPEED
    animate(n, ANI_IDLE)
    hide object n
next n

'geisha models for player 2 (opponent)
move_piece_to_tile(13, 1, 0)
move_piece_to_tile(14, 3, 0)
move_piece_to_tile(15, 5, 0)
move_piece_to_tile(16, 7, 0)
move_piece_to_tile(17, 0, 1)
move_piece_to_tile(18, 2, 1)
move_piece_to_tile(19, 4, 1)
move_piece_to_tile(20, 6, 1)
move_piece_to_tile(21, 1, 2)
move_piece_to_tile(22, 3, 2)
move_piece_to_tile(23, 5, 2)
move_piece_to_tile(24, 7, 2)
endfunction
```

Moving Pieces

The function move_piece_to_tile() is used many times in the game and is one of the key functions of the game because it performs such a key role. This function moves a given model to a specific location on the game board, represented by tile coordinates (x,y). Since the game board was positioned in such a way that the matrix surface is centered at the origin (0,0,0), it is a bit of a challenge to figure out where precisely each square is located. This function calculates the top left corner of the board and then jumps to the right and down by a specified number of tiles to arrive at the correct tile. A model is then displayed at the center of the chosen square. At the same time, the X and Y coordinates are inverted, which corresponds with the orientation of the board in 3D space.

```
function move_piece_to_tile(model as integer,tx as integer, ty as integer)
    'invert x and y since matrix is centered at the origin and the
```

```
'camera is facing toward z negative; matrix tiles are 100x100
if model > 0
  if object exist(model)
    'this is the only place where inversion is needed
    tempx = 300 - ty * 100 + 50
    tempy = 300 - tx * 100 + 50
    position object model, tempx, -100, tempy
    show object model

    'update board
    board(tx,ty) = model
  endif
endif
endfunction
```

Animating Models

The animate() function performs a simple call to the loop object command and is simply a time-saving device to cut down on the amount of code whenever a looping animation is needed from the anim array.

```
function animate(model as integer, frame as integer)
  loop object model, anim(frame).start, anim(frame).stop
endfunction
```

Initializing the Game

It might seem odd to have the game's initialization way down here in the code listing, but that is just to get it out of the way from the more commonly used functions above, which are closer to the run_game() function for convenience. This function sets the frame rate, color backdrop, lighting, and camera position.

```
function init_game()
  sync on
  sync rate 40
  hide mouse
  disable escapekey
  randomize timer()
  color backdrop rgb(0,60,60)
  set ambient light 50
  set normalization on
  set camera fov 0, 50
```

```
      POSITION CAMERA 0, -600, 500, 0
      POINT CAMERA 0, -150, 0, 0
endfunction
```

Creating the Mouse Pointer

The mouse pointer in Battle Checkers is a transparent sphere with an embedded point light source that lights up the game board when it is moved around.

```
function create_pointer()
    make object sphere 40, 20, 10, 10
    set point light 0, 0, 0, 0
    color light 0, 180, 180, 180
    ghost object on 40
    set object transparency 40, 1
endfunction
```

Creating the Square/Piece Selector

The selector is a large transparent cube that is positioned over a square when that square is selected. Since it is transparent, you can still see the piece on that square.

```
function create_selector()
    make object cube 50, 100
    color object 50, rgb(0,255,0)
    ghost object on 50
    set object transparency 50, 1
    hide object 50
endfunction
```

Summary

This chapter has been an astounding romp through the creation of a nearly complete checkers game with animated characters! Wouldn't you agree that this is a pretty cool game for its size? There is still much to be done with this game, and I'm counting on you to finish it, so get cracking!

Epilogue

Now, at the end of this final chapter, I find that we're also at the end of the entire book. This has been such a fun experience that I'm a bit sorry it's over and wish I could continue on by adding new material. But as they say, all good things must come to an end. On behalf of both authors of this book, we wish you farewell and happy coding.

If, in the process of writing games with DB, you find yourself stuck on some difficult piece of code, we welcome you to stop by our websites for some assistance or feedback. Joshua's website is located at www.delnar.com, while Jonathan's is at www.jharbour.com. We are usually too busy for one-on-one help, but do have discussion forums available.

If you are having difficulty with the DB compiler, we encourage you to take the issue over to www.thegamecreators.com where you will find help on matters of installation and upgrading of DB.

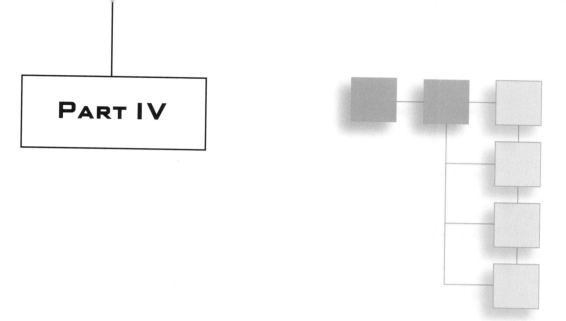

PART IV

APPENDICES

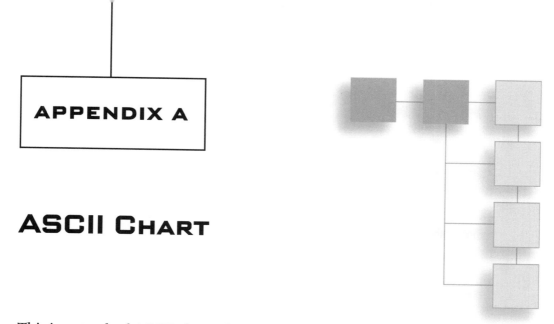

APPENDIX A

ASCII CHART

This is a standard ASCII chart of character codes 0 to 255. To use an ASCII code, simply hold down the ALT key and type the value next to the character in the table to insert the character. This method works in most text editors, including DarkBASIC. However, some text editors (such as DarkBASIC) are not capable of displaying the special ASCII characters (like codes 0 to 31).

Char	Value	Char	Value	Char	Value	Char	Value
null	000	¶	020	(	040	=	061
☺	001	§	021	)	041	>	062
☻	002	▬	022	*	042	?	063
♥	003	↕	023	+	043	@	064
♦	004	↑	024	,	044	A	065
♣	005	↓	025	-	045	B	066
♠	006	→	026	.	046	C	067
•	007	←	027	/	047	D	068
◘	008	∟	028	0	048	E	069
○	009	↔	029	1	049	F	070
◎	010	▲	030	2	050	G	071
♂	011	▼	031	3	051	H	072
♀	012	space	032	4	052	I	073
♪	013	!	033	5	053	J	074
♫	014	"	034	6	054	K	075
☼	015	#	035	7	055	L	076
►	016	$	036	8	056	M	077
◄	017	%	037	9	057	N	078
↕	018	&	038	:	058	O	079
‼	019	'	039	;	059	P	080
				<	060	Q	081

Char	Value	Char	Value	Char	Value	Char	Value
R	082	â	131	│	179	╒	213
S	083	ä	132	┤	180	╓	214
T	084	à	133	╡	181	╫	215
U	085	å	134	╢	182	╪	216
V	086	ç	135	╖	183	┘	217
W	087	ê	136	╕	184	┌	218
X	088	ë	137	╣	185	█	219
Y	089	è	138	║	186	▄	220
Z	090	ï	139	╗	187	▌	221
[	091	î	140	╝	188	▐	222
\	092	ì	141	╜	189	▀	223
]	093	Ä	142	╛	190	α	224
^	094	Å	143	┐	191	β	225
_	095	É	144	└	192	Γ	226
'	096	æ	145	┴	193	π	227
a	097	Æ	146	┬	194	Σ	228
b	098	ô	147	├	195	σ	229
c	099	ö	148	─	196	µ	230
d	100	ò	149	┼	197	τ	231
e	101	û	150	╞	198	Φ	232
f	102	ù	151	╟	199	Θ	233
g	103	ÿ	152	╚	200	Ω	234
h	104	Ö	153	╔	201	δ	235
i	105	Ü	154	╩	202	∞	236
j	106	¢	155	╦	203	φ	237
k	107	£	156	╠	204	ε	238
l	108	¥	157	═	205	∩	239
m	109	Pts	158	╬	206	≡	240
n	110	ƒ	159	╧	207	±	241
o	111	á	160	╨	208	≥	242
p	112	í	161	╤	209	≤	243
q	113	ó	162	╥	210	⌠	244
r	114	ú	163	╙	211	⌡	245
s	115	ñ	164	╘	212	÷	246
t	116	Ñ	165			≈	247
u	117	ª	166			°	248
v	118	º	167			·	249
w	119	¿	168			·	250
x	120	⌐	169			√	251
y	121	¬	170			ⁿ	252
z	122	½	171			²	253
{	123	¼	172			■	254
|	124	¡	173				255
}	125	«	174				
~	126	»	175				
⌂	127	░	176				
Ç	128	▒	177				
ü	129	▓	178				
é	130						

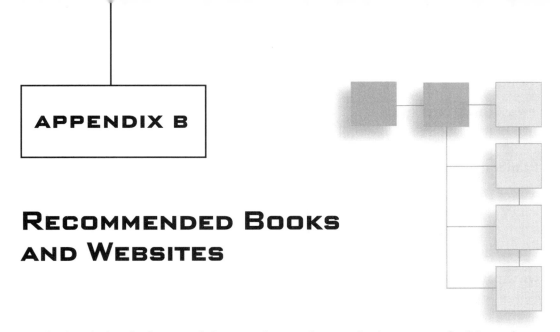

APPENDIX B

RECOMMENDED BOOKS AND WEBSITES

With the click of a button (okay, and some keystrokes) you can find just about everything on the Internet, from how to cook Mandarin chicken to implementing the latest 3D technology in your games. To make it a just a little easier for you, here is a collection of sites I greatly recommend if you are interested in game development or computing in general—and my favorite, computer humor.

Game Development and Programming

There are hundreds, if not thousands, of game development sites on the Internet. Some are good, some bad, but in my personal opinion, all in the following list fall into the first category. Not all of these are related to DarkBASIC, but you will find a lot of useful information from game development discussions and articles *not* specifically written for DarkBASIC. The important thing is the understanding of concepts, so you should be able to glean useful techniques for your games from any tutorial or article.

Jonathan Harbour's website:

www.jharbour.com

Joshua Smith's website:

www.delnar.com

Primeval Games:

www.primevalgames.com

University of Advancing Technology (UAT):

www.uat.edu

GameDev LCC:

www.gamedev.net

FlipCode:

www.flipcode.com/

Game Developers Search Engine:

www.gdse.com/

CFXWeb:

www.cfxweb.net/

CodeGuru:

www.codeguru.com

Programmers Heaven:

www.programmersheaven.com

AngelCode.com:

www.angelcode.com

OpenGL:

www.opengl.org

IsoHex:

www.isohex.net/

NeHe Productions:

http://nehe.gamedev.net/

NeXe:

http://nexe.gamedev.net/

Game Developer:

www.gamedeveloper.net/

Wotsit's Format:

www.wotsit.org/

News, Reviews, and Download Sites

Keeping up with all that is happening is a daunting task. New things happen every minute all over the world, and hopefully, the next set of links will help you keep up-to-date with it all:

Games Domain:

www.gamesdomain.com

Blue's News:

www.bluesnews.com

Happy Puppy:

www.happypuppy.com

Download.com:

www.download.com

Tucows:

www.tucows.com

Slashdot:

http://slashdot.org

Engines

Sometimes you should not try to reinvent the wheel. There are several good engines, both 2D and 3D out there. Below are some of the engines I have had the pleasure (or pain) to work with that I want to recommend to you. See which is best for you and start developing. Again, these are not directly related to DarkBASIC, but to C++. It's a good idea to broaden your horizons as much as possible.

Garage Games' Torque Engine:

www.garagegames.com

LithTech:

www.lithtech.com

CDX:

www.cdx.sk

Jet3D:

www.jet3d.com

Genesis3D:

www.genesis3d.com

RenderWare:

www.renderware.com

Crystal Space:

http://crystal.linuxgames.com

Independent Game Developers

You know, almost everyone started as you are starting, by reading books and magazines or getting code listings from friends or relatives. Some of the developers listed here struggled hard to get where they are now, and some are still struggling. Visit them, give them your support, and who knows, in the next book, it may be your site listed here.

Longbow Digital Arts:

www.longbowdigitalarts.com/

Spin Studios:

www.spin-studios.com/

Positech Computing Ltd:

www.positech.co.uk/

Samu Games:

www.samugames.com/

QUANTA Entertainment:

www.quanta-entertainment.com/

Satellite Moon:

www.satellitemoon.com/

Myopic Rhino Games:

www.myopicrhino.com/

Industry

If you want to be in the business, you need to know the business. Reading magazines and visiting association meetings will help you for sure. The following list contains links to both physical and online magazines, trade associations, conferences, and developers associations.

Game Developers Magazine:

www.gdmag.com

GamaSutra:

www.gamasutra.com

International Game Developers Association:

www.igda.com

Game Developers Conference:

www.gdconf.com

Game Developers Conference Europe:

www.gdc-europe.com/

Association of Shareware Professionals:

www.asp-shareware.org/

RealGames:

www.real.com/games

Computer Humor

Forget about Jerry Seinfeld and Ray Romano—now *this* is what I call real humor. The following online humor sites will keep you laughing for hours on end if you have some time to kill.

Home Star Runner:

www.homestarrunner.com

User Friendly:

www.userfriendly.org

Geeks!:

www.happychaos.com/geeks/

Off the Mark:

www.offthemark.com/computers.htm

Player Versus Player:

www.pvponline.com

Noteworthy Books

This is a list of books with a short description for each. They are either books I have written (plug!) or that I highly recommend because I've found them useful, relaxing, funny, or essential on many an occasion.

Beginner's Guide to DarkBASIC Game Programming

Jonathan S. Harbour, Joshua R. Smith; Premier Press; ISBN 1-59200-009-6

The first edition of this book is more relevant for the "classic edition" of DarkBASIC, which predates DarkBASIC Professional. If you have an older PC, or still own DB Classic, then this book will be helpful to you, while our second edition (which you are now holding) is devoted just to DB Pro.

Beginning Game Programming

Jonathan S. Harbour; Course Technology; ISBN 1-59200-585-3

This book teaches basic game programming using Visual C++ and DirectX 9. Keep a look out for the second edition, due out in 2006. This new edition will focus more on creating games and less time on the DirectX SDK.

C Programming for the Absolute Beginner

Michael Vine; Premier Press; ISBN 1-931841-52-7

This book teaches C programming using the free GCC compiler as its development platform, which is the same compiler used to write Game Boy programs! As such, I highly recommend this starter book if you are just learning the C language. It sticks to just the basics. You will learn the fundamentals of the C language without any distracting material or commentary. It includes the fundamentals of what you need to be a successful C programmer.

C++ Programming for the Absolute Beginner

Dirk Henkemans and Mark Lee; Premier Press; ISBN 1-931841-43-8

If you are new to programming with C++ and you are looking for a solid introduction, this is the book for you. This book will teach you the skills you need for practical C++ programming applications, and how you can put these skills to use in real-world scenarios.

Game Design: The Art & Business of Creating Games

Bob Bates; Premier Press; ISBN 0-7615-3165-3

This very readable and informative book is a great resource for learning how to design games—the high-level process of planning the game prior to starting work on the source code or artwork.

Game Programming All In One, Second Edition

Jonathan S. Harbour; Course Technology; ISBN 1-59200-383-4

This book explains how to create nice quality arcade style games using the awesome cross-platform Allegro game library. Topics covered include tile-based scrolling, animated sprites, level editing, and the development of several complete arcade games. Look for the third edition in 2006.

High Score! The Illustrated History of Electronic Games, 2nd Edition

Rusel DeMaria, Johnny L. Wilson; McGraw-Hill/Osborne; ISBN 0-07-222428-2

This is a gem of a book that covers the entire video game industry, including arcade machines, consoles, and computer games. It is jam-packed with wonderful interviews with famous game developers and is chock full of color photographs.

The Java Programming Language (Fourth Edition)

James Gosling, et al.; Addison-Wesley; ISBN 0-32134-498-06

This reference for the Java language was co-authored by the man who invented the Java language at Sun Microsystems. The fourth edition includes material from the latest version, J2SE 5.0.

J2ME Game Programming

Martin Wells; Course Technology; ISBN 1-59200-118-1

This book will teach you how to use the Java 2 Micro Edition to program games for cell phones and other portable devices using the Java language.

Java Programming for the Absolute Beginner

Joseph Russell; Course Technology; ISBN 0-7615-3522-5

Looking for a good introduction to the Java language? Look no further! This book will provide you with all the information you need to get started programming in Java.

Microsoft C# Programming for the Absolute Beginner

Andy Harris; Premier Press; ISBN 1-931841-16-0

Using game creation as a teaching tool, this book not only teaches C#, but also the fundamental programming concepts you need to grasp in order to learn any computer language. You will be able to take the skills you learn from this book and apply them to your own situations. *Microsoft C# Programming for the Absolute Beginner* is a unique book aimed at the novice programmer. Developed by computer science instructors, this series is the ideal tool for anyone with little-to-no programming experience.

Microsoft Visual Basic .NET Programming for the Absolute Beginner

Jonathan S. Harbour; Premier Press; ISBN 1-59200-002-9

Whether you are new to programming with Visual Basic .NET or you are upgrading from Visual Basic 6.0 and looking for a solid introduction, this is the book for you. It teaches the basics of Visual Basic .NET by working through simple games that you will learn to create.

Visual Basic Game Programming for Teens

Jonathan S. Harbour; Course Technology; ISBN 1-59200-587-X

This book is not about programming in Visual Basic or DirectX, although it uses these tools to good effect. The point of this book is to explain how to program a simple role-playing game using a tile-based scrolling game world and sprites.

Visual Basic Game Programming with DirectX

Jonathan S. Harbour; Premier Press; ISBN 1-931841-25-X

This book is a comprehensive programmer's tutorial and a reference for everything related to programming games with Visual Basic. After a complete explanation of the Windows API graphics device interface meant to supercharge 2D sprite programming for normal applications, the book delves into DirectX 7.0 and 8.1, covering every component of DirectX in detail, including Direct3D. Four complete games are included, demonstrating the code developed in the book.

Game Resources

The following list of websites provides game development resources such as game graphics, sound effects, music libraries, and other media.

Reiner's Tilesets: Royalty-free tiles and animated sprites

http://www.reinerstileset.de

Free Character Animation Graphics

http://www.vbexplorer.com/charpack1.asp

Free Sound & Music Clips

http://www.vbexplorer.com/gamesound.asp

Edgar Ibarra's Pocket Ideas (3D artwork)

http://www.pocketideas.com

Development Tools

The following list of websites focuses on development tools, game libraries, compilers, and related resources, including sites specifically maintained by Microsoft.

The Game Creators

http://www.thegamecreators.com

Microsoft DirectX Home

http://www.microsoft.com/directx/

Microsoft Games

http://www.microsoft.com/games/home/default.asp

Microsoft Games for PC

http://www.microsoft.com/games/home/gameslist.asp?platform=Windows

Microsoft Games for Xbox

http://www.microsoft.com/games/home/gameslist.asp?platform=XBOX

Microsoft Visual Basic Home Page

http://msdn.microsoft.com/vbasic/

Microsoft Visual Basic Online Product Documentation

http://msdn.microsoft.com/vbasic/technical/documentation.asp

Revolution 3D Engine

http://www.revolution3d.net/

INDEX

License Agreement/Notice of Limited Warranty

By opening the sealed disc container in this book, you agree to the following terms and conditions. If, upon reading the following license agreement and notice of limited warranty, you cannot agree to the terms and conditions set forth, return the unused book with unopened disc to the place where you purchased it for a refund.

License

The enclosed software is copyrighted by the copyright holder(s) indicated on the software disc. You are licensed to copy the software onto a single computer for use by a single user and to a backup disc. You may not reproduce, make copies, or distribute copies or rent or lease the software in whole or in part, except with written permission of the copyright holder(s). You may transfer the enclosed disc only together with this license, and only if you destroy all other copies of the software and the transferee agrees to the terms of the license. You may not decompile, reverse assemble, or reverse engineer the software.

Notice of Limited Warranty

The enclosed disc is warranted by Thomson Course Technology PTR to be free of physical defects in materials and workmanship for a period of sixty (60) days from end user's purchase of the book/disc combination. During the sixty-day term of the limited warranty, Thomson Course Technology PTR will provide a replacement disc upon the return of a defective disc.

Limited Liability

THE SOLE REMEDY FOR BREACH OF THIS LIMITED WARRANTY SHALL CONSIST ENTIRELY OF REPLACEMENT OF THE DEFECTIVE DISC. IN NO EVENT SHALL THOMSON COURSE TECHNOLOGY PTR OR THE AUTHOR BE LIABLE FOR ANY OTHER DAMAGES, INCLUDING LOSS OR CORRUPTION OF DATA, CHANGES IN THE FUNCTIONAL CHARACTERISTICS OF THE HARDWARE OR OPERATING SYSTEM, DELETERIOUS INTERACTION WITH OTHER SOFTWARE, OR ANY OTHER SPECIAL, INCIDENTAL, OR CONSEQUENTIAL DAMAGES THAT MAY ARISE, EVEN IF THOMSON COURSE TECHNOLOGY PTR AND/OR THE AUTHOR HAS PREVIOUSLY BEEN NOTIFIED THAT THE POSSIBILITY OF SUCH DAMAGES EXISTS.

Disclaimer of Warranties

THOMSON COURSE TECHNOLOGY PTR AND THE AUTHOR SPECIFICALLY DISCLAIM ANY AND ALL OTHER WARRANTIES, EITHER EXPRESS OR IMPLIED, INCLUDING WARRANTIES OF MERCHANTABILITY, SUITABILITY TO A PARTICULAR TASK OR PURPOSE, OR FREEDOM FROM ERRORS. SOME STATES DO NOT ALLOW FOR EXCLUSION OF IMPLIED WARRANTIES OR LIMITATION OF INCIDENTAL OR CONSEQUENTIAL DAMAGES, SO THESE LIMITATIONS MIGHT NOT APPLY TO YOU.

Other

This Agreement is governed by the laws of the State of Massachusetts without regard to choice of law principles. The United Convention of Contracts for the International Sale of Goods is specifically disclaimed. This Agreement constitutes the entire agreement between you and Thomson Course Technology PTR regarding use of the software.